Managing the
Multinational

W9-BMH-487

Managing the Multinational

Confronting the Global–Local Dilemma

Samuel Humes

Prentice Hall
New York   London   Toronto   Sydney   Tokyo   Singapore

First published 1993 by
Prentice Hall International (UK) Ltd
Campus 400, Maylands Avenue
Hemel Hempstead
Hertfordshire, HP2 7EZ
A division of
Simon & Schuster International Group

Typeset in 10/12pt Sabon
by Mathematical Composition Setters Ltd, Salisbury, UK

Printed and bound in Great Britain by
Dotesios Ltd, Trowbridge, Wiltshire

Library of Congress Cataloging-in-Publication data

Humes, Samuel.
    Managing the multinational: confronting the global–local
dilemma/Samuel Humes IV.
        p.   cm.
    Includes bibliographical references and index.
    ISBN 0-13-555137-4
    1. International business enterprises—Management. 2.
Comparative management. I. Title.
HD62.4H858 1993   92-24870
658′.049—dc20   CIP

British Library Cataloguing in Publication Data

A catalogue record for this book is available
from the British Library

    ISBN 0-13-555137-4 (pbk)

---

1 2 3 4 5   97 96 95 94 93

To Lynne
Who made this book possible

Contents

Part IV Reorganization: for managing transcontinental enterprises

List of Figures and Tables

Tables

Foreword

Managing the Multinational focuses on stimulating readers to reflect on how leading European, American and Asian companies strategically organize their international operations.

The research is extremely complete, precise and well developed. In one word, I would say that Dr Humes' book is a modern 'bible' for the managers of new generations; useful for day-by-day practice, and a fascinating instrument of consultation for analytical comparison of multinational aspects, in order to reach synthetic judgement on the dynamic world of enterprises.

The year 1993, when the mythic '1992' comes into operation, is the best year for producing such an important volume, immediately after the historical date of the Maastricht European Council and following the return of eastern European countries to market economy. Today, the truth that performing companies constitute the key-point of a democratic society, to assure real common welfare, *is a fact*, and Dr Humes has seized the right momentum to highlight *how the life of companies*, their strategies and organizational structure, *are essential* in our turbulent era of urgent solidarity and economic interdependence.

For multinationals, competing in a world comprising three major political/ economic areas will be the priority as they head towards the next century. I entirely share Dr Humes' philosophy. The successful business is led by managers who thrive on ambiguity, change and complexity – perhaps, may I add, 'motivating human resources to their full potential'!

I am convinced that the present extraordinary changes, all over the world, especially in Europe, call for imaginative ideas and for the best mutual understanding among people at all levels of social life. But one of the most precious elements of which we are in need, is a clear and complete knowledge of industrial realities, considered in a positive, interconnected and globalizing prospective.

Dr Salvatore Rossetti di Valdalbero
Head of Fiat Public Affairs, Brussels
Member of EC Social-Economic Affairs Committee

Preface

This book compares the ways leading American, European and Asian industrial corporations strategically organize and manage their multicontinental enterprises. It focuses on how multinationals are reorganizing their international operations with transcontinental structures, international staffing and globally shared values – designed to enable their product, functional and geographic parts to work together more coherently. The rapid development of the international operations of many major multinationals has accelerated efforts to reorganize, and especially to redefine and redevelop operating-division–international-affiliate relations.

As multinationals approach the end of the twentieth century, they are competing more fiercely, developing strategies more forcefully and reorganizing more frequently. Increasing inter- and intracontinental interdependence and intensifying global competition are forcing multinationals to recognize the inadequacies of their present organizational frameworks, especially for dealing with the global–local dilemma which fundamentally affects the management of their international operations. As a consequence, multinationals are introducing and testing new global arrangements for managing the disparate parts of their global operations. Twenty-first-century professors and practitioners may well recognize the final years of the twentieth century as the critical decades marking the transition to more coherent transcontinental organizations.

This book describes, compares and analyses the reorganizational efforts of a cross-section of leading American, European and Asian multinationals – in the context of the traditions that have shaped their organizational evolutions and the environmental factors now shaping their transitions – with the purpose of setting forth an agenda of multinationally tested ideas for creating more strategically coherent, and thus more competitive, global corporations.

Two interrelated premises have affected the preparation of this book. First, corporations generally achieve effective organizational change through vision-inspired incremental initiatives that build upon organizational traditions in an evolutionary manner. For this reason, the book focuses on the steps that multinationals are already testing and the way these steps flow from their organizational traditions and are affected by present conditions – as the basic source of ideas for creating more strategically coherent enterprises. Second, the creation of strategically coherent organizations requires an arsenal of mutually supportive organization initiatives. No matter how dearly some students and managers cling to the hope that there is a simple recipe for multinational organizational health, this book proceeds with the conviction that a well-orchestrated variety of mutually supportive structuring, staffing and value-sharing initiatives is required.

To facilitate this global comparison, this book introduces a $3 \times 3 \times 3$ comparative framework for comparing the way that leading multinationals on three continents – America, Europe and Asia – use three sets of management dynamics – structure, staffing and shared values – to manage three sets of organizational perspectives – product, function and territory. This $3 \times 3 \times 3$ framework provides a prism facilitating the identification and comparison of continental traditions, significant organizational types, and trends.

The different environments affecting the evolution of West European, North American and East Asian multinationals have led them to develop essentially different organizations for managing their international operations. Most European multinationals initially pursued an area-driven and staffing-stressed approach. Most American multinationals have developed a product-driven and structure-stressed organization. Japanese multinationals have relied upon a function-driven and shared-values organization. The accelerated efforts to globalize have, however, led to major shifts in corporate organizational strategies. As this book will note, a convergence of approaches appears to be emerging.

The challenge is thus more than a transnational one. It is a transcontinental one in which synergy among the product, area and functional perspectives – at the affiliate as well as the headquarters level – depends upon three organization dynamics: structures that enable the corporate parts to act independently and interdependently, staffing initiatives that develop a corporate-wide corps capable of balancing and blending the competing and complementary sets of perspectives, and shared values that transcend product and function as well as national borders. The broad, multidimensional comparison provides a general overview through which to appreciate the various specific and empirical studies, and which should encourage further study. My aim has been to provide sufficient specific information in the comparative survey to support the themes advanced.

Outline

The book comprises four parts: the introduction, the dynamic-by-dynamic comparison, the multinational case studies, and the conclusion. Part I defines the organizational issue and introduces the analytical framework, compares the different historical and environmental contexts in which West European, North American and East Asian multinationals have developed, and notes the conditions forcing changes, introducing those Global 50 multinationals on which the comparison focuses. Part II stresses the three sets of interdependent dynamics –

structure, staffing and shared values – that shape multinational organizations. Part III moves from general concepts to concrete examples selected among the Global 50 (see Table P.1) The corporate case studies present the strategic organizational initiatives which leading multinationals are now undertaking in the context of their evolutions and the present environment. The case studies have been arranged by continent, recognizing that multinationals based on the same continent have traditionally tended to take a similar approach to organizing their international operations. (Since different case studies illustrate different facets of the challenge and different features in the reorganization efforts, readers may wish to focus on particular case studies.) Part IV presents an agenda for change comprised of the more forward-looking strategic organizational initiatives that the leading multinationals are taking to confront the global–local dilemma.

The intent is that this aerial-type approach, by complementing more close-up portraits, will foster more understanding of the organizational transformations that multinationals are undertaking to globalize, localize and organize in their efforts to compete more effectively throughout the world.

Table P.1 Global 50 largest industrial corporations in the world: ranked by sales within country and industry ($bn), 1991

Continent / Countries / Corporations	Industries									
	Food	Soaps, cosmetics	Chemicals	Petroleum refining	Metals	Computers (and office equipment)	Electronic and electric equipment	Industrial and farm equipment	Aerospace	Motor vehicles and parts
AMERICA										
United States										
General Motors # *										124
Exxon # *				103						
Ford Motor # *										89
International Business Machines # *						65				
General Electric # *							60			
Mobil # *				57						
Philip Morris # *	48									
E.I. Du Pont de Nemours # *			38							
Texaco *				38						
Chevron *				37						
Chrysler *										29
Boeing *									29	
Procter & Gamble # *		27								
Amoco *				26						
United Technologies *									21	
Venezuela										
Petroleos de Venezuela				24						
EUROPE										
Britain/The Netherlands										
Royal Dutch/Shell # *				104						
Unilever # *	41									
Britain										
British Petroleum # *				58						
Imperial Chemical Industries # *			22							
France										
Elf Aquitaine *				36						
Renault *										29
Peugeot *										28
Alcatel Alsthom # *							28			
Total				25						

	C1	C2	C3	C4	C5	C6	C7	C8	C9	C10
Germany										
Daimler-Benz # *	57									
Volkswagen *	46									
Siemens *				45						
Hoechst *								28		
BASF *								28		
Bayer # *								26		
Thyssen										
Italy										
IRI *						22				
Fiat # *						64				
ENI *	47									
The Netherlands										
Philips Electronics #							41			
Switzerland										
Nestlé # *				30						36
Asea Brown Boveri			29							
ASIA										
Japan										
Toyota Motor *	78			56						
Hitachi # *				46						
Matsushita Electric Industrial # *					33					
Nissan Motor # *	43			27						
Toshiba *				22						
Honda Motor *	31			24						
NEC										
Sony										
Mitsubishi Electric #						23				
Nippon Steel				43						
South Korea										
Samsung # *				25						
Daewoo										
Totals										
Number of firms — Global 50	11	2	1	11	2	3	11	5	1	3
Number of firms — Global 500	45	16	27	45	15	35	53	45	10	47
Sales $bn (1990) — Global 50	602	51	29	415	99	110	549	143	27	125
Sales $bn (1990) — Global 500	853	169	219	650	210	339	931	397	71	397

Note: # corporations profiled in this book.
  * corporations listed in the Global 50, 1987, 1988, 1989, 1990, 1991
Source: *Fortune*, 27 July 1992:55.

Acknowledgements

For decades the focus of my research efforts has been the way that local units relate to and work within the larger organizational framework of which they form a part. From 1984, when I became director of Boston University Brussels and its graduate programmes, my research efforts have focused on the changing relations of international affiliates to the multinationals of which they are part, and the consequent changing responsibilities of international managers within large, diversified multinational corporations. Based on eight years of detailed in-depth study of more than a hundred American, European, and Asian multinationals, this book presents the essence of the global–local management challenge that multinationals face as they endeavour to compete more effectively throughout the world. The ideas presented flow from the close scrutiny of the evolution of these major multinationals, and of their efforts to confront the organizational issues that have magnified as they have diversified, globalized and localized their operations.

A major comparative endeavour such as this would not have been possible without the guidance, cooperation and sustained support of numerous international managers whom I interviewed for this book. Several were especially helpful. Charles De Meyer, a former IBM Belgium president, read the initial drafts of the study. Tetsuro Inaji, once the Mitsui Benelux president and now a member of the board of Mitsui & Co., introduced me to Japanese continental and country general managers. Jack Schmukli of Sony, Dr Salvatore Rossetti di Valdalbero of Fiat, Eric Bean of Matsushita, and Takashi Osawa of Nissan have been especially helpful in providing valuable insights into the ways their corporations and their countries approached organizational issues. All those who granted me interviews (and are listed in 'Sources and methodology') contributed to the character and detail of the study.

Dr Cecilia Andersen prepared a paper which I relied upon in the initial development of Chapter 2. Constance Wolf and Dr Robert Oresick likewise assisted in the initial preparation of Chapter 5. Diana Ibarra, Karl Brauckmann and Jerome Dortmans assisted in developing a few case studies. Helen Dumail and Lara Ham demonstrated patience in deciphering notes and retyping countless drafts. Cathy Peck, my editor, shepherded me through the publishing process.

O'Melveny & Myers financially supported the research expenses by selecting this project as 'runner-up' in their Centennial Grant Program. Management Development International, of which I am a partner, supported my efforts from conception to fruition. Most vitally, I am indebted to my partner and wife Lynne De Lay, who helped conceptualize this book, wrote the first draft of one chapter, queried every chapter, and endured my single-minded concentration on the book to the exclusion of almost everything else.

This multicontinental survey represents a milestone in my learning curve. I need hardly stress, though, that the errors of commission and omission are wholly mine.

Samuel Humes
Brussels

PART I
Organizational strategy: for global competitive advantage

CHAPTER 1
Strategy and organization: for corporate coherent advantage

To compete internationally: globalize, localize and reorganize

The world's largest companies are globalizing, localizing and reorganizing. The increasing pace of change and more aggressive global competition have forced multinationals to redevelop their traditional world-wide strategies. The new strategies have in turn forced them to redevelop the organizations they have long used to manage their international operations.

Changing strategies and organizations

To compete more effectively, the world's leading companies have stressed growth strategies to develop their economies of scale and scope (Chandler, 1990: esp. 17–18). They have diversified, expanding operations across business and industry borders to exploit technological or marketing skills or both. They have globalized, extending operations across country and continental borders to increase their world-wide customer base and global market share. And they have localized, moving more operations closer to their globally dispersed customers so that they can respond more effectively to local conditions and compete more effectively as 'local' companies. These strategic organizational efforts have multiplied the diverse parts comprising the multinationals. Consequently, they have also magnified the complexity of organizing and managing the multidimensional mosaic of product, geographic and functional parts that comprise the modern multinational – and increased the urgency of reorganizing.

A few reorganizations illustrate the sweeping impact of these efforts towards change upon the global divisions and the local affiliates:

- Du Pont has disbanded its international department and clarified the role of the surviving continental entities as staff support groups for the strengthened global product divisions.

- Philips has globalized the role of its product divisions, first by having them work in matrix with the national affiliates, and then by converting the latter into umbrella-type organizations containing the various product divisions' country units.
- British Petroleum (BP) has undertaken a similar reorganization, reducing their matrix from 11 business streams × 70 national affiliates to 4 business streams × 3 continental organizations, and has clarified the responsibilities of the territorial organizations as umbrellas with a limited supportive role.
- Sony, Nissan and Matsushita have developed continental organizations that manage the national sales affiliates and coordinate the continent-located operations of their production divisions. Matsushita's reorganization involved the absorption of its long-autonomous trading company.

These recent reorganizations highlight the latest phase of decades of evolution which cumulatively have revolutionized the way multinationals organize and manage their international operations. American companies long relied essentially upon international divisions, European companies upon their autonomous 'daughter' companies, and Asian companies upon their trading companies to manage their international efforts. By the early 1990s, however, almost all of the world's leading companies depended upon their global operating divisions to run their international operations.

With these changes has come an increasing readiness by multinationals to use a variety of management dynamics to unify their operations. Whereas until recently most American corporations tended to rely principally on structure and systems, European groups on management–staffing rapport, and Asian firms on shared corporate values to bind and bond the disparate parts of their international empires, today's multinationals are increasingly likely to rely on all three management dynamics. Thus what were once quite divergent American, European and Asian organizational traditions have undergone converging organizational transitions that point to several significant emerging trends.

The intent

Why and how have changing strategies led to major reorganizational efforts? What have been the organizational heritages from which these reorganizations have emanated? How have environmental conditions affected these reorganizations? How have changing operational distances, organizational perspectives and management dynamics reshaped multinational organizations? What trends may be perceived? As numerous and as noteworthy as the recent reorganizations have been, Peter Drucker has predicted that 'Businesses will undergo more and more radical restructuring in the 1990s than at any time since the modern corporate organization first evolved in the 1920s' (Drucker, 1989:22). The critical task for the multinational is to develop an organization with sufficient strategic coherency to mobilize the resources of the entire reorganization to focus on changing threats and opportunities. This task forms the central theme of this book.

This book compares the recent reorganizational efforts of a cross-section of leading American, European and Asian industrial corporations – with the intent of presenting an agenda of ideas that multinationals may wish to consider in undertaking future reorganizations. These ideas focus on developing more strategically coherent organizations – ones that can effectively identify transborder opportunities and mobilize cross-hierarchy collaboration towards common corporate objectives, and thus compete more advantageously. This book advances the theme that the creation of more strategically coherent organizations requires the concerted application of three sets of management dynamics – structuring, staffing and sharing values – to concert the three sets of organizational perspectives – product, geography and function – driving the various parts comprising the modern multinational.

In organizing and managing the modern mega-multinational, managers confront the global–local dilemma. The more successful a multinational has been in expanding its multi-industry and multicontinental scope and scale of operations, the greater the dilemma its managers face in developing a global organization capable of mobilizing its increasingly diverse local resources. The more a multinational provides global direction, the less opportunity the local parts may have in exercising local discretion and initiatives. The more successful multinationals have been in managing their vastness by 'pushing decisions down' and treating their global operating divisions as independent entities, the more difficult has been the challenge of mobilizing the interdependent resources. Thus the more a multinational has succeeded in walling-off its parts to enhance the advantages of their 'smallness', the greater the challenge it has in capitalizing on the 'bigness' advantages of scale and scope. How can a multinational promote global direction and local discretion? This is the dilemma this book addresses.

To manage size, diversity and complexity: the global–local dilemma

In developing an international organization with which to compete more advantageously world-wide, multinationals accommodate two sets of external pressures; those stressing global direction and those stressing local discretion (see Table 1.1.) Global direction stresses the responsibility for corporate-wide integration of product development and functional oversight. Local discretion enhances local responsiveness to the diverse demands of various geographic markets and flexible responsiveness to local conditions (see Prahalad and Doz, 1987:18). In their reorganizational efforts multinationals, more or less consciously, balance the pressures for global and local markets, global and local manufacturing and sourcing, and global and local resources.

Table 1.1 The global–local dilemma

Global direction	Local discretion
GENERAL	
Global Competition	**Domestic Competition**
The increased presence of multinational competitors and initiatives requires concerted responses.	The presence of local competitors may require a presence to assume flexibility and speed in competing.
Product Uniformity	**Product Demand Diversity**
Products which require little, if any, international adaptation across national markets may be produced and sold more economically on a transnational basis.	Geographic differences in customer needs and taste often require locally responsive strategies.
MARKETING	
Transnational Responsive Marketing	**Locally Responsive Marketing**
The presence of multinational customers who wish to purchase on a multicountry basis leads to a more international approach.	Differences in distribution channels in various countries and differences in pricing, product positioning, promotion and advertising require a local presence.
Marketing Industrial Products	**Multiproduct Customers**
The marketing of industrial products especially OEM (original equipment manufacturing) components is generally facilitated by an international approach.	Dealers who handle several lines of product may prefer to deal with the close-at-hand, general-purpose affiliate.
New Product Introduction	**Local Product Sensitivity**
The often costly introduction of new products and new brands into new national markets, which may, at least initially, affect the profit margins of profit-and-loss accountable national affiliates, may be facilitated by relying on global product divisions.	More sensitive to local conditions and tastes.

MANUFACTURING
SOURCING

Transnational Manufacturing
The need to exploit economies of scale by building plants that meet multicountry needs encourages firms to manufacture in a few locations serving multicountry markets.

Transnational Sourcing
Access to raw materials and opportunities for lower wages and lower other costs dictate a multicountry and perhaps a multicontinental approach to the location of production facilities.

Local Manufacturing/Sourcing
Where protectionism is strong, transportation costs are high, and/or the manufacturing process does not gain significantly from economies of scale. Local manufacturing/sourcing may be preferable.

OTHER

Transnational Financing
Intensive investments require access to global funding and world-wide strategies to be developed and implemented quickly to make the large initial investments.

Local Financing
For less intensive investments reliance on local financial sources may be sufficient.

Technology Transfer
Global integration facilitates the transfer of technical expertise and proprietary technology.

Global Image
Impact and interdependence of global image as means of promoting corporate and product recognition.

Local Interests
Host governments whose concerns range from local politics to country protectionism and national security may prefer dealing with one of 'our local companies'.

Global Professional and Management Resources
It is important to be able to shift expertise among countries and foster intercultural mixing and blending.

Host Country Personnel
Local staffing may be critical for local acceptance.

Many businesses such as food have organized to cope with more local pressures than global ones. Many others such as industrial electronics have organized to cope with more global pressures than local ones. The complex challenge facing multinationals is how to develop a corporate-wide organizational strategy for orchestrating the world-wide parts so that they have the capacity to work together in responding to changing conditions shaping both the local and global sets of pressures. This requires the meshing of global direction of product and functional strategies standards and systems with local discretion responding to geography-specific conditions. In diversified multinationals this issue has become so exacerbated that Drucker has called the problem the one that 'conventional organization theory cannot solve' (Drucker, 1973:747). Successful organizational strategies are not zero-sum games. To be globally competitive, multinationals need to find ways to exploit the advantages of smallness for their local entities as well as to exploit the advantages of bigness for the corporate whole.

A host of interrelated factors, ones that have long perplexed larger enterprises, provides the context for appreciating the global–local dilemma now confronting multinationals. Three significantly affect how a multinational divides and unites its international operations. They are as follows:

1. The operational distance that separates the management of a whole from the management of the entities comprising the whole, which reflects the extent of power and influence the management of the whole exerts on its parts, and affects the extent of operational autonomy that the parts exert.
2. The driving organizational perspectives that shape the distribution of power within the whole.
3. The management dynamics that provide the means for the whole exerting control over the parts.

These three criteria provide the cross-dimensions for a conceptual framework for comparing the major approaches to corporate governance.

Three degrees of operational distance and autonomy

A number of features reflect and affect the extent of operational distance separating the management of a multinational organization from the management of the entities comprising it (see Table 1.2 and Figure 1.1). Tighter and closer intraorganic power and influence occur when the multinational parts are subject to detailed instructions regarding not only what to do but how to do it, through various functionally specific sources of power. At the other pole, there exist looser/more open interorganic relations when the central headquarters' interest focuses on the meeting of general objectives. The coming of more convenient rapid transportation and instant communication has substantially increased the ability of an organization to direct and monitor the operations of its parts, and thus reduced

Table 1.2 Features reflecting/affecting operational distance/ autonomy

More operational distance – looser/more open	Less operational distance – tighter/more closed
General	
More independence/'arms length'	Less independence/'hands on'
Planning	
More decentralized	More centralized
Headquarters concerns	
Principally investments	Multiple product-specific
Financial control	and function-specific directions
Mode of oversight	
Advise and assist	Directing and controlling
General policy guidance	Detailed instructions
Standards	
Minimal and flexible	Comprehensive and detailed
Meetings	
Less frequent	More frequent
Generally of top executives	More levels
	Specialized functional and product oversight
Management systems	
Less integrated	More integrated personnel, financial and information systems

the operational distances dividing the constituent entities comprising the modern multinational.

In comparing multinational organizations with regard to the operational distance separating the management of the whole from that of the major members, one may distinguish a spectrum of types that range from undivisionalized companies that stress multiple intraorganizational ties to groupings of companies that possess limited interorganizational ties. The world's largest companies may be considered in three generic categories:

1. Multidivisional corporations such as Bayer which, while granting their divisions considerable autonomy, continue to manage certain staff support services centrally.
2. Multidivisional corporations such as Du Pont and General Motors which, while maintaining corporate staff services with an overview role, have developed their divisions as self-contained entities with a full range of staff services.

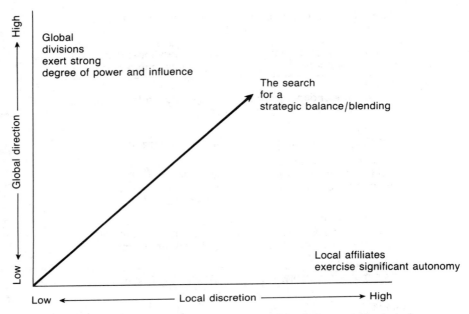

Figure 1.1   The global–local dilemma: the search for a strategic balance

3. Holding companies such as Royal Dutch/Shell and Nestlé which expect their
    operating companies to function with considerable operational autonomy. Core
    companies such as Toyota Motor operate with similar operational distance
    from other members of their group.

The basic organizational issue that a multinational needs to address in developing
the structure, staffing and shared-values facets of its organizational strategy is that
of whether the commonalities shared by all the organization are sufficient to support
the superstructure required to build coherence among the parts. This depends not
only upon the diversity of the parts but also upon the choice of driving perspectives
and management dynamics.

Three sets of interacting organizational perspectives

Three sets of organizational perspectives – function, product and geography – drive
the parts that comprise a multinational. These three, which compete with, conflict
with and complement one another, cut across management issues and converge
on specific management posts. These perspectives shape the way multinationals
divide their structures into manageable parts, develop staff to manage these
parts, and promote value sharing to facilitate communication and coordination

among the parts. Thus multinationals embrace three types of interlocked and interacting parts:

1. *Functional units*, which may focus on manufacturing and sourcing, marketing and sales, research and development, and such management resource/support services as finance, personnel and public affairs.
2. *Product divisions* – groups, sectors and subsidiaries which are generally responsible for a group of products related by technology or the customers/markets served. Many diversified multinationals refer to these as 'businesses'.
3. *Geographic or territorial entities*, such as national, regional and continental affiliates and offices, are responsible for the operations in one area. A multinational may consider these entities as markets or businesses.

Differences in outlook among differing national perspectives, differing product perspectives, differing functional perspectives – and between the differing sets of perspectives – inevitably generate tension, factions and friction. Tension is not only normal, it is vital for innovating, constructively appreciating, and balancing and blending perspectives. Differences enrich organizations; but divisiveness fragments them. The complexity of the organizational challenge springs from multinational dependence on these three sets of interactive and interdependent perspectives – which divide and bind the multinational organization in a multidimensional, mosaic-like framework (see Figure 1.2).

A basic issue which multinationals address is as follows: what perspectives, or combination of perspectives, does corporate leadership stress in routing commands and communications, developing management leadership and promoting core values? The ones it stresses reflect and affect the assignment of profit-and-loss responsibility, the control of financial and other management resources, and the prioritizing of professional loyalties and values – and thus determine how other perspectives are coordinated with or subordinated to the preordinate one(s). Multinationals have generally relied on one of these three major prototypes – product, geographic and functional – depending on which perspective has been stressed (see Figure 1.3).

Multinationals which stress the territorial or geographic perspective may be said to be area-divided and driven. The older European multinational 'groups', such as Royal Dutch/Shell, Imperial Chemical Industries and British Petroleum, initially developed with area-divided and driven strategies. Only in the last decades have BP, ICI and Philips moved to product-driven organizational strategies.

Multinationals which divide their operations primarily by product perspective may be said to be product-divided and driven. American corporations such as General Electric and Mobil may be described as having product-driven organizational strategies.

Multinationals whose global operations are divided essentially along functional lines may be said to be function-divided and driven. Japanese firms such as Nissan and Hitachi developed with function-driven strategies.

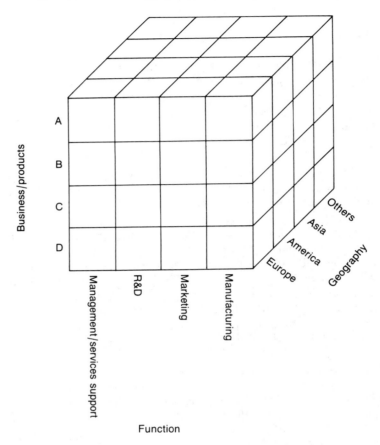

Figure 1.2   Three sets of perspectives driving multinational mosaics

Many multinationals combine these approaches (see Figure 1.4). Some, such as Exxon, use a 'mixed' approach, with part of the corporation stressing one approach and another part stressing another. Some use a 'matrix' approach; while in transition from the geographic to the product approach, Philips used a matrix that attempted to wed the product and geographic approaches. Some American companies, such as P&G, use an 'international division' approach in which domestic operations are divided by product and an international division manages overseas operations with an essentially matrix-like arrangement.

While multinationals combine these approaches, almost all stress one of these three. As noted at the outset, major multinationals on all three of the continents studied here are redeveloping their organizational strategies to place more stress on either an area or a product perspective. Many European firms, such as Bayer and more recently Philips, BP and ICI, have developed product-driven strategies. Some

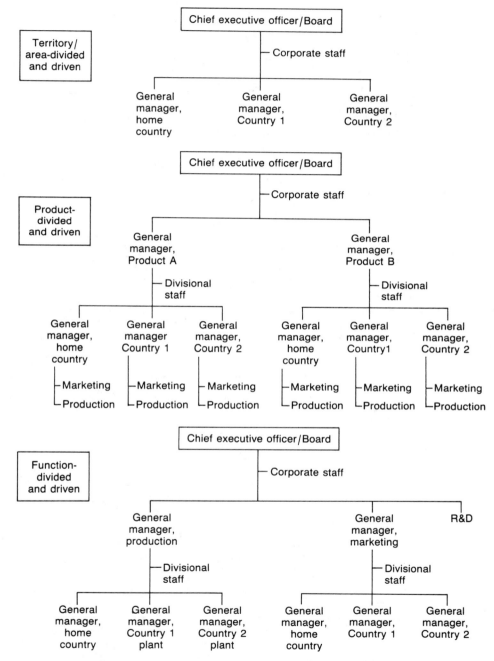

Figure 1.3 Simplified organograms depicting three prototypes (Source: Adapted from Chandler, HBS Case 373–369, revised June 1984b)

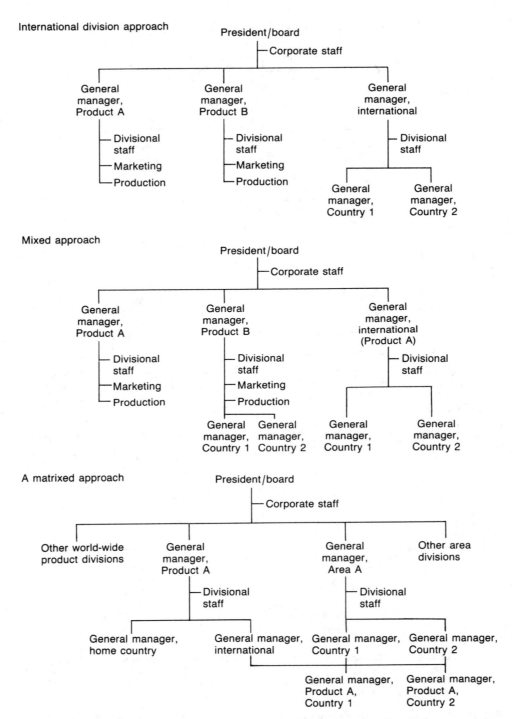

Figure 1.4 Simplified organograms depicting three approaches (Source: Adapted from Chandler, HBS Case 373–369, revised June 1984b)

American corporations, such as Du Pont, are reinforcing their product organizational strategies by eliminating their international divisions. And some Japanese firms, such as Sony, are tempering their function-driven strategies by establishing continental offices.

Three sets of management dynamics

To achieve organizational coherence, multinationals have relied on three sets of management dynamics: structure, staffing and shared values (see Figure 1.5). These have been the centripetal means by which multinationals have contained the centrifugal forces generated by the differing organizational perspectives. Successful organizational strategy seeks to employ these interacting dynamics in such a way that they not only ensure a coherent whole but also empower the component parts as follows:

- *Structuring*: what are the formal lines of command and systems of communications for exerting power and influence within the organization? Most American multinationals have stressed structure and their attended systems as means of exerting management control.
- *Staffing*: how do multinationals hire, educate, post and promote the corps on whom they rely to manage and lead the organization? Traditionally, most European multinationals have emphasized staffing with long-time associates for overseeing their international affiliates.
- *Sharing values*: how do multinationals develop the shared governing ideas affecting what employees believe about their organization – its mission, its vision and 'how we do things around here'? Traditionally, this cultural bonding

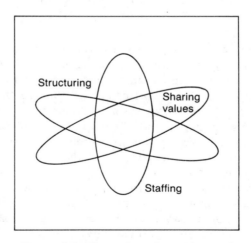

Figure 1.5 Dynamics of management

has been the major means by which Japanese companies have exerted hegemony over their international operations.

These three sets of dynamics are mutually reinforcing, but very few multinationals have stressed all three. A basic theme of this book is that all three are vital for competing successfully on a global scale; the larger and more complex the multinational, the more vital the combined, interactive use of all three. A series of complex strategic trade-offs affects how international responsibilities are structured, management positions staffed and corporate core values extended to the world-wide parts – and thus how the whole and the parts relate to one another. No organization will perform well in a competitive environment unless these dynamics drive the strategy and are consistent internally. The resolution of these critical issues affects resource development and allocation, marketing and production opportunities, and research and technological development – and the emergence of overall corporate leadership.

Multinationals may closely control some elements and not others. As Peters and Waterman have noted: The successful ones 'have pushed autonomy down to the shop floor or product development team [...but] they are fanatic around the few core values they hold dear' (1982:15). As they have developed, European, American and Asian multinationals have stressed different ways of exerting power and influence. The more successful major ones have, of necessity, strategically selected those issues on which they insist on corporate-wide hegemony and consistent standards – thus frustrating efforts to measure more than roughly the extent of power and influence a headquarters exerts over its component parts.

Introducing a 3 × 3 × 3 transcontinental comparative framework

The 3 × 3 × 3 transcontinental comparative framework, which this book introduces, facilitates cross-continental comparison of the organizational traditions and trends shaping the management of multinationals and their international operations. The transcontinental comparative framework comprises: the three degrees of operational autonomy; the three sets of organizational perspectives driving the product, territorial and functional parts; and the structure, staffing and shared-value dynamics employed to organize and concert operations. These three considerations provide the cross-dimensions for comparing the organizational evolution of American, European and Asian multinationals, and for noting the trends in their reorganizational transitions (see Figure 1.6). While there are variations and exceptions, this model facilitates comparison of the various European, American and Asian multinational organizational strategies, noting the variations in the stress they place on operational autonomy, organizational perspectives and management dynamics.

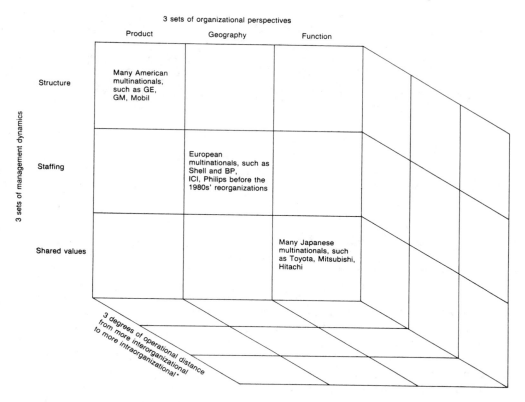

Figure 1.6 shows the following labels and content within the 3×3×3 framework:

3 sets of organizational perspectives

Product   Geography   Function

3 sets of management dynamics

Structure — Many American multinationals, such as GE, GM, Mobil

Staffing — European multinationals, such as Shell and BP, ICI, Philips before the 1980s' reorganizations

Shared values — Many Japanese multinationals, such as Toyota, Mitsubishi, Hitachi

3 degrees of operational distance from more interorganizational to more intraorganizational*

Note: *The American multidivisional multinationals have tended to provide their divisions with less operational autonomy than the European groups have allowed their national 'daughter' companies. The Japanese trading companies and sister companies have operated with significant organizational autonomy.

Figure 1.6   A 3×3×3 transcontinental comparative framework

By reviewing the circumstances and conditions under which these three traditional continental models evolved, one may appreciate the challenges facing each of them as they reorganize to confront the global–local dilemma.

CHAPTER 2
Reshaping organizational strategy: for continued growth

Forces shaping reorganization: traditions, trends, threats and opportunities

An organizational strategy outlines how an organization intends to manage its diverse organizational resources to attain its strategic objectives. A coherent organizational strategy enables the different parts to work together more effectively, more efficiently and more economically – by orchestrating the management dynamics of structuring, staffing and sharing values to balance and blend the diverse organizational perspectives driving the various pieces of the corporation. Concomitantly, structure, staffing and shared values – by their impact upon what perspectives an organization's leadership stresses and how it perceives its strengths, opportunities and threats – affect what strategies will be developed to advance an enterprise's objectives. Forces that have long shaped the evolution of organizational strategy include diverse continental traditions, dramatic global trends, and specific competitive threats and opportunities affecting various industries.

A corporation's organizational traditions, including the combination of organizational perspectives that has been stressed and the combination of management dynamics that has been used, have grown with and continue to guide its transitions. In part because of the different way their domestic operations have been organized, and in part because of the different conditions prevailing when many of these multinationals initially developed their present international affiliates, American, European and Asian multinationals have approached the organization of their international operations differently.

Global technological, economic and political trends have recast the intra-continental and intercontinental informational, social and economic communities. The increasing ease of global communication, growing trade and investment interdependence, and the emergence of three major continental trade blocs have led multinationals to develop and rationalize their presence on each continent. The development of a continental 'insider' presence reflects increasing economic interdependence and the need to compete locally in order to compete globally. The increased investment required to develop marketing, manufacturing, R&D and management infrastructure and expertise has fuelled the drive for internal growth, mergers (and streamlining and divestitures), a variety of marketing, manufacturing and R&D joint ventures, and other forms of strategic alliance.

The petroleum, motor vehicle, electronics/electrical equipment, chemicals and food industries – the fields in which all but a few of the Global 50 multinationals compete – have featured particular competitive conditions that have affected the development of the organizational strategy of these multinationals. As these conditions change, and the multinationals in the industries diversify, multinationals are led to reconsider how to face the global–local issue and its impact on the role of the country general manager.

All three sets of forces – the momentum of organization traditions, the growing integration of intracontinental and intercontinental communities, and the increasingly competitive industry conditions – affect the way multinationals use the management dynamics of structure, staffing and shared values to redevelop their organizational strategies.

Twentieth-century transitions: revolution through evolution

'What's past is prologue': an organization's past shapes its future. The ability of a multinational to change its organization is constrained not only by its external environment but also by its internal capability as shaped by its administrative legacy. A multinational organization, built over decades, develops a distinctive organizational heritage which cannot easily be changed (Bartlett and Goshal, 1989: 35; Stinchcombe, 1965). Thus a multinational's traditions not only provide building blocks but also present roadblocks in managing transitions.

A review of the successive organizational changes of multinational organizations over the course of the twentieth century demonstrates the impact of continuity upon organizations as they prepare for the twenty-first century. Four successive twentieth-century eras have left their distinctive imprint: pre-1945, 1945–59, 1960–74, and 1975–89. The pre-World War II years shaped the initial traditions of most of the 1990s' Global 50. The 1945–59 postwar period marked the decades of American multinationals' domination. The years 1960–74 witnessed European multinationals' resurgence. The post-1974 years have been ones of rapid Asian development (see Table 2.1).

Pre-1945 development

The latter decades of the nineteenth century and the early ones of the twentieth witnessed not only the emergence of the big industrial corporation but also the initial international expansion of many of the larger ones. Slower and more infrequent travel, limited and less convenient communication, high trade barriers and more marked national market differentiation characterized this era. 'In the United States,

Table 2.1   Global 50: by country, 1959–91

CONTINENTS/Countries	Five-year benchmarks								
	1959	1964	1969	1974	1979	1984	1989	1990	1991
NORTH AMERICA[1]									
United States	44	37	36	24	22	21	17	16	16
Total for continent	*44*	*37*	*36*	*24*	*22*	*21*	*17*	*16*	*16*
WEST EUROPE									
Britain	2	3	4	4	3	3	3	2	2
Britain/Netherlands	2	2	2	2	2	2	2	2	2
France				3	4	3	4	5	5
Germany		5	4	7	7	6	6	7	7
Italy		1	2	2	2	3	3	3	3
Netherlands	1	1	1	1	1	1	1	1	1
Switzerland	1	1		1	1	1	2	2	2
Total for continent	*6*	*13*	*13*	*20*	*20*	*19*	*21*	*22*	*22*
EAST ASIA									
Japan			1	4	6	6	10	9	10
South Korea							2	2	2
Total for continent			*1*	*4*	*6*	*6*	*12*	*11*	*12*
OTHER[2]									
Iran				1					
Kuwait						1			
Brazil				1	1	1			
Mexico						1			
Venezuela					1	1		1	1
Total for continent				*2*	*2*	*4*		*1*	*1*
Total overall	*50*	*50*	*50*	*50*	*50*	*50*	*50*	*50*	*50*

Notes: 1. Not including Mexico.
2. All are nationally owned oil companies.
Sources: Information collated from *Fortune*, 1960a,b, 1965a,b, 1970a,b, 1975, 1980, 1985a,b, 1990b, 1991a,b, 1992.

the modern industrial enterprise came into being and evolved' (Chandler, 1990:11–12) and expanded beyond its large domestic base. The bigger European enterprises expanded beyond their confining borders.

In the early decades of the twentieth century, there were many more modern industrial enterprises in the United States than in either Britain or Germany, the other leading industrial powers. Even before World War I, a number of American companies had directly invested overseas. One of the first to expand internationally was the Standard Oil Trust; by 1885 its exports to 'Europe, to the Middle East, and to the Far East [... accounted for] seventy percent of the Standard's business' (Sampson, 1988:43). Ford developed a few international affiliates before 1914. Others that developed extensive overseas investments then included General Electric, Vacuum Oil (a predecessor of Mobil), Otis Elevators (a predecessor of United Technologies) and Western Electric.

'Yet it is after 1914 that the blossoming and vast influence of the U.S. headquartered multinational corporation came of age' (Wilkins, 1974:VIII; see Wilkins for a detailed analysis of the development of American business abroad from 1914 to 1970). 'The large undivided size of the American domestic market, and the rapidly increasing American standards of living led the modern, integrated, multinational enterprise to appear in greater numbers and attain a greater size earlier in the United States than in other countries' (Chandler, 1990:52 – his book critically analyses the factors shaping the evolution of the larger American, British and German firms from the 1880s to the 1940s). 'In the main, a vast expansion of international business meant – as Alfred D. Chandler has pointed out – a company had to alter its overall management structure if it was to be efficient' (Wilkins, 1974:146). Thus, as the American companies developed and adapted the multidivisional organization with autonomous multifunctional operating divisions, they tended to develop an international subsidiary or division to develop and manage their international operations. General Electric formed an international division in 1919; Standard Oil did the same in 1927; General Motors (which had formed an export company in 1911 and replaced it with an Export and Overseas Group in 1924) firmly established national operations in Europe with the purchase of Vauxhall in England in 1925 and of Adam Opel in Germany in 1929, and in Latin America with the setting up of General Motors de Brazil in 1925. The American Telephone and Telegraph's manufacturing subsidiary Western Electric had well-developed international interests (which included the 1882-founded, Belgian-based Bell Telephone Manufacturing) until 1925, when it was forced by an anti-trust action to sell to International Telephone and Telegraph (ITT) (Sampson, 1973:25; Wilkins, 1974:70–1); the overseas holdings that comprised the initial components of the telecommunication business were sold in 1987 to CGE, now Alcatel Alsthom. By 1939, IBM's overseas affiliates, run by its 'foreign department', already accounted for about one-eighth of its sales (Watson and Petre, 1990:34). The American multinationals that had developed overseas affiliates before World War II were well poised to build upon these in the postwar decades.

The conditions of prewar Europe led European firms, as they expanded beyond their limited domestic bases across nearby frontiers, to create clone-like, relatively self-contained and autonomous affiliates. Together a parent company and its daughter companies formed a group in which the parent exerted strategic control. Nestlé had already begun assembling its multinational empire before World War I. Philips developed eighteen European affiliates – beginning with one in neighbouring Belgium – from 1919 to 1930; in 1933 it organized its US affiliate, which by World War II had become, next to the parent company, the largest national organization in the Philips group. The Anglo-Persian Oil Company (now British Petroleum or BP) developed affiliates throughout Europe in the interwar years, in part by purchasing what had been the prewar international affiliates of German oil companies. In their international efforts, these European firms tended to rely on trusted associates which operated with significant autonomy within well-understood, even though unwritten, guidelines. Those affiliates that survived World War II continued to exert considerable autonomy in their relations with headquarters.

The international efforts of Japanese companies before World War II were generally limited to the marketing activities of the international trading companies of their major *zaibatsu*.

1945–59: American domination

In the early postwar years, American firms continued to lead the way in overseas expansion. American firms, spurred on by war-propelled momentum, built on their well-developed American markets, productive capacity, and management structures and systems to expand overseas. Most of the firms organizing these affiliates continued to concentrate in the same industries as before the war: electrical equipment, motor vehicles, oil, chemicals and food. The extent of the American domination of the multinational arena in the 1950s is demonstrated by the fact that in 1959 all but six of the world's 50 largest multinationals were American. In 1959, the other six of the world's 50 largest companies in 1959 were European. Two were Dutch–British companies (Royal Dutch/Shell and Unilever); two were British companies (British Petroleum and Imperial Chemical Industries); one was Swiss (Nestlé) and one was Dutch (Philips – these last two had moved an international headquarters off-continent before the German occupation). These six had recovered and grown more quickly in the immediate postwar years than others. The boom years of the 1960s accelerated the pace of development of the European firms even more than that of the American ones.

1960–74: European redevelopment

The major European multinational groups grew dramatically from 1960 to 1974. Even while Servan-Schreiber was lamenting American domination in *The American Challenge* (1968), multinationals such as Siemens, Daimler-Benz, Volkswagen and Fiat had secured places in the Global 50 – soon to be joined by BASF, Hoechst, Bayer, Renault and British-American Tobacco. Within fifteen years the number of European multinationals had more than tripled so that by 1974 there were twenty.

This growth in size was accompanied by diversification. Philips, Fiat and Bayer, among others, expanded their product scope as well as their international spread. While Philips continued to rely on its international affiliates as the primary basis for developing its world-wide activities, the rapidly developing groups such as Fiat and Bayer relied upon their product sectors to provide the momentum for their international development. During this period, Philips first began the rationalization of its manufacturing operations, Bayer undertook a reorganization that would lead to its transformation into a multidivisional corporation, and Fiat with government assistance expanded rapidly, becoming a loosely administered conglomerate.

Several American companies increased their major international efforts during this period. Procter & Gamble, for example, accelerated its efforts with the 1963 establishment of a European Technical centre to coordinate and support its European activities. While many American multinationals continued the expansion of their international efforts, from 1960 to 1974, the number of US-based Global 50 firms declined from 44 to 24 – a decline accounted for not only by the dramatic European resurgence but also by the recessions of the early 1970s, which prompted a downsizing of the international operations of many major American multinationals.

> By the 1960s, most of the major American corporations with sizeable investments abroad had adopted the multidivisional structure to administer their foreign holdings. As they expanded their foreign direct investment, they put aside their international departments, which had long coordinated and monitored foreign activities, replacing them either by area divisions or by worldwide product divisions. (Chandler, 1990:611; see also Stopford and Wells, 1972:41)

It was during this period that a few Japanese companies began to secure a firm international base, with Hitachi joining the Global 50 by 1969 and Toyota, Mitsubishi Heavy Industry and Nippon Kokan (a Japanese steel company) by 1974, but most continued to rely on the trading companies for their international marketing efforts.

1975–89: Asian emergence

The 1970s and 1980s were the decades when many larger European groups diversified and redeveloped into product-driven multinationals, the American multinationals generally through their international divisions began to rationalize their marketing and manufacturing, and the Japanese and later the South Korean firms dramatically increased their presence. By 1989 there were twenty-one European multinationals in the Global 50, twelve Asian and only seventeen American.

As already noted at the outset of this chapter, the late 1970s and especially the 1980s witnessed dramatic organizational changes, in part accelerated by the emergence of continental trade blocs. The major American multinationals enhanced their multifunctional international presence by increasing and continentally rationalizing their manufacturing operations, strengthening their continental product coordination, and increasing localization of their support functions. European groups increased their diversification efforts; some firms, such as Philips and ICI, that had long operated as groups of country units began to undertake the major strides that would transform them into product-sector-driven multinationals.

The larger Japanese multinationals developed global functional networks of affiliates; first of marketing affiliates and later of manufacturing affiliates. In contrast, the Korean *chaebol* developed as product-driven conglomerates.

1990–?: Towards transformation

By the beginning of the 1990s, multinationals had developed a variety of approaches for organizing their international efforts. Most larger American corporations depend upon their highly structured product divisions; only a few have continued to rely on international divisions to work with most or all of their product divisions in coordinating international operations. An increasing number of European groups rely primarily upon their product divisions to manage their international affiliates; only a few corporations such as Royal Dutch/Shell and Nestlé continue to rely essentially on their globally dispersed operating companies. The Japanese firms have developed function-split global systems of marketing affiliates and of manufacturing affiliates. The South Korean *chaebol*, while sharing the Japanese corporate stress on corporate culture, are product-split conglomerates.

On all three continents, multinationals, conscious of the increasing pressures for change and the continuing need to improve their organizations, are developing a wider range of management dynamics. Some of the reorganizational steps that multinationals are taking appear more cautious and more piecemeal than others, but their cumulative impact upon corporate organizational traditions has been revolutionary. They have already led to converging transitions and pointed to prospective organizational trends (see Table 2.2).

Table 2.2 Successive organizational phases of prototypical leading multinationals

Continent	Earlier divergent traditions (thesis: divide by territory)	Recent converging transitions (antithesis: divide by product)	Prospective emerging trends (synthesis: bridging the divides)
American	International divisions manage foreign affiliates	Global multifunctional product divisions manage overseas affiliates – trend evident from 1960s	Global operating divisions supported by corporate-wide continental (marketing/sales/ service and/or management support) coordinating organizations
European	'Daughter' companies report to corporate board	Product divisions expand global and multifunctional roles – trend evident by 1970s	
Asian	Trading companies manage overseas business	Production division as well as sales divisions develop their own overseas affiliates – trend develops in 1980s	

A review of the events that surrounded the early twentieth-century major corporate transformation reveals three transitional stages 'that precede any great transformation' (Hickman and Silva, 1987: 7). First, there is a period of cumulated change during which organizations incrementally adjust approaches, methods, philosophies and orientation to fit the needs of a changing environment. Second, when the period of incremental change ends its acceleration and no longer 'satisfies' the organizational needs, the opportunity arises for a fundamental and comprehensive shift from past methods, approaches, philosophies and orientations. The old ways do not fade away gradually but rather provide the foundations on which management adjusts to the new transformation in view of the continuing changing conditions. 'Third, the transformation launches a new series of transitions and eras during which people adjust to the new approach in light of continually evolving conditions' (*ibid.*). In this process, there is often a leapfrog syndrome, with those that have been successful in meeting an earlier organizational crisis becoming somewhat complacent and then being forced to catch up in a later crisis. The case studies presented in this comparative survey provide ample evidence that the world's major multinationals, as they approach the twenty-first century, are in a state of flux. The creativity aroused by the increasing complexity and competition may, and appears headed in that direction, produce an organizational model more capable of coherently balancing and blending the diverse product, functional and territorial perspectives which drive the various mosaic-like parts of the multinationals.

Global trends: increasing inter- and intracontinental interdependence

A myriad of interacting global, social, political and economic trends continues to push multinationals to develop global strategies and transcontinental organizations. Symptoms of these trends have been the improved computer and telecommunication technologies which have facilitated cross-continental communication; increased customer concern for product quality, price, design, value, and brand image, whatever its national origin; and the economic integration of international communities. The more general trends have forced the pace of other changes. The rapid pace of technological change has multiplied the critical technologies on which most companies now depend, increased the dependence on technological transfer and the complexity of manufacturing and sourcing, and accelerated the speed with which new products come to market and are marketed. The accelerating pace of more sophisticated R&D, of building more technologically advanced manufacturing facilities, of extending distribution networks and promoting brand names, and of developing administrative support systems has dramatically increased fixed costs and forced multinationals to seek increased economies of scale, scope and synergy.

The desire to spread the costs and the risks and to speed up the development and distribution of new products has led not only to more mergers and acquisitions but also to a variety of forms of joint ventures and other types of alliances for R&D,

manufacturing and marketing (see Lewis, 1990, for a discussion of the variety of types and means of structuring and managing strategic alliances). Differences in the cost of staffing, raw materials, manufactured components and money – which change as currency exchange rates fluctuate – force multinationals to develop globally flexible sourcing strategies. The impact of these forces has been reinforced by differences in the extent to which countries exert protectionism, the variety of tariff and non-tariff means countries use to apply protectionism, and disparities in the application of their protectionism. All of these factors have increased the extent to which multinationals not only market but also manufacture and source multicontinentally.

A few particularly noteworthy interdependent trends have speeded globalization. They have accelerated continentalization even more. These trends include increasing inter- and intracontinental trade and investment, the emergence of continental communities and the significant growth of multinationals.

Increasing foreign investment and world trade: the triad

A review of world trade and foreign direct investment trends reveals not only their growing impact on the world economy but also the increasing extent to which world trade and foreign investment focus upon the United States, the European Community and Japan. (UNCTC, 1991, was a major source of information for this section.)

Since 1950, world trade has grown twice as rapidly as the sum of gross national products (GNP). A major factor contributing to this growth has been the postwar desire to liberalize and expand international trade. The most important expression of this desire has been the 1947 founding of the General Agreement on Tariffs and Trade (GATT), an integrated set of bilateral trade agreements aimed at reducing tariff duties and trade restrictions. The GATT negotiations have been spurred by a series of international conferences and negotiating 'rounds'. The stormy slogging that has marked the multilateral negotiations in the Uruguay round has, however, stimulated the negotiations regarding the European Community, the North American Free Trade Agreement, and Asia/Pacific cooperation. The expansion of world trade has been buttressed since the late 1970s by a 50 per cent real increase in foreign direct investment (FDI) accompanied by more dramatic growth in international stock, bond and foreign exchange markets (Nulty, 1990a:23). From 1984 to 1989 the flow of new foreign direct investment rose at an annual rate of 29 per cent – three times as fast as trade (*Economist*, 1991a:53).

By 1989, the total sales (more than $3,800 billion) generated by the 50 largest industrial corporations significantly contributed to the total GNP (less than $18,000 billion) of the countries of the world (*Book of Vital World Statistics*, 1990:33). A significant share of the multinational contribution to the world output is generated through intrafirm trade. Such intramultinational trade is an integral aspect of multinationals' activities that involves international dispersed sourcing of raw

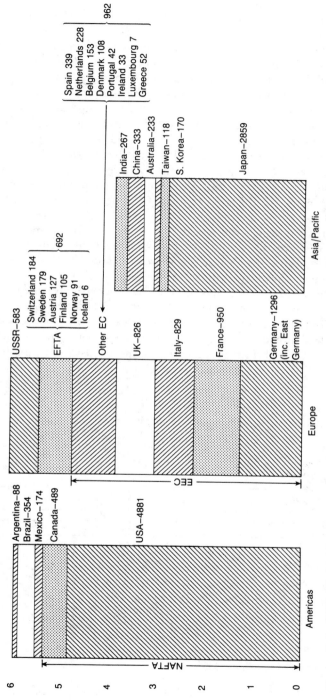

Figure 2.1 GDP ($bn) of 'richest' nations compared by 'macrocontinent', 1988 (Source: *Book of Vital World Statistics*, 1990:33)

materials and manufacturing of components and the use of transnational distribution channels.

Three major economies have become not only the foci of major trade blocs but also the principal sources of investment. As Figure 2.1 demonstrates, the economies of the United States, the rapidly integrating European Community (EC) and Japan dominate their continents. The extent to which these three continental economies shape the patterns of world trade is illustrated by Figure 2.2. The dominant role of the United States within the Americas is indicated by the fact that more than 70 per cent of the exports of Canada and Mexico are USA-bound. The extent of European intracontinental interdependence is illustrated by the facts that not only are more than 70 per cent of the export of the European countries to other European countries, but also only three European countries count the USA among one of their three major markets (the UK exports 12.9 per cent, Italy 8.9 per cent, and Switzerland 8.5 per cent) (*Book of Vital World Statistics*, 1990:158).

The extent to which the world is splitting into three investment 'clusters' is illustrated by Figure 2.3. Until 1980, foreign direct investment (FDI) was dominated by the United States, which was the source for about half of FDI. Since then, the USA's dominance has waned; investment by cash-rich Japanese firms has increased exponentially; and the EC has become an increasingly integrated source and destination for investment. Together the three continental blocs now account for more than 80 per cent of foreign direct investment – with the EC's share (including intra-EC flows) already matching that of the USA, with Japan rapidly catching up. Investment by these three was stimulated in the 1980s by non-EC-based companies

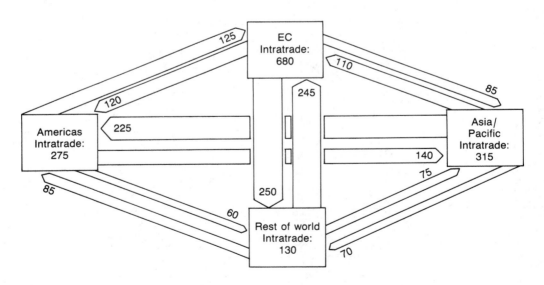

Note: *Figures rounded to nearest $5bn

Figure 2.2 World trade flows ($bn)*, 1989 (Source: *Economist*, 1991d:20)

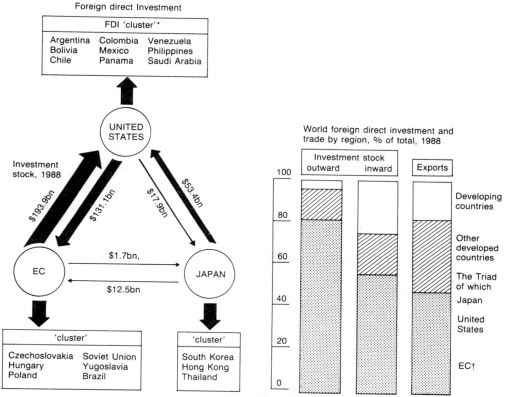

Figure 2.3   Foreign direct investment, 1988 (Source: *Economist*, 1991a:53)

rushing to position themselves within the EC before the creation of the single market, and by Japanese companies' efforts to dodge rising costs at home and growing protectionism abroad.

FDI has tended to focus on opportunities in the same continental region. The USA has long been the major source in the Americas, and Japan has become the major source of investment in Asia. The EC countries, especially Germany, are the major source for new investment throughout Europe, including Eastern Europe. For example, 'American firms account for 61 per cent of all FDI in Mexico, Japanese firms for 52 per cent in South Korea. Often this reflects attempts by multinationals to build up regional networks naturally starting near their home base' (*Economist*, 1991a:53). The tri-focal pattern of foreign direct investment provides evidence that continental neighbours will continue to associate more closely in trading blocs, further motivating multinationals to look and think continentally rather than nationally as they develop globally.

Continental trade areas

The intracontinental trade and investment patterns have reflected and stimulated efforts to develop continental free-trade areas. The EC, born with the signing of the Treaty of Rome in 1956, initially consisted of the Federal Republic of Germany, France, Italy, the Netherlands, Belgium and Luxembourg. It added the United Kingdom, Denmark and Ireland in 1973, Greece in 1981, and Spain and Portugal in 1986. The extent to which EC interaction has stimulated each EC country's external trade, and especially the intra-EC trade, is illustrated in Figure 2.4.

The EC, which forms the nucleus of a much larger trade area, may more than double in membership in the next decade. An agreement has already been negotiated between the twelve-nation EC and seven-nation European Free Trade Association (EFTA) – Austria, Finland, Iceland, Liechtenstein, Norway, Sweden and Switzerland – to form a nineteen-nation European Economic Area (EEA) (see Figure 2.5). The accord provides not only a type of affiliate membership in the EC but also a transition phase easing the entry of countries into the EC – and thus sets the stage for an enlarged EC which may include not only more Western European countries but also some of what have been called East European countries (and perhaps even a few non-European Mediterranean countries). An irony of the EEA agreement is that it was initially conceived as a way for the EC to avoid early enlargement and for applicant countries to avoid the internal political divisions that applying for the EC membership may involve; but it has in fact spurred countries to apply to join the EC club. With the accord, EFTA members recognize that they have to assume many of the economic obligations without the accompanying political decision-making capacity to determine these obligations. Already Turkey, Austria, Malta, Cyprus, Sweden, Finland and Switzerland have applied for EC membership. In 1991 the EC granted Poland, Czechoslovakia and Hungary the status of associate members.

The Single European Act (SEA), adopted in 1985 and ratified in 1987, committed the EC member countries to the progressive establishment of a single market by 31 December 1992 – a step that has significantly enhanced the EC. The single market goal has required the development of new legislation in company law, competition policy, consumer protection, environmental policy, financial services, industry, transport, public procurement, telecommunications and free movement of persons. The agreement removed the need for unanimity in the Council of Ministers when deciding single-market issues. By 1992, the Council of Ministers and the European Parliament had approved over 70 per cent of the 282 single-market directives; the implementation of many of these directives has been delayed because they depend upon legislation being passed by all twelve member states.

These SEA efforts began to affect corporate organizational strategies well before 1992. For European firms, the initial SEA efforts have encouraged investment and

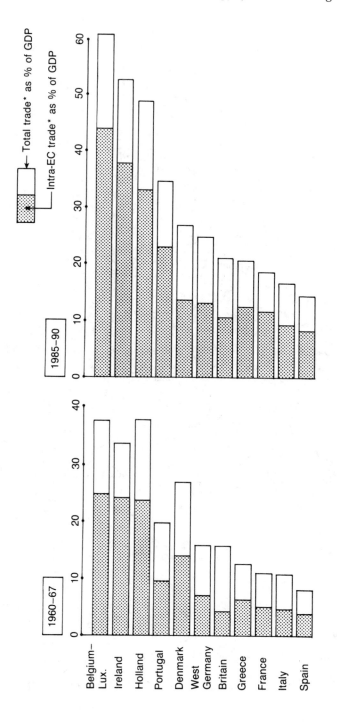

*Average of merchandise imports and exports

Figure 2.4 European Community 'togetherness' in trade 1960–7, 1985–90 (Source: *Economist*, 1991i:35)

EC countries

EFTA countries

(A)   Countries that had applied for EC membership by April 1992

Figure 2.5   Broadening the European Community

the rationalization of production because the cost of exporting was being reduced. For non-European firms, the protective impact of a common external tariff and expectations of a strengthened European competitiveness have led to their increasing their EC-located investments – to 'localize' manufacturing and in many cases R&D as well – in order to participate as insiders as quickly as possible. Japanese investment especially has surged; according to the Export–Import Bank of Japan, from 1988 to 1989 Japanese multinationals increased their European investment by 68 per cent. Anticipation of 1992 has also encouraged numerous cross-border mergers, acquisitions and alliances. These have included the merger of Asea with Brown Boveri to form ABB (Asea Brown Boveri), the CGE (now Alcatel Alsthom) acquisition of the ITT telecommunication business, and the Fiat alliance with Alcatel Alsthom. These represent only the largest of a wave of mergers and acquisitions.

The issue of breadth versus depth has provoked debate. Some, including most vocally the United Kingdom, have preferred to stress the broadening of membership and the slowing down of economic–political integration. Others, including France, have preferred to proceed as quickly as possible with economic integration, including the creation of a common currency, thus setting the terms on which additional countries would join or associate themselves with the EC. The Treaty of Maastricht, which was negotiated in December 1991, was intended to propel the European Community further towards European union. The treaty as written has proposed enhancing the powers of the European Parliament, virtually committing the countries to a monetary union and common currency by 1999, providing for an intergovernmental common foreign and security policy 'which might in time lead to a common defence', and delegating responsibility for decisions and actions that have defence implications to the Western European Union. It has also proposed providing for a common European citizenship, establishing a new 'cohesion fund' to aid poorer member states and endowing the EC with new responsibilities in social policy, culture, consumer protection, telecommunications, environment and immigration. Thus the treaty has proposed not only extending the EC's competence on common-market issues but also expanding its capacity to make common policy, and supervising member state policies in such critical fields as monetary, fiscal, foreign and security affairs. While the narrow defeat of the Maastricht treaty in the Danish referendum, the narrow victory in the French referendum, and the growing caution of British and other national leaders may lead to rewriting, revising, clarifying, or otherwise modifying the Maastricht treaty, the tide towards a continued strengthening of EC institutions appears unrelenting – albeit at a slower pace with a greater stress on 'subsidiarity'.

The way the European Union evolves will not only shape the continuing political integration of Europe and the multinationals' organizations for managing the European market. The speed with which it develops its supra-sovereign powers will affect the urgency with which countries on the American continents and those in the Asia/Pacific region address the issue of strengthening their trade associations.

The 1987 Canada–United States Free Trade Agreement, which will eliminate tariffs between the countries over a ten-year period, has already begun to have an impact on American and Canadian multinational organizations. The agreement will benefit US and Canadian exporters as the tariffs are phased out (depending on the product) either immediately, over five years or over ten years. The reduction of tariffs will also affect the sourcing of components used by corporations in both countries. Discussions are already well under way with respect to Mexico's interest in becoming an additional participant in the North American Free Trade Area. President Bush's invitation to other countries on the American continent to consider some form of association with the North American Free Trade Area has aroused some interest. The USA has already signed sixteen so-called framework agreements, the first step in the process towards a free trade area.

Asian/Pacific countries, whose growth rate in recent years has doubled that of the USA and the EC, have strengthened their regional ties. Japan has played a key role in the process (see Figure 2.6), in part by corporate investment in the region and in part by government aid. Hong Kong, Singapore, South Korea and Taiwan have substantially increased their exports to Japan as well as to other countries.

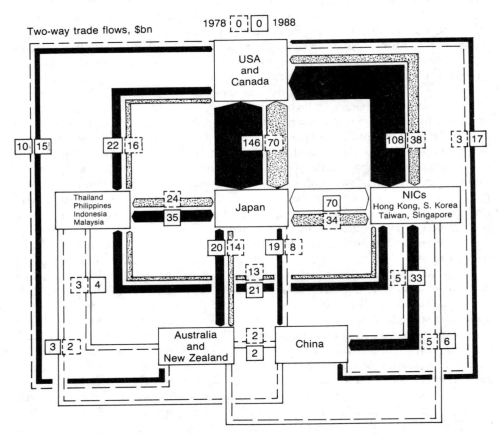

Figure 2.6   East Asia/Pacific Rim: two-way trade flows 1978–88 (Source: *Economist*, 1989b:7)

A stronger Asia/Pacific bloc would assist these countries in diversifying their investments, and create larger markets for their products (*Economist*, 1989b:9). The regional recipients of Japanese foreign aid are interested in increasing their share of exports to Japan because the earned yen is needed to service their debt payments. Japan, which gains a source of lower-cost production, has worked out a Pacific economic cooperation policy whereby Japanese aid, technical assistance and measures to open the Japanese market are linked with private capital and technology.

While the potential economic gains from Asian/Pacific economic cooperation would be significant, the emergence of such a bloc faces serious political barriers and historic animosities. Many of the Asian/Pacific countries in which Japan is investing so heavily continue to harbour bitter memories of World War II and its efforts to develop the Greater East Asia Coprosperity sphere. Critical issues are which countries will participate and on which matters they will cooperate. Already a number of overlapping associations have been formed. These include ASEAN (Association of South-East Asian Nations) and APEC (Asia–Pacific Economic Cooperation). ASEAN comprises Brunei, Indonesia, Malaysia, the Philippines, Singapore and Thailand. APEC includes not only the six ASEAN members, but also the United States, Canada, Australia, New Zealand, Japan, South Korea, China, Hong Kong and Taiwan (see Figure 2.7). ASEAN has proposed a free trade area to be called the East Asia Economic Caucus; Japan, China, South Korea, Taiwan and Hong Kong have been invited to join. The proposed pact aims to reduce tariffs on manufactured goods gradually on a sector-by-sector basis over a fifteen-year period, but the framework avoids dealing with trade in agriculture and services. The ASEAN free-trade-zone proposal is an attempt to counter the emergence of free-trade areas in Europe and North America. But the limited nature of the plan, strong national reservations regarding the role of Japan and the continuing trade links of individual ASEAN members with the United States and European countries continue to present dilemmas that must be overcome.

The future of international economic integration in Latin America, Africa, West and South Asia and East Europe is uncertain. Several multicountry groupings have long functioned in Africa, Latin America and the Middle East. It is not yet clear how closely associated the Commonwealth of Independent States formed by the ex-Soviet republics will become. The potential in some of these markets is substantial. The number of joint ventures and other terms of strategic alliances between local companies and global ones goes on growing. As these markets continue to open up for multinational corporations, the overall strategies of the companies will change dramatically.

While the final forms of the three major trade areas are unclear, what does appear obvious is that these forms will differ dramatically. The EC is moving rapidly to some form of political union (but not a 'federation' as the USA and Germany have role-modelled the concept: see Wheare, 1946: Part I): such a union would provide a barrier-free zone for products, people and money, and perhaps have affiliate as well as full members. The very size of, and discrepancies in living standards in, the American countries appear to limit the North American Free Trade Area's

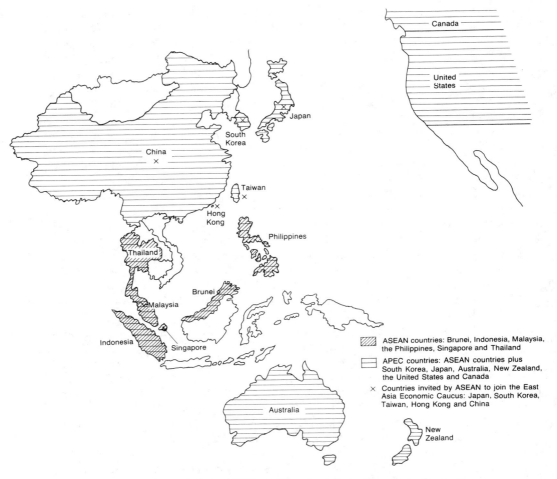

Figure 2.7   ASEAN, APEC and the East Asia Economic Caucus

foreseeable prospects. The Asia/Pacific community appears to face even more difficult issues. However they develop, though, these emerging blocs provide each of the three continental communities with a more effective means not only of reducing intracontinental trade barriers but also of negotiating the alleviation of intercontinental ones.

Just as the strength of the American and Japanese economies has encouraged the EC to develop closer ties, so does the evolution of the EC encourage the American and Asian communities to do the same. The increasing intra- as well as intercontinental interdependence of world trade and world investment reinforces this trend. So do the continuing efforts of multinationals to expand multi-continentally – and to coordinate at continental levels.

Global 50 growth: multi-industry as well as multicontinental

The 1990 Global 50, the world's 50 largest industrial corporations as ranked by sales, differ significantly in many regards (see Table 2.3). In 1991 their sales ranged from almost $124 billion (General Motors) to $21 billion (United Technologies), their assets from over $180 billion (General Motors) to less than $14 billion (Petroleos de Venezuela or PDVSA), their stockholders' equity from more than $53 billion (Royal Dutch/Shell) to less than $3 billion (Thyssen), and their employees from more than 750,000 (General Motors) to about 40,000 (Texaco). While Exxon generated a 1991 profit of over $5 billion, General Motors recorded a loss of over $2 billion. While Du Pont traces its history to the beginning of the nineteenth century, Samsung considers itself to have started from scratch in the latter half of the twentieth. While most of the Global 50 have widely dispersed shareholdings, one family controls a substantial portion of the equity in each of Fiat, Samsung and Daewoo, a bank controls Daimler-Benz, and other Mitsubishi grouping companies own 17 per cent of equity in Mitsubishi Electric. The national government owns a majority of the equity in France's Renault and Elf Aquitaine, Italy's IRI and ENI, and Petroleos de Venezuela (see Table 2.4).

A dramatic feature of the Global 50 has been their growth. In 1959, fewer than 25 industrial corporations generated sales of more than $1.5 billion. By 1990, after three decades of remarkable growth of the leading industrial corporations, 50 recorded more than $21 billion. This is more than the total government expenditure of Ireland, Portugal, Turkey or Israel (*Book of Vital World Statistics*, 1990: 136–7). Even a conservative projection of their rate of growth indicates that by the year 2000 more than 50 multinationals will generate sales exceeding $40 billion and more than 10 will generate sales exceeding $100 billion (see Table 2.5).

This growth has been fuelled not only by multicontinental expansion, but also by multi-industry diversification. While a few Global 50 companies have remained highly focused, most have diversified across a number of industrial fields. A few, such as Samsung, Hitachi, Du Pont, General Electric and Fiat, cut across many (see Table 2.6). In fact, a few companies have so diversified that their primary focus has shifted or blurred. *Fortune* continues to list IRI under 'metals', even though IRI's telecommunication subsidiary STET 'does earn the most money in total revenue sales [but] the majority of IRI's revenue still comes from the manufacturing sector, and within the manufacturing sector, steel ranks as the top revenue earner' (personal letter from Mattern (of *Fortune*), 5 November 1990). The extent of diversification magnifies the complexity and the consequent organizational challenge.

The evolution of the 50 biggest firms reflects the changes in the postwar industrial structure. Not only has American multinational dominance been reduced by the rise of West European and East Asian companies, but also, increasingly, the multinationals now compete principally in one of five industries: petroleum, electric/electronic equipment, motor vehicles, food and chemicals (see Table 2.7). For decades, more than 60 per cent of the Global 50 have focused on one of these five industries (see Table 2.8). By 1990, 42 of the Global 50 competed principally

Table 2.3 Global 50: sales, profits, assets and employees, 1991

1991	1990	Company	Country	Sales $ millions	Sales % change from 1990	Profits $ millions	Profits Rank	Profits % change from 1990	Assets $ millions	Stock-holders' equity $ millions	Employees Number
1	1	GENERAL MOTORS[X]	US	123,780.1	(1.1)	(4,452.8)	490	—	184,325.5	27,327.6	756,300
2	2	ROYAL DUTCH/SHELL GROUP[X]	Britain/Neth.	103,834.8	(3.1)	4,249.3	2	(34.0)	105,307.7	53,890.1	133,000
3	3	EXXON[X]	US	103,242.0	(2.5)	5,600.0	1	11.8	87,560.0	34,927.0	101,000
4	4	FORD MOTOR[X]	US	88,962.8	(9.5)	(2,258.0)	488	(362.5)	174,429.4	22,690.3	332,700
5	6	TOYOTA MOTOR[X]	Japan	78,061.3	21.0	3,143.2	3	5.0	65,178.7	33,197.6	102,423
6	5	INTL. BUSINESS MACHINES[X]	US	65,394.0	(5.3)	(2,827.0)	489	(147.0)	92,473.0	37,006.0	344,553
7	7	IRI[G]	Italy	64,095.5	4.3	(254.1)	459	(127.4)	N.A.	N.A.	407,169
8	10	GENERAL ELECTRIC[X]	US	60,236.0	3.1	2,636.0	5	(38.7)	168,259.0	21,683.0	284,000
9	8	BRITISH PETROLEUM[X,F]	Britain	58,355.0	(2.0)	802.8	55	(70.9)	59,323.9	16,648.5	111,900
10	11	DAIMLER-BENZ[X]	Germany	57,321.3	5.6	1,129.4	30	8.4	49,811.8	11,996.1	379,252
11	9	MOBIL[X]	US	56,910.0	(3.2)	1,920.0	8	(0.5)	42,187.0	17,534.0	67,500
12	12	HITACHI[X,F]	Japan	56,053.3	10.6	1,629.2	16	10.3	60,641.0	19,993.9	309,757
13	17	MATSUSHITA ELECTRIC INDUSTRIAL[X,F]	Japan	48,595.0	11.7	1,832.5	10	11.1	62,312.5	24,429.2	210,848
14	15	PHILIP MORRIS[X]	US	48,109.0	8.5	3,006.0	4	(15.1)	47,384.0	12,512.0	166,000
15	13	FIAT[X]	Italy	46,812.0	(2.0)	898.7	46	(33.3)	69,736.4	18,531.2	287,957
16	16	VOLKSWAGEN	Germany	46,042.2	5.3	665.5	65	2.1	46,111.8	9,294.1	265,566
17	24	SIEMENS	Germany	44,859.2	14.4	1,135.2	29	24.3	41,785.0	10,408.1	402,000
18	14	SAMSUNG GROUP[X]	South Korea	43,701.9	4.4	347.3	126	4.1	43,290.3	5,835.8	187,377
19	20	NISSAN MOTOR[X,F]	Japan	42,905.7	6.7	340.9	128	(57.8)	45,916.4	12,662.9	138,326
20	21	UNILEVER	Britain/Netherlands	41,262.3	3.2	1,842.6	9	29.2	25,340.3	13,299.0	298,000
21	18	ENI[G]	Italy	41,047.3	(1.7)	872.0	48	(48.6)	N.A.	14,158.5	N.A.
22	22	E.I. DU PONT DE NEMOURS[X]	US	38,031.0	(4.5)	1,403.0	22	(39.3)	36,117.0	16,739.0	133,000
23	19	TEXACO	US	37,551.0	(8.9)	1,294.0	26	(10.8)	26,182.0	9,828.0	40,181
24	23	CHEVRON	US	36,795.0	(6.3)	1,293.0	27	(40.1)	34,636.0	14,739.0	55,123

25	26	ELF AQUITAINE[G]	France	36,315.8	10.3	1,737.1	12	(11.0)	46,539.7	16,505.7	86,900
26	25	NESTLE[X]	Switzerland	35,583.7	6.7	1,722.3	14	5.4	28,732.3	11,149.5	201,139
27	29	TOSHIBA[F]	Japan	33,232.5	10.1	855.4	49	(7.3)	39,334.1	8,383.7	162,000
28	38	HONDA MOTOR[F]	Japan	30,567.3	12.9	539.8	83	(5.6)	21,005.2	7,736.2	85,500
29	28	PHILIPS ELECTRONICS[X]	Netherlands	30,217.6	(2.1)	642.8	70	—	29,087.4	6,735.4	240,000
30	30	RENAULT[G]	France	29,432.4	(8.1)	545.8	82	145.6	41,375.4	6,432.3	147,195
31	27	CHRYSLER	US	29,370.0	(4.9)	(795.0)	483	(1,269.1)	43,076.0	6,184.0	126,500
32	36	BOEING	US	29,314.0	6.2	1,567.0	18	13.1	15,784.0	8,093.0	159,100
33	35	ABB ASEA BROWN BOVERI	Switzerland	28,883.0	4.3	587.0	78	109.6	30,754.0	4,753.0	214,399
34	34	HOECHST	Germany	28,468.2	2.6	661.8	67	(28.6)	23,498.0	7,813.2	179,332
35	31	PEUGEOT	France	28,403.3	(6.5)	979.9	39	(42.4)	23,466.6	9,955.3	156,800
36	38	ALCATEL ALSTHOM[X]	France	28,390.7	4.7	1,095.9	33	16.2	44,485.1	8,450.4	213,100
37	32	BASF	Germany	28,130.4	(3.6)	627.0	73	(8.4)	24,652.8	9,571.5	129,434
38	41	PROCTER & GAMBLE[X,F]	US	27,406.0	12.4	1,773.0	11	10.7	20,468.0	7,736.0	94,000
39	40	NEC[F]	Japan	26,675.4	9.4	384.9	113	(35.5)	27,948.3	6,265.5	117,994
40	51	SONY[X,F]	Japan	26,581.4	27.0	825.1	52	14.6	32,734.7	10,500.8	112,900
41	33	AMOCO	US	25,604.0	(9.5)	1,484.0	20	(22.4)	30,510.0	14,156.0	54,120
42	39	BAYER[X]	Germany	25,581.3	(1.8)	1,100.5	32	(5.4)	24,945.4	10,736.2	164,200
43	45	DAEWOO	South Korea	25,362.6	13.9	N.A.		—	N.A.	N.A.	81,607
44	42	TOTAL	France	25,361.7	5.7	1,030.3	38	34.7	21,954.8	7,423.1	56,156
45	43	PDVSA[G]	Venezuela	24,000.0	2.3	N.A.		—	14,000.0	8,000.0	52,000
46	49	MITSUBISHI ELECTRIC[X,F]	Japan	23,976.3	12.9	564.5	81	5.0	23,599.3	5,634.7	97,002
47	50	NIPPON STEEL[F]	Japan	23,141.6	9.4	641.8	71	(21.5)	31,358.0	7,445.3	54,062
48	48	THYSSEN[F]	Germany	22,465.0	4.5	294.1	158	(34.8)	14,327.1	2,929.2	148,557
49	44	IMPERIAL CHEMICAL INDUSTRIES[X]	Britain	22,339.4	(4.3)	958.4	42	(19.9)	20,554.0	8,941.9	128,600
50	47	UNITED TECHNOLOGIES	US	21,262.0	(2.4)	(1,021.0)	485	(236.0)	15,985.0	3,961.0	185,100

X = Corporations profiled in this book.
G = Government owned.
F = Fiscal year does not end 31 Dec.

Source: *Fortune* 1992 © The Time Inc. Magazine. All rights reserved.

Table 2.4 Global 500: majority-owned corporations, by country and industry, 1991

Industry group	Aerospace	Chemicals	Computers, office equipment	Electronic electrical equipment	Industrial and farm equipment	Metal products	Metals	Mining, crude oil production	Motor vehicles and parts	Petroleum refining	Tobacco	Total government owned	Total Global 500
Americas													
Argentina										1		1	1
Brazil										1		1	1
Chile								1				1	1
Mexico										1		1	2
Venezuela										1*			1
Europe													
Belgium							1					1	4
France	2	3	1	1		1			1*	1*		10	32
Italy							2*			1*		3	7
Portugal										1		1	1
Spain					1					1	1	3	4
Austria							1					1	1
Finland		1					1			1		3	6
Norway		1					1			1		3	3
Asia													
Japan											1	1	119
India							1	2		3		6	6
Malaysia										1		1	1
Taiwan										1		1	1
Thailand										1		1	1
Africa/Middle East													
Turkey										1		1	3
Zambia							1					1	1
Total Government owned	2	5	1	1	1	1	6	3	1	16	2	41	
Total Global	16	45	15	45	27	18	35	12	45	53	6		500

*One Global 50 company; five of 1991 Global 50 were government majority owned.

Source: *Fortune*, 27 July 1992:55–66.

in one of these industries; and others competed in very closely related ones (computers, and soaps and cosmetics). These are industries in which, for different combinations of reasons, organizing for strategies of global growth is essential for survival.

Petroleum

Of the eleven Global 50 multinationals now competing in the petroleum industry (as Table 2.9 indicates), seven have ranked among the leading 50 industrial corporations for three decades. Of these seven, four have a common parentage: Exxon, Mobil, Chevron and Amoco were once Standard Oil companies – and British Petroleum has acquired a fifth. Exxon, Royal Dutch/Shell, Mobil and British Petroleum (BP) have by sales ranked among the world's ten largest companies since the early 1970s.

A number of factors have affected the organizational strategy of the larger petroleum multinationals. First, the more profitable 'upstream' sources have seldom been located close to the more lucrative 'downstream' markets, thus requiring complex logistical infrastructures for linking sources and markets. Second, the magnitude of investment costs for R&D, for exploration and developing the 'upstream' production sites and for the 'downstream' refining and distribution capacity requires large capital investments and a well-developed global financial management. Third, the similarity of the competitive major consumer products leads petroleum companies to invest major amounts of money in promoting brand recognition. Fourth, since oil is a basic critical resource for every country, and a major source of income for many producing companies – as well as a major source of tax revenue in many countries – petroleum companies have been involved in national politics (a fact that the oil crises of the 1970s and the impact of nationalizations made manifest) and the country heads have key roles. Fifth, while some major oil companies have remained largely focused on 'upstream' and 'downstream' oil operations, the diversification initiatives of many of them, undertaken in part to exploit petroleum by-products and in part to invest the profits that many companies have generated, have complicated organizational arrangements. As the corporate profiles of BP and Exxon in Part III show, the desire to exert more global direction on the various diversified product businesses has affected the role of the country general managers.

Motor vehicles

Motor vehicle corporations entered the Global 50 (as Table 2.9 demonstrates) in three waves. The three American entrants (General Motors, Ford and Chrysler) were already established well before the 1950s. Three European companies joined in the early 1960s (Daimler-Benz, Fiat and Volkswagen). Renault, Toyota and Nissan joined in the 1970s, and latecomers Peugeot and Honda in the 1980s. The aggressive development of American and Japanese markets by the Japanese

Table 2.5 Global 50, 1959–91

Ranking	1959	1964	1969	1974	1979	1984	1989	1990	1991
1	GM	GM	GM	EXXON	EXXON	EXXON	GM	GM	GM
2	S.O. NJ	S.O. NJ	S.O. NJ	SHELL	GM	SHELL	FORD	SHELL	SHELL
3	FORD	FORD	FORD	GM	SHELL	GM	EXXON	EXXON	EXXON
4	SHELL	SHELL	SHELL	FORD	MOBIL	MOBIL	SHELL	FORD	FORD
5	GE	GE	GE	TEXACO	FORD	FORD	IBM	IBM	TOYOTA
6	UNILEVER	SOCMOBIL	IBM	MOBIL	BP	BP	TOYOTA	TOYOTA	IBM
7	US STEEL	UNILEVER	CHRYSLER	BP	TEXACO	TEXACO	GE	IRI	IRI
8	SOCMOBIL	CHRYSLER	MOBIL	S.O. CAL	S.O. CAL	IBM	MOBIL	BP	GE
9	GULF	US STEEL	UNILEVER	NATIRANOIL	GULF	DUPONT	HITACHI	MOBIL	BP
10	TEXACO	TEXACO	TEXACO	GULF	IBM	AT&T	BP	GE	DAIM-BENZ
11	CHRYSLER	IBM	ITT	UNILEVER	GE	GE	IRI	DAIM-BENZ	MOBIL
12	SWIFT	GULF	GULF	GE	UNILEVER	S.O. IND	MATSUSHITA	HITACHI	HITACHI
13	WESTELEC	WESTELEC	WESTELEC	IBM	ENI	CHEVRON	DAIM-BENZ	FIAT	MATSUSHITA
14	DUPONT	DUPONT	US STEEL	ITT	S.O. IND	ENI	PHIMORRIS	SAMSUNG	PHIMORRIS
15	BETHSTEEL	SWIFT	S.O. CAL	CHRYSLER	FIAT	ATLANTIC	FIAT	PHIMORRIS	FIAT
16	S.O. IND	NATCOAL	L-T-V	PHILIPS	FRANPET	TOYOTA	CHRYSLER	VOLKSWAGEN	VOLKSWAGEN
17	ARMOUR	S.O. IND	DUPONT	US STEEL	PEUGEOT	IRI	NISSAN	MATSUSHITA	SIEMENS
18	GENLDYN	BP	PHILIPS	S.O. IND	ITT	UNILEVER	UNILEVER	ENI	SAMSUNG
19	BP	S.O. CAL	VOLKSWAGEN	FRANPET	VOLKSWAGEN	ELFAQU	DUPONT	TEXACO	NISSAN
20	BOEING	WESTINGH	WESTINGH	NIPPONKOKAN	PHILIPS	MATSUSHITA	SAMSUNG	NISSAN	UNILEVER
21	NATDAIRY	BETHSTEEL	S.O. IND	THYSSEN	ATLANTIC	CHRYSLER	VOLKSWAGEN	UNILEVER	ENI
22	GOODYEAR	INTLHAR	BP	BASF	RENAULT	PEMEX	SIEMENS	DUPONT	DUPONT
23	S.O. CAL	NAAVIAT	GTE	HOECHST	SIEMENS	HITACHI	TEXACO	CHEVRON	TEXACO
24	ICI	ICI	ICI	WESTELEC	DAIM-BENZ	US STEEL	TOSHIBA	SIEMENS	CHEVRON
25	UNIONCAR	GOODYEAR	GOODYEAR	ENI	HOECHST	FRANPET	CHEVRON	NESTLE	ELFAQU
26	RCA	VOLKSWAGEN	RCA	CONTOIL	BAYER	PHILIPS	NESTLE	ELFAQU	NESTLE
27	P&G	BOEING	SWIFT	ICI	BASF	NISSAN	RENAULT	CHRYSLER	TOSHIBA
28	INTLHAR	PHILIPS	MCDONDOUG	DUPONT	PETROVEN	PETROBRAS	ENI	PHILIPS	HONDA
29	IBM	NATDAIRY	UNIONCAR	ATLANTIC	TOYOTA	SIEMENS	PHILIPS	TOSHIBA	PHILIPS
30	LOCKHEED	P&G	BETHSTEEL	SIEMENS	THYSSEN	UNITDTECH	HONDA	RENAULT	RENAULT
31	NESTLE	ARMOUR	BRITSTEEL	VOLKSWAGEN	ELFAQU	VOLKSWAGEN	BASF	PEUGEOT	CHRYSLER
32	SINCLAIR	UNIONCAR	HITACHI	WESTINGH	NESTLE	PHILLIPSPE	NEC	BASF	BOEING
33	FIRESTONE	RCA	BOEING	BAYER	US STEEL	OCCIDENTPE	HOECHST	AMOCO	ABB
34	PHILLIPSPE	GTE	EASTMANKO	DAIM-BENZ	NISSAN	DAIM-BENZ	AMOCO	HOECHST	HOECHST
35	CONTCAN	SIEMENS	P&G	MONTEDISON	CONOCO	BAYER	PEUGEOT	ABB	PEUGEOT
36	AMERCAN	THYSSEN	ATLANTIC	HITACHI	HITACHI	KUWAITOIL	BAT	BOEING	ALCATEL

Rank	1959	1964	1969	1974	1979	1984	1989	1990	1991
37	PHILIPS	LOCKHEED	NAROCKWEL	TOYOTA	NIPPONSTEEL	NIPPONOIL	ELFAQU	HONDA	BASF
38	GTE	GENLDYNAM	INTLHAR	ELFAQU	DUPONT	TENNECO	BAYER	ALCATEL	P&G
39	UNIAIRCR	ITT	KRAFT	OCCIDENTPE	CHRYSLER	HOECHST	CGE	BAYER	NEC
40	REPSTEEL	FIAT	MONTEDISON	MITSUBISHI	MITSUBISHI	SUNOIL	ICI	NEC	SONY
41	GENLFOOD	NESTLE	GENLDYNAM	NESTLE	ICI	BASF	P&G	P&G	AMOCO
42	NAAVIATON	BAYER	TENNECO	BETHSTEEL	TENNECO	MITSUBISHI	MITSUBEL	TOTAL	BAYER
43	INTLPAPER	FIRESTONE	SIEMENS	RENAULT	MATSUSHITA	ITT	ABB	PETROVEN	DAEWOO
44	ARMCO	MONSANTO	CONTOIL	BRITSTEEL	WESTELEC	PETROVEN	NIPPONSTEEL	ICI	TOTAL
45	CITIESSER	PHILLIPSPE	UNIAIRCRA	UNIONCAR	SUNOIL	FIAT	BOEING	DAEWOO	PDVSA
46	SPERRYRAND	GENLFOOD	BRITLEYLA	GOODYEAR	PETROBRAS	BAT	OCCIDENTPE	OCCIDENTPE	MITSUBEL
47	USRUBBER	DAIM-BENZ	DAIM-BENZ	BAT	OCCIDENTPE	ICI	DAEWOO	UNITEDTECH	NIPPONSTEEL
48	BORDEN	BORDEN	FIAT	TENNECO	PHILLIPSPE	NESTLE	UNITEDTECH	THYSSEN	THYSSEN
49	EASTMANKO	SPERRYRAND	FIRESTONE	PETROBRAS	BAT	P&G	FUJITSU	MITSUBEL	ICI
50	DOUGLASA	REPSTEEL	THYSSEN	PHILLIPSPE	P&G	RENAULT	EASTMANKO	NIPPON	UNITEDTECH

Note: Sales (to nearest $bn) for firms ranked 1, 10, 20, 25/6(median), 30, 40 and 50

Rank	1959	1964	1969	1974	1979	1984	1989	1990	1991
1	11	17	24	42	79	91	127	125	124
10	3	4	6	16	23	33	49	58	57
20	2	2	4	9	17	20	35	40	41
25/6	1	2	3	7	14	18	29	33	36
30	1	2	3	7	14	16	26	30	29
40	1	1	2	6	12	14	22	24	27
50	1	1		5	9	12	19	21	21

Selected abbreviations

ALCATEL: Alcatel Alsthom
AMERCAN: American Can
ATLANTIC: Atlantic Richfield
BAT: British-American Tobacco
BETHSTEEL: Bethlehem Steel
BRITLEYLA: British Leyland
BRITSTEEL: British Steel
CITIESSER: Cities Service
CONTCAN: Continental Can
CONTOIL: Continental Oil
DAIM-BENZ: Daimler-Benz
DOUGLASA: Douglas Aircraft
EASTMANKO: Eastman Kodak
ELFAQU: Elf Aquitaine

FRANPET: Francaise des Petroles
GENLDYN: General Dynamics
GENLFOOD: General Food
INTLHAR: International Harvester
INTLPAPER: International Paper
MITSUBEL: Mitsubishi Electric
MITSUBISHI: Mitsubishi Heavy Industries
MCDONDOUG: McDonnell Douglas
NAAVIAT: North American Aviation
NAROCKWEL: North American Rockwell
NATCOAL: National Coal Board
NATDAIRY: National Dairy Products
NATIRANOIL: National Iran Oil
OCCIDENTPE: Occidental Petroleum

PHILLIPSPE: Phillips Petroleum
PHIMORRIS: Philip Morris
REPSTEEL: Republic Steel
SOCMOBIL: Socony-Mobil
S.O.CAL: Standard Oil (California)
S.O.IND: Standard Oil (India)
S.O. NJ: Standard Oil (NJ)
UNIAIRCR: United Aircraft
UNITEDTECH: United Technologies
UNIONCAR: Union Carbide
WESTELEC: Western Electric
WESTINGH: Westinghouse

Sources: *Fortune*, 1960a,b, 1965a,b, 1970a,b, 1975, 1980, 1985a,b, 1990b, 1991a,b.

Table 2.6 Extent of multi-industry diversification of 25 leading multinationals: by industry, ranked by sales

Multinationals	Transport: Motor vehicles and parts	Transport: Transportation equipment	Equipment: Aerospace	Equipment: Industrial and farm	Equipment: Electronics	Equipment: Computer and office	Equipment: Scientific and professional	Materials: Textiles	Materials: Building	Materials: Forest products	Materials: Metal products	Materials: Metals	Energy: Mining	Energy: Petroleum	Chemicals: Chemicals	Chemicals: Rubber and plastics	Chemicals: Pharmaceuticals	Consumer pkgd: Soaps and cosmetics	Consumer pkgd: Food	Consumer pkgd: Beverages	Consumer pkgd: Tobacco	Other mfg: Apparel	Other mfg: Publishing	Other mfg: Toys and sporting goods	Services: Trading	Services: Diversified finance and banking	Services: Insurance	Services: Construction/engineering	Services: Entertainment	Services: Computer information services	Services: Land development	Services: Hospitals	Services: Education
Motor vehicles																																	
GM	x	o	o	o	o			o																		o				o	o		o
Ford	x	o	o	o	o																					o							
Toyota	x	o	o	o	o																					o							
Daimler-Benz	x	o	o	o	o																						o	o		o	o		
Fiat	x	o	o	o	o																												
Nissan	x	o	o	o	o																												
Equipment																																	
IBM					o	x																								o			
GE		o	o	o	x	o	x								o								o			o	o		o	o	o	o	o
Hitachi		o		o	x	o						o	o		o											o							
Samsung	o			o	x	o		o							o																		
Matsushita Electric					x	o									o			o											o				
Philips					x	o												o			—			—									
Alcatel Alsthom		o			x	o																						o					
Mitsubishi Electric					x	o						o													o	o		o					
Sony					x	o																	o	o					o				

Petroleum
Royal Dutch/Shell
Exxon
BP
Mobil

Chemicals
E.I. Du Pont
Bayer
ICI

Consumer packaged goods
Philip Morris
Nestlé
P&G

x = Industry in which company generates plurality of sales, as reported by *Fortune*, 1991a,b.
O = Industry in which a corporate unit generated less than a plurality of sales as reported in corporate annual report.
Specific industry categories are those used by *Fortune*.
Source: recent annual reports of each company.

Table 2.7 Global 500: by country and by industry, 1991

Industry Groups → / Countries ↓	Aerospace	Apparel	Beverages	Building materials	Chemicals	Computers, office equip.	Electronics, electrical equip.	Food	Forest products	Furniture	Industrial and farm equip.	Jewelry, watches	Metal products	Metals	Mining, crude-oil production	Motor vehicles and parts	Petroleum refining	Pharmaceuticals	Publishing, printing	Rubber and plastic products	Scientific and photo equip.	Soaps, cosmetics	Textiles	Tobacco	Toys, sporting goods	Transportation equipment	Total
Argentina																	1										1
Australia				2										2	1		2		1	1							9
Austria																	1										1
Belgium				1	1									1			1										4
Brazil																	1										1
Britain	2		4	4	4		2	8	1		1		1		2	2	2	3	2	1	1	1	1	1			43
Britain/Netherlands								1									1										2
Canada						1	1	1	1				1		1	1	1		1								9
Chile									1																		1
Finland				3	1		1							1													6
France	4		2	3	4		3	4						3	1	3	2		1	1		1					32
Germany				3	4		3	1					2	2	2	7	3	1	1	1	1	2					33
India					1									2	1	1	1										6
Italy						1	2	1								1	1			1							7

																						Total
Japan	3	3	13	4	15	9	5	8	2	6	10		18	7	2	2	3	1	2	4	1	2	119
Luxembourg										1				1									1
Malaysia														1									1
Mexico	1													1									2
Netherlands		2		1	1					1		1											7
New Zealand					1																		1
Norway		1						1						1									3
Panama								1															1
Portugal														1									1
South Africa						1					1	1											4
South Korea	1	1			3				1	1			2	3						1			13
Spain										1	1			2					1				4
Sweden		1		2			1		2			1	2	1	1								14
Switzerland		1					3		1						2					1			10
Taiwan						1																	1
Thailand														1									1
Turkey	1							7			1	1	1	1									3
USA	10	5	11	9	15	18	12		4	6	1	7	15	10	4	6	3		6		7		157
Venezuela													1										1
Zambia									1														1
Total number of companies	16	18	45	15	45	47	25	27	18	35	12	45	53	19	12	9	10	6	6	2	2		500
Total sales in $ billion	169	112	397	210	650	397	142	219	92	339	67	853	931	126	64	78	71	42		7	10		5,188
Median sales in $ billion	8	4	6	7	8	6	5	6	3	6	5	8	10	7	5	6	5	6	4	5			

Source: *Fortune*, 1992.

Table 2.8 Concentration of Global 50 in major industries, 1959–91

Industries/Benchmark years	1959	1964	1969	1974	1979	1984	1989	1990	1991
Petroleum	11	9	11	18	19	19	9	11	11
Motor vehicles	3	6	7	7	10	9	11	11	11
Rubber	3	2	2	1					
Electronics	6	9	10	7	7	7	11	11	11
Aerospace	6	4	4			1	2	2	2
Industrial and farm machinery	1	1	1	1	1	1	1	1	1
Computers and office machines	1	1	1	1	1	1	2	1	2
Scientific and photographic	1		1				1		
Chemicals	3	5	4	7	5	5	5	5	5
Food	7	7	3	2	2	3	4	4	3
Soap and cosmetics	1	1	1		1	1	1	1	1
Tobacco				1	1	1	1		
Metals	4	4	5	5	3	2	2	3	3
Metal products	2								
Mining		1							
Forest	1								
Total	*50*	*50*	*50*	*50*	*50*	*50*	*50*	*50*	*50*

Source: Information integrated from *Fortune*, 1960a,b, 1965a,b, 1970a,b, 1975, 1980, 1985a,b, 1990b, 1991a,b, 1992. (This table includes all companies included in the Global 50 in each benchmark year – whether or not they ranked in the 1991 Global 50. Table 2.9 includes under each benchmark year only the 1991 Global 50 companies.)

manufacturers has been a major factor forcing the motor vehicle manufacturers to streamline their organizations in order to compete successfully to increase, or at least maintain, their market share.

A number of other factors have affected the organizational strategy of the leading motor vehicle corporations. First, the motor vehicle industry involves the manufacture or sourcing of an array of components for a complex assembly process requiring sophisticated logistical systems, especially to sustain just-in-time, cost-competitive efficiency. Second, massive sums of capital are required to develop customer-attracting new models, develop and improve efficient production facilities, and develop and build the brand image and distribution system to compete effectively. Third, several motor vehicle corporations have diversified. General Motors, Ford, Fiat and Daimler-Benz have, by acquisition or growth, developed major businesses in related industries such as aerospace and information systems technology. Toyota and Nissan have, less dramatically, also begun to diversify. The market brand visibility as well as the workforce size of the various manufacturing facilities has made automobiles more sensitive than most products to protectionist pressures and the need for well-networked national managers. Perhaps more important, the increasing market share of the Japanese firms is forcing American and European firms to streamline their efforts. Those whose markets have long been especially well protected such as Fiat, Renault and Peugeot – or already weak ones such as Chrysler – are particularly threatened.

Electronics and related

The third major concentration of Global 50 companies is electronics and businesses closely related to electronics. Of the eleven major players in 1990, only three (General Electric, Philips and Siemens) had established themselves as Global 50 players before the mid-1960s. Alcatel Alsthom did not become a major player until after its denationalization and purchase of ITT's telecommunications business in the late 1980s. Seven East Asian electronics firms, led by Hitachi and Matsushita in the 1970s, entered the Global 50 in the late 1980s. In the process they have forced American competition out of several segments of the electronics industry and have threatened such European manufacturers as Philips.

A number of factors have had a particularly significant impact on the organizational strategies of electronics businesses. First, the rapid pace of technological change requires not only massive investment but also close coordination of the R&D, manufacturing and marketing processes in order to minimize the time required to develop, manufacture or source and market a new product – in order to beat the competition and recoup the investment costs. Second, as several of the profiles in Part III will show, the diversity of the product range of several of these companies is vast. Samsung includes such diverse activities as electronics, chemicals, textiles, a hospital, a newspaper and insurance. General Electric includes industrial and power systems, appliances, aerospace, telecommunications, lighting and medical systems, and semiconductors – as well as a TV and broadcasting company, financial services, a motor vehicles company and an oil company. Hitachi embraces power systems, appliances, information and communication systems, industrial machinery and parts – as well as metal and chemicals. The diversity of products has forced General Electric to reorganize over and over again to develop a more effective means of managing its fragmented empire. Philips was finally forced to discard its largely autonomous national organizations to develop effective global product divisions.

The very different marketing requirements for industrial and consumer electronics have even forced most Japanese firms to split their international sales divisions along these lines, with industrial electronic marketing being managed more globally, and consumer electronics more locally. Many of the Japanese national sales affiliates handle only consumer products and are locally managed.

International Business Machines (IBM) has been for more than three decades the only Global 50 corporation whose principal business is computers and office equipment. Though, in fact, several diversified electronics firms include computers and office equipment among their 'businesses'; and Toshiba has so expanded its

Table 2.9 1991 Global 50 by sales: changing rank within Global 50, 1959–91

Industry/Company	Continents			Five-year benchmarks								
	Americas	Europe	Asia	1959	1964	1969	1974	1979	1984	1989	1990	1991
PETROLEUM												
Exxon	USA			2	2	2	1	1	1	3	3	3
Mobil	USA			8	6	8	6	4	4	8	9	11
Texaco	USA			10	10	10	5	7	7	23	19	23
Chevron	USA			23	19	15	8	8	13	25	23	24
Amoco	USA			16	17	21	18	14	12	34	33	41
Petroleos de Venezuela	V							28	44		43	45
Royal Dutch/Shell		B–N		4	4	4	2	3	2	4	2	2
British Petroleum		B		19	18	22	7	6	6	10	8	9
ENI		I					25	13	14	28	18	21
Elf Aquitaine		F						31	19		26	25
Total		F					38	46	25	37	42	44
MOTOR VEHICLES												
General Motors	USA			1	1	1	3	2	3	1	1	1
Ford Motor	USA			3	3	3	4	5	5	2	4	4
Chrysler	USA			11	8	7	15	39	21	16	27	31
Daimler-Benz		G			47	47			34	13	11	10
Volkswagen		G			26	19	31	19	31	21	16	16
Fiat		I			40	48			45	15	13	15
Renault		F					43		50	27	30	30
Peugeot										35	31	35
Toyota Motor			J				37	29	16	6	6	5
Nissan Motor			J					34	27	17	20	19
Honda Motor			J							30	37	28

Company	Country	1960	1965	1970	1975	1980	1985	1990	1991	1992
ELECTRONICS AND RELATED										
IBM (computers)	USA	29	11	6	13	10	8	5	5	6
General Electric	USA	5	5	5	12	11	11	7	10	8
Boeing (aerospace)	USA			33				45	36	32
United Technologies (aerospace)	USA	39	27	45				48	47	50
IRI (metals)	I							17	11	7
Philips Electronics	N	37	28	18	16	20	26	29	28	29
Siemens	G		35	43	30	23	29	22	24	17
Thyssen (metals)	G		36	50		30			48	48
Asea Brown Boveri	S							43	35	33
Alcatel Alsthom	F							39	38	36
Hitachi	J					36	23	9	12	12
Matsushita Electric Industries	J					43	20	12	17	13
Toshiba (computers)	J							24	29	27
NEC	J							32	40	39
Sony	J									40
Mitsubishi Electric	J								4	46
Nippon Steel (metals)	J							44	50	47
Samsung	SK							20	14	18
Daewoo	SK							47	45	43
CHEMICALS										
E.I. Du Pont de Nemours	USA	14	14	17	28	38	9	19	22	22
Imperial Chemical Industries	B	24	24	24	27	41	47	40	44	49
BASF	G				22	27	41	31	32	37
Hoechst	G					25	39	33	34	34
Bayer	G				33	26	35	38	39	42
FOOD AND RELATED										
Procter & Gamble (soaps, cosmetics)	USA	27	30	9		50	49	41	41	38
Philip Morris	USA	6	7		11	12		14	15	14
Unilever	B-N	31	41		41		18	18	21	20
Nestlé	S					32	48	26	25	26

Source: Information integrated from *Fortune*, 1960a,b, 1965a,b, 1970a,b, 1975, 1980, 1985a,b, 1990b, 1991 and 1992.

computer business that by 1991 this had actually become its principal business (*Fortune*, 1991a:55). As one of the world's least diversified mega-multinationals, IBM's organization challenge is not its diversification, but the fact that, as one of its senior managers points out: 'its businesses are so inter-related and inter-dependent that it is difficult to separate them' (interview, William Bumpas, 12 September 1990).

Asea Brown Boveri (ABB), the industrial giant formed by the 1988 merger of Swiss-based Brown Boveri and Swedish-based Asea, presents itself as a federation of national companies, of which one of the strongest is the German-based one. Its focus has been power systems, industrial equipment and transportation equipment, a field in which it competes with such firms as Alcatel Alsthom and Hitachi.

Two American aerospace firms, Boeing and United Technologies, manufacture electronic products, and thus their businesses overlap with those of the major electronic multinationals. In addition, three Global 50 firms whose primary focus is metals engage in electronics: IRI, an Italian state-owned conglomerate whose subsidiary STET is a major player in telecommunications; the German firm Thyssen, which is in both heavy industrial equipment and electronics; and the Japanese firm Nippon Steel, which has expanded into electronics and chemicals as well as steel products.

The rapid technological advances in electronics thus have not only created a variety of subindustries ranging from telecommunications to consumer electronics to electronic components; they have also made electronic technology a vital part of a number of industries and concomitantly forced multinationals which once focused their efforts in one industry to diversify into electronics. Thus the whole range of machinery industries – from office machines to industrial equipment, aerospace and motor vehicles – has moved towards becoming one mega-industry in which many of the larger players span several industries. Since their businesses share common technologies, and depend on global markets, the need for developing organizations and managers with border-transcending capacity is imperative.

Chemicals

The chemicals industry continues to be dominated by European and American firms. Du Pont and ICI have been Global 50 players for several decades. The three German firms – Bayer, BASF and Hoechst – which demerged from I.G. Farben after World War II entered the Global 50 ranks in the 1970s.

The larger chemical firms have tended to diversify into a number of related industries, including pharmaceuticals and rubber and plastics. Du Pont has even diversified into the petroleum business with its purchase of Conoco – a move which, like those of some of the major oil companies into chemicals, signifies the increased intermeshing of these two industries.

Factors that have increased the propensity of chemical firms to diversify include the rapid development of technology and the increasing scope of applications of technological innovations, the rapidly increasing costs of product development and the consequent need for increasing scope and scale of efforts to fund the massive investments required, and the need to spread the risks, which are especially high in several of the chemical-related fields such as pharmaceuticals. The extent of the diversification of ICI and Du Pont was a major factor leading to their recent moves to strengthen the global role of their product sectors and convert their territorial organizations into administration support units and has led ICI to propose splitting their corporation in two.

Foods and related packaged consumer goods

Three firms have long been major players in the foods and related packaged goods industries: Unilever, Nestlé and Procter & Gamble (P&G). While each has developed its international organization differently, they have all relied on country-based operating companies which have continued to exercise considerable local autonomy. Unilever and Nestlé have essentially operated as confederations of companies, most of which have retained their original company names and continued marketing their products under individual brand names. P&G has managed its international affiliates more closely through its international division. Thus the food industry has not yet been as affected by the trend towards globalization as the electronics, petroleum, chemicals or motor vehicles industries.

A number of interdependent factors, though, may have begun to move its companies towards globalization. First, the tastes of consumers in the more developed countries, as they have gained more discretionary income and become more familiar with the specialities of other cultures, have tended to overlap and thus have more commonalities. Second, the advent of mass communication has increased the capacity of multinationals to promote brands world-wide. Third, the interest in acquiring food companies has continued to accelerate. These trends are leading the companies to take a more active role in managing global brand strategies. As a consequence, whereas selling and new product promotion used to be left largely to local management, the central staffs now take a far more active role in new product development, financing the introduction of new products and promoting global brands and global marketing techniques. Multinationals are beginning to reorient arrangements at the country level for coordinating the operations of their various products: P&G has begun to strengthen European-wide category management, Unilever has strengthened the role of global product 'coordination', and so has Nestlé. Philip Morris's rapid growth through the acquisition of Kraft, General Foods and Jacob Suchard has intensified the competitive nature of the industry and the need to develop organizations which can bring products to market more quickly. As food companies move in these directions, the geography vs. product organizational issue has become more complex, and the need to face it more demanding.

The multi-industry multicontinental enterprise

The effort to compete successfully has driven multinationals to expand across continents and across industries. By superimposing a diversity of business on a diversity of countries, these multinationals have created a multidimensional mosaic of parts which conventional organizational approaches have not yet mastered. The discrepancy in the global–local balance of pressures in different businesses introduces an additional set of challenges (of variable consequent complexity) for multinational leadership to develop approaches which can more coherently organize and manage such multicontinental, multi-industry mosaics.

PART II

Management dynamics: to concert differing perspectives

CHAPTER 3
Structuring: for multicontinental systems

Formal dynamics of power: framing multicontinental systems

Structure shapes strategy by determining who is primarily responsible to whom for what. Not only profit-and-loss accountability but also planning, budgeting, personnel, information and other management systems generally follow the formal structure (Business International Corporation, 1979:27). Formal lines of power significantly affect which perspectives most influence the mind-sets with which decisions are made and through which they are conveyed. Mounting pressures for global product development and distribution, coupled with the increasing homogenization of tastes and the decreasing impact of national frontiers, have accelerated the pace of multinational efforts to alter the balance between global and local perspectives by restructuring.

This chapter addresses several sets of structuring issues that multinationals face in their globalization, localization and organizational initiatives. The first focuses on top corporate governance – especially how the composition and distribution of collective and individual responsibilities at corporate board level(s) fundamentally reflect and shape a multinational's organizational priorities regarding operational distance, driving perspectives and management dynamics, and thus its capacity for global coherence. The second focuses on how a multinational splits its international operations and specifically how organizing the major corporate parts along product, functional or territorial lines has affected globalization, localization and coordinative efforts. The third focuses on continental/regional organizations – specifically how their coordinative/supportive roles have been affected by global initiatives and have influenced how multinationals localize. The fourth focuses on international affiliates – specifically how the role of many has been, and has continued to be, affected by continuing global integration of product and functional efforts. The fifth focuses on lateral linkages – specifically how multinationals have developed horizontal ties such as committees, matrices and teams that overlay the pyramid-like vertical hierarchies comprising the modern multinational. How differently do the American, European and Asian multinationals approach these issues? Do these differences affect and reinforce a product, geographic or functional emphasis in headquarters–affiliate relations? These questions are addressed.

Top corporate governance: parochial or global-minded

Top corporate governance, which determines the corporate strategy and organization of a firm, generally consists of two often overlapping institutions. The corporate chief executive officer (CEO) often heads both; but in some cases he or she only heads one of these bodies. The first is the corporate board (of directors) which, as the ultimate trustee of an enterprise, makes its major strategic decisions including in what businesses the enterprise will engage, in what countries it will operate, how much resources it will invest, what results it will expect, and, most critical, in whom it will trust to lead the firm – thus the hiring and firing of the CEO. The second is the corporate executive team, headed by the CEO, which is responsible for the overall management leadership of a firm. The heads of an enterprise's various major corporate parts are responsible to this team and one or more may be members of it.

The way a multinational structures its corporate board and corporate executive team fundamentally shapes the way the corporate leadership mixes and manages the differing sets of perspectives driving the various parts comprising a multinational mosaic. Which perspectives are represented within the corporate leadership and how they are represented affects whether a multinational is myopic- or multiple-perspective-minded – and thus shapes the direction of its corporate strategy and organization. Who comprises the corporate governance? What interests do they represent – and what responsibilities do they shoulder? How these issues, individually and collectively, are handled affects the corporate vision as well as the organizational perspectives stressed in developing staffing and shared values as well as corporate strategy and structure.

The corporate board

The differences in the composition of American, European and Asian corporate boards mirror and reinforce their perspectives in overseeing corporate operations and appreciating their global opportunities. Particularly significant in this regard are two differences: the extent to which the board is composed of its own executive 'insiders', as compared to non-executive 'outsiders', and the extent to which the board posts are monopolized by home country nationals.

Multinationals differ significantly in whether, and to what extent, their corporate boards include their own senior executives (see Figure 3.1). The non-executive or 'outsider' board members may be retired 'insiders', active or retired senior executives of other companies, representatives of banks or other interests holding significant equity in the firm, representatives of labour, or those appointed

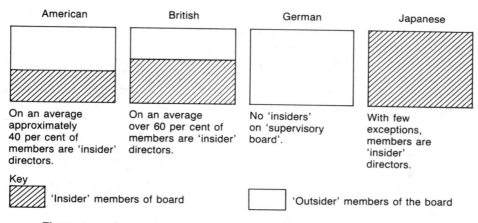

American	British	German	Japanese
On an average approximately 40 per cent of members are 'insider' directors.	On an average over 60 per cent of members are 'insider' directors.	No 'insiders' on 'supervisory board'.	With few exceptions, members are 'insider' directors.

Key

▨ 'Insider' members of board   ☐ 'Outsider' members of the board

Figure 3.1 Comparison of board composition: 'insiders' and 'outsiders'

to reflect specific interests. Most of the larger American, British, Swiss and Italian multinationals tend to mix 'outsider' directors with 'insider' executives on their boards. American corporations have tended to have two-fifths of their seats held by 'insiders' (Mills, 1985:269). British 'insider' executives tend to hold more than three-fifths of the board seats; in a few British multinationals such as British Petroleum, the senior executives hold all the board seats (Mills, 1985:265). Swiss and Italian multinationals tend to include only one or a few of their top officers on their boards.

Major German multinationals include only 'outsiders' (that is, non-executives) on their 'supervisory boards' (*Aufsichtsrat*), which are separate and include no members of the corporate executive team (*Vorstand* or 'management board'). The 'supervisory board' is chaired by an 'outsider' as the non-executive corporate chairperson. By law the boards of the larger German multinationals consist of seven non-management employees, three union nominees and ten representing shareholders (including one or more shareholding banks). The larger French and Dutch multinationals have similar two-tier arrangements. While the inclusion of 'insiders' on the board integrates the responsibility for corporate governance, the separation allows the 'outsiders' to focus on their trustee-like responsibilities in an atmosphere less likely to be dominated by the CEO and his or her other 'insider' colleagues. In contrast, senior executives of the major Japanese and South Korean multinationals generally hold all of the seats on their boards, which usually range in size from 30 to 50 members. A few of these multinationals have included as 'outside' board members one or more representatives of the banks with which they have long been closely associated.

The inclusion of 'outsiders' on a multinational board facilitates the introduction and consideration of fresh insights and different points of view. The disparate approaches of the Japanese, American, British and German enterprises to 'non-executive' members tend to reflect home country values. The lack of 'outsiders' on most Japanese and South Korean boards reflects the stress on group homogeneity and the multinational refrain of culture distinctiveness. The inclusion of workers' representatives on German boards reflects Germanic social values. The fact that in 1989, 59 per cent of American corporations had women board members and 31 per cent included ethnic minorities (Korn-Ferry International, 1990:15) reflects the emergent American gender and ethnic 'equal opportunity' consciousness. The application of these home country values appears to have taken priority over developing more globally representative boards.

Despite the global nature of their businesses, relatively few multinationals have selected foreigners as 'outsider' board members. From 1984 to 1989 the percentage of American corporations with non-American directors actually declined from 17 per cent to 12 per cent (Korn-Ferry International, 1987:15; 1990:15). Those American companies that do include a non-American tend to have only one or a few: for example, Exxon has one Englishman, and IBM one Swiss and one German. Philip Morris, with three 'insider' and two 'outsider' board members, is the exception. Several European multinationals have progressed further in their efforts to globalize their boards. Philips has two Americans, a German, a Frenchman, a Belgian and a Briton on its supervisory board. ICI includes two Germans and two Americans among the eight 'outsiders' on its board. Fiat, Alcatel and Bayer also include nationals of other European countries. Among Asian companies Sony is an exception: it has three non-Japanese on its board, one 'outsider' and two 'insiders'. The lack of international representation on multinational boards often impedes the development of a global vision and an appreciation of the diversity of national cultures and markets.

The CEO and the corporate executive team

The multinational structure focuses on its CEO and his or her senior colleagues who comprise the corporate executive team. The increasing size and complexity of the role of the mega-multinational CEO has led many companies to institutionalize some form of corporate executive team to share the top management leadership responsibilities. Many Japanese firms have an executive committee comprised of the senior members of the board of directors. In British and American corporations the corporate executives sitting on the board of directors generally comprise at least the nucleus of a corporate executive team. In continental European firms with a two-tier board arrangement, the second tier is the corporate executive team. Multinationals may label this corporate executive team the *Vorstand* (Bayer), Group Management Committee (Philips), Committee of Managing Directors (Royal Dutch/Shell), Management Council (Nissan), Executive Committee (Hitachi and Sony), Management Committee (IBM and Exxon), Corporate Executive Office (GE) or Office of the Chairman (Du Pont). Typical titles of this executive team's members are CEO/chairman, vice chairman, president, chief operating officer (COO), (executive/senior/group) vice-president, and (senior/executive) managing director. An executive team may or may not include those who have the operational responsibility for the major operating divisions and major corporate support services of the corporation.

Members of an executive team share responsibility for formulating and implementing the overall multinational strategy. The way they share this leadership depends on two major factors. The first is the extent to which the CEO dominates or shares power with his or her principal associates. The second is what responsibilities are assigned to the other members of the corporate executive team; whether they are primarily oversight or operational; and how they are divided. The way each multinational approaches these issues affects not only which organizational perspectives tend to receive more consideration, but also the capacity of the CEO to resolve 'turf' issues, impose consensuses and develop strategic coherent capability.

The extent to which a CEO dominates, or shares power with, his or her corporate executive team colleagues depends upon the formal prerogatives of the post, the individual's style, drive and charisma, and the values of the corporation and home country. Formal authority may be vested solely in the CEO, or it may be shared (at least formally) with colleagues in a plural executive arrangement. Japanese companies rely on a corporate executive committee, comprised of the chairperson, the president and a few senior executives, to determine the major issues affecting the company; but its 'representative directors', typically the chairperson and president, may individually commit the firm. In the Federal Republic of Germany since 1971 by law corporations may no longer vest corporate management authority solely in the CEO; such authority must be formally shared among the *Vorstand* members. Royal Dutch/Shell and Philips also possess such a first-among-equals collegial executive. In comparison, the American, French and Italian CEOs generally have long exerted one-above-others authority with the colleagues functioning as lieutenants. Whatever the formal sharing of power, however, the CEO in every system possesses extraordinary opportunities to propose and to impose consensus.

In every country forceful executives – by sheer strength of personality – play a powerful role. When they are the founders (such as Henry Ford of Ford, Gerard and Anton Philips of Philips, Giovanni Agnelli of Fiat, Kenosuke Matsushita of Matsushita, Akio Morita of Sony and B.C. Lee of Samsung), or quasi-founders (such as Alfred P. Sloan of General Motors, T.S. Watson Sr. of IBM and Harold Geneen of ITT), who transformed and dominated their companies for several decades, their influence is pervasive. So has been that of many heirs to the throne, such as Henry Ford II and Thomas S. Watson Jr. Gianni Agnelli of Fiat has developed a powerful role, partly because of his style, partly because his grandfather built the company, partly because his family owns a significant share of the Fiat equity, partly because of his extensive governmental and corporate connections and partly because the Italian culture sustains a charismatic leader. In contrast, K.H. Lee, B.C. Lee's son and successor as chairman, has adopted a far more participative style.

Other CEOs, such as Edzard Reuter of Daimler-Benz, Pierre Suard of Alcatel Alsthom and Jack Welch of General Electric, have, even in a few years, been able to dominate the leadership of their companies with their vision, drive and personality. A CEO's management style affects the zeal his or her executive team colleagues exert for integrating product, geographic and functional points of view.

So does the degree to which his or her immediate colleagues' responsibilities so focus on advocating and protecting specific interests that their capacity to consider general interests is muted.

The roles of corporate executive team members vary, depending upon whether their responsibilities tend to stress operational or oversight tasks – and upon whether their duties embrace a more general and more diverse responsibility or focus on one product group, function or territory. Each of these sets of contrasting terms are in fact poles at opposite ends of a spectrum. As illustrated in Figure 3.2, the crossing of these two spectrums distinguishes four types of corporate executive team members. A corporate executive team consists of a CEO and one or more of these four types of members. One type is the officer who has general control over all or almost all the operations of the company. An example is Cesare Romiti, the Fiat managing director who, along with the chairman Gianni Agnelli and his brother and vice-chairman Umberto Agnelli, comprise the close-knit Fiat high command. Other examples are Ronnie Hampel, the COO of Imperial Chemicals Industries (ICI), who serves as a member of an eight-person executive team; Norio Ohga, Sony's president and COO; and Edward E. Hoab Jr., the vice-chairman of General Electric (GE) and number two on its two-member corporate executive team.

A second type of corporate executive team member is the one specifically responsible for the management of a product sector, a geographic area such as 'international' (generally the area outside the home country), or a major function such as manufacturing, marketing and sales, research and development, or finance. The corporate executive team at Minnesota Mining and Manufacturing (3M), for

Extent of diversity of assignment

	More general	More focused
More operational	COOs whose operational responsibilities embrace a broad range of corporate products, functions and/or area responsibilities	Operational heads who are operationally responsible for the management of product groups/divisions sectors; marketing, R&D, manufacturing or finance or other support services units; and/or international or continental divisions
More oversight	Corporate executive team members with oversight responsibility for one or multiple portfolios such as marketing, North America and one product group	Corporate executive team members with oversight role in advising, assisting and coordinating one cluster of product-, area- or function-related activities

(left axis label: Extent of hands-on/direct control)

Note: A corporate executive team consists of a CEO and one or more of the above-described types of corporate executive team member.

Figure 3.2 Types of corporate executive team member

example, consists of the CEO, the executive vice-presidents who head the four product sectors, the executive vice-president who heads international operations, and the four senior vice-presidents who head the corporate staff services. Philips's corporate executive team, once composed mainly of those heading functional services, now includes the heads of the product sectors. The Du Pont Office of the Chairman includes the CEO, the vice-chairman who heads CONOCO, the vice-chairmen who oversee chemicals operations, the finance head and the human resources/corporate planning head. Such executive team members thus have a dual role: as a general member of the corporate executive team considering the best interests of the overall company, and as the executive directing one specific part of the corporation.

A third type exercises an oversight, but not an operational, role for one part of the corporation. Such an executive team member guides, advises and 'coaches' the leadership of one or more divisions and represents their interest in the board. In Nissan and Matsushita, for example, senior members of the corporate executive team look at issues with a more general perspective and divide the oversight roles along functional lines: for example, one member oversees marketing, one R&D, one production and one corporate staff services (Kono, 1984:24–9). IBM's corporate executive team has similarly divided responsibilities, with one member generally in charge of overseeing international activities, another generally in charge of US operations including the businesses, and the CEO overseeing the corporate staff services.

The fourth type holds multiple portfolios assignments. For example, most of the six members of the Shell corporate executive team have oversight responsibilities which include one territorial, one (or more) function, and one (or more) product line portfolio. Since its 1971 reorganization, Bayer too has delegated operational responsibilities to lower tiers and assigned its *Vorstand* members multiple oversight portfolios, mixing area, functional and product responsibilities. Nestlé and BP have similar arrangements.

The establishment of a corporate executive team as an inner circle of members who focus on general oversight roles rather than on the operational direction of specific parts has extended the circle of executives who are depended upon to direct and coordinate the specific corporate parts. In Japanese companies, the executives of this extended circle are included on the board of directors. Other companies, including Bayer, ICI, GM and Du Pont, have formally institutionalized committees (or councils) that constitute a second layer or an outer ring of senior executives. ICI, for example, has a Performance and Policy Committee which includes not only the corporate executive team (the 'insider' board members with multiple portfolios) but also the heads of the seven business groups and the finance head. Du Pont's Operating Group consists of its 23 senior vice-presidents. General Motors' almost 30-member administration committee includes its seven-person management committee and all vice-presidents/group executives, plus specified other vice-presidents.

The way the corporate executive team and its outer ring assign responsibilities among the team's members affects corporate leadership's ability to develop and implement a focused multinational strategy. As corporations have grown and become more mosaic-like, complex and difficult to manage, they have moved to develop multiple-person executive teams to lead the corporation. Whether or not the executive team members have specific operational responsibilities has shaped the extent to which these senior executives work separately – and sometimes at cross-purposes – to protect and promote their 'turfs', or work collegially to develop coherent corporate strategies and to focus corporate resources more effectively. The way the executive team is composed also shapes the extent to which the corporation brings to its decision-making a global mind-set.

Global versus home country mind-set

Many multinationals have so organized their corporate executive teams that the members have tended to be so preoccupied with home country issues that global ones have too often been viewed myopically. Several phenomena reflect and prolong this mesmerization with domestic concerns (see Table 3.1).

First, with a few exceptions such as Nestlé, domestic activities initially constituted the overwhelming share of the sales of most corporations. The domestic sales of most American corporations continue to account for the majority of revenue. Notable exceptions have been Exxon, Mobil and IBM. In contrast, the European and Asian firms have tended to become more dependent on international sales, and thus less tempted to perceive international efforts as peripheral to domestic ones.

Second, most multinationals have concentrated their manufacturing facilities and other assets in their home country. Such a concentration manifests a continuing home country orientation.

Third, relatively few multinationals have separated their world headquarters from their home country headquarters. Few multinationals organize their domestic operations as a country affiliate organizationally comparable to their foreign ones. Thus the corporate leadership has a dual role: running the domestic operations and overseeing global activities. Such a role discourages the viewing of global issues other than through a headquarter-country prism. Since its 1907 formation as a binational company, the Royal Dutch/Shell central offices in London and The Hague have dealt comparably with all the country affiliates, including those in the two 'home' countries. Nestlé's Swiss-based affiliate is separate from and operates similarly to those based outside the headquarters country. Philips has set up a domestic company separate from the international one. In 1992, IBM combined IBM USA with IBM Canada to form IBM North America, which along with IBM Europe/Middle East/Africa, IBM Asia Pacific and IBM Latin America constitute the four marketing and source companies responsible to the IBM world headquarters.

Fourth, multinationals (with the notable exception of Nestlé) have long located the head offices of all, or most of, their major operating parts in the home country, thus further fostering a home country mind-set. Only a few multinationals have

Table 3.1 A few factors affecting/reflecting global-mindedness

Continent/Country	% sales, foreign, 1989/90	Extent corporate management internationalized	
		Board of directors/ supervisory board	Corporate executive team/ senior management
AMERICA			
Exxon	73	1 British 'outsider' and 1 Canadian vice-president on board	
Mobil	65	All-American	
IBM	59	1 Swiss and 1 German on board	Canadian, Japanese, German and Italian vice-presidents
Du Pont	44	Canadians on board	
P&G	40	1 German group vice-president on board	8 of 25 corporate officers not US natives
GE	40	Italian executive team member also board vice-chairman	
Ford	40	All-American	
Philip Morris	35	Former British CEO, Australian COO, German CFO, and an Australian and a Venezuelan 'outsider' on board	2 Australians, 1 German and 1 Canadian in top posts
GM	30	1 British-born 'outsider'	
EUROPE			
Nestlé	98	Spanish, German, French and US board members	German CEO/chairman; Spanish, English and Austrian 'general managers'
Philips	94	Non-Dutch majority on supervisory board	1 Briton, 1 American, 1 Swiss and 1 Norwegian on GMC
ICI	78	2 Germans and 2 Americans among 8 'outsiders' on board	
Royal Dutch/Shell	N.A.	3 Dutch and 3 British comprise board/executive team	
BP	N.A.	Two Americans, 1 German and 1 Irishman on board	
Bayer	65	All-German supervisory board	1 Belgian on *Vorstand*: 6 of 25 group heads not German
Alcatel Alsthom	63	Board includes 1 Italian and 1 Belgian	
Daimler-Benz	61	All-German	
Fiat	44	1 Belgian, 1 Dutchman and 1 German on board	
ASIA			
Sony	66	1 American 'outsider', German head of Sony Europe and American head of Sony Software on board	
Nissan	47	All Japanese	
Matsushita	42	All Japanese	
Toyota	41	All Japanese	
Mitsubishi Electric	N.A.	All Japanese	
Samsung	N.A.	All South Korean	
Hitachi	14	All Japanese	

Sources: Include annual reports and personal information.

to locate the headquarters of a major product division – or even a product subdivision – in a foreign country. Two of Alcatel's major product divisions are headquartered outside of France. IBM has just moved its communications system division headquarters to southeast England. Bayer left the headquarters of two acquired divisions (of its health care product sector) in the United States (at the headquarters of its Miles, Inc. acquisition). Philips has moved approximately 25 per cent of the headquarters of its subdivisions outside the Netherlands, including moving its major appliance headquarters to Italy and more recently its headquarters for X-ray tubes and generators to Germany. GE locates its international division headquarters in London.

A fifth factor is that, with relatively few exceptions, home country nationals hold all or almost all the top management posts. Similarly, only a few American multinationals have promoted non-Americans to top corporate posts. Four Philip Morris senior executives, including its president-COO, are foreign-born. In 1988–9, a European served as vice-chairman of IBM. Eight of Procter & Gamble's 25 senior executives are foreign-born and bred. But these are noteworthy exceptions to a long-standing American syndrome. Only a few European multinationals, especially those based in small countries, have been more internationally minded in their senior appointments. Nestlé's CEO is German. Philips now includes an American, a Swiss and a Norwegian on its corporate executive team. Sony is the only Global 50 Asian company that has promoted 'foreigners' to board-level executive positions. In many multinationals, the capacity to develop global-mindedness at the corporate level is impeded not only by the scarcity of foreign-bred executives in the top ranks, but also by the lack of appreciation of international experience as a significant criterion for being promoted to top posts.

A sixth factor, which has affected American corporations that have relied on international divisions to manage their overseas operations, is that the international head (who may or may not have had foreign experience) has generally been overshadowed at the corporate level by those whose experiences and responsibilities have been essentially domestic. (Procter & Gamble, whose present CEO previously served as international head, and as European head before that, is an exception.) While Japanese and South Korean multinationals similarly focus the responsibility for overseas sales and development on the head of the international (sales) group, the fact that globalism has been considered basic to the multinational's development has mitigated the problem. European multinationals, such as Bayer, Shell, Nestlé, ICI and Philips, by assigning geographic or continental portfolios to several executive team members, have the potential for overcoming this syndrome – if the geographic portfolio assignments are considered to be as important as their product and functional portfolios. The capacity for developing a global-mindedness has affected the way multinationals have organized their companies and developed their international operations from the domestic base.

Many factors, then, have tended to encourage a myopic vision of corporate issues. The way the multinationals organize their corporate parts – whether and how they separate the international operations from the domestic ones – further affects their global localization efforts.

Splitting international operations: by product, by function and by territory

As already noted, two major factors have long shaped the way a company has organized its international operations. First, the strength of national trade barriers at the time the company began the development of its present affiliates has affected the extent of autonomy they have traditionally been allowed to exercise. The earlier a company developed its international affiliates the more likely it is that they were organized as semi-autonomous daughter companies, with or without an international divisional umbrella to coordinate their efforts. Second, the organizational architecture of the parent firm has affected the reforming of the earlier established affiliates and the forming of the more recently established ones. Many product-divided multinationals have in recent decades extended this split to their international operations. Increasing globalization and diversification, and the growing size of the various international parts of the mega-multinationals, have led them to modify their traditional approach to organizing their international operations.

As a consequence three approaches to the corporate organization of international operations may be distinguished (see Figure 3.3). American and European multinationals, most of which once organized their non-domestic activities principally by country, are now modifying the organizational relations so that they more closely respond to the product-oriented organization of the corporate whole. Only a few of the American and European multinationals continue to organize their international operations primarily by country. The Japanese companies are tempering their functionally organized overseas operations so that there is greater opportunity for continental coordination. The case studies in Part III note that a few American and European multinationals have continued to organize their international operations primarily on a territorial basis – even though product has become the principal rationale for dividing the corporate activities.

Splitting international operations by product

The rapid increase in product-split, multidivisional corporations, coupled with the host of factors making economies more interdependent, have expedited the trend away from multinationals splitting the management of their international activities from their domestic ones. While initially most American firms relied upon their international divisions (or subsidiaries) and European firms upon their sister companies for the management of foreign operations, an increasing number now depend upon their global product divisions to open new country marketing and develop new sources for raw materials and manufactured goods, and managed their own network of affiliates. While a few American multinationals, such as P&G and 3M, have retained their corporate-wide international divisions, others,

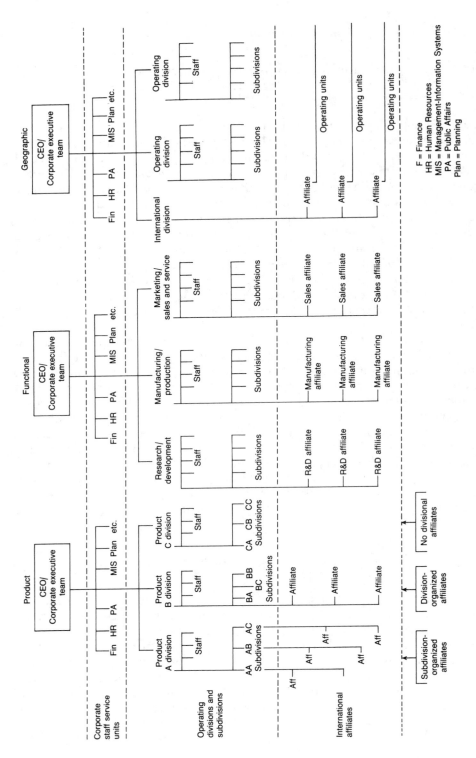

Figure 3.3 Comparison of the three international organizational prototypes

F = Finance
HR = Human Resources
MIS = Management-Information Systems
PA = Public Affairs
Plan = Planning

such as Exxon and Ford, use the international organization only to manage the international operations of their major business(es); Ford International Operations manages Ford's overseas motor vehicle operations; Exxon Company International manages Exxon international oil ('upstream' and 'downstream') but not the chemical operations. Many more, such as Mobil, now depend on each of their product subsidiaries, sectors and divisions to coordinate its own sets of international affiliates. Philip Morris is distinctive in its recent move to bring together all its overseas operations under one executive vice-president.

As European multinationals developed and diversified in the latter decades of the twentieth century, those that had retained their pre-World War II affiliates continued to depend on these sister companies. On the other hand, those multinationals that rebuilt their international operations tended to develop affiliates whose role was generally limited to the manufacturing or selling of one product line. The events of the 1980s, however, hastened the consideration of approaches that strengthened the global role of their product divisions.

Splitting international sales and marketing operations

Japanese companies have long separated their sales operations from their production divisions. As they expanded overseas they initially relied upon a trading partner (such as Mitsui & Co. or Mitsubishi Corporation), an international trading/sales subsidiary (such as Matsushita Trading Co. or Toyota Motor Sales), an international division (such as Sony's and Nissan's) or a combination of these options (as Hitachi does) to handle their international marketing and sales. As Japanese multinationals have expanded their international operations, their production divisions have developed their own overseas manufacturing affiliates, thus extending the functional split internationally. The Canon organization diagram (see Figure 3.4), for example, demonstrates the structural split into three 'global systems': one for research and development, one for production and one for marketing (which includes the geographic area affiliates). Only in the late 1980s did a few Japanese companies begin to temper their function-split overseas operations with continental cross-hierarchy organizational arrangements.

Splitting international operations territorially

Many multinationals have continued to rely principally on omnibus international affiliates for the multifunctional management of (almost) all of their international operations. Mega-multinationals have used a variety of arrangements for coordinating these omnibus affiliates. European multinationals such as Royal Dutch/Shell and Philips have tended to divide the responsibility for the oversight of international operations – by continent – among several board members, each assisted by regional offices. Those American multinationals that have continued to rely on

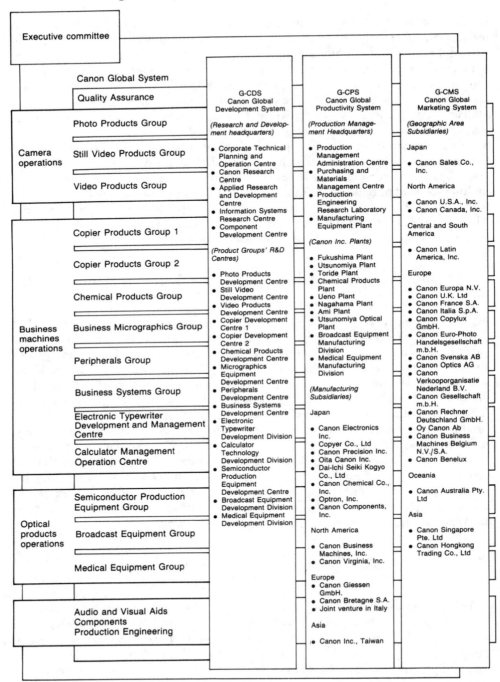

Figure 3.4   Canon organogram, 1989 (Source: Canon, 1989:21)

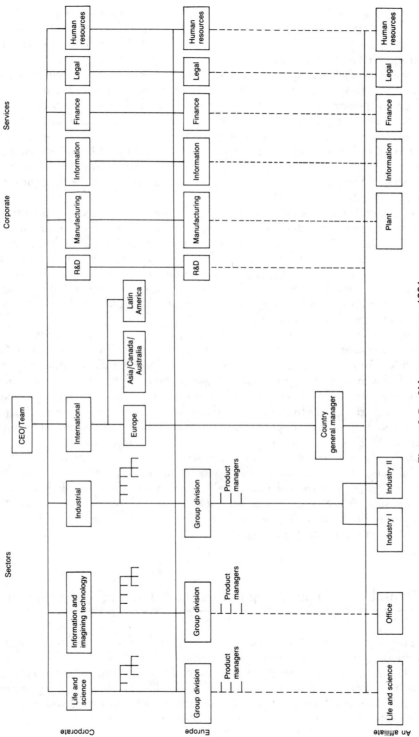

Figure 3.5 3M organogram, 1991

omnibus-type international affiliates have depended upon an operational international division to coordinate these efforts.

International divisions work with other corporate divisions in a wide variety of ways, ranging from a broad (omnibus-like multifunctional and multiproduct) operational responsibility with accompanying profit-and-loss accountability to a more limited staff support role. The extent of the geographic area for which they are responsible may vary from everything 'international' – that is, the area outside the borders of the home country (the area generally embraced by an 'international division/group') – to a continental region (such as the Americas, Europe or Europe/Africa/ Middle East, and Asia/Pacific), to an intracontinental region such as Benelux, Scandinavia, the Middle East or one country.

Many American multinationals long favoured the corporate-wide, operationally responsible international division. In this approach, an international division converted product division strategies into international affiliate programmes. Increasingly these international divisions have worked through continental organizations. Procter & Gamble and 3M have followed this model (see Figure 3.5). A few, such as Exxon and GM, have tempered the arrangement by using the corporate international entity to manage the major part – but not the full extent of their corporate overseas businesses.

A supportive rather than operational approach to the coordination of international operations has been developed by General Electric (GE). GE's London-based International Division, which is headed by a corporate senior vice-president (who in 1992 was appointed as one of two corporate vice-chairmen), is not an operational but essentially a staff service division that supports the product divisions, and their subdivisions, by scouting and promoting new business opportunities, facilitating cooperation and consultation, and providing support activities for GE's new business ventures. GE's product divisions and their subdivisions manage their own sets of product-focused international affiliates.

The functionally split nature of Japanese companies has meant that their 'international groups' have been essentially single-function marketing, sales and service organizations. Nissan uses an Overseas Group to oversee the efforts of their affiliates whose operational responsibilities embrace marketing, sales and service – but excludes manufacturing affiliates.

Continental coordination: operating, coordinating and supporting

Continental organizations have emerged in response to the global expansion of multinationals, the growing number of international affiliates, and the increasing need for continentally localized coordination and rationalization of the efforts of neighbouring affiliates, especially when their economies have become significantly integrated. Continental offices assist in converting global product strategies into country-specific efforts. A continental organization may serve a major fraction of a continent (such as the European Community) or more than a continent (such as Europe, Africa and the Middle East).

American corporations, particularly IBM (Sobel, 1981:131–7), pioneered the continental concept as they expanded into Europe. As Asian firms, such as Canon, Nissan, Matsushita, Sony and Samsung, have expanded their international operations, they too have organized continental coordinating centres. In the early 1990s, BP and ICI did the same.

European multinationals have generally limited their continental coordinating efforts to a global headquarters-located operation. Nestlé, Shell, Bayer, BP, Philips and ICI have corporate executive team members with continent-specific portfolios. Philips and Shell have organized bureaus whose task is to coordinate the effort to advise and assist the national affiliates within its continental overview and to advise the corporate executive team members responsible for overseeing that continent. But such offices have a more limited role than the continental organization that has been developed by many American and a few Asian multinationals. ICI and BP are the only European multinationals that have organized European continental organizations; but ICI disbanded theirs after one year, and the role of BP's corporate-wide European office has focused on representational responsibilities.

Continental offices vary in the extent to which they exert a strong or weak coordinating role. 3M, IBM, P&G and Sony have well-developed continental offices staffed with product-specific and function-specific expertise. Led by a continental executive with a strong power base, they have large staffs which exert significant power in directing the country affiliates in integrating and modifying world-wide directives. On the other hand, AT&T's continental office has a more facilitating role: its head does not outrank the heads of some affiliates, and many of the staff comprising the continental headquarters report principally to their product or functional bosses in the US headquarters.

A critical way in which continental centres differ is the extent of their responsibilities. A continental centre's responsibilities may vary, like those of an international affiliate, (as will be described later), in the extent of its product responsibility and of functional responsibility (see Table 3.2). The combination of these spectrums of possibilities provides a number of organizational approaches.

Omnibus approach

An omnibus approach, both multi-product and multifunctional, is the one used by 3M. 3M Europe, based in Brussels, coordinates all of 3M's European operations. Essentially it is the means by which the product sector strategies are transmitted to the sixteen European international affiliates, each of which is responsible for the marketing and manufacturing operations within its national borders. The continental organization, headed by the vice-president for Europe, who reports to the executive vice-president for international operations, comprises such staff offices as finance and human resources, marketing offices for each of 3M's product sectors, and a manufacturing office. These 3M Europe continental, office-

Table 3.2   Comparison of roles of continental centres

Extent of functional responsibility	Extent of product responsibility	
	Corporate-wide, multiproduct	Narrow, limited product
Broad, multi-functional operational role	Omnibus responsibilities include management coordination/direction of: – Marketing, sales and services – Manufacturing – Administrative staff support – (Sometimes) research & development	Multifunctional operational responsibilities for limited range of products
Functionally focused plus coordination role	Responsibilities include: – Marketing, sales and services – Administrative staff support – Coordination of other functions	Functionally focused, operational role plus coordinative responsibilities for limited range of products
Functionally specific operational role	Responsibilities include: – Management coordination/direction – Marketing, sales and services – Representation, etc.	Functionally specific operational role for limited range of product
Limited functional support	Responsibilities include: – Providing administrative support – Services and representation	Functionally specific and product-specific support role

based managers maintain administrative relationships with the vice-president for Europe as well as an operational reporting relationship with their respective sector bosses at the corporate headquarters in St Paul, Minnesota. The 3M heads of the country affiliates report to the vice-president for Europe or his deputy. The 3M Europe product and functional managers have long had no line authority over national affiliate personnel. They are expected, however, to work closely with the affiliate product and functional managers and are held accountable for business decisions by their product sectors in the United States.

Limited product or limited function

Whereas 3M Europe serves as the multifunctional agent for all 3M's sectors, many continental centres are the arm of only part of their multinationals. GM Europe, for example, manages only GM's motor vehicle operations in Europe; other GM sectors, such as GM Hughes, have their own European centres. Likewise, Exxon Company International manages the Exxon overseas oil businesses, but not its chemical businesses.

Another type of continental centre is one whose responsibilities focus on marketing, sales and service but also coordinate and support manufacturing operations. In these multinationals the global business divisions manage their own international manufacturing, and the continental centres essentially exercise an administrative support role. IBM Europe, whose primary mission has been the management of the national affiliates (essentially marketing, sales and service companies), provides an example. While Sony Europe is essentially a multiproduct sales and service entity managing the national marketing affiliates, it also serves as the organizational coordination and support base for the Europe-based arms of Sony's business groups, whose continental heads sit on the Sony Europe executive committee.

The Mitsubushi Electric and Matsushita Electric continental centres have a role even more focused on marketing, sales and service. They do, however, exert a limited coordinating role with regard to manufacturing operations. Matsushita, for example, accomplishes this by naming executives in its essentially marketing and sales continental centres to additional supervisory posts in the various overseas manufacturing companies.

Du Pont's European office provides management support services to the manufacturing and marketing efforts of their multinationals' product sectors. BP Europe has an even more limited role – principally, the coordination of public affairs efforts; the product division continental offices (for example, BP Oil) handle most of their own support services.

A continental centre with limited product scope and limited functional responsibility is the Hitachi Sales European Coordinating Office; it oversees the continental sales efforts for Hitachi consumer products, which constitute less than 12 per cent of the Hitachi group's total sales.

Changing continental affiliate relations

Growing economic interdependence and the potential of even more interdependence have fuelled European integration. The challenge for business has been to develop a flexible organization which can adapt as the new political, supranational arrangements unfold over the coming decades. The increased continental consciousness of multinationals has pushed them to continentalize their operations; that is, rationalize manufacturing and other functions on a continental basis. Increased continental economic integration, particularly in Europe, has led multinationals to strengthen the pan-European perspectives within the continental offices and rationalize the manufacturing on a transcontinental basis. The development of continental offices has motivated multinationals to control the country affiliates with a more continental perspective, tightening the product and functional integration. It has also provided a means of allowing host country nationals to run the country affiliates while retaining greater flexibility in using home country and third country nationals in the continental headquarters. The presence of continental offices also provides opportunities for multinationals to keep informed and even influence continental developments. The lessons learned from the development of continental offices and the changing relations with affiliates in Europe has already had an impact on the creation and redevelopment of continental organizations on other continents.

International affiliates: omnibus and *ad hoc*

International, country and multi-country affiliates have long been the basic components of the non-domestic parts of a multinational's global mosaic. They differ in many ways: size, ownership, area covered, scope of products, and power.

Differences

Size differences could hardly be more dramatic. With respect to sales, Shell Oil (USA), the US international affiliate of the Royal Dutch/Shell group, ranked as the 14th largest US corporation in 1990. Five other international affiliates rank among the world's largest 100 firms in terms of sales income. Canada's two largest companies have been General Motors of Canada and Ford Motors of Canada. Two of Germany's thirteen largest companies are also affiliates of General Motors and Ford: Adam Opel (GM) and Ford Werke. GM, IBM and Shell control major affiliates in Japan, the United Kingdom and France (see Table 3.3). At the other end of the spectrum, many affiliates employ only a few people.

International affiliates vary significantly in the extent to which one parent company owns them. Since 100 per cent corporate ownership of an affiliate allows

Table 3.3 Wholly or majority-owned affiliates with sales sufficient to rate in the Global 200, 1988 (if they had been independent companies)

Affiliate	USA	Canada	Germany	UK	Japan	France
General Motors		(16)	(10)			
Ford		(13)	(11)	(11)		
Chrysler		(7)				
Shell	(27)	(7)				
IBM			(7)	(7)	(8)	(6)
Hanson	(7)					
Unilever	(6)					
Total	*3*	*4*	*3*	*2*	*1*	*1*

Note: ( ) = Sales revenues in $bn
Source: Compiled from *Fortune*, 29 April 1989a, 161–209; 31 July 1989b, 33–80.

a multinational the opportunity to move surplus and capital more freely, some firms, such as IBM until recently, have avoided joint venture arrangements. On the other hand, joint ventures and other forms of strategic alliances facilitate the development of new products, new markets, and new manufacturing facilities. Furthermore, some countries, such as India, have long insisted on at least 50 per cent host country ownership, a policy relaxed as recently as 1991.

Affiliates differ, too, in the area they cover. Typically, they cover one country, but a few cover one or more neighbouring countries as well. For example, Mitsui Benelux covers the Netherlands, Belgium and Luxembourg. The IBM Italian affiliate serves North Africa, and the Mobil French affiliate serves the francophone African countries.

International affiliates also differ dramatically in their role. As with continental organizations, two major factors shape differences in national affiliate roles. One is the scope of products for which the multinational holds the affiliate responsible – whether the scope spans the broad range of the corporation's product line or only a limited fraction (such as only the products of one division). The other is the extent of functional control for which the management of the affiliate is held responsible. These two factors affect the initiatives that affiliates are encouraged or allowed to take in developing local product strategies and setting functional standards. Together they affect the extent of loose or tight control exerted by multinationals over their affiliates, and thus the degree of integration achieved among the various multinational efforts in any one geographic area. These factors generate a broad, two-dimensional spectrum of types – with a wide assortment of variations and combinations of approaches. The schema extends from the more omnibus affiliates (which are both multiproduct and multifunctional) to the more *ad hoc* (which are single-product and single-function, such as marketing cameras or manufacturing car phones) (see Table 3.4).

Table 3.4 Comparison of roles of national affiliates

Functional responsibility embraces	Scope of product responsibility embraces	
	Narrow-scope product	Broad-scope product
Limited functional role	Limited product Limited function	Multiproduct Limited function
Focused functional plus coordinative role	Limited product Limited function plus coordinative role	Multiproduct Limited function plus coordinative role
Extensive multi-functional role	Multi-functional limited product	Omnibus Multiproduct and multi-functional (Some may have highly unified management such as Shell; others, such as Philips, may have less unified country management)

More omnibus

The more omnibus affiliates manufacture, market and manage a broad, multiproduct range of the products produced and sold in that country by the multinational of which they are part. With regard to how closely their omnibus affiliates integrate their product and functional units, they vary from being highly unified through being federated or confederated to being umbrella-type entities in which the parts are only loosely associated.

The unified affiliate, with broad operating responsibility for a wide range of its multinational's products, is a distinctive feature of the sister company approach to the management of international operations. Such an area-sensitive or country-driven approach features a strongly empowered affiliate executive and a well-developed sense of local organizational identity. An example of unified omnibus affiliate is a Royal Dutch/Shell operating company – one which manufactures, markets and manages whatever products are produced and/or sold in the country. While the affiliates are expected to seek advice and assistance regarding their products and functional expertise, it is the country general manager with the support of his or her management team in whom corporate headquarters has focused the integrated responsibility for the management of Royal Dutch/Shell's operations in that country.

In the more frontier-conscious pre-1960s era, as has already been stressed, most European and many American multinationals relied upon such unified omnibus-type affiliates. The American firms that initially relied upon international divisions to develop their overseas businesses tended to develop such integrated affiliates. With their continued growth and diversification in the postwar years, though, the larger and more diversified American multinationals have either tended to leave the management of the affiliates to their product sectors or, upon rationalizing their manufacturing, converted their affiliates into essentially marketing ones. By the late 1980s and early 1990s, several European firms, such as Philips and BP, had also internationalized their product divisions and thus converted what had been their unified 'sister companies' into more federated-, confederated- or associated-type entities.

The federated and confederated affiliates are hallmarks of a matrix-like approach to the management of international operations. Such an approach features an affiliate executive whose colleagues are directly responsible to product or functional superiors in higher echelons. Such affiliates may have been converted from unitary affiliates – as the Philips ones have recently been. Most Philips country affiliates now consist of units working closely with and under the direction of the global product divisions and subdivisions, which not only direct the product strategy but also have world-wide profit-and-loss accountability. Such country general managers continue to have representative and administrative support responsibility, but they are no longer the 'feudal lords' they once were.

The BP affiliates are even less integrated. While an omnibus country BP embraces the BP Oil and other BP country units, and represents BP interests as a whole, the country product units' primary chain of command is a vertical hierarchy line (BP Oil Deutschland reports operationally to BP Oil Europe, which reports to BP Oil).

The Bayer affiliates are less integrated again. They are essentially associations of product units which have been brought together under one 'roof'. The country management board (composed of the heads of the major local units) that coordinates this confederate-type arrangement is led by a 'spokesperson' who maintains contact with a Bayer corporate executive team (*Vorstand*) member. Nestlé and Nissan have taken similar steps in organizing one all-embracing, confederate-like American affiliate.

Each of these arrangements reflects the balance of product versus territory emphasis that a multinational has decided to stress in its international organization strategy.

Single purpose: marketing affiliates, manufacturing affiliates and product-specific affiliates

A few varieties of the *ad hoc*, single-purpose type affiliate may be distinguished. One type is multiproduct but essentially function-specific. A Sony country affiliate's role is limited to sales of a broad range of its multinational's products. The IBM affiliates' role is largely focused on sales, but they do have an administrative coordinating role for the manufacturing and other units located in their country.

Another type is the multifunctional limited product company. Electronic Data Systems' international affiliates, for example, have a multifunctional responsibility for selling and producing one of GM's products in one defined territory.

A third type is the single-product and single-function affiliate. An Hitachi sales international affiliate, for example, only sells consumer electronics, a small fraction of Hitachi products, in one country. Its overseas manufacturing companies are likewise single-product and function-specific. Other single-product and single-function affiliates may have only manufacturing responsibilities.

The tendency of American and Asian multinationals to control manufacturing more closely from international or continental headquarters reflects the fact that they have taken a continent-wide approach to developing and rationalizing manufacturing operations on other continents. Increasingly European multinationals, such as Philips, follow this strategy in order to compete more effectively in an integrated Europe (Taucher, 1989).

Thus there is a spectrum of national affiliate arrangements ranging from the more omnibus, multifunctional and multiproduct approach to the more pluralistic, *ad hoc* approach with different global divisions managing their own sets of affiliates. The in-between approaches, such as IBM's multiproduct marketing affiliates and Philips' federated-type affiliates, are alternative strategies aimed at balancing the virtues of product, territorial and functional approaches to global competition.

Lateral linkages: binding the vertical hierarchies

The way a multinational structures its major operational divisions and affiliates shapes the pyramid-like vertical hierarchies that comprise the modern multinational. The way it structures the lateral cross-hierarchy linkages that enable the vertical hierarchies to collaborate effectively in cross-border efforts vitally affects the corporate capacity to achieve synergy among business units, concerted use of common resources, and collaboration efforts towards common, corporate-wide objectives. To facilitate the achievement of this objective, multinationals have developed a number of structural mechanisms to aid cross-communication and coordination. Committees have long been used; the matrix has had its advocates; and teams and teamwork have more recently been advanced as a means by which multinationals may more effectively achieve cross-hierarchy coordination.

The matrix

However organized, the superimposing of one set of organizational command relationships upon another produces a matrix; that is, a situation with a multiplicity of reporting relationships. When a multinational stresses one set and subordinates another, thus creating or allowing an 'unbalanced' equilibrium, the power exerted by the more potent set outbalances the secondary set (which may be described as a 'dotted line' relationship). When multinationals equally, or almost equally, stress two (or more) sets and expect coordinated action, they legitimize a more or less 'balanced' multiplicity of command (see Figure 3.6). As multinationals have attempted to integrate and blend two or more sets of perspectives, many have increasingly experimented with and adopted arrangements that have attempted matrixing of product and function, product and area, or function and area, and in some cases matrixing three or more. Such multiplicity of lines of command/ coordinated relationships may generate confusion without achieving coordination. (In an interview for this book, one American corporate manager, upon reading the corporation organizational manual, 'discovered' a reporting relationship which he had either never known or had forgotten.)

The European multinationals that have retained their traditional reliance upon daughter companies have tended to limit the matrix to one in which the area perspective has been stressed. For example, the Shell headquarters is organized in a matrix, but the multiplicity of command relationships does not extend beyond headquarters. On the other hand, as Philips has gradually globalized the role of its product sectors, the balance of power between the product divisions and the national organizations has shifted – whereas once there was a matrix arrangement unbalanced in favour of the affiliates, it is now unbalanced in favour of the product sectors.

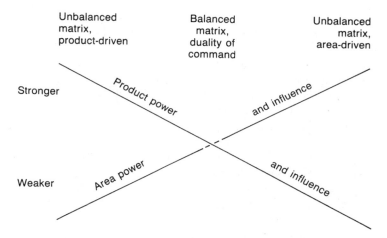

Note: This is the spectrum of a two-dimensional matrix relationship. Function communication/command relations may provide a third dimension.

Figure 3.6   Spectrum of matrix-like arrangements

American multinationals, as they have diversified and developed product-driven corporate models, have constructed the unbalanced line-and-staff matrix to reconcile the product and functions perspectives. As they have extended overseas, they have had to add a geographic dimension. Those that have relied on international divisions have matrixed the geographic perspective and the product perspective; the more the geographic perspective has been stressed, the more autonomous the affiliates. The more and the greater the efforts to mesh the two sets of perspectives, the more difficult the challenge of making a more-or-less balanced matrix work. Those American multinationals that rely wholly on their product divisions to manage their international operations have clearly stressed the product perspective over the area one. Japanese multinationals, with their strong indoctrination in the company's corporate culture and the accompanying premium on harmony, *ringi* and consensus, appear to have had more success in alleviating the tensions that generally accompany matrixed arrangements.

Variations in the matrix arrangement have affected the degree of 'formal power' vested in positions, the people to whom managers primarily relate, and the degree of difficulty that managers have in working together both vertically and laterally. Some forms of matrix-like arrangement are an inevitable feature of complex management, but the more 'balanced' they are the more they promote a lack of clarity regarding who is accountable; and they often fuel power struggles, 'turf' battles and frustration. To work successfully in such a complex environment, managers have needed a sophisticated understanding of power and the ability to work cooperatively to accomplish objectives.

Teams

Disappointed by earlier, more formally structured matrix arrangements, and pressed to develop arrangements that further facilitated lateral coordination across vertical hierarchies, multinationals have sought more inclusive and more flexible arrangements. Many have moved to the concept of teams as a neo-matrix means of embracing managers from different parts of the enterprise and facilitating their participation in decisions whose impact transcends intracorporate borders. As competitive pressures force more and more companies into global-type organizations, many companies are relying more upon teams and networks of teams to bridge the pyramidal hierarchies on which they have long depended. The key players in these hierarchy-spanning efforts have been the international general managers, who have catalyst-like roles in mobilizing the teams and thus bringing the various parts of the organization together.

Teams and networks may embrace diversity by including people from different functions, different products, different nationalities and different areas (corporate headquarters, continental affiliates and national affiliates) as well as different languages and cultures. A European product team of eight people might represent six countries, four different languages and cultures, and affiliate and headquarters people, as well as the usual technical services, financial and product representatives. When such diversity is combined with growing structural interdependence and scarce or shared resources, the challenge in seeking concerted direction is magnified. Teamwork which requires more lateral working relationships is such a way of life at IBM that they have introduced a course called Cluster Management, which deals with group dynamics and managing conflicts across traditional boundaries. Working in these diverse teams clearly requires increased general management knowledge, sophisticated interpersonal skills and flexible attitudes. Nowhere is the diversity and interdependence greater than with product or business teams in companies such as Philips, 3M and Exxon. Although the dynamics may vary, depending upon the structure and reporting relationships, the overall theme is consistent – eroding professional and affiliate fiefdoms and increasing work-related interdependence.

The way the international operations are structured is therefore a critical aspect of the corporation's organizational strategy and affects the role of the affiliate in developing and implementing overall corporate strategy. Those multinationals whose organizational strategy has long consciously or unconsciously considered the national affiliates as their 'businesses' have held the country general manager responsible for profit-and-loss. Those multinationals which stress a product perspective hold the product parts responsible for profit-and-loss. The critical issue is finding a fit between corporate headquarters and the affiliate that better utilizes the product and functional expertise in headquarters and the local sensitivity of the affiliate. This requires not only improved structural arrangements, but also improved processes for developing managers who can work in power-sharing arrangements extending across functional, country and product borders.

Structure affects and reflects the perspectives, mind-sets and power bases of the key players, and thus their priorities. Hence, when a multinational organizes by product sectors at headquarters level, the key headquarters players will have predictable perspectives and values. When these key players interact with key players at the continental and country level, differences in perception, priorities and value emerge. As the multinational parts become more interlocked, it is vital for the differences among the parts to be consciously surfaced, acknowledged as legitimate, and managed constructively in order for the multinational to work together successfully. Such an effort requires corporate-wide staffing and shared values as well as structures that enable cross-hierarchy concerting of resources and collaboration of efforts toward common, corporate-wide objectives.

CHAPTER 4
Staffing: for international general management skills

Human dynamics of power: affecting cross-border coordination

As multinationals have expanded their product scope, their geographic spread and their span of professional specialisms, the responsibilities of their management posts have become far more complex. International general managers increasingly have had to deal with a greater variety of more complex strategies and structures involving more complicated issues and interests. They have had to work in harness, with some degree of harmony, with more 'bosses' and more colleagues outside of their primary chain of command or coordination or both. Conflicting company perspectives have increasingly placed international general managers in the cross-fire not only between headquarters and affiliates but also among their various contending corporate, product and functional hierarchies. They are under constant pressure to accommodate atypical local situations to a variety of global directives, systems, standards and bottom-line expectations. As global pressures have forced changes in corporate strategies and structures, the roles of international managers have required more power sharing, more participative management styles, and more eclectic and less predictable general management career paths. Consequently, multinationals face the need to refocus their international management staffing efforts in order to develop the management leadership skills that can integrate the differing perspectives and concert the diverse parts into cohesive wholes.

Effective staffing for international general management skills requires not only securing those with potential management leadership capability and developing that potential, but also using that capability to maximum advantage. Such international management staffing efforts depend upon an appreciation of what skills the changing international general manager role demands, whom to recruit for the management corps from which such managers are selected, and how to develop managers with the leadership skills required for international general manager posts. This chapter focuses on these issues.

Changing international general management roles: towards power-sharing

International general managers – that is, those who hold positions with multifunctional and/or multibusiness responsibility outside the multinational home country (see Kotter, 1982, for a broader definition of a general manager) – are generally responsible for geographic areas such as countries, regions or continents, and/or all international operations. This chapter focuses primarily on country and continental general managers who have the linchpin roles linking the geographically specific product and functional parts of international operations.

Country general managers head all or most of a multinational's operations within a specific country. They may be titled president, managing director, general manager or country general manager. For example, there is a managing director of 3M UK, a president of Mitsui Benelux, a general manager of Belgian Shell, and a country general manager of Olivetti France. Their roles and responsibilities may include the full range of sales and marketing services for all or most of the company's range of products. They may also direct or coordinate manufacturing. In fewer cases, their responsibilities embrace research and technical development.

Continental general managers head all or most of a multinational's operations on a continent, most of a continent, or a continent plus all or parts of one or more adjacent continents. Thus a European continental organization may not include (what has long been called) Eastern Europe; on the other hand, it may include not only all of Europe but also all or parts of North Africa and West Asia. European continental general managers carry titles such as President of Canon Europe, Chairman ICI Europe, and General Manager AT&T Europe. The extent to which these international managers are responsible for the performance of all European activities varies substantially.

Two interdependent factors distinguish the scope of responsibility and power base of these international general managers. The first is that of to whom the manager is responsible: generally, the broader the scope of responsibility and the stronger the authority base of the general manager's 'boss', the stronger the potential support for exerting power that transcends intracorporate borders. The second is that of what the manager is responsible for: generally, the more the multinational holds a general manager accountable for profit-and-loss, the stronger the power base and the more varied the systemic means through which the international general manager may exert power and influence and coordinate local efforts effectively. These systemic means include control of capital and operational budgeting, input regarding management staffing assignments and evaluations, access to functional and product-driven information sources, and opportunity to shape the corporate local 'public face'. Clearly, the fewer means a general manager has for exerting power, the less he or she may rely on the authority to command and the more he or she must depend upon his or her ability to exert influence. Just as clearly, the more an international general manager must share power with colleagues, the more he or she must depend on his or her ability to negotiate and collaborate with them.

Even in intrahierarchy situations, a general manager must seek more aid and negotiate more with his or her colleagues, who are no longer subordinate in the traditional sense. In situations calling for cross-hierarchy collaboration, the capacity to exert leadership, even without the authority to command, is indispensable.

With regard to the authority vested in positions of country or continental general managers, there is a broad spectrum ranging from (at one end) significant formal authority vested in the general manager's position to (at the other end) no such general post existing. Along this spectrum several types of arrangement may be discerned at the country and continental level (see Figure 4.1). Clearly this affects job demands.

Executive head

The executive-head type of international general manager is responsible for all or most of the unified operations of a multinational in one or more countries outside a multinational's home country. While his or her subordinates may and generally do communicate with counterpart superiors in headquarters, these relationships are clearly secondary to their relationship to the executive head, who is accountable for the affiliate meeting its profit-and-loss and other headquarter-set objectives. The executive head is the classical 'boss' whose role stresses vertical relationships. To the extent that a multinational has executive-head type general managers at the country or continental level, they have stressed multiproduct and multifunctional coordination at the local level more than global product or global functional integration.

The executive-head type of country general manager was the norm before World War II. While many European and American multinationals continued the arrangement in the postwar era, few Global 50 firms continue to do so. Traditionally the most important ties in this arrangement have been the personal ones between the parent company 'overlords' and the country 'lords'. The country manager's surrogate role depended at least as much upon corporate headquarters rapport as upon formal organizational processes and reporting relationships. A country manager of this sort had absorbed the values and practices of the parent company over decades and had become 'one of the boys'; he or she had also developed a strong local power base. Written rules and reports were generally not stressed. Consequently, such country general managers exercised significant autonomy, but within well-understood yet unwritten constraints. As long as constraints were respected and profits generated as anticipated, headquarters rarely interfered with – or even asked for much detailed information from – their international affiliates (Franko, 1976: 113–19). While in recent decades the multi-national headquarters have increased their contacts, required more information and exerted more control, the tradition of relative autonomy has continued, albeit abated, in a few multinationals such as Royal Dutch/Shell and Nestlé.

Jan DeSmedt, who heads a Royal Dutch/Shell national operating company, provides an example of an executive-head type general manager. DeSmedt, a

Executive head (of unified-type structure)
Within territory, he or she is directly responsible for all or almost all of a multinational's operations; all product and functional support subordinates are directly responsible to him or her. The executive head is the 'boss', who has been perceived by many as ruling like a baron over a feudal fief.

Strong operational coordinative head (of federated-type structure)
Within territory, he or she is directly responsible for representation, management and general administration oversight/coordination of all activities; profit-and-loss and reporting relationships of subordinates/colleagues may vary by activity. Most of his or her senior colleagues have a 'boss' in their product/functional hierarchy as well as him or her.

Weak/administrative coordinative head (of confederate-type structure)
Within territory, he or she is directly responsible for representation, management support and general coordination of all activities; some staff support subordinates may report to him or her, but business unit heads report primarily to product/function bosses.

Representative head (of association-type structure)
Within territory, he or she has general representation and promotion responsibility for all operations, usually as a role in addition to direct responsibility for one unit. Colleagues report to product/function bosses, not to him or her. He or she may be the senior management person, but not the 'boss'.

No single overall territorial head
All units report directly to functional/product boss.

Key

──────	Lines of communication and control
- - - -	Lines of communication and technical advice
ʌ	Report to higher business or functional unit
GM	Country general manager
B	Business units (functionally integrated – sales, marketing, manufacturing, etc.)
S	Staff support units (finance, human resources, etc.)

Figure 4.1 Simplified comparison of country general manager roles (with regard to all or most of a multinational's activities in a country or multicountry area)

Dutchman and so a home country national, along with the affiliate management committee composed of department heads who are mostly host country nationals, directs all Royal Dutch/Shell activities in the country (except for a research laboratory which is only administratively coordinated by the country management). The department heads not only have contact with but also are expected to consult with headquarters on significant issues; such consultation, however, is advisory. The strength of the affiliate executive head has been enhanced by well-developed contacts in corporate headquarters and a successful track record which fosters his staff's respect and deference.

The coordinative head: from strong to weak

Two types of coordinative head may be identified: stronger and weaker. A stronger one – that is, one who heads a more unified organization (more federative than confederative) – has profit-and-loss and operational responsibility for all or a major part of the activities of the affiliate, and directs all or most of its staff support functions. While his or her role includes the coordination of the operations of the affiliate, his senior colleagues (unlike those of the executive head) report as well through their operational divisional hierarchies. A major factor affecting the strong coordinative head's strength is his or her ability to concert the affiliate's various resources: by preparing and controlling an integrated operational and capital budget, by preparing performance reviews and participating in personnel decisions affecting persons assigned to the affiliate, by managing the flow of information critical to measuring the affiliate's operations, and by handling its public affairs. In some cases, another factor affecting the strength of a country general manager may be his or her power emanating from another role as one who heads the principal product unit or a multicountry manufacturing facility.

A weaker coordinative head – that is, one who heads a less cohesive organization (more confederative than federative) – has less control of product units and staff support activities. His or her role is more one of administrative coordination: his or her senior colleagues generally view their operational 'boss' in the product or functional divisional hierarchy as the more important one.

Organizations which have established a stronger coordinating role for their country and continental general managers have tempered global direction with relatively strong opportunity for local discretion. The continental head of Sony Europe controls the continental support services, directs the country sales affiliates and chairs the Sony Europe executive committee, which includes the European-based continental business group heads who are responsible for the marketing strategy as well as the manufacturing of their sector's products. Despite the fact that these continental production group heads are operationally responsible to their Tokyo-based bosses, Jack Schmukli, the president of Sony Europe, has pointed out with a smile: 'If they don't cooperate, they will be moved to new positions' (interview, 29 June 1991 – he did not elaborate on what the new positions might be). Schmukli's membership of the Sony board of directors and his direct reporting relationship to the Sony president facilitates his strong operational hegemony.

Organizations which have established the weaker type of coordinative role have tempered global direction with less opportunity for local discretion. With the shift in the balance of power in Philips from the country affiliates to the product group, the head of Philips France, who once was a strong head, no longer has profit-and-loss responsibility for product group activities within France. Nor does he have control of the product unit budgets and staff assignments within his affiliate. His position remains prestigious; but as a consequence of his weaker role, to achieve coordination he must depend on his close rapport with corporate leadership and his ability to lead and negotiate rather than on his authority to command.

The presence of two 'bosses' – one in the affiliate and another in the product or functional division hierarchy – creates a matrix-like arrangement. Such arrangements generate conflicting loyalties and directives. The way such conflicts are resolved varies from product to product, function to function, issue to issue and individual to individual, depending on such factors as priorities, power, personality and profit-and-loss responsibility. The coordinator-type general managers whose positions have not been endowed with budget control and personnel review authority are disadvantaged in their ability to exert power and influence over or with their colleagues. Thus coordinator-type managers and their subordinates operate in an environment in which a relatively evenly balanced matrix generates ambiguity and confusion. They must rely not only on the force of their personality and their career-developed prestige and networks, but also on their ability to lead teams, negotiate consensus and ensure follow-through without full operational authority.

Roberto Vitorio, a relatively strong country general manager (of an American multinational's Italian affiliate) who is responsible for the company's diverse range of sales and marketing activities, articulates the tension this way:

> My biggest challenge is to balance headquarter directives with local
> plans and local input. I spend a lot of time negotiating with our
> continental headquarters. Some of my subordinates work in teams led
> by European product managers. These teams are good at making
> decisions from a product perspective but they seldom appreciate
> sufficiently the complexities of the Italian culture and market. Sometimes
> I don't support certain team decisions which I believe will adversely
> affect affiliate performance. The product specialists in headquarters don't
> fully appreciate that their strategies, if not adapted sufficiently for the
> Italian market, are a waste of the company's money. (Interview, 2 May
> 1990)

Needless to say, this push/pull between headquarters and affiliates affects not only the country general managers but their colleagues in the affiliates as well.

Such country and continental general managers, when interviewed, stress the need to develop effective interpersonal negotiating skills as well as the ability to work collegially and orchestrate direction in groups. In cases where a colleague's professional loyalties and values are closely tied with those in headquarters, general managers at the country and continental level may experience difficulty influencing their nominal subordinates. One coordination-type general manager remarked: 'In some cases they are more loyal to their counterparts in headquarters than they are to me.' He noted that this was particularly true when he has little input regarding a colleague's/subordinate's next assignment and promotion. Coordinator-type general managers also reported that lateral relationships are demanding. 'Sometimes,' one coordinative-type general manager wryly noted, 'my immediate boss does not fully appreciate my situation. If I do a good job he takes it for granted. If I am having difficulty handling things successfully, I'm told to be a better leader, whatever that means.'

Several coordinator-type general managers voiced frustration with the evolution of their role from what they saw as one of control to 'one of the team'. One country general manager with a strong engineering background put it this way: 'My job used to be more fun. All this power sharing is frustrating. It slows down decision-making.' As the general manager roles have become more complex, participative management styles have become more vital to the diverse perspectives and bridge the borders separating the disparate parts.

The multicountry business or product managers, whose posts have grown more critical as the country general manager's role has lost power, also tend to find their roles frustrating. Ian Walker, a 36-year-old European product manager for an American multinational, leads a multifunctional product team made up of sales and marketing managers, as well as manufacturing, finance and technical services representatives, from different affiliates throughout Europe. The affiliate product sales managers are primarily responsible to their own country general managers. Together the team is responsible for reconciling global product directions and local conditions, to make pan-European business decisions. Ian spends hours persuading, negotiating, influencing and trying to understand each country situation, so that collectively the group members will buy in to an agreed-upon strategy. Ian reports that his biggest challenge is getting the agreed strategy implemented. 'My people go back to their local affiliates, where they try to sell the decision to their staff and the country general manager. These managers often get caught between their loyalty to their affiliate with its markets and their friends and the company's efforts to develop pan-European strategy. They don't like it very much.' Ian believes that his team members are generally more loyal to their own country or function than they are to him:

> My marketing manager has worked in our French affiliate for 21 years.
> As a Frenchman, he is more loyal to French affiliates and the French
> market than he is to the company's pan-European strategy. While many
> managers outwardly comply, the strength of their loyalty to their
> affiliates or functional support services undermines their commitment
> and thus the degree of enthusiasm and energy required to implement a
> team decision.

Representative head

The representative-head type country or continental general manager has no formal authority for coordinating the range of corporate operations within a territory. This arrangement stresses lateral relationships among colleagues who are operating in different corporate hierarchies and with their own 'bosses'. A representative head's relationship with those heading operational units in his or her territory depends upon some combination of such leverage-generating factors as personality, seniority in rank, home office rapport, local networking, and perhaps responsibility for a 'leading' business unit and control of one or more staff support services. But his or her responsibilities do not include operational, budget or staffing control of the various business units. They do include projecting a corporate presence and a 'unified corporate face', working with the host government, dealing with the media, attending socially and politically critical functions, identifying new business opportunities in the country and promoting cooperation among the various affiliates. While the representative head is Mr/Ms GE, or Mr/Ms BP, or Mr/Ms ICI, his or her role compares more to that of a head of state than a head of government.

Multinationals that have established representative heads have stressed global product and global functional integration more than local coordination among the various operational units. Thus American multinationals such as General Electric (GE) and American Telephone & Telegraph (AT&T), whose businesses report directly through the product divisional hierarchies (and have international divisions with a supportive rather than a coordinating or controlling role), have representative heads at both country and continental levels. Japanese firms, such as Matsushita, similarly have continental affiliates that have relatively loose oversight regarding their company's continental manufacturing and R&D activities.

Art Davie, who has been the continental general manager (entitled regional vice-president) for AT&T Europe, has been responsible for promoting coordination among all AT&T's businesses in the European, Middle East and African regions. In each country he has relied upon representative-type country general managers whose major responsibility has been heading a major business unit in their country. All AT&T's country business heads at the country level have reported directly to their own business units in the region or in the United States. Davie has viewed his biggest challenge as building a team from these diverse business heads and creating a coordinated business presence in Europe: 'I have had to do all this without direct accountability. I can only suggest and recommend to people.' To accomplish this objective, he has spent 65–70 per cent of his time out of the office either in the United States or with the various business heads in the region. When he draws an organizational chart at the continental level, he no longer shows solid and dotted lines: 'In my situation they have been meaningless. I have just drawn one big box and placed all the positions in it' (interview, 19 June 1989). But at least there is an organizational means of promoting cooperation; pointing out areas in which cooperation would be fruitful, initiating mutually beneficial projects and representing a common front on continent-wide issues to the corporate hierarchy as well as the public. Where there is no such institution or individual, there is little opportunity for such common efforts.

No single country general manager responsible for most of a multinational's operations in a country

Some multinationals have chosen not to have a single country or continental general manager for their international interests. They have not established an executive position with responsibility, however limited, which spans all or even a significant share of their business interests in that country. In such cases, each corporate division generally has its own network of affiliate operating units. Sales and manufacturing, as well as the R&D units, may also be organized separately.

General Motors provides a good example. While General Motors Europe oversees all the European motor vehicle operations, EDS (Electronic Data Systems), Hughes and Component Parts maintain separate European networks. In Nestlé, there has been little effort to coordinate the activities of various Nestlé companies' operations within any one country (until the recent establishment of an umbrella-type entity in the United States and in the United Kingdom). Hitachi, too, has a fragmented continental operation. Clearly, the way a multinational establishes its international general management posts affects their job demands and their management style.

The inevitability of complexity

As multinationals have responded to global pressures by globalizing their strategies and structures, the role of international general manager has become more complex and challenging, not only because the span of external and internal responsibilities has multiplied, but also because many of their principal colleagues now must satisfy one or more international functional or product 'bosses' as well as the geographic one. The trend has placed these general managers at critical pressure points that require linchpin-like positions to tie together an increasingly maze-like web of interdependent relationships. The greater the effort to globalize the product divisions, as American and European multinationals are doing, or to coordinate the functional operations geographically, as Japanese firms are doing, the more complex the coordination required.

As a consequence of these more complex relations, an increasing proportion of country and continental general managers have roles which involve responsibility-sharing and influence-extending skills. This increase in power-sharing roles has magnified the challenge that the general manager faces in attempting to develop coherent local strategies.

The diminution in the formal power of continental and country general managers has made the responsibility even more complex and challenging. Even with significant formal power, it has been difficult to reconcile headquarters'

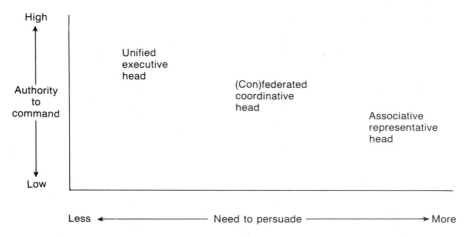

Figure 4.2 Differences in country general manager job demands

directives with local conditions. With less formal power a general manager needs to exert leadership with considerable ingenuity and flexibility. As power has become shared, the need to develop coalitions and consensuses has tended to encroach on the energy and enthusiasm a manager can devote to long-term strategy. While his or her role has changed from 'one above others' to 'first among equals', or even 'one among equals', his or her boss or bosses have often appeared to view the responsibility for 'getting something done' as undiminished. Figure 4.2 notes the degree of difficulty in lateral relationships: the less the authority to command, the greater the need to persuade. Power-sharing has increased the importance of building lateral working relationships at the lower as well as higher levels of the organization. Multinationals have increasingly recognized that their country or continental general managers – as well as many continental and country product and functional managers – require not only well-developed interpersonal skills, but also a well-developed appreciation of the diversity of strengths contributing to the corporate mission, in order to work effectively in an ever expanding and border-divided environment.

Developing international general managers: for linchpin roles

The increasing complexity and changing character of international general manager positions have magnified the task of developing potential managers for these posts. The way a multinational develops its international management staffing policies and practices reflects and reinforces the way an enterprise expects its international managers to share and exercise power. The organizational mind-set underlying a multinational's international management staffing efforts shapes how these efforts are organized and managed, which people become international general managers, what combination of geographic, product and functional skills and perspectives they bring to their positions, and ultimately how they manage their responsibilities. To function effectively in border-spanning roles, international general managers require a multifaceted appreciation of the different perspectives driving the disparate parts of an organization. To develop such a multifaceted appreciation, many multinationals have reassessed the interdependent aspects of management staffing, policies and practices, including the way they recruit and assign, evaluate and promote, and educate and train their prospective international general managers.

The way multinationals have responded to the need to develop the coherency/capability of managers has been shaped by two factors. First, to what extent does a corporate staff unit coordinate early career recruiting, facilitate cross-border assignments, promote corporate-wide management educational training, and develop a corporate-wide evaluation and executive development process? Second, to what extent does a multinational include non-home country nationals in its early recruitment, cross-border assignments, corporate-wide management education and training, and executive development efforts? The way a multinational addresses these issues shapes the pool of candidates from which international general managers are chosen and their capability for bridging the multiple and competing business perspectives effectively (see Table 4.1).

The way multinationals approach these critical interdependent issues reflects an enterprise's commitment to make the long-term investment in human resources necessary to develop a corps of well-selected, well-educated, well-experienced, border-spanning managers. A key element of this commitment is the extent to which multinationals centrally coordinate the recruitment, postings, promotions and management education of host as well as home country prospective general managers.

Table 4.1   Four approaches to management staffing

Division/Country	Division-specific/ corporate-divided	Division-spanning/ corporate-coordinated
Country-specific	Each corporate division manages its own recruitment, assignments, training, etc; home country nationals are more likely to receive varied international postings.	Corporate office coordinates recruitment, assignments and training, and monitors high-flyers; headquarters nationals are more likely to secure varied international assignments.
Country-spanning	Each corporate division essentially develops its own managers; host and home country nationals have quite equal opportunities for education and international postings.	Corporate office coordinates recruitment, assignments, training and monitoring of high-flyers; non-headquarters nationals have access to management education and international posting opportunities.

Recruitment, postings and promotions of international management staffing

The extent to which a multinational, through a corporate office, coordinates on a corporate-wide basis the management staffing of its operating divisions and international affiliates affects the corporate capacity to develop the generalist capabilities and commitment needed for international general managers to undertake border-spanning responsibilities. In this respect, the approaches of American, European and Asian multinationals have tended to differ; but there have been notable exceptions to continental tendencies and a few remarkable converging trends.

Many major American multinationals, in a way that is consistent with their multinational organizational strategy, push the responsibility for management recruitment, assignments and promotions on to the corporate divisions, many of which in turn delegate responsibilities for staffing all but the top international posts to their affiliates. With this arrangement, each major unit recruits its own managers and prospective managers, and within general corporate guidelines determines their postings and promotions – which, with few exceptions, have been intradivisional and intra-affiliate. Most American multinationals have no or severely limited corporate-wide means for identifying talent on an interdivisional or international basis, or for facilitating transfers for those who seek or whose careers would be advanced by cross-divisional or cross-national transfers and promotions. In most multinationals, even home country nationals' careers have tended to be division-bound. Host country nationals' careers have tended to be territorially bound as well as division-bound, which contributes to the specificity of their mind-sets. Some American multinationals that have relied upon international divisions or continental organizations, or both, to manage their international operations have developed a variation of this arrangement. While the corporate product and functional divisions have selected Americans for financial and other specialized overseas postings, home country nationals have been promoted to other senior posts in the affiliates.

A number of American multinationals have developed noteworthy variations of these arrangements. In GE the International Division has inaugurated a 'global brains' effort, through which it attempts to orchestrate the careers of potential international managers. They recruit and identify potential 'high-flyers' in order to provide them with the education and cross-border experiences to prepare them for senior management posts. Exxon has established 'compensation and executive development' (COED) committees at each level in the organization to evaluate their senior personnel; such evaluations are quantified on a 0–100 scale so that managers can, at least in principle, be compared across divisional borders. Such scorings are intended to facilitate cross-border comparisons of especially promising managers and monitoring of their progress. IBM, which has long staffed its affiliates, almost without exception, with home country nationals, has increased its reliance on home continent nationals to staff its European offices. The Procter & Gamble international division provides extensive opportunities for cross-border experiences (see Table 4.2). While several of their country managers are now serving in their home country, all have had experience in other countries, often in other continents.

Many European multinationals, in a way that is consistent with their multicountry group organizational strategy, long managed their staffing on a country-by-country basis. The omnibus affiliates managed their own staffing. Staff expertise from the parent company was assigned with the concurrence of the affiliate management. Royal Dutch/Shell and Nestlé have continued to rely on operating companies, most of whose management has been locally recruited and developed. But both companies also recruit directly on a multicountry basis for an international corps from which personnel are posted to various affiliates. One country manager, for example, began his career in the legal department of the corporate headquarters 21 years ago. Later he was posted to Nigeria, and then to London with the public affairs unit when 'Royal Dutch/Shell was looking for a Dutch lawyer with African and operating company experience' (interview, 26 June 1989). Then he was moved back to The Hague as the General Manager of Shell Real Estate, and then to Shell's regional organization, where he was responsible for external matters with the EEC. Now he is the general manager for a national Shell affiliate.

Other European multinationals, such as Philips, BP and ICI, have moved from the multicountry to a more multidivisional staffing approach. As they have done so, several multinationals have continued to rely on a headquarters-located management development office to increase its efforts to recruit and orchestrate the careers of the non-home country as well as home country senior personnel. As an ICI corporate human resource manager stated: 'We consciously try to move the more promising managers who want international careers into a variety of assignments which cross corporate product, functional, and area borders. The effort is to determine what experiences the international managers of the next decade will need and to provide the opportunities to gain these experiences' (interview, 13 March 1991). As Philips has globalized its product divisions, the corporate headquarters product divisions, in conjunction with the corporate management resources office, have more assertively moved senior and middle-level staff from country to country, with or without the consent of the affiliate management.

Those European multinationals that redeveloped their international operations after World War II have long tended to maintain central control over staffing. When Bayer developed its multidivisional organization, it retained its centralized human resources division and a central staff office. A Fiat central office coordinates executive development throughout the corporate divisions and affiliates. A Fiat corporate subsidiary, ISVOR, centrally runs the Fiat training programme and also reviews and approves management appointments throughout the Fiat organization, as well as arranging interdivisional transfers.

Japanese multinationals, in a way that is consistent with their more functional approach to organizational strategy, have long taken a corporate-wide approach to management staffing. They have generally recruited their home country nationals on a corporate-wide basis. Only after their recruitment and their corporate-sponsored training are they assigned to the division which will be their home base. It has not been uncommon for a senior manager to have a broad range of job assignments

Table 4.2 Cross-border assignments in Procter & Gamble Europe

	CGM 1	CGM 2	CGM 3	Division manager Europe A	Division manager Europe B	Division manager Europe C
Nationality	Belgian	Italian	British	German	French	French
Career path						
Post 1	Product mgr./Belgium	Product mgr./Italy	Manufacturing/England	Product mgr./Germany	Product mgr./France	Product mgr./Italy
Post 2	Asst. adv./Holland	Asst adv./Italy	Product mgr./Switzerland	Asst. adv./Germany	Asst. mgr./USA	Asst. adv./Italy
Post 3	Advert. mgr./Belgium	Advert. mgr./Peru	Asst. adv./Switzerland	Advert. mgr./UK	Advert. mgr/France	Advert. mgr./Italy
Post 4	CGM/Belgium	CGM/Belgium	Asst. adv. mgr./Switzerland	CGM/Austria	CGM/France	CGM/Argentina
Post 5		CGM/Italy	CGM/Greece	CGM/Belgium	Div. mgr./Europe	CGM/Benelux
Post 6			CGM/Taiwan	Div. mgr./Europe		Div. mgr./Europe
Post 7			CGM/UK			
Education	Law	Business Admin.	Chemical Engineering	Business Admin.	Business Admin.	Business Admin.
Last degree	Doctorate	Master	Master	Doctorate	Master	Master

Source: Courtesy of Jozef F. Doppler.

including ones in finance, personnel, sales and data processing. Some of the more diversified multinationals though, such as Hitachi, have begun to plot careers within one operating division in order to develop their specific expertise.

One of the features of the multidivisional approach to the development of executives in Asian multinationals has been the assignment of especially promising managers to stints in the corporate head office. Each Samsung division regularly assigns its most promising Korean managers for a multiyear stint at corporate headquarters. Mitsui and Company annually selects several especially promising young Japanese executives for assignments as 'assistants to' the chairman, president and executive vice-presidents, so that they may enlarge their corporate-wide perspective and provide senior management with an opportunity to assess their potential. But such corporate efforts have been limited to home country staff. Matsushita's 1991-announced initiative to bring 100 non-Japanese to Japan for one year to work alongside Japanese colleagues has been a pioneering effort.

While most American and European multinationals generally use a hierarchy of pay grades based essentially upon an assessment of job responsibilities, Japanese staffing has long featured a system of pay by rank based on seniority. This has facilitated interdivisional transfer and has also impeded integrating non-Japanese into the system. A manager's pay depends principally (if not wholly) on his or her rank, not on the job. At Mitsubishi, for example, managers are promoted in status-grade more on length of service than on merit; a minimum number of years must be spent in each status-grade, and beyond a maximum number of years promotion occurs automatically, even if one is working on the same job (Kono, 1984: 323–5). At Nissan, one manager estimates that promotion is based 75 per cent on seniority, 25 per cent on merit (interview, Kato, 2 May 1989). Such a system does not generate high-flyers who rise rapidly and earn salaries significantly above others of their age group, but those who more fully demonstrate their competence are more likely to reach senior ranks eventually, while those who less fully demonstrate their competence retire at an earlier age or are 'parachuted' to a subsidiary or sister company to finish their career.

While the pay-by-grade system facilitates the ease with which managers may be shifted and rotated into a variety of challenging assignments (which may vary dramatically in responsibility as well as in the expertise required), it handicaps rewarding, and perhaps retaining, particularly promising candidates who have the opportunity to be hired by another company, as some of the more promising of Matsushita's younger non-Japanese managers have done (interview, Eric Bean, 16 March 1990).

Management education and development

The larger and more diverse a multinational's mosaic of parts, the more varied the perspectives driving its various parts, and the more educationally and experientially specialized its managers, the more critical is the challenge of providing management education and development programmes. Such programmes provide an integral and vital element in the host of efforts to develop international general managers capable of cross-hierarchy linchpin roles. Multinationals concerned with the development of generalist managers have tended to stress the development of communication and leadership skills – and they have relied upon corporate-wide institutions to take the lead in developing and delivering these programmes.

To meet the need, many multinationals have increased the scope as well as the scale of their management education efforts. Their efforts have taken a variety of forms including external sessions sponsored by educational institutions and internally delivered education and development. Such initiatives have included efforts to develop specific professional competencies and industry issues, interpersonal skills in communicating and working together, and distinctive corporate values affecting the 'ways we do things around here'.

While the bulk of multinational management education continues to be designed to develop specific professional skills, it is the development of interpersonal skills and the promotion of corporate-wide values that deserve special attention as means of fostering organizational coherence. The ability to work in and lead teams is vital for facilitating cross-border teamwork. Shared corporate-wide values are essential for establishing the foundation for consensus-building.

Developing specific professional competence and appreciating specific industry issues continue to be important as companies compete with broader spectrums of specialists in more fields. It is this accelerated demand for specialists that escalates the critical need for persuasive styles and skills often called leadership, as well as the shared values and cooperative spirit required to support leadership. While the issue of management education, interlocked as it is in the disparate education tradition of countries as well as the strategies of companies (Handy *et al.*, 1987) is far too complex to be explored here, it is appropriate to note the more salient features of management education efforts, and especially those shaping communication skills and corporate culture.

Multinationals differ not only in the extent to which education and training are emphasized, but also in how much is off the job (as contrasted with on the job) and how much is designed to develop a general managerial competency and a corporate-wide perspective (as contrasted with a limited divisional or subdivisional perspective). While some firms, such as Olivetti, generally limit training to on-the-job efforts, many multinationals have extensive off-the-job general management programmes. With few exceptions, the major multinationals in the United States, Germany, France and Japan devote at least five days to off-the-job training per year for each manager (Handy *et al.*, 1987:1). Asian firms stress training throughout their careers, beginning with an extensive indoctrination programme, and continuing with periodic on-the-job as well as off-the-job training at corporate training centres. Such management development is planned in conjunction with rotating such personnel through a variety of posts in different departments to ensure the development of generalist capability. IBM has long pioneered the way among American firms, not only in the extent of its commitment to education (8–9 per cent of personnel budget for educational programmes) but also in its job rotation practices. Other multinationals such as Fiat, Daimler-Benz, GM and GE support extensive in-house training establishments.

American and European multinationals have generally tended to continue to focus on the development of specific skills. A number of American multinationals have begun to recognize the potency of shared values, and have accented corporate-wide staff development efforts which strengthen the individual manager's sense of identification with the overall corporate precepts and *esprit de corps*. GE has launched an extensive series of 'work-out' sessions involving all ranges of management from the top down. 3M has used European-wide training to 'socialize' its managers, in order to encourage teamwork across country and functional borders and slowly to refocus their thinking to accommodate a more product-driven strategy. A few European firms, too, have begun to stress communication and other skills in order to improve the multicultural leadership ability of their managers. Fiat emphasizes 'capacity of communication' and 'intercultural competence' as well as 'professional know-how' in the development of their managers.

East Asian multinationals' training programmes are noteworthy not only for the amount of time each manager spends in training but also for the extent to which training efforts indoctrinate managers as Matsushita or Mitsubishi or Nissan people. New employees begin with a corporate in-company indoctrination programme which typically lasts for three to eight months. This generally starts with a multi-week orientation into the company that includes lectures in its distinctive philosophy and history, and way of thinking and working. This is followed by multi-month training periods in marketing and production. Regular on-the-job and off-the-job training follows at regular intervals throughout a manager's career. Samsung follows this up every year with a 'spiritual renewal' session particularly regarded for the in-career assignments. But the East Asian multinationals have historically left the non-headquarters nationals out of the mainstream of their training efforts.

Not surprisingly, the multinationals that have been most ardent in the development of communication and leadership skills have been those that have developed and supported corporate-wide management education and training institutions. The Japanese multinationals, the extremely diversified Korean ones, Fiat, IBM and GE have long relied on corporate institutions to provide and oversee the management educational training efforts throughout their corporate domain. Increasingly these efforts have extended to include their international staff.

Whether or not the efforts to develop international cross-border managers are limited to home country nationals has a major impact on the extent to which a multinational has globalized its senior cadre of managers in their international affiliates, as the next section discusses. The Japanese and Korean multinationals have tended to limit their efforts to identify and maximize the cross-border experience of high-flyers to home country nationals. 'Through naivete or foresight,' as one European executive put it, 'American multinationals have led the way in internationalizing' the senior cadres in their affiliates (interview, 4 September 1990). The approach of 1992 expedited the efforts of European firms to do the same.

Identifying, evaluating and nurturing potential general managers

An increasing number of major multinationals are taking particular efforts to identify and promote the careers of those who show promise as potential international linchpin managers. The corporate executive teams of many corporations and many of their corporate divisions set aside major blocks of time to assess their managers. They identify potential high-flyers, monitor their progress, and consider assignments which will broaden their cross-border perspectives as well as enhance their management capability and credibility. In many American and European firms, potential high-flyers tend to be put on the management fast track soon after they graduate and join the company – in their early twenties in the United States and the United Kingdom, in their late twenties in Germany where potential high-flyers are more likely to stay at university longer. In many Japanese companies, where managers-to-be spend their twenties learning their companies from the ground up in three or four different company divisions and do not reach the junior level of management until their early thirties, the grooming of high-flyers may begin even later.

In order to identify and evaluate the potential of their managers more readily, some multinationals require each layer of management not only to evaluate the next level below, but also to appraise the performances of the level below that. Some go beyond this to gather multiple evaluations, not only from the hierarchical 'boss' but also from those with whom the managers must work, including in some cases those they supervise. Such multiple evaluations, intended to provide a broader portrait of the performance and potential of staff members, indicate what additional education and experience would be most fruitful. Corporate oversight of this process and corporate-wide comparison of the evaluations have the additional advantage of fostering cross-hierarchy postings.

A number of companies use more senior managers to act as mentors to younger managers. At IBM, such mentors have a particularly vital role when younger managers are assigned overseas, when out of sight may mean 'out of mind'. In Shell, the more promising the candidate, the more senior the mentor; thus a change in mentorship reflects a downgrading or upgrading of management assessment of the younger person's career potential.

The corporate approach to career-long employment, pay and promotion affects such issues as job mobility and job security. The traditional Japanese low-pay and slow-promotion systems have worked in a culture that stressed 'hire young, promote from within and fire only for cause', by providing security in return for being virtually career-locked in one company. In contrast the American environment has long offered far more mobility, but also far less security. From 1980 to 1990 alone, the top 500 American corporations reduced personnel by 21 per cent (*Fortune International*, 23 April 1990a:188). Such reductions have always been a means by which American companies have met crises. Increasingly, European companies such as Philips and BP, as well as American ones, are also being forced to reduce headcount as they seek to remain competitive. The perception of whether the corporation considers its management resources as a long-term investment and commitment, or as a commodity that may be turned on or off as needed, fundamentally affects not only the corporate manager's commitment to the corporation but also a corporation's willingness to undertake, on a long-term, continuing basis, the efforts needed to develop the management corps required to lead the competitive multinational in the future.

The magnitude of the job of developing the multidimensional capacity of international general managers sufficiently to lead transborder teams has been one of the factors leading a number of companies to apply vigorously a policy of 'hire young and promote only from within'. Such a policy provides aspiring managers with the opportunity to undergo a variety of management education programmes and stretching managerial experiences that facilitate their learning the art of leading transborder teams, appreciating the extent of the diversity and complexity in the multinational operations, developing widespread, cross-hierarchy networks of managers with whom they can interact to expedite common efforts, and understanding the corporate core principles and practices sufficiently to be successful 'culture carriers'.

Particularly when coupled with a policy of discharging only for cause, such a policy presents a challenge. As Harald Einsmann, president of P&G Europe, has pointed out: hiring young and promoting from within requires a company to anticipate its senior management needs decades in advance, a challenge that involves not only accurately forecasting the multinational's growth and future needs but also guessing how many of the new recruits will depart and how many will successfully develop the requisite skills (interview, 4 June 1986). The magnitude of the job is such that it requires a corporate-wide, recruitment-to-retirement effort. To develop a sufficient corps of managers capable of respecting the perspective driving the various parts of the corporation and with the leadership skills to achieve unified direction from the diversity composing the teams they lead requires the skilful guidance of promising careers.

Multinationals that hire directly into senior positions generally do so because there appears to be a lack of qualified candidates for the specific post, often the result of not having made sufficient earlier efforts to develop an adequate pool of promising managers. Such direct-hirings may adversely affect the morale of those aspiring to higher posts and force the newcomer to become a fast learner regarding the disparate parts of the firms, and thus his or her initial capacity to function effectively in situations requiring transborder efforts. The greater the stress on early career hiring and career-long, multifaced development, the less the likelihood the multinational may need to hire directly into senior posts.

Internationalizing global management: mixing and meshing cultures

The effectiveness of affiliate management depends on their capacity to accommodate the global–local dilemma – to respond to global direction with local discretion. To perform such a mission effectively requires an affiliate management with an internationalized view of the affiliate objectives. Such internationalization may be fostered by international assignments, management evaluations that enhance an awareness of transnational issues, and the way they mix home, host and other nationalities in the senior management of an affiliate.

Multinationals have long varied in the extent to which they have relied upon home country nationals or host country nationals for staffing the senior management posts in their affiliates. As noted in Table 4.3, the use of home, host or 'third country' nationals tends to be interdependent on a number of factors. One is the extent to which the local affiliate has matured sufficiently to have generated senior managers from their own ranks. Another is the extent to which headquarters depend on affiliate management who share a common background and a home country mind-set. A third is the importance of projecting an image as a 'local' company.

The American emphasis on the use of home country nationals stems in part from the long-term overseas presence of many affiliates of American multinationals, in part from the high cost of maintaining American nationals overseas, and perhaps in part from American reliance on structure and systems which alleviate the difficulties of fitting those with different backgrounds into the organization. In contrast, the affiliates of Japanese firms have shorter histories and their management style has depended upon managers who shared similar backgrounds and values.

As noted in Table 4.4, US-based multinationals rely more on host country nationals and Japanese-based multinationals rely more on home country nationals.

Headquarters country nationals

The Japanese multinationals have tended to stress home country nationals in part because their country-based corporate culture, which is considered so distinctive and so vital to the values to corporate success, is not so easily shared. A further reason is that overseas affiliates of the leading Japanese firms have generally been more recently established than those of the leading American and European ones. One 53-year-old Japanese head of a multinational's continental coordinating centre, like his fellow Japanese corporate executives, had graduated from a prestigious Japanese university, and had spent most but not all of his career in Japan in a variety of positions designed to give him an overall view of the company's operations. His previous job assignments had included sales, corporate planning, finance, data processing and personnel.

European and American companies have continued to post a significant number of headquarters-country nationals as general managers of their foreign affiliates. A typical American country general manager of an American multinational may not have had an earlier assignment outside the United States. Before the overseas assignment, the manager may have had a number of challenging assignments in the United States, but none of these may have been outside his or her division or professional specialization.

Table 4.3 Management staffing of affiliates: home, host and 'third country' approaches

Aspects of the enterprise	Home	Host	International ('third country' nationals)	
			Continental	Global
Complexity of organization	Complex in home country, simple in affiliates	Varied	Highly interdependent on a regional basis	Increasingly complex and highly interdependent on a world-wide basis
Authority: decision-making	High in headquarters	Relatively low in headquarters	High regional headquarters and/or high collaboration among affiliates	Collaboration of headquarters and affiliates around the world
Evaluation and control	Home standards applied for persons and performances	High level output	High regional input	Standards which are universal and local
Rewards and punishments; incentives	High in headquarters, low in affiliates	Wide variation: can be high or low rewards for affiliate performance	Rewards for contribution to regional objectives	Rewards to international and local executives for reaching local and world-wide objectives
Communication: information flow	High volume of orders, commands, advice to affiliates	Less to and from headquarters, little among affiliates	Little to and from corporate headquarters, but may be high to and from regional headquarters and among countries	Both ways and among affiliates around the world
Geographical identification	Nationality of owner	Nationality of host country	Regional company moves people within region	Truly world-wide company, but identifying with national interests
Perpetuation (recruiting, staffing, development)	Home country personnel developed for key positions everywhere in the world	Host country personnel developed for key positions in their own country	Regional people developed for key positions anywhere in the region	Best people everywhere in the world developed for key positions everywhere in the world

Source: Adapted from Heenan and Perlmutter, 1979: 18–19.

Table 4.4 Comparative use of headquarters country nationals (HQCN), host country nationals (HCN) and third country nationals (TCN) (as reported in 1982)

	US multinationals			European multinationals			Japanese multinationals		
	HQCN	HCN	TCN	HQCN	HCN	TCN	HQCN	HCN	TCN
NORTH AMERICA[1]									
Senior management	25	74	1	29	67	4	83	17	0
Middle management	1	99	0	18	82	0	73	0	0
Lower management	3	96	1	4	96	0	40	60	0
WEST EUROPE									
Senior management	33	60	7	38	62	0	77	23	0
Middle management	5	93	2	7	93	0	43	57	0
Lower management	0	100	0	4	96	0	23	77	0
EAST ASIA									
Senior management	55	38	7	85	15	0	65	35	0
Middle management	19	81	0	25	75	0	41	59	0
Lower management	2	96	2	5	95	0	18	82	0
SOUTH/LATIN AMERICA									
Senior management	44	47	9	79	16	5	83	17	0
Middle management	7	92	1	37	58	5	41	59	0
Lower management	1	96	3	0	100	0	18	82	0
AFRICA									
Senior management	36	47	17	75	15	10	50	33	17
Middle management	11	78	11	35	65	0	0	100	0
Lower management	5	90	5	0	95	0	0	100	0
WEST ASIA									
Senior management	42	34	24	86	14	0	67	33	0
Middle management	27	63	10	50	29	21	83	17	0
Lower management	9	82	9	7	86	7	33	67	0

Notes: [1]Data for Canadian affiliates of US multinationals and US affiliates of European and Asian multinationals.
Source: Adapted from Tung, 1982, 60–1.
There are, however, dramatic variations concealed by some of these statistical averages. For example, 1988 US Department of Commerce data indicate that in the USA British multinationals are more likely to depend on host country nationals (Americans) than are French multinationals, which depend heavily on headquarters country nationals (Frenchmen) (*Business Week*, 17 December 90:52).

Host country nationals

Management staffing with host country nationals stresses the importance of familiarity with the local language, culture, customs and conditions. The increasing use of host country nationals reflects multinational recognition of the strategic advantage of developing a local image and establishing relationships with customers, clients, government agencies, employers and the general public. The tendency for major American multinationals to rely on host country nationals may stem from a number of factors, including their long-time overseas presence as well as the high cost of maintaining Americans overseas.

IBM has long relied on host country nationals to staff their affiliates. Charles De Meyer, whose career has been fairly typical for an IBM country general manager, graduated in commercial engineering from the Solvay School, Belgium's top engineering college, and entered IBM as a sales trainee in 1956. Having been identified as a 'high potential manager', he was promoted to branch manager, and three years later was transferred to Paris to become assistant to the general manager of IBM Europe. Two years later, he was posted to the IBM Europe Finance Department, and after another two years, he moved back to IBM Belgium to become the finance manager, then sales and marketing manager, and finally president of IBM Belgium. The career path of his successor as president of IBM Belgium was similar.

Japanese multinationals have begun to appreciate that their biggest challenge is to integrate non-Japanese into key management positions. Presently, most senior management positions at the country as well as the continental level are filled by Japanese. This is changing. Mitsui as an experiment has hired European managers in its Benelux affiliate. The European managers have been provided with Japanese assistants to help them understand the Japanese headquarters' way of thinking, and also to translate European conditions to Tokyo-based executives in ways they can understand. The path towards unity, however, has not been easy on either side, as a country general manager, now on the board of his company, has noted:

> I have had to reduce Tokyo's scepticism about using Europeans in key management positions and the Europeans' scepticism that the company is as much theirs as ours. In my years here I have finally convinced them that I am sincere. However, my assignment is coming to an end and I have little control over my successor. The scepticism is re-emerging. They now ask whether the next country general manager will feel the same way. This issue is critical for the Japanese because having employees believe that the company cares about them, and having them devoted to the company, is integral to the Japanese management philosophy. (Interview, Tetsuro Inaji, 21 November 1988)

Japanese multinationals recognize that staffing their national affiliates with qualified non-Japanese will be difficult. In the past Japanese companies have hired local people, but there was little corporate intention to develop these people beyond a particular level. Many local people who have worked for Japanese multinationals and understand the culture may not be presently capable of taking over significant responsibility at the country and continental level.

Third country nationals

A third possibility is to assign third country nationals, those that are nationals of neither the headquarters nor the host country. In practice most third country nationals have been posted to countries in the same continent (generally the same subcontinent) as their home country. A variety of factors may account in part for the more extensive American multinational use of third country nationals in West Europe, East Asia and Latin America (as indicated earlier in Table 4.4). These may include American naivety or relative insensitivity to country cultural differences, American vision regarding the values of transborder staffing and staff development, and the high cost of sending and maintaining Americans in expatriate status. As already described, companies such as Shell and P&G, with fairly extensive international operations, have long developed cadres of international managers whom they regularly transfer among their affiliates. With the increasing economic integration of Europe, more European and Asian as well as American multinationals are posting their managers to third country assignments.

The growing recognition of the need to develop diversity-appreciative managers for international operations has begun to affect multinational executive development programmes. The thrust of management development initiatives demonstrates the increased recognition by multinationals of the need to develop a unifying world-wide culture, as well as an international structure and management staffing, as the centrepiece of organizational dynamics.

Many multinationals are appreciating the need for management teams at the country and continental levels that mix home, host and third country nationals, as well as different product and functional perspectives. Such a mixture not only provides the means to blend perspectives but also develops managers from every part of the corporate mosaic. To be effective, cross-border managers, whether they are headquarters-country or not, profit from headquarters as well as affiliate experience. Such a cross-pollenization within the ranks of senior management at country and continental level is indispensable to global localization.

'The need for effectiveness in multinational management leadership is so important,' says Basil Zirinis, an Exxon Company International vice-president, 'that we cannot afford not to develop our younger managers to their fullest potential and provide them with opportunities to reach the top country, continental, and corporate positions, whatever their nationality, product focus, or professional specialization' (interview, 23 April 1991). Meeting this challenge will require a variety of initiatives, depending on the organizational traditions and the specific conditions facing multinationals. To foster the ability to work together effectively will require not only staffing policies and practices designed to extend mind-sets, but also the promoting of shared values which focus perspectives and energies towards common corporate goals.

CHAPTER 5
Sharing values: for a unifying spirit and style

Ideological dynamics of power: forging corporate mind-sets

Every organization, in the course of its evolution, develops its own culture; that is, 'a pattern of basic assumptions invented, discovered or developed as it learns to cope with its problems of external adaptation and integration – that has worked well enough to be considered valid and, therefore, has to be taught to new members' (Schein, 1985b: 6). The pattern of ideas focuses on the broad query: 'Who are we? What do we believe? What values do we (intend to) share?' The broader query involves responses to the following three questions (see Senge, 1990:223–4):

1. What do we (intend to) do? or what is our mission or purpose?
2. For what do we (intend to) strive? or what is our vision or plan?
3. How do we (intend to) behave? or what are our principles and practices?

Together, the articulation of purpose, plan and principles comprises the governing ideas or philosophy that shape a company's sense of direction, fashions its distinctive style and energizes its spirit of commitment.

The extent to which the corporate governing ideas become ideas personally shared throughout an enterprise affects the ease with which the inevitable differences that arise among the disparate corporate parts are recognized and resolved. These ideas shape the development of the corporate strategy, the binding that holds diverse parts together and the bonding among the staff. Corporate beliefs and accompanying corporate patterns of behaviour that have been legitimized by experience and nourished with companies' stories and symbols, heroes and myths, slogans and songs, and rites and rules have enhanced the prospects for a corporate *esprit de corps*, a corporate style and a corporate-wide commitment to a common objective. By cultivating, clarifying, communicating and celebrating corporate ideology, multinationals encourage and 'entice rather than force people' (Fallows, 1989:13) to accept and to carry out corporate objectives with the desired corporate 'way we do things around here' behaviour. Shared beliefs and behaviours speed communication, foster understanding and facilitate decision-making and coordination. They allow for greater reliance on consensus and less dependence on commands. For corporate mosaics with diverse polyglot parts, a bonding set of values provides an indispensable cohesive force.

While strategic corporate policies, cohesive structures and cross-hierarchy management development systems vitally affect the strategic coherent capability of a multinational enterprise, shared ideas provide an indispensable force securing commitment to corporate objectives and ways. 'In an environment where potent short-term economic pressures and parochial politics can easily come to rule behavior, just such a force may be necessary to keep line management focused on any centrally important corporate objective, and that is what we seem to find in firms with superior management' (Kotter, 1988: 100). In fact, of the major corporations which compete effectively, 'most have strongly shared values' (Peters and Waterman, 1982: 8).

As multinationals diversify their product lines and develop manufacturing and management as well as marketing competence across continents – to gain efficiencies of scale, scope and maximize their economic clout – the need for unifying values becomes even more critical as well as increasingly difficult to define and communicate. In international operations, values exported from the home country frequently conflict with host country mores, customs, conventions and laws. Multinationals depend upon professional specialists (such as engineers, accountants and lawyers) and increasingly upon subspecialists (such as petrochemical engineers, cost accountants and tax lawyers), whose prolonged specialized education and experience foster guild-like professional loyalties which, especially in America, may exceed corporate loyalty. Diversified multinationals embrace corporate parts that often serve different markets, rely on different technologies and operate with different styles of management. As corporations expand across professional, industrial, geographical and other cultural boundaries, sharing visions and values becomes critical for productive cross-border working relationships.

The extent to which a corporate culture embraces and complements subcultures, or clashes with them, depends upon the aspiration, sensitivity and skills of management leadership in proactively shaping and promoting sharing of corporate-wide beliefs and behaviours. The variations in the receptivity of the parts present a challenge in developing a unifying rubric which accommodates the diverse cultures of the multinational parts. The more varied the parts comprising the corporate mosaic, the more necessary the task of stressing superordinate values – the sharing of which nurtures a corporate-wide sense of community, *esprit de corps* and style. Communication barriers impede coherence in every multinational. Coping with these barriers presents an especially demanding challenge in managing newly developed affiliates, new joint ventures, newly acquired companies and newly merged enterprises, where divergent sets of beliefs need to be accommodated and reconciled.

A particular challenge facing a multinational as it develops its global network is to develop corporate-wide core values that accommodate the distinctive values of its international parts. Yet a paradox exists. International affiliates are expected to apply global strategies to local situations. but to be effective in doing this, they need to accommodate these strategies to the local realities of national laws, tax codes, customs barriers, market characteristics, work practices and cultural preferences. Thus tension exists between the corporate aim of promoting shared values throughout the organization and an international affiliate's predisposition to reflect and respond to local cultural norms. This fundamental conflict generates trade-offs in developing a unifying vision and values for diverse parts of a multinational enterprise.

Over the course of the evolution of a multinational, a number of sets of forces have shaped the values driving it and its diverse parts. One of these sets has been the panoply of cultural norms that have shaped the business environment of the multinational's home country. The way these norms have been mixed and blended with the host country's cultural norms has determined the unique set of operative values developed in each international affiliate. Another set of forces has been the variety of cultural norms practised by the professions upon which a corporation relies and the industries in which it competes, and the extent to which these disparate norms can be focused upon the development of a corporate core strength. Interacting with these sets has been the impact of founder and successor change-agent corporate leaders, whose personalities and preferences continue to shape the ideas and the actions that determine the extent to which corporate values are shared throughout the organization.

The cumulative impact of these forces shapes whatever beliefs are shared by the mosaic of parts comprising the corporation. These forces may conflict; they may also reinforce one another. The IBM, Philips and Matsushita cultures, for example, reflect the combined impact of the personalities of their early leaders, the culture of their home base, and the professional and industrial expertise which these men personified and cultivated.

Through an evolutionary, interactive process these forces generate an intricate pattern of values and behaviours which comprise a multinational's ideological traditions. The combined impact of these forces so pervasively affects the subconscious as well as conscious ideology, which forge corporate structure and staffing as well as beliefs and behaviour, that corporate leaders are constrained in their modification efforts. For core values shape how structures are formally divided and less formally united, who is recruited and who succeeds, and what values are pre-eminent in the decision-making and decision-implementing processes.

To appreciate the challenge of developing corporate core values as an instrument of centripetal power requires considering several interdependent questions. How striking are the country cultural differences that pose challenges to developing corporate-wide shared values? How have multinationals attempted to overcome the potential friction of differing professional and industrial factions by forging a corporate core competence and a common identity? What is the essential role of leaders in picking, proposing and practising core values throughout the organization? These are the issues facing American, European and Asian multinationals that this chapter considers.

Managing cultural diversity: mixing and blending country values

Multinationals derive many of their values consciously and subconsciously from the culture in which they originated and continue to locate their headquarters. These home-grown and home-derived values have often contributed to the competitive advantage that a country's multinationals have exploited (see Porter, 1990, for a discussion of the competitive advantage of nations in a different context). American cultural values have profoundly affected GM and Ford, GE and IBM, Exxon and Mobil, P&G, and Philip Morris and Du Pont. Japanese culture pervades Mitsui and Mitsubishi, Matsushita and Hitachi, and Nissan and Sony. German values underlie the management beliefs of Bayer and Daimler-Benz, and Italian culture pervades Fiat.

Influenced as they have been by a home-based culture, multinationals face a challenge in reconciling home and host country values in their international affiliations. The impact of the IBM American-oriented headquarters culture on IBM affiliates manifests itself in the IBM-promoted confrontational style of decision-making as well as in its more evident conforming code of dress. A comparison of the striking features of a few national cultures, as reflected in their business practices, demonstrates the tensions, frictions and frustrations which arise when efforts are made to mix and mesh home country culture and host country cultures in an international affiliate. The basic differences that exist among country cultures vitally affect the quest of multinationals for superordinate values (Hofstede, 1980, 1983).

In many companies the corporate culture has been affected not only by the home country but more specifically by the home city or region in which the company has been headquartered. Daimler-Benz has not been just a German company: it is a Stuttgart-Württemberg (southwest Germany) one. Philips manifests its Eindhoven-Brabant (southwest Netherlands) heritage, Fiat its Turin-Piedmont (northwest Italy) traditions, Matsushita its Osaka heritage and Du Pont its Wilmington, Delaware origins. Exxon reflects Texas despite the fact that its corporate headquarters was long located in New York. The home-nurtured corporate culture that multinationals have exported to their foreign affiliates has sometimes been accompanied by a home country, 'not invented here' syndrome that has not facilitated two-way communication. Understandably, such cultural colonialism has encountered resistance. While headquarters–affiliate tensions are evident – and inevitable – in every multinational, they may be constructive when the home and host values are mutually appreciated as vital complementary inputs in developing transnational – and transcontinental – cultures.

In every multinational, these tensions pose problems which demand attention. They particularly demand attention in situations where two established corporate cultures have been forced to mesh or meld, as in a joint venture, a merger or a takeover. General Electric's experience in the 1988 takeover of the French medical equipment maker Compagnie Générale de Radiologie (CGR) demonstrates the hazards of even the most well-intended efforts. At an initial management training session GE gave out GE T-shirts with a note: 'Wear this to show you are a member of the team.' The move generated resentment:

> That gaffe began what was to become a bitter and prolonged cultural clash at GE–CGR. The French company – formerly a sedate state-owned concern that had been run much like a government ministry – found itself in the hands of swaggering, all-American, profit-hungry GE. After two years of nonstop restructuring, massive layoffs and a continuing flight of French managers and engineers (the work force has shrunk to about 5,000 from 6,500), GE–CGR is still losing money. (Nelson and Browning, 1990)

The story illustrates the profound importance of appreciating variations in corporate culture and identifying and promoting the elements with which to comprise an overarching rubric. In developing global organizations with their ever-expanding web of affiliates and alliances, securing the shared values with which to make an organization workable is critical for success. Since the differences in underlying home-culture-driven values and perspectives fundamentally affect the way corporations expect to do business and the frustrations they will encounter internationally, cultivating a corporate-wide cultural rubric is a critical element in the organizational challenge facing multinationals. A brief review of the salient differences between American, European and Japanese business cultures, along with an insight into their variations, illustrates the challenge (see Table 5.1).

American management culture

The American management style long pervaded international business, in part because American multinationals were so omnipresent on the international scene

Table 5.1   A continental comparison of a few management cultural characteristics

	North America (USA)	Western Europe	Eastern Asia (Japan)
Group values	'Individualism'	Personal relationships	'Collectivism'
Decision criteria	Structure systems and standards	Personal trust	Cultural homogeneity and consensus
Job roles	Specialists well defined	Quasi-generalists loosely and ambiguously defined	Generalists loosely and ambiguously defined
Results orientation (growth/profit)	Short term	Middle term	Long term
Government	Confrontive	Supportive	Collaborative

and the American approach to business so consciously articulated. As Brooke and Remmers noted:

> Currently the American business style is dominant because it appears to produce the efficiency required. Commenting on this, a European executive of a United States company has emphasized five major traits in the American managerial philosophy which have produced a successful penetration into other cultures. One is the belief in growth as a vital need in its own right; another is the belief in profit as a mark of efficiency and performance, and as a producer of social benefits. The third is a belief in free initiative and private enterprise as a system which, in spite of its imperfections, has hitherto performed more effectively than any other. The fourth element in this philosophy is that hard decisions must be accepted for the sake of the well being of the whole organization. Such decisions include the elimination of inefficient businesses, the dismissal of weak executives, and the down-grading of conventional status symbols. The final feature is that change must be accepted in every aspect of the working existence. (1978a:52)

While American businesses are no longer so dominant, and their style no longer so copied, its features remain essentially the same. The American stress on 'rugged individualism', which has been fostered by the mythology of the American pioneer, pervades American culture – and hence American business culture. This 'rugged individualism' has made confrontation a salient feature of American life, interaction within and among corporations and relations between corporations and government. It has husbanded a distrust of government that has caused business and government relations to be adversarial. This confrontational atmosphere has been all-pervasive in the hostile political rhetoric, shaped the antitrust and other regulatory legislation and generated concentrations of lobbyists in the state and national capitals. This tension contrasts with the more supportive business–government relations found in Europe, and what have been the far more collaborative relations in Japan and South Korea.

Paradoxically, the 'rugged individualism' phenomenon may have contributed to the traditional American corporate stress on hierarchical structure, systems, standards and specialization as the means to fit and knit individuals into corporate organizations. As American corporations, abetted by American universities and especially their business schools, have confronted the issues of size, diversity and complexity, they have developed a disposition for sophisticated structures and systems. American companies have long been concerned to develop structures that clearly prescribe the distribution of authority and responsibility (see Brooke and Remmers, 1978a:51). American organizational structures and job descriptions have long been more formally and more clearly defined and developed than the European or Asian. American-based multinationals have also stressed quantifiable standards, prescriptive manuals and the latest management fads. American managers have tended to trust 'scientific management' and quantitative data in their efforts to evaluate and improve job performance. Americans have become preoccupied with more easily measured and compared short-term results as reflected in growth and profits set forth in yearly, quarterly and even monthly statements. This predisposition has been fostered by American financial markets that can analyse short-term results more easily than long-term potential, by business schools that can teach quantitative methodology better than qualitative judgment, and by shareholders who prefer an immediate return on their investments. Thus American businesses have stressed goals that can be quantified, progress that can be measured and the tools for these efforts. In the eagerness to define and develop concepts which further the profession of management, professors and practitioners have defined, developed (and later refined, redeveloped, rebottled) and applied new management concepts often beyond the point of practical or sustained application.

Current management concepts or 'fads', as articulated by management gurus and accepted widely if only superficially by corporations, have played a major role in shaping the corporate cultural rhetoric of many American corporations. What corporation has not proclaimed their commitment to excellence and quality, entrepreneurship and innovation, customer satisfaction and employee empowerment? Interestingly, fads have been largely an American phenomenon. While the latest management books sell fads throughout the world, non-Americans have been more likely to read them 'as grist for thought, not as prescriptions to be acted upon' (Pascale, 1990:20). The American mesmerization with new techniques and fads has stemmed in part from an American perception of 'professional management' based upon a set of generic concepts underlying managerial activity anywhere. The mass marketing of these new concepts, or more often recycled ones with a catchy title and novel twist, has often led to their less-than-critical acceptance and piecemeal application without an in-depth appreciation of their roots, their interdependence with other phenomena, or the conviction necessary to implement them (see Figure 5.1).

Specialist expertise has long been a hallmark of American management. Classical management itself, which has influenced business school as well as corporate thinking, has defined roles in terms of specific job descriptions and well-designated responsibilities. The increasing specificity of these roles has been concomitant with the proliferation of technical and professional specialisms and societies and specialized educational programmes. American managers have generally begun their careers as specialists and their rise to management ranks has been based upon their success as specialists. Consequently American corporations are more likely than non-American ones to hire on the basis of specialist qualifications; and they are more likely to go outside the company to find someone with specific qualifications. Thus US MBA programmes include a specialist concentration while European ones do not. US executives have long tended to be more vocationally specialized, more likely to identify their career interests with their professional specialism than with their company, and more likely to identify with a specialized faction of the company than the whole company.

American management has radiated faith in the ability to solve problems successfully. The pace has been quick and decisive. Conflicts and competition have been the norm. The preferred tools of managements have been definition and

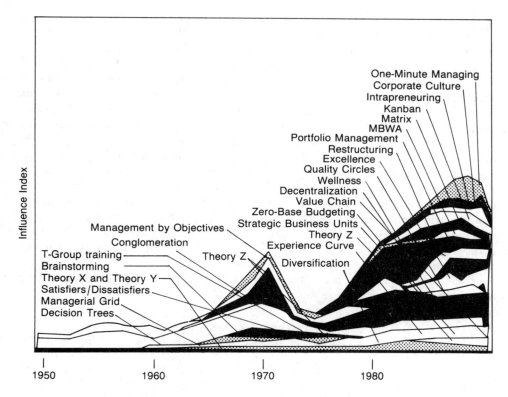

Curves shown are for illustrative purposes. Empirical foundation of chart based upon frequency of citations in the literature. However, increased interest in business topics in the past decade tends to exaggerate amplitude of recent fads when compared to earlier decades. As a result, the author has modified curves to best reflect relative significance of trends over entire period.

Figure 5.1 Ebbs, flows and residual impact of business fads, 1950–88 (Source: Pascale, 1990:20. Copyright © 1990 by Richard Pascale; reprinted by permission of Simon & Schuster, Inc.)

manipulation of organizational structures, policies, rules, job descriptions and task objectives. The American mesmerization with the most current thinking, and consequent rhetoric, had enhanced the appearance of commonalities. The American business hero (enshrined in Horatio Alger stories) has been the individual achiever, taking risks, acting quickly and decisively, and reaping rewards. Americans have tended to judge themselves and others by what their jobs are, how successful they are, and how much money they make or have made. Lee Iacocca has exemplified the American tendency to self-promote and glorify the self-made man. Risks and achievement have been the hallmarks of the American business hero.

As noteworthy as the similarities in American corporations are, however, the dissimilarities are as remarkable. American corporations vary significantly not only in their emphases but also in the extent to which they have adapted aspects of the predominant American business culture. Some corporations overtly encourage a 'survival of the fittest' culture; others, such as IBM, while encouraging a confrontational atmosphere actively cultivate a family spirit, not only through rhetoric but also through assignment and training policies. ITT has long stressed management by the numbers; Apple has prized creativity to the extent that it appears to encourage a clash of cultures. GM continues its hierarchical management style; others, such as GE, have begun to promote participative styles. 3M stresses innovation far more than AT&T with its more cautious management style. Not only do such corporate cultures vary significantly from one American corporation to another but also, as the Exxon profile in Part III demonstrates, such cultures often vary substantively from one division to another within one corporation. While American multinationals share the predilection for growth and profits, they often differ in the way they attempt to achieve these results. Only someone who is vaguely familiar with more than one American corporate culture misses the significant distinctions among them. The commonalities and the conviction with which corporate values have been exported and cultivated in American affiliates throughout the world have increased the consciousness of the differences between American and other business cultures – and the tensions that arise when attempting to mix and mesh these differences.

Asian management cultures

Japanese and South Korean business cultures, like the American ones, are embedded in their national cultures. Japanese national and corporate culture has stressed 'consensus' as a style of management and encourages deference to authority. Managers have functioned within an interlocking system of personal relationships in which individuality, at least in the Western sense, is repressed. The ruling groups have been an elite who share a common socialization, including education at leading universities. The corporate loyalty exacted by Asian multinationals has provided an organizational glue somewhat comparable to that once owed to feudal lords. The South Korean business culture has stressed many of the same values, abetted (as the Samsung profile in Part III shows) by their patriotic need and their governmental support of efforts to develop the Korean economy.

Thus Japanese business culture has stressed a collective approach to society and management. Members have subordinated themselves, and their families, to the overall good of the organization with which they have identified and have been identified. Employee status has come from their company and their role within the corporate family in which they have expected, and been expected, to spend their whole career. The more prestigious the company and the more senior the post, the more highly regarded the status. Since Japanese multinationals have rarely hired Japanese at mid-career, Japanese multinational managers have long been virtually career-locked, with few options but to trust their careers to their company and their mentors; with mid-career opportunities in non-Japanese companies increasing, this syndrome has begun to lessen, but the career-locked tradition remains strong.

Multinationals have expected their well-indoctrinated and career-locked members to perceive their whole career as an opportunity to develop their skills and knowledge. The work ethic has been reinforced by continued off-hours as well as on-hours interactions with others in the work group. The corporate *esprit de corps* has been reinforced by group exercises, singing of company songs and other rituals that are less appreciated in Western environments. The sense of belonging and the shared beliefs and behaviour that these efforts achieve appear to have mitigated the need for developing clear-cut organizational structures, the absence of which has characterized the loosely defined relations among the companies that comprise the extended corporate families (*keiretsu*) such as Hitachi, Toyota and Matsushita.

The Japanese approach to business has stressed harmony and cooperation more than speed. Decisions are made by the *ringi* system. Proposed actions are circulated to, considered by and agreed to by everyone affected. While everyone from the bottom up appears to be included and respected, Akio Morito, the Sony chairman, has noted:

> The concept of consensus is natural to the Japanese, but it does not necessarily mean that every decision comes out of spontaneous group impulse. Gaining consensus in a Japanese company often means spending time preparing the groundwork for it, and very often the consensus is formed from the top down, not from the bottom up, as some observers of Japan have written.

He goes on to say, 'My second son, who worked for Morgan Guarantee Trust... finds the Japanese way of reaching consensus and planning tedious' (Morita, 1986: 198–9).

Japanese management has long emphasized generalists. Employees work for the whole organization and are expected to understand and perform a wide variety of roles. As noted in the previous chapter, this value is reflected in the Japanese corporate recruitment, its orientation programmes, job training and job rotation. Japanese management development programmes reflect the corporations' willingness to invest for the long-term development of their staff; they stress an appreciation of corporate philosophy and corporate spirit as well as an understanding of all parts of the company. Job rotation in a variety of assignments is an integral aspect of the career development effort. The focus on investing for the long term applies to financial as well as human resources. Perhaps in part because they are more dependent on cross-holding investors than on outsiders, Japanese companies have long been prepared to invest with a longer-term view of results – not demanding visible results each quarter.

A sense of community and collaboration pervades Japanese corporate life, and this embraces governmental bureaus, which have long had extraordinary powers for awarding licences and other permissions for commercial pursuits, and of withholding advantages like subsidies, tax privileges or low-interest loans at their own discretion. Ministries have resorted to 'administrative guidance' to force organizations to adopt 'voluntary' measures. It is by such means that the Ministry of International Trade and Industry (MITI) has shaped industries to make them more internationally competitive. The Ministry of Finance and the Bank of Japan have also exercised powerful control. While large corporations are no longer as dependent upon them for loans as they once were, these institutions still maintain 'a very large voice in allocating funds for all really big investments' (van Wolferen, 1989:44–5).

As among American and European multinationals, there are striking organizational and cultural differences among Japanese corporations. To illustrate the differences, it is useful to compare the Mitsui and Mitsubishi trading companies and the groupings of which they are a part. The Mitsubishi culture tends to emphasize the organization more than Mitsui, whose individual companies, divisions, national affiliates and individuals pride themselves on having far more autonomy. Similarly, Sony and Matsushita differ substantially in their approach to management staffing and development.

The differences between companies – even those within the same industry – are so striking that they have affected mergers. Daiichi Kangyo Bank, formed from a merger more than two decades ago, continues to have two parts so clearly delineated that care is still taken to choose top executives and successive CEOs so that both sides remain fairly represented. While the Japanese corporate stress upon culture acts as a means to extend networks and integrate operations, the close intracorporate bonds generate cultural clashes when efforts are made to merge two companies. The cross-corporate differences are especially difficult to overcome when the Japanese multinational attempts to accommodate its values to non-Japanese cultures.

European management cultures

European multinationals are based in countries with such strikingly different histories, languages, traditions and educational systems – and management cultures – that European integration, no matter how readily or rapidly achieved, will not overcome these differences in the foreseeable future. Even when viewed from across oceans, Europe – even just Western Europe – appears as a collection of cultures. The disparity discourages attempts to present a common description. As Barzini's (1983) description of the imperturbable British, the mutable Germans, the quarrelsome French, the flexible Italians and the careful Dutch illustrates, it appears easier to note the distinctive cultures and dissimilarities than the commonalities. The differences between the business cultures of Italy and Britain continue to appear to be more remarkable than the differences between the United Kingdom and the United States, which have long shared so many cultural traditions and contacts. Like overlapping circles, European business cultures share characteristics, but each has distinctive features (see Figure 5.2).

The British culture has tended to stress common sense, resourceful pragmatism, adaptability, class and club-consciousness in the approach to business management. By others, British managers are often perceived as monolingual, insular and non-European in outlook. Traditionally British managers have been 'gentlemen

(a) Individualism/power–distance

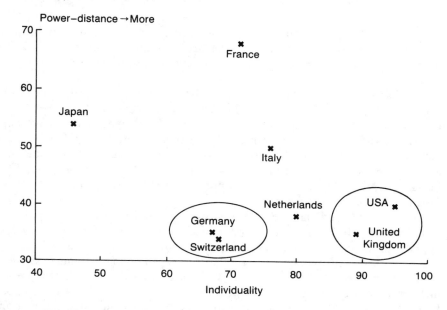

(b) Risk avoidance and job equality content (masculinity)

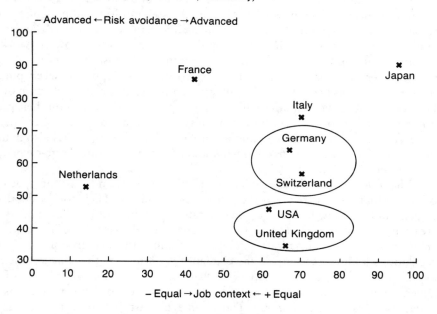

Note: The purpose of these graphs is to illustrate the degree of divergence and convergence of selected national work-related characteristics. In both cases, Japan is separated and the English-speaking countries are clustered, as are the German-speaking ones.

Figure 5.2 International differences in work-related values (Source: Adapted from Hofstede, 1980:77, 122, 158, 189)

amateurs' – with non-graduates along with liberal arts graduates and accountants providing a significant share. With the drive to apply more business acumen to management, accounting has provided an increasing source of executives (Handy *et al.*, 1987).

German managers have tended to emphasize order, discipline and efficiency. By others, German managers may be perceived as arrogant. A high proportion have earned doctorates in economics, science or law. As a Bayer executive has expressed it: 'We Germans respect disciplined professional expertise, capable of setting and achieving demanding objectives.' He went on to say, 'Many non-Germans, especially Americans, have difficulty setting about a task without their objectives being determined for them. Germans prefer to set their own' (interview, Vossberg, 18 July 1989).

French managers have tended to stress logic and cartesian rationality, as well as *élan*, as the basis of organizational success. To others, French managers often appear intolerant and xenophobic. The networks of graduates of the Grandes Ecoles, whose curricula have emphasized engineering, applied sciences and management, pervade the higher ranks of business (Ardagh, 1987:488–92). While in most countries an educational pedigree is an entry ticket into a company, in France Grandes Ecoles graduates have 'an employment passport guaranteeing prestigious and powerful posts for life' (Barsoux and Lawrence, 1990:24–46). As a former ITT executive, now with Alsthom Alcatel, put it: 'Nothing quite compares to the elitist self-confidence and the autocratic hauteur of these Grandes Ecoles graduates' (interview, 6 June 1990). With their shared values and networks, they dominate the top echelons of both government and industry, cross over from one to the other and communicate easily. The resulting rapport between public and private sectors has been reflected in government support for the protection of French business. Both Peugeot and Renault, for example, have depended on their protected domestic market for their continued viability, a fact that approaching EC-promoted integration is threatening. Blending of public and private spheres is also manifested in the fact that two of the five French Global 50 companies are state-owned, as are ten of their 32 Global 500 ones.

The Italian culture has prized charisma, spontaneity and a macho-type flair. By others, Italian managers are perceived as undisciplined. Their top leaders, such as Agnelli and De Benedetti, have demonstrated hauteur and flamboyancy as well as creativity in directing their enterprise. As one Olivetti executive phrased it: 'A little chaos is seen as necessary to maintain an innovative environment. Rules and regulations inhibit creativity so the challenge is to manage this chaos sufficiently to avoid anarchy' (interview, Craen, 2 August 1989). The willingness of Italian governmental institutions to provide investment for private as well as public enterprises (as described in the Fiat profile in Part III) indicates one aspect of business–government relations in Italy.

Even within these countries, though, corporate cultures range widely. The swift pace of the 1990 reorganization undertaken by British Petroleum contrasts with the deliberate pace at which Shell has moved towards organization change. The energetic pace of the entrepreneurial-oriented, Turin-based Fiat contrasts with that of the two state-owned and south-Italy-based conglomerates IRI and ENI.

When viewed together, the traditional European styles can be described as less formal and less carefully defined than the American one. Whereas American companies have been more concerned to develop and implement a clear-cut structure as far as the distribution of authority and responsibility are concerned, European ones have long been accustomed to less closely defined arrangements. Similarly, the European job descriptions have long tended to be less specific than American ones.

Several characteristics do appear to have pervaded European multinational business culture – at least as compared to American and Japanese business cultures. Europeans have tended to stress personal relations. They have not appeared as individualistic as the American nor as group-oriented as the Japanese. Europeans have tended to value their personal time and security more than Americans or Japanese – a value which has become imbedded in European governmental regulations. For many Europeans, personal and family security has tended to be more important than 'success', at least as Americans and Japanese define the term. Having noted these traditional characteristics, one must also recognize the extent to which, in the face of global competition, values which have long been more associated with American businesses appear to be replacing the more traditional European ones – albeit with notable resentment and resistance. While business–government relations differ from one European country to another – ranging from strong government support in France and Italy to more complementary relationships in Germany and the Netherlands – the relations generally appear less adversarial than in the US, and less orchestrated than in Japan.

The European multinational groups have historically accommodated a variety of cultures and approaches, and therefore many have not as assiduously and consciously developed a corporate-wide culture. Unlike the American and Japanese efforts to extend some degree of their national cultures to corporate parts, Europeans appear to have tolerated or appreciated more variety.

The differences among countries throughout the world have long reflected and supported corporate organizational arrangements that split international operations from domestic operations. As the multinationals reorganize to facilitate transnational coordination, they face the challenge of developing organizations that can flourish in a constant state of flux generated by the continuing unevenness of the rates of cultural as well as economic homogenization. As long as such differences remain, multinationals will continue to face the challenge of accommodating differences while sustaining organizations that are sensitive to these differences.

Managing occupational cultures: focusing corporate strength

While differences in national cultures have long divided the mind-sets of multinational employees along geographic lines, differences in professional, industrial and cultural values have also divided corporate loyalties along product and functional lines. Each of the various specializations, such as engineers, marketers and accountants, and each industry, such as motor vehicles, chemicals and oil, project their own predispositions, priorities and 'ways of looking at things'. These disparate values have been shaped by their differing educations, dissimilar experiences and their continued association and bonding with others in the same field. Increasing industrial diversification and increasing functional specialization have magnified the issue. Corporate stress on 'every unit on its own bottom', with the accompanying implications regarding profit-and-loss expectations and divisional control of resources, severely restrict cross-border communication, collaboration and coordination. Division-bound staffing processes virtually mandate division-bound and division-myopic careers. Division-specific information systems reduce cross-division communication and coordination. Corporate reluctance to shift divisional fiscal and other resources across hierarchical borders handicaps efforts to refocus strategies upon emerging opportunities.

Thus, just as multinationals face the issue of reconciling the national cultures that interact within an international affiliate, so they also face the issue of focusing the often competing occupational cultures of the various professions and diverse industries, so that they complement one another in the common effort to increase the corporate competitive advantage. Increasing diversity frequently accompanies growth. Such increased diversity may add synergy to scale and scope as a rationale for continued growth. But the greater the diversity in occupational specialization and industrial diversity, the greater the danger that factionalism may divide the organization. Such factionalism, whether manifested by infighting or indifference, adversely affects not only the prospects for cooperation among the parts but also the possible benefits of scale and scope. In the effort to develop norms that transcend the diversity of interests, the leaderships of many multinationals have focused on a specific core competence or a common identity or both.

Core occupations

In many multinationals a single profession or occupational group, whose knowledge, skills and orientation have long been closely identified with the organization's principal perspective(s), has provided the principal source of leadership, established an 'elite' network and fashioned the preordinate organizational values (Bledstein, 1976:83–6; Mosher, 1975:112; Pascale, 1990:60–3). Such an occupational group may be marketing, engineering or accountancy, or it may be a subprofession such as industrial marketing, chemical engineering or cost accountancy. As corporations have diversified across industries, those whose occupational backgrounds have been in the core business have tended to promote these values throughout the company. Such a core occupational group may focus on a generic industry such as motor vehicles, chemicals or electronics, or on a specific industry such as prestige automobiles, polyurethanes or telecommunications. A corporate core 'elite' may comprise one or more, or a combination, of these occupational groupings. Such a core group has perpetuated its culture by recruiting and promoting these who 'fit in'. Those who have sought employment, conformed and advanced have tended to be those whose own values, as derived from their education, experience and socialization within the company, have been consistent with those that have long been legitimized and developed within the corporation (see Figure 5.3). Thus the educational and experiential background of the company's past, present and potential future major 'players' have tended to be consistent with the company's traditional culture.

The accent on different professions has long tended to distinguish companies. In General Electric the finance/auditing elite have long dominated the scene (Pascale, 1990:237–8). Procter & Gamble managers have long tended to rise primarily through marketing. The top Exxon executives have tended to be petro-engineers. The top ranks of Shell have long been comprised principally of Dutch engineers, primarily from Delft University, and British liberal arts graduates' principally from Oxford and Cambridge. Over 75 per cent of the Bayer top management have doctorates, most in scientific fields.

The commonality of shared values profoundly affects the ideology of many companies. The marketing orientation of IBM has long dominated its company culture; most of those at the top have risen through marketing posts. Finance men have long tended to win the turf battles within General Motors and Ford (Halberstam, 1986:237–8; Pascale, 1990:116). The more diversified the multi-national, the less is the likelihood that any one elite occupational group may extend a common corporate culture throughout the company. General Motors' efforts to integrate the more entrepreneurial Electronic Data Services (EDS) have been frustrating. Philips has straddled the more conservatively cautious culture of its lighting division (its longtime major revenue producer) and the more fast-paced, innovative culture of its electronics-related divisions. The extent to which the

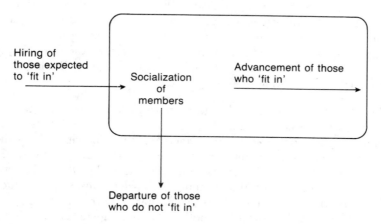

Figure 5.3   How core cultures perpetuate themselves

Mercedes-Benz division of Daimler-Benz will be able to extend its culture through the recently acquired AEG and aerospace divisions is an open question.

The phenomenon of professional diversity and professional dominance by a core elite has been complicated by the diversification of corporations. Diversification has increased the number of industry occupational groupings sprawling across corporate cultural landscapes, even while that of the core industry has generally remained pre-eminent. While the presence of a core occupational elite facilitates the imposition of corporate-sponsored values, such an imposition of values may cause resentment, resistance and the consequent loss of the cross-border 'pollenizing' that enhances the multinational's initiative and ability to compete more effectively. To overcome this dilemma, many multinationals have taken steps to concentrate on a core competence and corporate identity that focus and integrate the energies of the diversity of professional and industrial interests and values.

Focusing on core competence

A critical means by which a diversified multinational may focus its diversity, increase its cohesiveness and improve its competitiveness is concentration on a core competence. Such a focus may provide a sense of purpose that concerts the perspectives driving the diverse parts in such a way that the scarce common resources are used to maximum advantage in meeting corporate objectives. Prahalad and Hamel have pointed out the relationship between a core competence and coherent advantage as follows:

> In the long run, competitiveness derives from the ability to build, at lower cost and more speedily than competitors, the core competence that spawns unanticipated products [. . .] The diversified corporation is a large tree. The trunk and major limbs are core products, the smaller branches are business units, the leaves, flowers, and fruits are end products. The root system that provides nourishment, sustenance and stability is the core competence. You can miss the strength of competitors by looking only at their end products, in the same way you miss the strength of a tree if you look only at its leaves. (Prahalad and Hamel, 1990:80: see Figure 5.4)

The real sources of competitive advantage are to be found in management's ability to harmonize its corporate-wide technologies, production skills and market understanding into competences that increase the capacity of its individual businesses to adapt the changing opportunities quickly and effectively. Such core competences provide a unifying focus to a multinational's efforts, determining its corporate-wide priorities, and thus shaping its border-transcending values.

A core competence is thus the knowledge shared by the variety of professional perspectives that feed the corporate mosaic. Core competences are the source of competitive strength generating strategies of market entry diversification, sourcing

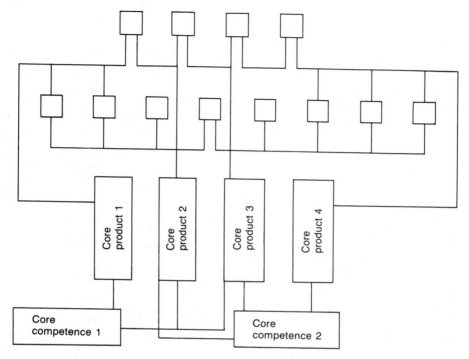

Figure 5.4 Core competences: the root of competitiveness (Source: Adapted from Prahalad and Hamel, 1990:81)

and alliance-building. Examples of such a core competence have been Sony's capacity to miniaturize, Philips optical-media expertise and 3M's focus on surfacing technologies. These multinationals have leveraged their core competences to develop a wide diversity of products.

To develop core competences throughout the organization, multinationals need to view their resources on a multidivisional basis. A core-competence development strategy requires viewing R&D, manufacturing and marketing efforts of the diverse parts of a corporation from a corporate-wide point of view. Such an organizational strategy treats human, fiscal, technological and other common resources as assets that cannot be divided among enclave-like parts of the corporate whole. The fragmentation of resources becomes inevitable when a company's information system, communicative networks, career paths, management rewards and processes for strategy development do not transcend divisional and country borders. Thus the development of a border-spanning core competence depends not only on structures that foster cross-border communication and employee development policies that foster cross-divisional transfers, but also on a corporate-wide sense of identity that reflects a common vision based on the core competence.

Projecting a common corporate identity

Projecting a common corporate identity provides a complementary and reinforcing means for an enterprise to focus its diverse elements on a common goal. A company projects its distinctive identity not only with logos, colours and typography, but also by consistent emphasis of the features for which it wants to be appreciated. Corporate advertisements are the most visible manifestation of the efforts to project a corporate identity. The more diversified the multinational, the more geographically dispersed, and the more its growth has been fuelled by mergers and takeovers of companies with ready-made cultures, the more difficult has been a multinational's task of presenting itself coherently. The advantages, however, of being able to present a single coherent identity appear to be sufficient to make such an effort rewarding.

A focused effort to identify what a corporation stresses helps the corporate staff, its customers and other stakeholders to appreciate what the company produces, why it exists and how it behaves – provided, of course, that the company appears to practise what it proclaims. A strong, well-recognized, well-appreciated, coherent corporate image may provide a valued corporate asset for endorsing specific ventures and for speeding the introduction of new products and the opening of new markets. The ability to project a single corporate image across product and national borders leverages a company's resources.

Multinationals have differed dramatically in the extent to which they have used corporate branding to project the corporation and its products. The spectrum of approaches ranges from focused/monolithic through 'endorsed' to diffused/multiple (see Figure 5.5: see Murphy, 1990:46–69, for discussion of a similar typology). While corporations may not be consistent in following one approach, depending in part on the corporate message being marketed and to whom it is marketed, the cumulative effect of these presentations affects the corporate ability to concert corporate efforts.

Corporations which stress a focused (sometimes called monolithic or comprehensive) option have developed a clear, cohesive single identity for the corporation as a whole. A single name and visual identity, such as Mitsubishi's three diamonds, Royal Dutch/Shell's shell and IBM's blue, serve as a rallying point for the staff and 'purport to give customers a clear idea of what they can expect – in terms of product, service, and price – in the belief that customers will stay loyal to the organization that respects their needs and with which they are familiar' (Olins, 1989:82–3). It is the concentration on the development of a single clear identity that creates a name recognition and message that the multinationals can transfer across products and country borders. By developing a global brand umbrella, companies like 3M, Philips and Sony – and even alliances such as Mitsubishi – have facilitated the building of a more readily identified image, customer loyalty and access to distribution channels (see Prahalad and Hamel, 1990:87).

The 'endorsed' approaches cover the spectrum of options in which both the parent and the part are projected in corporate communication efforts. At one end

Focused/
monolithic

Endorsed

Diffused/multiple

Figure 5.5   Spectrum of branding strategies projecting corporate identity (Sources:
Bayer, General Motors, Procter & Gamble, reproduced with permission)

are those in which the parent company's name is stressed, at the other are those in which the name of the corporate part is emphasized, with only a fine print or small logo reference to the general company to which it belongs (as GM's logo is almost lost in Opel's advertisement, shown in Figure 5.5). Both approaches represent efforts to recognize the diversity of parts while stressing the unity of the overall organization.

The diffused or multiple approach is that in which the corporate parts project their own image without identifying their parents. The Procter & Gamble advertisement for Pampers in Figure 5.5 provides an example. Companies may also wish to maintain a separate identity for one or a few specific products. Procter & Gamble, along with other packaged consumer products companies such as Philip Morris and Nestlé, have long advertised their brands rather than their company. While Fiat has bought Alfa Romeo and merged it into its Fiat Auto Sector, Fiat continues to project a separate image for the prestige car which has long had a distinctive clientele.

There are arguments for the more focused approach, but the decision is one which a multinational takes with caution.

> If Daimler-Benz wants to introduce real Mercedes standard of
> behaviour, performance measurements and quality into its acquisitions
> [. . .] if it wants the world and its own people to see that Mercedes
> standards now apply in AEG, MTU, Dornier, and for the future in
> MBB too, the simplest, most direct action [. . .] is to replace or modify
> existing financial reporting systems, quality, control methods,
> production processes, and marketing techniques [. . .] and bring them
> up to what it regards as Daimler-Benz standards [. . .], and replace all
> existing names and identities with the Mercedes name and star. (Olins,
> 1989: 139)

Such an approach, however, may not only encounter violent opposition from the acquired parts and disrupt traditional processes and systems, but may also risk the loss of the marketing value of the displaced names. Given the clash of cultures between the more conservative, older parts of GM and the more aggressive EDS one, GM would have an even more difficult challenge in attempting to establish an overall GM culture.

Orchestrating value-sharing: the critical leadership task

As so widely diverse a group as the Tom Watsons, Jack Welch, Gianni Agnelli, Konosuke Matsushita and Akio Morita amply demonstrate, the most important factor contributing to the potency of a corporate culture may be the leader who clarifies, communicates and celebrates 'what we believe', the governing ideas regarding the corporate vision, purpose and principles. In fact Schein insists that 'the unique and essential function of leadership is the manipulation of culture' (Schein,

1985b:317). Such leadership focuses corporate resources on the continued development of the core corporate strength in their people, their products and their markets, and motivates people to do their best. Leaders do this by what they choose to consider and control, how they react to critical events, on what criteria they allocate resources, how they decide staffing issues and confer rewards and status, and – most important – what values they stress, how they articulate them and how they live them.

The philosophy and principles of potent leaders, especially founders and transforming successor CEOs, become shared and passed on formally and informally. Ultimately these perspectives are consensually validated into the values and assumptions with which new members are indoctrinated. These values then shape the corporate perception of the external environment and how to survive in it. And they outline how to organize relationships – to optimize the survival prospects in the environment through effective performance and the creation of internal comfort (see Schein, 1985b:50). In a new organization, in a company with a new leader, or in a company determined to modify its culture, the role of the leader is critical in (re)developing the corporate values. Such leaders shape organizational cultures to the extent that they are able to indoctrinate their subordinates with their own beliefs, or cultivate ideas that their subordinates adopt as their own (see Dyer, 1985:158). While not externally as apparent, the heads of the corporate parts – especially the product divisions and the country affiliates – play a vital role in infecting their corporate part with the energy to pursue subcorporate goals, which may complement, conflict with or transcend the overall corporate ones.

Confronted with the urgency of organizing more effectively, and inspired by recent writings about cultural management, multinational leaders have become more proactive in developing corporate culture as a powerful instrument of corporate strategy, particularly as they have faced mergers and joint ventures with companies with a differing ethos, expanded into countries with different ways of life, diversified into product lines requiring diversified strategies, and experienced rapid growth or retrenchment, or serious conflict between groups (Wilkins, 1983:24). Their efforts have depended upon the corporate leadership's ability to define the corporate mission, to set worthy goals and articulate distinctive means for achieving their objectives. Japanese multinationals, as well as some American ones such as IBM and P&G, have long understood the power of common values and beliefs, and proactively manage their company's culture. Many European companies have begun clarifying values. As a brief review of some of the more evident practices affecting the development of shared values demonstrates, strategy structure, staffing and cultural development steps are closely related. These steps have involved clarifying the strategic elements of the corporate culture, communicating these values to the internal and external stakeholders, and involving others sufficiently to achieve the momentum crucial for competing successfully.

Clarification

As stressed at the outset of this book and this chapter, the initiative to define and evangelize common values and beliefs is an integral aspect of defining and developing corporate strategy. The basic task is to identify and position those guiding beliefs and values that transcend product, functional and geographic borders, or that can be cultivated to transcend these frontiers. From this follows the promotion of what may be called operational culture: identifying the corporate heroes and myths, creating corporate logos and mottoes, establishing office decor and dress codes, and developing styles of communication and decision-making. It is noteworthy that those corporate leaders which have been the most successful in developing energetic organizations have actively cultivated distinctive ones.

Kenosuke Matsushita, the founder who led Matsushita for 70 years, as early as 1932 articulated his philosophy of business in the corporate mission which was to guide his company: 'The mission of a manufacturer is to overcome poverty, to relieve society as a whole from the misery of poverty and bring it wealth [. . .] thus creating peace and prosperity' (Matsushita, 1984:22). 'When Matsushita employees sing the company song about "Sending our goods to the people of the world, endlessly and continuously, like water gushing from fountains", they are proclaiming the corporate vision' (Senge, 1990:224). And by daily repetition of laudable principles 'about service, honesty and teamwork [. . . the employees] gradually take them to the heart' (Yamashita, 1987:89). PHP Institute, the trust created by the founder, continues to publish and distribute his books which stress the company's responsibility to society, the importance of harmony, the need to contribute to national industrial development, the improvement of people's lives and the development of the people who comprise Matsushita.

Probably no company has laboured so self-consciously for so long as IBM to develop its distinctive corporate culture. IBM has canonized Thomas Watson Sr. and Jr., who stressed the customer as its focus, encouraged a dark-suit-and-white-shirt dress code, popularized distinctive slogans such as 'THINK' as well as the blue IBM logo, and emphasized its code of ethics.

Jack Welch has faced a far more difficult challenge in his effort to develop a unifying corporate-wide culture for GE. GE is not only more diversified but well beyond its formative years. To define the core of the shared corporate values which he is attempting to cultivate throughout the company, Welch has relied on such phrases as 'No 1 and No 2' and 'shared management practices' to describe the (albeit slim) common 'thread that binds them [the diverse businesses] together and creates what we call integrated diversity' (GE Annual Report, 1989:4).

European multinationals have not generally been so self-consciously assiduous in cultivating a common corporate image; while a few have. Royal Dutch/Shell has long had a well-developed corporate culture, distinguished not only by the common logo but by its accent on decentralization. The Agnelli charisma and flair have contributed a distinctive aspect to the Fiat corporate culture. Daimler-Benz has long stressed quality; the newly developed company stresses not only quality but also transportation (not only road but also air, with the high technology to keep it on the cutting edge) as the rubric unifying its diversified operations. Each of these efforts to identify the overarching corporate values has required vision and energy. Implementing them has been at least as difficult.

Communication

The audiences to which a corporate culture needs to be communicated include the staff, the customers and potential customers, and other stakeholders. Communicating the distinctiveness of the multinational to its own staff may be the most difficult as well as most essential element of developing a world-wide culture. The challenge has been to communicate what the corporate objectives are, why they have been selected, who is responsible for what, and how they are going to be carried out. As multinationals expand across national and cultural borders, and through linguistic curtains, the task of communicating effectively becomes far more difficult. Not only do the customs and perceptions differ more widely, but also the possibility of communicating in a common language whose nuances are widely appreciated is significantly reduced.

Multinationals have demonstrated their increasing concern for disseminating information, especially among their employees. Corporate news magazines, newsletters and releases have proliferated. Perhaps most importantly, multinationals have increased their management development efforts to promote cross-border communication and socialization. GE's 'Work-out' efforts and 3M's (EMAT and related) management development efforts in Europe are examples of bringing together groups to discuss how to work together to achieve common objectives. Top management has increasingly recognized that without major attention to such training-cum-socialization activities the lower echelons lack an appreciation of what they are (supposed to be) doing and how they fit in. While such efforts may resemble evangelism and even brainwashing, they can serve to arouse a common spirit, encourage participant networking and provide more direct contact between the top and lower levels of management.

Celebration: involving and inspiring

For corporate culture to have an impact on behaviour and motivate performance it must involve and inspire. To use corporate culture to bind the diverse parts of the enterprise, multinationals depend upon managers throughout the organization to celebrate the shared values 'by how they walk as well as how they talk'. To secure compliance and to encourage commitment requires corporate-wide involvement in the attempt to inspire the staff to undertake the efforts vital to compete successfully.

Efforts to cultivate a transcontinentally unifying and motivating corporate culture require the involvement of the managers with sufficiently broad perspectives to share the leadership role of communicating a comprehensive corporate vision, appreciating the interdependence of the corporate parts, and promoting common practices. They must individually help create the common vision and share the common values in order for these beliefs to be driven throughout the organization, bridging the national, product and functional chasms dividing it. Increasingly multinationals recognize that the corporate commitment required to be globally competitive demands diversity of nationality, educational and experiential perspective, and linchpin managers who can serve as 'culture carriers' binding the parts of the multinational mosaic. As multinationals depend more and more upon multifunctional teams whose effectiveness requires mutual appreciation, the need grows for an abundant supply of diversely experienced and diversity-appreciative management leaders for key management posts throughout the organization.

To compete globally, multinational leadership must inspire and motivate by role-modelling from the top down. Dynamic CEOs such as Matsushita of Matsushita, Lee of Samsung, the Watsons of IBM, Welch of GE and Reuter of Daimler-Benz have attempted to articulate and propagate a corporate *esprit de corps* which motivates the whole company. To be effective the practices of the would-be role models must conform with the precepts which are being propagated. To change or revitalize the already existing corporate culture not only requires a vision, it also depends upon generating strategic and symbolic messages to signal what will be rewarded and not rewarded, freshening the history and legends, pointing out the role models to be emulated and persuading the staff to trust leadership (see Dumaine, 1990).

CEOs who have successfully undertaken this challenge have first made efforts to understand their company's old culture before framing their vision of the new. They have avoided tackling the old culture head-on. They have looked for the subculture which provided the best example of the vision they wanted to achieve, and held it out as a model. They have encouraged and rewarded staff whose ideas and practices exemplified the culture they were trying to develop. They have been patient, not expecting a vision to be implemented without years of effort and persistent role-modelling. Most of all, they have managed culture by mingling throughout the enterprise. They have met and interacted with countless employees, seeking out their ideas and sizing them up in order to flesh out the specific articulation of the vision and values as well as to propagate the cultural gospel. B.C. Lee of Samsung sat in on all recruitment interviews to meet and evaluate not only those interviewed but also the interviewers. Welch has used his 'Work-out' sessions not only to spot problems but also to cultivate the new corporate cultural faith.

Top managers recognize that the function of corporate communications is one to which they must devote a major portion of their time. It cannot be delegated. Inspiring the troops is the essential magic required to achieve the momentum for successfully competing throughout the world. The critical task of corporate leadership is to clarify, communicate and role-model the governing ideas that answer these questions: what is our vision, what is our purpose, and what are our principles? The development of these ideas underlies the effort to concentrate the diverse corporate resources on strengthening their corporate core competence, corporate identity and the core of leadership, which inspire the corporate stakeholders to do their best.

Together with a global strategy, a transcontinental structure and a world-wide management staffing, these corporate-wide and globe-spanning cultural initiatives are vital elements, encouraging unity among the diverse parts of the multinational. The disparate parts of the corporate mosaic have become so diverse, so dependent upon common resources, and thus so complex that structural and staffing initiatives are no longer sufficient for achieving the corporate-wide synergy vital for global competitiveness.

PART III
Case studies of organizational change and continuity: differing perspectives driving leading multinationals

CHAPTER 6
American corporations: globalizing product perspectives

From international divisions to global product divisions

While most US multinationals long relied upon corporate-wide international divisions to develop their overseas operations, by the 1990s most of the major ones had globalized their product divisions and concomitantly dispensed with their corporate-wide international divisions. Major factors driving the changes were the accumulated impact of cross-industry diversification, the spread of multidivisional organizations, and the desire to reorganize the long geographically divided overseas operations to conform to the product-driven corporate organization. More recently, growing intercontinental competition, increasing continental economic integration and decreasing growth and profits have speeded up efforts to reorganize. Most American multinationals, though, have continued to view their foreign operations as peripheral to their domestic operations, a fact that has continued to affect the way US multinationals manage their overseas operations.

Many of the major 1991 Global 50 American multinationals had already developed overseas affiliates by the 1950s; some, such as Ford, GM, GE, Exxon and Mobil, had significantly developed overseas decades before World War II. Nine of the fifteen had ranked among the 50 largest American companies in term of assets as early as 1917 (see Table 6.1). Fourteen of the fifteen largest (by sales) American companies have been Global 50 companies for more than three decades. The exception – Philip Morris – has acquired companies that had once ranked among the top 50 American companies by sales.

Many American multinationals began their overseas expansion while they were less diversified, while national economies were less internationalized, and while communication was less convenient. To add marginally to their large domestic base, they tended to rely on a single international division that, working alongside the domestic operating divisions, organized and managed relatively self-contained international affiliates which handled relatively limited ranges of products. By the 1980s though, not only were national economies significantly internationalized and

Table 6.1 The largest US industrial enterprises: by assets, 1917–91

Ranking	1917	1930	1948	1965	1979	1991
1.	US Steel	US Steel	Standard Oil (New Jersey)	Standard Oil (New Jersey)[1]	Exxon	General Motors
2.	Standard Oil (New Jersey)	Standard Oil (New Jersey)	General Motors	General Motors	General Motors	Ford
3.	Bethlehem Steel	General Motors	US Steel	Ford Motor	Mobil[3]	General Electric
4.	Armour	Internat'l Paper & Power	Standard Oil (Indiana)	US Steel	IBM	IBM
5.	Swift[2]	Standard Oil (Indiana)	Socony-Vacuum[3]	Texaco	Ford	Exxon
6.	Midvale Steel	Ford	Texaco	Socony Mobil[3]	Texaco	Philip Morris
7.	International Harvester	Gulf Oil	Gulf Oil	Gulf Oil	Standard Oil (California)[4]	Chrysler
8.	Du Pont	Anaconda Copper	Du Pont	Standard Oil (California)	Gulf Oil[5]	Mobil
9.	US Rubber	Standard Oil (New York)[3]	General Electric	Gen'l Telephone & Electronics	Standard Oil (Indiana)[6]	Du Pont
10.	Phelps Dodge	Bethlehem Steel	Ford	IBM	General Electric	Chevron
11.	General Electric	Shell Union Oil	Standard Oil (California)	Standard Oil (Indiana)	Shell Oil	RJR Nabisco Holding
12.	Anaconda Copper	Du Pont	Bethlehem Steel	General Electric	ITT	Rank Xerox[6]
13.	American Smelting	Standard Oil (California)	Cities Service[7]	Du Pont	Atlantic Richfield	Amoco[6]
14.	Standard Oil (New York)	Texaco	Western Electric[8]	Chrysler	Tenneco	Shell Oil
15.	Singer	General Electric	Union Carbide	Bethlehem Steel	US Steel	Texaco
16.	Ford	Armour[9]	Sinclair	Shell Oil	Dow Chemical	Dow Chemical
17.	Westinghouse Electric	Sinclair Oil	Westinghouse Electric	Western Electric	Conoco[10]	Atlantic Richfield
18.	American Tobacco	Allied Chemical Dye	American Tobacco	Union Carbide	Standard Oil (Ohio)[11]	Eastmann Kodak
19.	Jones & Laughlin Steel	Union Oil	International Harvester	Phillips Petroleum	Du Pont	P&G
20.	Union Carbide	International Harvester	Anaconda Copper	ITT	Union Carbide	Westinghouse Electric

Note:
1. Renamed Exxon.
2. Acquired by Esmark.
3. Merged with Vaccuum to become Socony-Vacuum, then Socony Mobil, then renamed Mobil.
4. Renamed Chevron.
5. Gulf merged into Chevron.
6. Renamed Amoco.
7. Cities Service merged into Occidental Petroleum.
8. Merged with AT&T.
9. Acquired by Greyhound.
10. Merged into Du Pont.
11. Merged into BP.

Sources: Chandler, 1990: Appendix A; Fortune, 1980:276–7, and 1991a,b:71–2.

communication simplified, but also the leading multinationals had significantly diversified and developed.

While the reasons for organizing international operations separately from domestic business were becoming less germane, the rationale for increasing diversification and developing international businesses along product lines was becoming more compelling. As American anti-trust legislation developed and impeded growth within one industry, the propensity to merge and acquire – manifested conspicuously in 1897–1904, 1925–30, 1965–72 and the 1980s – was increasingly applied to diversifying across industries (see Chandler, 1984c).

The multinational organization and the international division

As described earlier, in the initial decades of the twentieth century a few American corporations were already pioneering the multidivisional organization. By the late 1960s the increasing size and diversity of the larger American corporations had led 90 per cent of them to adopt this product-driven type of organization (Fouraker and Stopford, 1968:59; Rumelt, 1979:63). Increasing diversification, expanding international business, and tension between the product-divided divisions and geography-divided affiliates fostered the gradual globalization of the role of the product divisions. The 1980s quickened the pace of change. Increasing intercontinental competition, the more interdependent multicontinental economy, and declining profits (in some cases losses) have forced efforts to reorganize in order to compete more effectively in a rapidly changing environment.

As a consequence, only a few major American multinationals have continued to rely upon an international division to manage all or almost all of their international operations. Procter & Gamble, 3M, Exxon and Ford present diverse examples of corporations that have maintained an international division for managing overseas operations. Procter & Gamble's international division is responsible for managing the whole range of its packaged goods outside its domestic market. Highly diversified 3M continues to use an international division and what have long been omnibus geographic affiliates, but the company has moved towards weakening the role of what have been their baron-like country general managers. Exxon's international division is responsible for the upstream and downstream oil affiliates, not the chemical affiliates. Similarly, Ford's international division embraces the motor vehicle international operations, but not the company's other such operations. GE's international division, a latterday addition to its multidivisional organization, has a supportive cooperation-promoting role rather than an operational one.

A few multinationals have dispensed with their international division and now rely on continental organizations. While IBM has long eliminated its international divisions, it now relies on continental entities, which the international division parented, to blend the product and geographic perspectives. In 1990, Du Pont discarded its international department; its continental entities are now support operations. Philip Morris run counter to the trend by combining its international tobacco and foods operations under one executive vice-president in its 1991 reorganization. While Mobil, GM and Ford have strengthened continental organizations, these have been intradivisional not corporate-wide operations.

Overseas operations generally peripheral

The large size of the American domestic market has allowed several American corporations to rank in the Global 50 despite the fact that their overseas operations have continued to be peripheral. Chrysler sold off its foreign operations, including Talbot, in an earlier period of crisis. Texaco, Amoco and Chevron have not developed their overseas sales operations nearly as intensively as Exxon and Mobil. Boeing maintains sales offices overseas. Only two of United Technologies' businesses, Carrier (air conditioners) and Otis (elevators), have extensive manufacturing as well as sales presence overseas.

As the American case studies show, the multinationals have shaped their organizations through successive transitions that have evolved with significant variations. Differences in the structure are reflected in the extent the companies have developed staffing patterns and practices that are limited by divisional and country borders. The American corporate penchant for dividing its organization into product-divided strategic business units (SBUs) has appeared to direct attention away from developing a common sense of corporate-wide staffing and values.

Stress and structure systems

As described in the last chapter, the early domestic growth of many American firms into gigantic complexes led not only to the rise of the multidivisional organization but also to developing business administration as a field of study that spawned a host of concepts designed to improve the practice of business management. Spurred by the need to find more and better means of managing their large and complex businesses, American corporations developed well-defined structures, sophisticated systems and precise job specifications. Increasingly, their systems and processes have stressed the 'harder' quantitative data which facilitate more rigorous comparison and calculation than does the more elusive, 'softer' qualitative information. Numbers, especially financial numbers, have not only become the common denomination of diversified businesses, they have also lent themselves to more rigorous comprehensive scrutiny. Business schools, by stressing courses focusing on systems and number crunching, have promoted these principles and practices.

It was this American business culture that American companies have promoted in their affiliates throughout the world – not consciously as an 'American culture' but simply as the most up-to-date, effective and efficient way of doing business. As one American business management professor (who has consulted extensively in Europe) has said somewhat superciliously: 'The only difference between the American way of doing things and the way the rest of the world does things is that the rest of world hasn't caught up yet' (interview, George Labovitz, April 1985). The success of American corporations in the postwar decades led to the unquestioned adoption of many American principles by European and Asian as well as American companies. Only with the international challenge of recent decades have many American businesses and business schools begun to seriously question the extent of their traditional emphasis upon the more accountable subdivisions and SBUs, more sophisticated systems, more comparable statistics and more readily taught management dynamics.

Only a few American-based major multinationals have self-consciously long promoted a distinctive culture and the development of human resources. IBM has for decades promoted distinctive slogans, symbols and styles. Procter & Gamble has similarly developed a distinctive culture. The extent to which IBM's and P&G's younger managers have been recruited by other companies provides testimony not only to their distinctiveness but also to their success in developing managerial potential. In more recent years, other companies such as General Electric have recognized the need to increase the stress on management development and shared values – as complements to the structure and systems efforts – in order to enhance synergy across hierarchies as well as within hierarchies. The case studies that follow, by tracing the organization evolution of selected American major multinationals, point to the trend towards experimenting with a greater variety of ways of achieving organizational coherence.

One international division runs all overseas operations

Procter & Gamble (P&G): continental centres with 'dual matrix responsibility'

Procter & Gamble (P&G), which began as a producer of soap, has so diversified over several decades that its product line includes not only soaps, detergents and cosmetics but also foods and beverages, medicine and health care products, disposable diapers and tissues, and pharmaceuticals and industrial chemicals.

P&G has long been noted for its marketing orientation and acumen, strong ethical standards and well-developed *esprit de corps*, which stem in part from its rigorous selection and promotion-from-within policy. P&G developed the 'brand', and later the 'category', management system, in which the brand or category manager has coordinated all elements of the development, manufacturing, financing and marketing of one brand or category of brands. P&G's strategic stress on brands has shaped its marketing strategy, which advertises not the company but the individual brands; these include Tide, Ariel, Ivory, Crisco, Head and Shoulders, Camay, Oil of Ulay, Lenor, Mr Clean, Folgers, Pampers, Duncan Hines and Vicks.

P&G remains one of a declining number of mega-multinationals which continues to manage its international operations through one corporate-wide international division, whose four regional offices manage the operation of P&G's multiproduct international affiliates. The international division and the continental centres are the means by which P&G converts the strategies of its US-based product divisions into the operational objectives of the international affiliates.

From soap to over 40 categories

On 31 October 1837, William Procter, a candlemaker, and James Gamble, a soapmaker, founded the Procter & Gamble Manufacturing Company in Cincinnati, Ohio. Both partners were devout Protestants who practised a puritan ethic that the company still promotes. The P&G concern for research and development, intensive use of creative marketing techniques, the constant introduction of new products and the development of the brand management concept fostered its growth from a local soapmaker to a global company with more than 40 categories including detergents, shampoos, dentifrices and sanitary napkins (Schisgall, 1981:1–185).

P&G began its major move outside North America with the purchase of Thomas Hedley & Sons in England in 1933, building a new, state-of-the-art plant and developing its marketing skills to cut into Lever's market share. By World War II it had developed operations in Cuba, the Philippines and Indonesia. Shortly after the war, Procter & Gamble adopted a multidivisional, product-divided structure (Chandler 1990:159, 169, 181, 385). The P&G entry into Europe was accelerated in 1963 with the establishment of its European Technical Center in Brussels to serve its Common Market affiliates in product research, purchasing, engineering and manufacturing. By the early 1980s P&G had standardized its European products, rationalized their production and marketed them on a European-wide basis. The 1992 goals have accelerated the trend towards a more integrated approach.

P&G first began developing its Japanese business in 1983. It recently began construction of a new technical centre in Japan which will provide the capacity for product and packaging innovations in the Far East to match what already exists in America and Europe. P&G's 1985 $1.2 billion purchase of Oil of Ulay and Pantene from Richardson-Vicks was followed by the 1989 $1.3 billion purchase of Cover Girl and Noxema from Norell. P&G's 1991 $1.4 billion purchase of Revlon's Max Factor and Beatrix cosmetics businesses clearly extends its scope, establishing it as a leading global player in the cosmetics business.

P&G's gross sales in 1990 exceeded $24 billion. Its major affiliates in 50 countries sold more than 200 brands in more than 140 countries, and employed about 80,000 persons, of which about 40 per cent served outside the USA. The percentage of sales generated overseas rose from 29 per cent in 1986 to 46 per cent in 1991.

US by product, international by area

Six of the eighteen (all North American with the exception of the 1991 German appointee) board members are P&G senior executives. The senior executive ranks (see Figure 6.1) comprise the chairman/CEO, the vice-chairman/president P&G International, two executive vice-presidents (one heads domestic operations and the other heads some of the staff services), plus the following:

- five senior vice-presidents who head staff resource units;
- seven group vice-presidents who head the US-based product groups;
- four group vice-presidents who head the overseas continental groups.

One of the staff support divisions is Product Supply, which is the result of a 1987 combining of Purchasing, Engineering, Manufacturing and Distribution into a single organization.

The seven US-based product divisions are Beverages and Food, Laundry and Detergents, Paper Products, Industrial Chemicals, Food Services and Lodging, Health, and Beauty Care (the last two were separated in the late 1980s). These divisions are composed of categories, which in turn are divided into brand groups. In the effort to cut costs, P&G has begun to consolidate some of its brand groups.

The international division comprises four continental groups. All of these regional groups 'have a dual matrix responsibility for reviewing the product development needs of the regions in which they are located, while contributing innovative product and packaging technology to the Company's world-wide business' (Artzt, 1990:6). One group handles Asia/Pacific operations. Another oversees Canada and Latin America operations. As a consequence of the 1985 Richardson-Vicks acquisition there are two sets of European operations. The Richardson-Vicks centre in England is responsible for health and beauty care products. The European Technical Center, located in Brussels, coordinates beverages, laundry detergents, fabric softeners, and household cleaners and disposables (it is by far the largest of the P&G continental organizations; its head, who is German, was appointed to the board in 1991).

The European Technical Center operations comprise staff functions (paralleling those at corporate headquarters) and five line units (each headed by a vice-president): Northern Europe, Southern Europe, Central Europe, Africa/Middle East and General Export, and Disposables and Beverages. The vice-presidents/general managers heading the North Europe, South Europe and Central Europe regional offices have additional portfolios as European-wide category managers: one for laundry detergents, one for household cleaners, and one for fabric softeners. The organizational separation of disposables and beverages in Europe reflects the fact that profit-and-loss responsibility has been established on a European-wide product base. There is some speculation regarding how quickly P&G may move to shift from primarily an area basis to a product basis with the other categories. For the present, though, the country general managers are responsible for the 'bottom line' (market shares, volumes and profit) and report to the subcontinent division heads. Their direct subordinates have secondary reporting relationships to category coordinators (who, as has been noted, are also regional vice-presidents). In Europe, where (as has also been noted), two continental offices

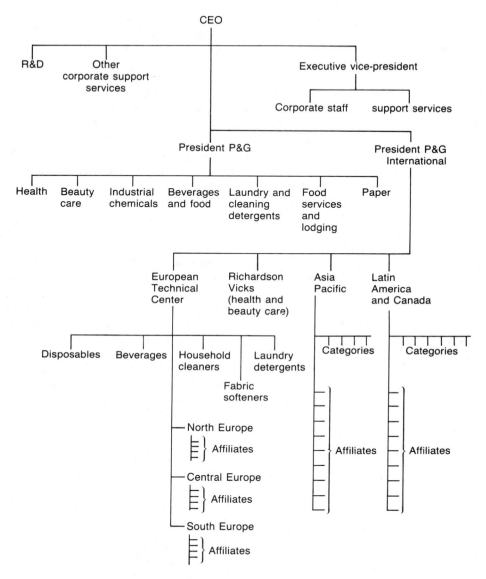

Figure 6.1   Procter & Gamble organogram, 1991

divide the responsibilities along category lines, the smaller countries tend to have one combined operation covering the range of P&G European product lines, and the larger countries tend to have two country organizations (one handling health and beauty care products for Richardson-Vicks, and the other handling the products for the European Technical Center).

International staffing

P&G recruits directly from university, starts new employees from the bottom, varies their assignments, and trains them continuously. P&G stresses that it recruits the most qualified people without any distinction of race, sex or other irrelevant characteristics. P&G's marketing reputation contributes to its ability to attract recruits.

P&G rigorously applies the 'promotion from within' principle. It stresses continuous on-the-job training, technical training and management education. Managers are evaluated not only on their personal achievements but also on how well they develop the skills of their subordinates. Because of P&G's reputation for recruitment and training, many firms 'head hunt' its managers.

P&G is a company in which marketing has been the dominant profession. As noted in Chapter 4, the typical career path of a country general manager has begun in advertising (usually as brand assistant) and then moved up through an advertising manager post. From that point he or she is eligible for a country general management post.

On the basis of the 'promotion from within' principle, the senior executive officers of the company have begun as first line managers in the company. They have been regularly promoted to reward their overall performance and their concern for the business. Generally managers serve a series of two-year stints, but there is increasing concern that the assignments should be longer. Postings to a variety of countries assure the development of an international perspective. A typical 31-year veteran has served in nine different countries. By now P&G no longer depends on Americans for top assignments; Europeans occupy the senior European posts. Host country nationals head most national organizations; their management teams include a Europe-wide mix.

Procter & Gamble is one of the few American corporations with several non-Americans in top executive posts. Among the 25 corporate officers, eight are not US natives. Most P&G top executives have had extended international experience. The new CEO previously served as President P&G International, and before that headed the European Technical Center.

The P&G image

P&G has built its strong marketing reputation on its ability to market its separate brands, not the company. But after decades of not actively promoting its name, the consumer product giant has begun to market itself and various corporate projects as well as its famous brands. For example, P&G has begun to advertise its environmental efforts. This responds to competitive pressures and a growing consumer predisposition to judge a product not only by its brand but also by the company that stands behind the brand. While P&G has placed the P&G logo on its brand packaging in Japan, it has not changed its traditional approach in the USA or Europe.

P&G's strong ethical culture stems from the founding fathers who brought their ethical principles into the business, and from the 'promotion from within' principle that maintains the culture by promoting people acting the P&G way. The company stimulates internal competition. Brands are competing with each other and people are eligible for a limited number of higher positions. P&G has developed a reputation for dealing fairly with its employees and provides employment security, retirement plans and insurance. Jobs are designed to give each employee a challenging and self-actualizing job that suits his or her competence. The salaries and fringe benefits are aimed to attract young, qualified managers.

P&G strives to meet the consumers' needs and wants with adequate products showing the best quality/price ratio. In the past, it has withdrawn products from the market because it could not give the expected quality standard. A few years ago, it initiated total quality systems (TQS) as an approach not only to minimize rework and maximize efficiency but also to ensure that each individual activity supports supplier–customer relations.

Teamwork is a key word at P&G. The training programmes are aimed at giving managers an overall view of the business of the company and an understanding of the jobs and responsibilities of other employees. The atmosphere at P&G is businesslike. There is no formal protocol to be followed, neither is there an architectural style or a clothes style for the managers. The offices themselves are not luxurious but aimed at functionality and thoroughness – another key word at P&G. This is the P&G culture which the company has promoted throughout the world.

The future

The P&G CEO, Edwin L. Artzt, points to a vision for P&G that stresses continued globalization, strategic use of acquisitions and alliances, restructuring by 'reducing the layers of management structure, eliminating insular barriers between functions, while continuing to expand both category management and matrix management as fundamental models for running our business, [and . . .] organization development increasing the involvement of our employees at all levels in the process of recruiting, training, and retaining valued employees'. Artzt goes on to say that

> Our concept of globalization does not mean that we plan to run our business globally [. . .] We are managing our business and our brands regionally and locally. But increasingly, these will be world brands, sharing global technology and common positioning but with appropriate regional tailoring of product aesthetics and form, packaging materials, advertising and promotion executions – whatever it takes to best satisfy local consumer demand for quality and value. (Artzt, 1990:5,6)

P&G thus plans to meet its global challenge by exploiting its global marketing strength and developing its local presence throughout the world. The globalization of its category management and the increased emphasis on the P&G image as the company that stands behind a wide range of products are salient structural and cultural aspects of the globalization efforts.

While P&G has long organized its domestic operations by products, it has continued to rely upon an international division and area-driven international affiliates to manage its overseas operations. The increasing efforts to globalize the brands, combined with the economic integrating of national economies, may lead to P&G reorienting its international operations to conform more with the home country organization, to do so P&G is strengthening the continental product hierarchies so that they surpass the country hierarchies as the principal source of communication and command. The fact that the subcontinent directors already wear two hats would facilitate such a move.

Philip Morris: from tobacco no. 7 to consumer packaged goods no. 1

By aggresssive exploitation of its Marlboro brand and bold acquisitions, Philip Morris has developed from the US no. 7 tobacco manufacturer to become the world's largest consumer packaged goods company with core businesses in three industries: tobacco, food and beer. It is the only American Global 50 corporation that before 1985 had never ranked among the world's 50 leading industrial enterprises. Philip Morris's rapid growth and diversification may be attributed principally to its 1950s repositioning and successful marketing of its Marlboro brand, and to its 1980s acquisition of two major food companies, both of which had once been Global 50 companies. In 1990 Philip Morris doubled its European food presence with its acquisition of Jacobs Suchard, the Swiss coffee and confectionery giant. Other acquisitions may be under consideration. While the tobacco and foods parts of Philip Morris have operated independently of one another, in 1991 Philip Morris combined the international operations of both food and tobacco under one executive vice-president. This may lead to more integration of the international affiliates.

Multicontinental origins

Philip Morris traces its origins not only to the company that Philip Morris, the London tobacconist, started in 1847 but also to the companies founded by 'Mr. Miller the brewer, Mr. Entenmann the baker, Mr. Kraft the cheese manufacturer, Mr. Birdseye the frozen food king [...] and Oscar Mayer, C.W. Post, and Louis Rich' (*Tobacco International*, 1990:4). With the acquisition of Jacobs Suchard, Philip Morris has added three more European 'founders' – Philippe Suchard, Johan Jacobs and Johan Tobler – to its pantheon.

'In 1919, the rights to the Philip Morris name were bought by a New York group' (Williams, 1991:44). In 1930 it not only trailed behind six other American tobacco manufacturers but was dwarfed by the American Tobacco Company (the core company remaining after a tobacco trust, organized by James Buchannon Duke in 1903, was dissolved in 1911 as part of the antitrust efforts that also broke up Standard Oil and Du Pont). In 1948 Philip Morris continued to trail far behind not only American Tobacco, but also R.J. Reynolds and Liggett and Myers (Chandler 1990:78, 639, 645).

Philip Morris took off in 1954 when it repositioned its former women's brand by marketing the Marlboro man that became the symbol of the leading brand in the USA and the world. It has provided Philip Morris with a lucrative source of profits with which to diversify, beginning in the late 1950s with the purchases of Milprint, Burma-Shave, the American Safety Razor Company and Clark's Gum. In 1961–2 Philip Morris strengthened its European business by entering into licensing agreements with SEITA (the French state-owned tobacco monopoly), Monital Monopoli de Stato (the Italian government-owned tobacco monopoly) and Austria Tabakwerke AG (the Austrian government-owned monopoly) (*Tobacco International*, 1990:5). In 1970 Philip Morris acquired the Miller Brewing Company. It also acquired Seven-Up in 1978 but sold it to Pepsico in 1986.

Philip Morris undertook even larger diversification efforts shortly after Hamish Maxwell took command in 1984. In 1985 he engineered what was then the company's largest acquisition, the $5.6 billion purchase of General Foods that put the company into branded packaged foods. In 1988, the same year that arch-rival R.J.R. Nabisco's CEO launched his disastrous attempt to take his company private, Maxwell paid $12.9 billion for Kraft Inc. Philip Morris has continued its acquisition streak with its $4.1 billion purchase of Jacob Suchard, the Swiss-based coffee and confectionery maker, in 1990 and the $1.5 billion one for Freia Marabou, Scandinavia's biggest maker of sweets and chocolate, in 1992. These acquisitions made Philip Morris a major European food company as well as the continent's largest manufacturer of tobacco products.

In its takeover of General Foods and Kraft, Philip Morris acquired the second and third largest food companies in the USA (just behind the since-dismembered Beatrice). General Foods, the product of a 1928 merger bringing together brands such as Calumet, Maxwell House, Postum, and Jell-O, had, through its international division, invested abroad as early as the 1930s. (Chandler, 1990:157, 165). Its purchase of Oscar Mayer in 1981 was its most recent major acquisition before it was taken over by Philip Morris in 1985. Kraft, too, had developed a wide range of brands, extended with the late 1960s' purchase of National Dairy Products (which as recently as 1964 had been the world's 29th largest manufacturer, trailing only Swift among food companies).

Philip Morris's urge to diversify from cigarettes has been driven by the rising public concern regarding the health hazards of tobacco (which also drove R.J. Reynolds to become R.J.R. Nabisco). To consolidate its entry into the foods business Philip Morris merged General Foods and Kraft to form the world's second largest packaged foods company, trailing only Nestlé. Philip Morris has merged the

Jacobs Suchard operations in Asia/Pacific and Latin America into Kraft General Foods; in Europe these two sets of operations, with some minor rationalizations, have been left to operate in parallel. Food now accounts for more than 50 per cent of Philip Morris's sales and 30 per cent of its operating profits.

The food and tobacco split

The 1991 reorganization which accompanied the retirement of British-born Hamish Maxwell signals the extent of the shift from cigarettes to food. Michael Miles, the new chairman of Philip Morris, was the second-in-command of Kraft Inc. from 1982 until its purchase in 1988, and later named CEO of the combined Kraft and General Foods businesses. William Murray, the new president and COO, is an Australian whose assignments have included Europe-based ones and the presidency of Philip Morris International. Also foreign born are the new head of Philip Morris USA (Canadian), the international division head (Australian) and the chief financial officer (German). The international orientation of Philip Morris is reflected in its board which includes its retired British CEO, Australian COO, German CFO, and two outsiders (an Australian and a Venezuelan).

The reorganization separated the international wings from the pre-1991 tobacco and food divisions to form a new international division whose executive vice-president ranks with the heads of the food, tobacco and beer parts of the Philip Morris organization (see Figure 6.2). The effort to reduce costs led to a late 1991 restructuring initiative to consolidate manufacturing and distribution facilities, discard several unpredictable losses, and merge the sales forces for its General Food, Kraft, Oscar Mayer, and KGF Frozen Foods lines.

The organization which the new international executive vice-president takes over comprises two major parts. The tobacco side consists of one Philip Morris European operation for the EC, another one for East Europe, Middle East and Africa (EEMA), a third organization for Asia/Pacific, and a fourth for Latin America. Each of these sets of continental organizations coordinates a number of country affiliates. The long-established tobacco country affiliates operate with significant autonomy. While an affiliate brand manager receives advice and assistance from a continental brand manager and a factory manager also receives guidance from Lausanne, their 'boss' is the country general manager. On the food side the situation is more complicated, with the continental office exerting more direction with some factories and some brands than for others (interview: Sean Murray, 22 November 1991).

The challenge of coordinating rapidly achieved diversity

Philip Morris has faced the challenge of diversifying into foods in order to avoid the risk of relying for the long term on cigarettes. As it continues to scout for new acquisitions, it faces the challenge of merging two distinct sets of staff and two different cultures. The 1991 reorganization was intended to facilitate these efforts.

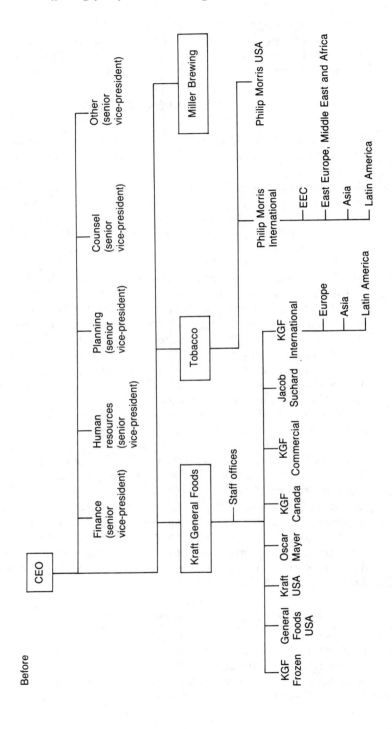

Before

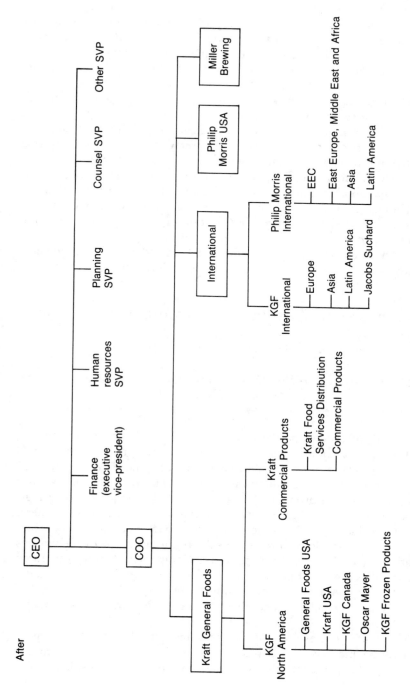

Figure 6.2 Philip Morris organogram: before and after the 1991 reorganization

The effort to integrate the international operations may provide an indication not only of how the overall integration will proceed, but also of whether the long-term intent is to integrate the domestic and international operations of both businesses more closely into two global businesses, or coordinate the international operations of tobacco and food more clearly so that each country has one omnibus affiliate, or attempt both organizational strategies simultaneously.

Philip Morris provides a prototype of a multinational that has significantly shifted its focus. By its rapid diversification, it has become a major player in the international food business. Having already merged its two major food company acquisitions, Philip Morris, like P&G, has demonstrated its predisposition to take a more integrated approach to the management of its component parts.

The appointment of an executive vice-president for its international tobacco and food business signifies another unusual feature of Philip Morris: it is the only major multinational that has recently created a corporate-wide international division. This move may indicate the prospect of further integration of international operations. Such reorganization efforts, along with those being undertaken by P&G, may signal the beginning of an organizational trend within the food industry similar to those that have already occurred in the electronics, motor vehicles and oil industries.

One international division manages major overseas business(es)

General Motors (GM): a massive agglomeration of multidivisional multinationals

General Motors (GM) presents in outsized form many of the features that have long characterized American conglomerates. The massive multinational, which in 1990 employed many more persons (over 760,000) and generated more sales (over $125 billion) than any other industrial corporation in the world, not only manufactures motor vehicles (in America, Europe and Asia) but also runs major motor vehicle parts, aerospace, electronic data services and financial services businesses. General Motors is so massive that not only its motor vehicle groups but also several other parts generate sales comparable with the total sales of all but a few of the world's largest multinationals. In 1990 GM's Automotive Components Group generated about $30 billion sales, GM Europe (which includes Opel and Vauxhall) roughly $25 billion, GM Acceptance Corporation more than $14 billion, GM Hughes Electronics more than $11 billion, and Electronic Data Systems more than $6 billion.

Among GM's joint ventures are a 50 per cent one with Toyota (New United Motor Manufacturing Inc.), a 38.2 per cent stake in Isuzu (the Japanese motor vehicle firm), and a 50 per cent stake in Daewoo Motors (a subsidiary of a

Korean *chaebol* which GM was attempting to sell in 1992). More recent ventures have been the 1990 alliance with Saab-Scania, in which GM acquired half of Saab-Scania's Saab motor vehicle division, and the 1992 marriage of convenience with Toyota Motor to form United Australian Automotive Industries, Ltd. (This formation reduces the number of Australian-based car manufacturers to three. There were fourteen before Australia began, in 1984, to abolish import quotas and gradually cut tariffs from over 55 per cent, with an eye to reaching 15 per cent by the year 2000.) GM's overseas efforts have generated about 30 per cent of its sales, almost two-thirds of which has been Europe-derived.

In the early 1980s, GM's North American motor vehicle market share, which had once exceeded 50 per cent, continued dropping and its profits declined. To meet this threat and restore its profitability, in 1984 GM undertook a reorganization that broke down the time-honoured walls separating six North American motor car divisions by combining them into two major groups – a reorganization that was intended to lead to a new openness, facilitating the transfer of manufacturing technologies. This caused considerable trauma; the effort was insufficient to stop the continuing decline of GM's share of the US motor vehicle market and accelerating losses in the North American vehicle operations.

To improve its unprofitable European motor vehicle operations, in 1986 GM established GM Europe as a continental organization embracing the Opel and Vauxhall operations. In 1988 GM also set up a continental headquarters for its European automotive components operations. The purchase of EDS in 1984 and Hughes Aircraft in 1985 were undertaken to diversify and enhance GM's technology and computer capability. The Saturn Corporation was created in 1985 to develop a GM niche in the small car market with a new company, a new facility and a substantially Japan-influenced approach. The acquisition of Lotus in 1986 and the 1989 half-acquisition of the Saab motor vehicle division increased GM's European presence.

These efforts, some of which may have been misguided and others insufficient, did not prevent GM from undergoing increasing trauma in the late 1980s and early 1990s. With the onslaught of global competition, GM's US car share dropped from 47 per cent in 1980 to 35 per cent in 1991. As a consequence of the drop in market share, the recession, and GM's inability to organize its cumbersome bureaucracy and cut costs sufficiently for changing conditions, GM lost almost $2 billion in 1990 and $4.5 billion in 1991 – despite $1.8 billion in profit from its European operations and other profits from GM Acceptance Corporation. These losses have led to continued cost-cutting efforts aimed at reducing positions in North American operations to half of the 1985 numbers. An April 1992 board-initiated top management reshuffle installed an outsider board member (the retired CEO of P&G) as chairman of the executive committee, and replaced the president and the chief financial officer. In effect these dramatic changes placed the CEO on notice to expedite the reorganizational and accompanying cost-slashing and bureaucracy-reducing efforts, especially those required to revive the slumping North American vehicle operations.

Building the GM empire

In 1908, William C. Durant, who headed Buick, formed General Motors by merging Buick, Olds and a few smaller companies. Following the merger, GM under Durant's leadership continued adding companies, including Cadillac in 1909 and both Chevrolet Motors and United Motors in 1918, acquisitions that enabled GM to challenge and by 1930 overtake Ford in sales (see Table 6.2).

The rapid, and reckless, growth combined with Durant's failure to create a corporate office and the corporate management capabilities sufficient to manage the various constituent companies led to repeated financial difficulties – in 1910, 1917 and 1920. As a consequence the Du Pont family invested in General Motors and replaced Durant with Pierre Du Pont as president in 1920 (Nevins and Hill, 1954:414). Shortly thereafter, Du Pont and his protégé Alfred P. Sloan introduced a product-driven, multidivisional structure, similar to the one the Du Pont company itself had only recently developed (see Chandler, 1962:114–62, 206, and Sloan, 1986: 3–56, for an account of the reorganization effort).

Partly to increase capacity, partly to keep in closer touch with the needs of the major foreign markets, but primarily to get under increasingly high tariffs, GM decided in the mid-1920s to purchase existing, integrated overseas enterprises. Through its export company, which had been organized in 1911 'to sell GM products overseas' (Sloan, 1986:8), GM in 1925 obtained Vauxhall, a British producer of trucks and medium-sized cars, and in 1929 purchased Adam Opel, Germany's largest producer of passenger cars (Chandler, 1990:209). In Latin America, General Motors established General Motors de Brazil in 1925, and in the Asia/Pacific region General Motors–Holden's Pty was created by merging GM Australia and Holden's Motor Body Builders Ltd. 'By 1937, General Motors exported 180,000 vehicles (normally assembled abroad), and manufactured 188,000 more abroad. By then it had assembly plants in Belgium, Sweden, Denmark, Spain, Egypt, Brazil, Argentina, Uruguay, Australia, New Zealand, India, Canada, South Africa, Java, China, and Japan' (Chandler, 1990:209). But GM, along with Ford, stopped its Japanese production ventures almost two years before Pearl Harbor because 'Life was made so difficult' (van Wolferen, 1989:394); the war also stopped GM operations in China, Belgium and Denmark.

The post-World War II years brought a period of rapid growth for General

Table 6.2 American motor vehicle companies' rank among US industrial enterprises: ranked by assets, 1917–91

	1917	1930	1948	1964	1979	1991
General Motors	29	3	2	2	2	1
Ford	16	6	10	3	5	2
Chrysler		47	24	14	26	7

Sources: Chandler, 1990: 663–4; *Fortune*, 1965a,b: 221; 1980: 276; 1991a,b: 122; 1992: 55.

Motors. By 1955, GM had captured more than a 50 per cent share of the American market (Halberstam, 1986:327). In the 1960s GM developed manufacturing plants in Brazil and Argentina and assembly plants in other locations (Sloan, 1986: 314–16). The energy crisis of the 1970s, combined with the increased marketing efforts of Japanese manufacturers, led to a rethinking of GM's corporate strategy, massive investment programmes, and a major reorganization of its North American passenger car operations.

GM diversified its operations by its 1984 acquisition of EDS (which, with more than 20 per cent of the world's market, is the largest supplier of computer services). This acquisition was followed by its 1985 purchase of Hughes Aircraft Company to facilitate the application of high technology to GM cars. It continued the expansion of its European vehicle operations by the 1986 acquisition of the Lotus group, a UK-based engineering consulting and performance car manufacturing firm, and the 1989-implemented 50 per cent acquisition of the Saab-Scania Saab Motor Vehicle Division, which GM now manages.

To coordinate its European motor vehicle operations, GM formed General Motors Europe (GME) in 1986. The 200-person operation located in Zurich played a major role in arranging the GM–Saab deal, in increasing GM's share of the European market, and in making GME one of the most profitable parts of the GM empire. In 1988, GM established a European automotive components operation in Paris to coordinate the various European automotive components groups. Although GM has not taken such dramatic steps in Asia, it has set up a regional office in Hong Kong and sales offices in Thailand, Malaysia and Indonesia.

Its conglomerate structure

In 1990 Robert Stempel succeeded Roger B. Smith as the GM CEO, Lloyd E. Reuss was appointed president and John F. Smith, Jr. was made a vice-chairman, while International Operations, which John Smith headed, was separated from the other motor vehicle operations. The next impact of the 1992 top management coups was to appoint outsider board member (and former P&G CEO) John G. Smale to replace Stempel as board chairman, to appoint John Smith as CEO and to oust several GM executives as well.

Following the April 1992 coups (in which the demoted president and another GM executive lost their board seats), the GM almost all-American board included the GM CEO, and its new chief financial officer. GM's management committee consists of these three plus the executive vice-presidents and senior executives heading GM's major parts. Its almost 30-person administration committee, whose role is to ensure communication among the various component parts, includes the management committee, all vice-presidents/group executives, and specified other vice-presidents. The Detroit-based headquarters controls the multidivisional structure through its direction of such functions as investments, employment, product development, personnel and finance.

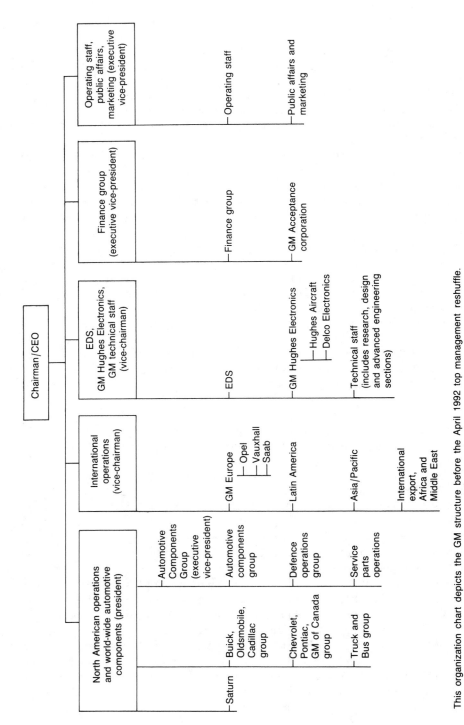

Figure 6.3 General Motors organogram, 1991

This organization chart depicts the GM structure before the April 1992 top management reshuffle.

Roger Smith, GM CEO from 1981 to 1990, had reorganized GM's American operations with the goals of cutting costs, improving both quality and productivity, and winning back the American car buyers. The 1984 reorganization combined Buick, Olds and Cadillac into one group and Chevrolet, Pontiac and GM Canada (which is the largest Canadian industrial corporation) into another (see Figure 6.3). The reorganization involved substantial cost-cutting, including reducing by thousands the number of white-collar as well as blue-collar workers, massive and costly upgrading in production facilities and automation, and training programmes for employees emphasizing quality, teamwork and employee involvement.

The reorganization of the American motor-vehicle-related product groups continues to be refined as GM seeks a balance between centralized management and flexible response to the market. While the product divisions have not previously been responsibile for their production facilities (which have been handled by the automotive assembly divisions), the North American motor vehicle groups are now more responsible for the quality performance and profitability of their products (Taylor, 1989:36). GM has reduced parts complexity and duplication by combining two separate engine operations and one transmission division into a Powertrain Division to coordinate the design of new engines and transmissions more effectively. Further changes may involve combining such staff functions as planning. These reorganizational moves were accompanied by a 1991-announced cut that will further reduce the American staff by 25 per cent, reducing the salaried positions in North American operations from 90,000 to 70,000 and the hourly paid workforce from over 300,000 to 250,000 – the cumulative impact of which will be to reduce the workforce to one half of the 1985 numbers. The efforts will be expedited by the plan, announced shortly after the board-led coup, that the new president, who will head both North American and International automotive operations will merge the North American automotive groups.

GM International Operations consists of four parts: General Motors Europe (GME), Latin American operations (which consists principally of General Motors de Brazil), Asian and Pacific Operations (which in 1990 set up a regional headquarters in Hong Kong), and International Export, African and Middle East Operations.

As part of the reorganization effort, with the goal of ensuring the profitability of the European operations and responding to the integration of the European market, General Motors Europe (GME) was established in 1986 to coordinate the Opel and Vauxhall motor vehicle operations. The size of GME may be appreciated by recognizing that, as a stand-alone operation, GME would rank sales-wise among the world's top 100 industrial corporations. The Zurich-headquartered GME is divided by both product and function, as shown in Figure 6.4. The three major operational parts are Adam Opel in Germany (almost $10 billion in 1988), Vauxhall ($3.6 billion in 1988) in the United Kingdom, and the Saab motor vehicle division, whose heads are thus in the fourth tier of GM management. There are major motor vehicle assembly operations in Belgium and Spain; the other manufacturing facilities produce components. The GME sales, services and parts operation oversees the sales operations for the European motor vehicle lines.

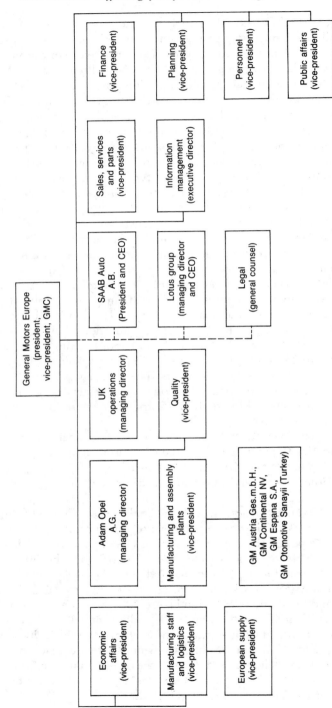

Figure 6.4 General Motors Europe organogram, 1991

Adam Opel A.G. has three manufacturing sites in Germany as well as its own product development group, and develops its own car designs with inputs from the US headquarters; but as noted it depends on GME for its marketing and sales. Opel employees see themselves as working for a German company, not an American company; and most Europeans think of Opel cars as German. Nevertheless, it is an integral part of GME, with an American managing director. Vauxhall is similarly organized and views itself as a British operation. GME is essentially a self-contained product group; compared with GM's arch-rival Ford, there have been few efforts to coordinate motor vehicle operations world-wide. GME does not even coordinate the export sales of GM's American-manufactured models (Cadillac, Buick, Oldsmobile, Pontiac and Chevrolet); their European and other international sales are managed by the US-based GM export unit.

GM's Automotive Components Group, 'a huge organization with 200,000 employees and annual sales of $30 billion' (GM, *Annual Report* 1990:5), formed its Automotive Components Group Europe (ACGE) in 1988 to coordinate its various European efforts. In the new Paris-based set-up, the business directors of GM's ten automotive component divisions continue to report operationally directly to their US-based divisional general manager; but they now also report administratively to the head of ACGE, which coordinates the strategy and the support for all the European automotive component operations. So whereas GME is essentially a directive/coordinative operation, ACGE is essentially a supportive/coordinative one.

When GM acquired Hughes Aircraft, Delco Electronics was combined with it to form GM Hughes Electronics, which employed 51,000 people and earned over $11 billion in 1990. GM Hughes Electronics has still another European headquarters arrangement. Its production groups run their own overseas manufacturing companies (see Figure 6.5), and reporting to its senior vice-president (international and marketing) are not only the domestic sales operations but also the four international offices: in Europe, the Middle East, Asia and Latin America. This European headquarters (which predates the GM acquisition of Hughes) has recently reduced its national offices from seven to four (in the United Kingdom, Sweden, Germany and Italy); it services the rest of Europe and backs up the single-person national offices with the European headquarters-based, product-specific sales force.

Other major parts of GM are Electronic Data Services (EDS) and General Motors Acceptance Corporation (GMAC). Both have continental offices in Europe, GMAC's in Zurich and EDS's in Geneva. Since GM Hughes Electronics, EDS and the Automatic Components Group, have major clients that are GM competitors, they maintain their own separate identity; there are no efforts to promote GM-wide collaboration at either a country or a continental level.

The Brussels-located General Motors Coordination Center houses several support units. One is the economic and public affairs unit which reports to a GM vice-president; its head has several additional responsibilities, one of which is to serve as the representative head of the Coordination Center. Another support unit located in the Coordination Center is the GM Regional Treasury Center (which

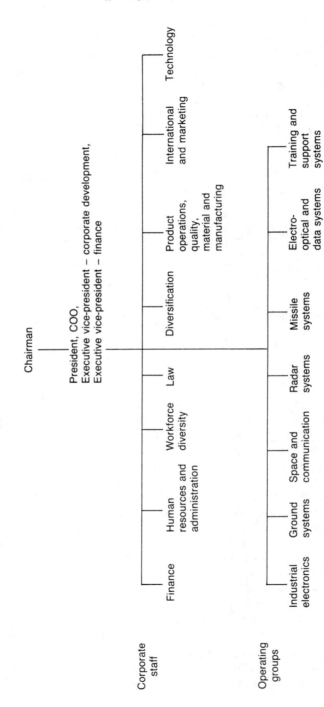

Figure 6.5 GM Hughes Aircraft organogram, 1991

reports to GM's financial office in New York). A third is the GM Acceptance Corporation Regional Finance operations (which is separate from the GMAC regional office), which reports directly to GMAC's New York headquarters.

Product-split staffing

Typically, GM's various parts hire employees and develop their careers inside their individual units over long periods of time. There is little rotation among divisions, and none among the major parts, except at the very top.

The intent of the present training programmes has been to change the way people think and respond to their jobs. As one GM manager explained: 'Changing people is difficult. First line supervisors and top management are the most difficult. They must now do more coordinating and motivating than in the past' (interview, 30 April 1990). Presently, a massive training programme is under way in Europe. The focus of the training is to encourage the employees to become active participants in their work environment in order to ensure overall quality and customer satisfaction. People are encouraged to work together to find solutions through teamwork and feedback communication loops.

Trying to merge conflicting cultures

GM has conventionally been portrayed as the paragon of a conservative, complacent and bureaucratic culture. One reason why Roger Smith as chairman initiated the purchase of the two high-tech firms Hughes and EDS was to change the corporate culture. Instead, the merger has attracted attention to the extent to which the traditional GM culture differed from the far more aggressive culture of EDS.

Increased competition in both Europe and the USA has led General Motors to make substantial changes in the past few years, but it continues to face the issue of how to achieve more synergy among its disparate parts. The difficulties confronting GM have been especially complex due to its size and diversity, and to the bureaucratic complacency that has stifled change. The massiveness of the structure presented a challenge before the corporation added Hughes and EDS. The challenge has been exacerbated with their merger and the continued conservativism of the GM culture. The mechanics for coordinating the separate networks of overseas affiliates do not appear to provide sufficient means for achieving synergies between domestic and overseas endeavours. The separate staffing of the various divisions provides little opportunity for managers to perceive how their operations fit into the overall GM mosaic. There has been insufficient effort to develop a superordinate GM culture which transcends its corporate parts. And GM continues to look at the increasingly competitive world through an American corporate perspective. These are symptoms of the challenge GM faces.

General Motors presents in exaggerated form the challenge facing the mega-sized corporation. Its large size in the early decades of the twentieth century led it to pioneer the multidivisional structure which supported and sustained its long-time lead in the American automobile industry. While GM has modified its structure over the years, its size, diversification and globalization have long since outgrown the capacity of its organization to provide the coherency required to compete effectively. GM's dominance of the American automobile industry from the late 1920s to the late 1970s generated such complacency that insufficient steps were taken to develop an organization capable of coherently aligning its massive mosaic of parts. The increased intercontinental competitiveness of the last decades of the twentieth century, and the consequent haemorrhaging losses, have demonstrated GM's organizational weaknesses. Just as GM's cumbersome organization and heavy losses in the early decades of this century encouraged the company to introduce the multidivisional organization, so its unwieldy massiveness and losses at the outset of the last decade of the twentieth century may challenge it to develop more creative approaches to organizing its diverse parts into a coherent whole.

Ford: strategic development of international alliances

Ford Motor Company pioneered the development of the vertically integrated manufacturing company. More recently, it has been an 'industry leader in the use of alliances' (Lewis, 1990:XIV). In 1990, Ford had manufacturing, assembly or sales affiliates in 24 countries outside the United States, international business relationships with automotive producers in nine countries, and a total network of more than 10,000 dealers in more than 200 countries. In 1990 Ford's international operations generated 40 per cent of its total sales.

In addition to producing cars and trucks, and the steel, glass, plastic, components and electronics for them, Ford subsidiaries engage in financial and leasing services. In order to sharpen its focus on its automotive and financial services core businesses, in 1990 Ford sold its aerospace business to Loral Corporation. It also spun-off Ford New Holland, Ford's farm and industrial equipment operation, into a $5 billion 80–20 joint venture, of which Fiat is manager and majority equity holder. Those moves contrast with the 1980s' diversification efforts of GM, Fiat and Daimler-Benz.

Like GM, Ford splits its North American vehicle operations from its international vehicle operations. Each of the three continental operations that comprise the international grouping is responsible for its own product development, manufacturing and sales. By itself, Ford of Europe, with sales exceeding $25 billion in 1990, almost equals Peugeot and Renault.

Rapid growth

Henry Ford, a mechanical tinkerer, auto-racer and entrepreneur, and eleven other investors incorporated the Ford Motor Company in 1903. This third effort of Henry Ford to found an automobile company grew rapidly (Nevins and Hill, 1954:169–252). By 1915, in an industry crowded with more than 100 competing companies, Ford with its Model T had captured a 35 per cent market share, four times that of its strongest rival, Willys-Overland (Nevins, 1957:9). In his efforts to keep well ahead of the competition, Ford articulated and acted upon the recipe: 'Expand the operations, and improve the article, and make more parts ourselves, and reduce price' (Nevins and Hill, 1954:93).

The efforts to develop a vertically integrated company led Ford to develop the Rouge plant as an integrated 'self contained auto city with twenty-seven miles of conveyers and ninety-three miles of railroad' (Hayes, 1990:18), whose 93 buildings embraced such varied activities as an open hearth and rolling mill, and a motor assembly plant. Thus, by 1926, the Rouge plant was the core of a vertically integrated production capacity in which raw material flowed from Ford coal mines in Kentucky and West Virginia and from Ford glass plants in Pennsylvania and Minnesota, the products travelled on Ford ships and Ford-owned rails, and the variety of Ford parts had expanded to include starters and generators, batteries and tyres, cloth and wire (Nevins, 1957:249–300, especially 257). The vertical integration approach of Ford contrasted with that of General Motors, which 'had a policy of controlling one-quarter of its suppliers, and Chrysler [which] obtained nearly all its supplies from independent producers' (Chandler, 1990:38).

Ford bought out his partners in 1919, so he, his wife and son Edsel became the sole owners of the empire. The growth of the corporation was achieved with a notable lack of organization. Ford's principal lieutenants were assigned to various functions, but these arrangements were informal: he disliked titles and organization, and rarely permitted an experimental task under one man to start without surreptitiously launching someone else on a similar project to promote competition. As one executive explained: 'we're not allowed to have an organizational chart' (Nevins and Hill, 1962:57–8). The frustration of working in this environment accelerated the departure of top men from Ford. One of them, William Knudsen, left Ford for General Motors and, as head of the Chevrolet division, contributed to GM's overtaking of Ford as the world's leading auto-maker in the 1920s (Chandler, 1962: 207; Halberstam, 1986: 96). The introduction of the Model A as the successor of the Model T did not stop the fall in sales.

The lack of organization combined with Henry Ford's authoritarianism, his loss of key executives, and his advancing age almost caused the collapse of the company in the early 1940s. Henry Ford II succeeded his grandfather as president in 1945. In 1946, Henry Ford, with the aid of Ernest Breech and the 'Whiz Kids', reorganized the company into two major parts: basic manufacturing and motor vehicles, with the latter embracing a Ford division and a Lincoln–Mercury division (Nevins and Hill, 1962:329, 382). With the death of Henry Ford in 1949, 95 per cent of the stock – albeit the non-voting stock – became the property of the Ford Foundation; the Ford family retained the voting stock (Nevins and Hill, 1962:334–51, 411).

The company's first major postwar effort to introduce a new model, the Edsel, failed dismally in 1957. Ford's introduction of the Mustang in 1964 was a major success, increasing Ford's profits and abetting the rise of Lee Iacocca, who became one of a troika of three presidents in 1969 (Iacocca headed North America, another headed International Operations, and a third headed 'Diversified Products'). He became Ford's president in 1970, but was fired in 1978. (He then became CEO of Chrysler.) When Henry Ford II retired as CEO in 1979 he was succeeded by Philip Caldwell, who led a massive retrenching effort.

The oil crises of the 1970s facilitated a dramatic growth of Japanese imports, which led to their capturing 25 per cent of the American market. From 1979 to 1982, Ford lost $2 billion a year. The plight of the American motor vehicle industry was so severe that the US government negotiated 'voluntary' import quotas with Japan to protect it. The Japanese development of American-based assembly plants, and the increase in American content, have brought about a production overcapacity that continues to challenge Ford as well as General Motors, and more especially threatens Chrysler.

International development

The Ford Motor Company began to export automobiles to Europe and Canada in 1903, less than six months after the company's founding. Ford Motor of Canada Limited was established in 1904, just across the Detroit River in the province of Ontario. By 1909, business prospects in Europe were so encouraging that a branch of the parent company was opened in England. Two years later, Ford organized a British company and built a car assembly plant. Ford followed up this effort by establishing companies in a number of countries in Europe, Asia/Pacific and Latin America from 1916. The highly protectionist environment of the era led Ford to develop plants in many of these countries (see Table 6.3).

While General Motors expedited its development by acquiring Opel and Vauxhall and using these names, Ford for the most part developed its own plants and used the Ford name. An exception was the 1934 purchase of the French firm Mathis, which became Matford (Nevins and Hill, 1962:88). These concerns operated with little regard for one another, and the oversight exercised by the corporate head office through travelling auditors and district supervisors, occasional roving agents and an intermittent flow of letters and cables lacked consistency and force (Nevins and Hill, 1962:78). All these overseas operations reported directly to Detroit where control, consistent with the lack of organization there, was divided among several men (Nevins, 1957:358–9).

In 1928, in order to unify all its European operations, Ford organized in England the Ford Motor Company Ltd, which held 60 per cent of most of the European companies. The British-based company functioned as an overlord of the various European fiefdoms, with Sir Percival Perry and his lieutenants keeping in close touch with them. Later, the French and the German companies, which had their own manufacturing capability, were separated from this arrangement and managed directly from the USA.

In 1948, following Perry's retirement, Ford created an international division to coordinate the various overseas sales; but Ford product divisions managed the overseas manufacturing (Wilkins and Hill, 1964:371–2). To achieve this, the role of the UK company was changed from that of a continental overlord to that of a purely national company which, along with the other national sales affiliates reported to the international division. In 1967, under the international operations umbrella, Ford created Ford of Europe Inc., based in Brentwood in England, to coordinate the European sales affiliates in 15 countries, the manufacturing facilities in Germany, France, Spain, the United Kingdom and Belgium (the Belgian one is owned and operated by Ford Werke, the German affiliate), and the product development centres in the United Kingdom and Germany. The importance of Ford of Europe and the quality of its leadership may be indicated by the fact that in 1972 its chairman was Philip Caldwell, its finance director Harold Poling, and its president Bill Bourke – the first two later became Ford CEOs and the other almost made it (Hayes, 1990:130–1, 155–63).

Ford of Europe has aggressively sought means to strengthen its European operations. In the 1980s Ford and Fiat discussed merging their European operations, but the issue of control was not resolved. Following this, Ford attempted to buy Alfa-Romeo, but Fiat's intervention and purchase frustrated this effort (Friedman, 1989:1–8). Ford did enter into a joint venture with Iveco, the commercial vehicles sector of Fiat, to create a British-based joint venture (Iveco-Ford) for producing and marketing trucks, in which Ford has a 49 per cent equity and Fiat 51 per cent. This was followed up by the spin-off of Ford New Holland into a Fiat-80–Ford-20 joint venture. Ford purchased Jaguar in 1989 and in 1992 began a 50–50 joint venture in Portugal with Volkswagen to produce multipurpose vehicles, which will be sold competitively through each company's European dealer network.

In 1970, Ford followed up the reshuffle of the European operations by organizing a Latin American automobile operations grouping (headquartered in Dearborn) to coordinate the affiliates in Venezuela and the Ford–Volkswagen joint venture, Autolatina (in Brazil and Argentina), in which Ford has a 49 per cent stake. To create the joint venture, which is 'the biggest private employer in Latin America and the eighth largest auto firm in the world', Ford and Volkswagen 'had to work through two corporate cultures, four different languages (English, Spanish, Portuguese and German), and four national cultures (American, Argentine, Brazilian, and West German)' (Lewis, 1990:131–2, 253).

In the same year, Ford also established Ford Asia/Pacific, headquartered near Melbourne, for the coordination of Ford affiliates in Australia, New Zealand and Taiwan, and a joint venture in Malaysia. In 1979, Ford acquired a 29 per cent equity interest in Toyo Kogyo, a car, truck and machine tool producer based in Hiroshima, Japan, and now known as Mazda Motors. In 1986, Ford established a Northern Pacific Business Development office (NPBD), headquartered in Tokyo, to coordinate its interests and develop business in Japan, Korea and other Northern Pacific countries. In Korea, Ford acquired a 10 per cent stake in the Kia Motor Corporation in 1986. In Japan, Ford now markets a variety of Ford-badged, Mazda-manufactured vehicles which are sold through Autorama, a 38 per cent

Table 6.3 Ford around the world

CONTINENT/ Country	Dates operations begun				1991 affiliates operations					
	Branch	Affiliate	Assembly	Manufacturing	Sales	Sales and assembly	Sales and manufacturing	Business alliances	Employees	Dealers
NORTH AMERICA										
Canada		1904		1904			X		16 000	680
Mexico		1925	1926	1983			X		9 700	130
EUROPE										
Ford of Europe		1967								
Austria		1947			X				70	290
Belgium		1922	1922^c		X		Plant owned by Ford-Werke		22 000	120
Denmark		1919	1919^c		X				88	74
Finland		1926			X				150	55
France	1908	1916	1913–54 1973				Transmission plant		4 500	1 400
Germany		1925	1926	1931			Manufacturing, plastics and R&D		50 000	2 100
Ireland		1917			X				80	60
Italy		1923	1922^c		X		Chemical design subsidiary		300	250
Netherlands		1924			X				174	210
Norway		1960			X				130	61
Portugal		1932	1964			X		Multi-purpose vehicle w/VW – 1992	680	40
Spain		1919	1919–54	1976			Manufacturing		10 800	106
Sweden		1924	1949–58		X				210	85
Switzerland		1948			X				140	364
United Kingdom	1909	1911	1911	1931			Manufacturing	Iveco Ford Truck w/Fiat	45 000	1 000

					Manufacturing			
LATIN AMERICA								
L.A. Automation Operations								
Argentina	1970	1913	1959	1922^c		Auto-Latina-Argentina w/VW – 1987	7 000	200
Brazil		1917	1968–87	1987 / 1922^c		Auto-Latina-Argentina w/VW – 1987	50 000	400
Venezuela	1911	1959	1959–87	1987	x		1 000	90
ASIA/PACIFIC								
Ford								
Asia/Pacific								
Australia	1909	1970	1925			Model sharing agreement with Nissan – 1987	12 000	350
Japan		1925–39, 1974	1925–39					
Korea						24% Mazda – 1979 / 10% Kia Motors – 1986	450	Mazda* 50
Malaysia	1926							
New Zealand		1936				Anim Holding – 1985 / With Mazda – 1987	300	71
Taiwan		1972					400	40
Turkey	1928					30% in Otosan – 1983	3 000	

Note: ^c = Later closed
*Ford has used the Mazda network of dealers rather than develop its own dealer network.

Source: Collated from Ford International 'Ford Around the World' – August 1989; Nevins, 1957; Nevins and Hill, 1954, 1962.

Mazda-owned network of dealers in which Ford acquired a 34 per cent stake in 1989. In the same year, with the shift of Ford Asia/Pacific in focus, Ford moved its Asia/Pacific headquarters from Melbourne to Tokyo.

Two major groupings

Ford Motor Company and its many subsidiaries are organized into two major groups: Ford Automotive Group and Ford Financial Services Group (see Figure 6.6). Presiding over this complex is an all-American seventeen-member board, of which five are executive officers and three others are Ford family members (William Clay Ford, Henry II's younger brother, who is a retired vice-chairman, and two fourth-generation Fords, both of whom are middle-level Ford executives). The Office of the Chief Executive, first created on the recommendation of McKinsey & Co. in 1977 (Hayes, 1990:174–9), consists of the chairman/CEO, the president/COO, the head of the Ford Automotive Group and the chief financial officer.

The Ford Financial Services Group, which in the early 1990s was the sole source of Ford profits, includes Ford Credit, First Nationwide Bank and its associates, and US Leasing International. Ford Credit, which provides credit to car buyers, has its own international affiliates. First Nationwide is one of America's largest thrift institutions. US Leasing leases office equipment as well as automobiles.

The Ford Automotive Group, the company's principal core business, separates North American from international operations. North American Automotive operations splits along functional lines, separating car product development, manufacturing operations (which includes the Mexican company) and sales operations. Sales operations include a Ford division, a Lincoln–Mercury division, and Ford Motor Company of Canada. In order to reduce the lead time required to develop and bring a new model to the market, Ford has pushed the concept of simultaneous engineering, which brings the sales and manufacturing people together with the product design and engineering people to work together on the development of new models. The creation of the Powertrain Operations unit has facilitated the effort.

In contrast, the International Automotive Operations splits by continent, with European, Latin-American and Asian-Pacific components, each of which is divided functionally. Ford of Europe, for example has organized itself as an analogue version of North American Automotive Operations with product development, manufacturing, sales and finance and administration separated – each with its own vice-president, who together with the Ford of Europe chairman and president form the executive committee managing the European operations. The European sales vice-president oversees the fifteen European sales affiliates; the engineering and manufacturing group vice-president directs the European manufacturing operations; and the product programmes and Powertrain group vice-president manages the product development. Within the various affiliates, in addition to the sales corps, there are sales support units. The company considers itself a European company with American parentage. As Jan Candries, Ford's Director of European

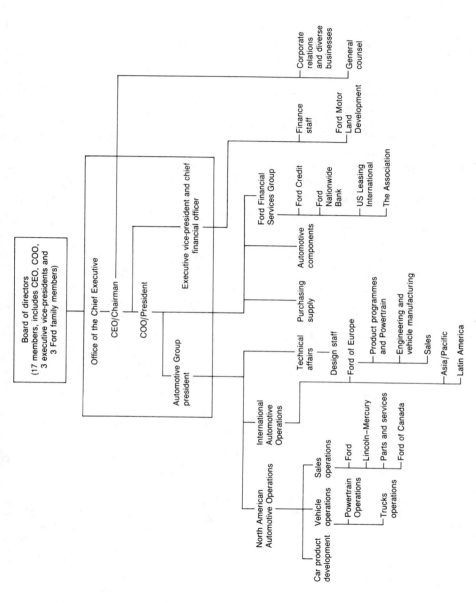

Figure 6.6 Ford Motor Company organogram, 1991 (Source: Adapted and simplified from Ford Company organization chart, 1 May 1991)

Affairs, noted: 'With our continentally dispersed operations, in a sense, we are more European than Fiat, which is basically a national championed company' (interview, 20 November 1991).

Function-specific and increasingly country-specific

Ford recruits its professional and managerial corps by continent and by country. Following initial testing, but without initial training, Ford assigns the new hirees to their first posts. Ford recruits generally expect to remain for their career in the functional operation to which they are initially assigned. Only at the higher ranks does Ford make an effort to shift executives into different operations in order to broaden their experience. As in other sharply divisionalized companies, the lack of opportunity for mobility for many in the more specialized functional areas has frustrated those Ford managers who perceive this as limiting their chances for advancement. To overcome this Ford of Europe has taken a few steps to broaden the perspective of its managers, increase their mobility, and thereby improve its organizational effectiveness.

Ford has undertaken efforts to internationalize the staffing of its international operations. 'Overseas, each of Ford's fifteen European companies is headed by a European executive. Virtually all have either worked in or are nationals of other countries. Moreover, an increasing number of Europeans are moving to senior management posts at Ford headquarters in the United States' (Lewis, 1990:286). In 1991 Ford of Europe created a common management development organization for Europe. Until then Ford's European training efforts had been fragmented among its various units, thus there had not been a concerted effort to develop a sense of shared corporate values, an appreciation of the diversity of efforts, and the leadership skills required in cross-unit collaboration. Ford's major world-wide leadership development effort, which regularly brought a cross-section of managers together from throughout the world to Detroit to focus on corporate strategy, was discontinued in the budget crunch several years ago.

A 1991-initiated effort to reduce costs may have further impact on the cross-fertilization efforts so necessary to team efforts. Ford of Europe's '30–30–30' staff reduction programme intends to cut 30 per cent of the higher level managers, 30 per cent of its staff in 'indirect services' (that is, those not directly producing) and 30 per cent of those serving outside their home countries. The cutback in those assigned outside their home country will reduce the possibility of the mutual appreciation of diversity which is vital to international teamwork.

In order to develop its sense of commonality, Ford has not only sold and spun off ancillary businesses, but has also developed and distributed widely a statement of mission as the basis of its shared values. As in many companies, though, without active promotion and application throughout the organization the statements tend to go into drawers and stay there. One Ford executive told me that given a little time he was sure he could find it (he did).

Ford as a continental competitor

Ford has moved adroitly and aggressively to develop its continental presence – in Western Europe, Australia, South America and East Asia. The recent development of the alliances in South America with Volkswagen and in East Asia with Mazda and Kia have significantly increased its presence on these continents. The efforts to ally Ford of Europe with Fiat would have significantly enhanced its European presence. The Portuguese-based Ford–Volkswagen joint venture may be an indication of further efforts to develop and solidify its grasp of a major share of the European market.

The rapid expansion and integration of the European market is forcing Ford and other volume car manufacturers long-established in Europe – General Motors, Volkswagen, Fiat, Peugeot and Renault – to consider how to strengthen their competitive position. The Japanese manufacturers – Toyota, Nissan and Honda – have already cut into the European market and expect to double their car sales in the European Community by the year 2000, and to increase their Europe-based manufacturing capacity to sustain these sales. Ford, like longer-established European manufacturers, has suffered financial losses. Especially concerned are Fiat, Peugeot and Renault whose home markets have long been protected but will not continue to be so. Many are seeking acquisitions, mergers and strategic alliances such as Renault's with Volvo, GM's purchase of half of Saab, and Ford's purchase of Jaguar and joint venture with Volkswagen.

Exxon: Exxon International runs foreign oil, not chemical, businesses

Exxon's two major businesses have long been upstream oil and downstream oil. With its multidivisional reorganization in 1927, Standard Oil of New Jersey (as the company was then named) created an international division to develop and manage its operations outside the USA and Canada. In 1966, while the company continued to separate its upstream oil and downstream oil operations domestically, the international operations were divided into four regional groupings that managed both upstream and downstream operations. In 1986, driven by the effort to economize, Exxon created Exxon Company International and closed the regional headquarters by merging their operations into the US-based international company.

While Exxon Chemical, organized in 1966 as a separate business, generates only a fraction of Exxon's total sales, as a stand-alone company its $10 billion sales would rank it among the world's major companies. Exxon combines its international upstream and downstream oil operations into one international organization, but the different conditions facing the oil businesses and the chemical ones have led Exxon to organize the international operations of Exxon Chemical separately from the oil businesses.

A Rockefeller progeny

John D. Rockefeller founded Standard Oil in 1870. By 1883 he had, ruthlessly by many accounts, 'gobbled up his rivals [. . . and] formed the Standard Oil Trust on a continental scale. [. . .] By 1885 seventy percent of the Standard's business was overseas' (Sampson, 1988:41–9). To avoid Ohio antitrust litigation, Rockefeller reconstituted the corporate interests into a holding company called Standard Oil (New Jersey). Later in 1911, following lengthy federal antitrust litigation, the Standard Oil trust was divided into more than 30 companies. Four of these progeny continue to rank among the world's eight largest oil companies. Standard Oil (New Jersey) has changed its name to Exxon but continues to market its oil products overseas under the brand name Esso. Standard Oil (New York), which early on merged with Vacuum to form Socony-Vacuum, has become Mobil. Standard Oil (California), long called Socal and now named Chevron, has absorbed Gulf. Standard Oil (Indiana) has renamed itself Amoco. A fifth offspring, Standard Oil (Ohio) or Sohio, has been merged into British Petroleum.

Following the break-up of the trust, Standard Oil (New Jersey), which inherited a major share of the crude oil production strength of the old trust, moved rapidly to expand its domestic refinery and marketing. In the early 1920s shortages of American crude oil led the other major American oil companies to develop crude oil sources in many parts of the world in order to assure themselves of adequate supplies. But the opening of new fields in Louisiana and Texas in the 1920s and the depression of the 1930s caused many firms to sell their foreign holdings – principally to Standard Oil (New Jersey), Socony-Vacuum (now Mobil) and Texaco. These firms, together with Gulf, Standard Oil (California), Royal Dutch/Shell and British Petroleum – the so-called Seven Sisters – thus dominated the world oil industry for several decades (Chandler 1990:99–100).

The rapid development of Standard Oil (New Jersey) led to a recognition of structural weaknesses and to several attempts at *ad hoc* reorganization in the 1920s. In 1927, it created a multidivisional, more decentralized structure (Chandler, 1962:163–224). 'Among the operating divisions were Imperial Oil, Ltd (which operated in Canada and supervised subsidiaries in Peru and Colombia), and the "European and Latin American Group" (the equivalent of other corporations' "international company" or "overseas and export group")' (Wilkins, 1974:148). In the surge of American business overseas expansion in the postwar years, the American oil companies were especially aggressive. As a consequence, 'in the 1960s, the largest international oil companies reorganized their businesses to leave the old international division (or any variant of it) behind. [. . .] In 1966, Standard Oil of New Jersey announced "a major reorganization" of its overseas businesses. It transferred much of its foreign operations to four regional groups' (Wilkins, 1974:388). By the 1980s these groups were labelled Europe, Asia/Pacific, Inter-America (South and Central America) and Middle East. Twenty years later, in 1986, in an effort to improve competitiveness by reducing costs, Exxon again reorganized. With the intention of reducing overlapping responsibilities and layers of management, Exxon not only eliminated many executive positions and cut its corporate headquarters in New York from over 2,000 to less than 300 (principally by transferring many to other offices), but also merged its four regional offices into one US-based international company. At the same time, its Exxon Chemical subsidiary began a series of reorganizations in which it adjusted and readjusted the product area matrix with which it runs its overseas operations. By 1990 Exxon operated in 80 countries.

A geography-divided and product-divided structure

Exxon Corporation, whose headquarters moved in 1990 from the Rockefeller Center in New York to Irving, Texas, consists of several major subsidiary operating companies (see Table 6.4). Three of these divide oil and natural gas, both upstream (exploration and production) and downstream (refining and marketing), along geographic lines:

- Exxon Company USA, headquartered in Houston, which manages Exxon's US-based upstream and downstream oil businesses.
- Exxon Company International, headquartered in Florham Park, New Jersey, which manages all Exxon upstream and downstream oil businesses outside the USA and Canada.
- Imperial Oil Limited (Canada), 69 per cent owned by Exxon, which embraces all Exxon's upstream and downstream oil and chemical businesses in Canada.

The non-oil businesses are as follows:

- Exxon Chemical, formerly headquartered in Darien, Connecticut, and now in Houston, Texas, which generated almost $11 billion in 1988.
- Exxon Coal and Minerals, located in Houston, which generated less than $2 billion in 1988.

Table 6.4 Exxon Corporation companies and their businesses

Subsidiary company	Upstream	Downstream	Chemicals	Coal/mineral power
Exxon USA	x	x		
Exxon Company International	x	x		
Imperial Oil (Canada)	x	x	x	x
Exxon Chemical			x	
Exxon Coal and Minerals				x

In addition, there are two research and development subsidiaries, one Central Services division, and one world-wide explorations division, established in 1991 by bringing together parts from Exxon USA and Exxon Company International. Thus a mixture of product and area considerations has shaped the organization of the principal parts of Exxon Corporation.

Central headquarters

   The Exxon Board of Directors consists of fifteen persons, six of whom are the senior Exxon executives; that is, the chairman, the president and four senior vice-presidents. All but two of the directors are American, one is the British chairman of United Biscuits (Holdings) and one is a Canadian senior vice-president. The chairman, president and four senior vice-presidents constitute the Exxon Corporation management committee as well as its 'compensation and executive development committee (COED)'. Each of the six management committee members has a portfolio as the contact executive with the various parts of the multinational mosaic (see Figure 6.7). Each of the six oversees one of the subsidiary/operating companies. Five of the six have functional portfolios, and two have 'business portfolios' ('upstream' and 'downstream' oil) which transcend three of the operating companies: Exxon Company (USA), Exxon Company International and Imperial Oil (Canada).

Exxon Company International

Prior to 1986 Exxon's international petroleum business was managed via five offices:

1. Esso Europe (based in London), which also included Middle East/Africa downstream.
2. Esso Eastern Asia/Pacific (headquartered in Houston).
3. Esso Inter-America Central and South America (headquartered in Coral Gables, Florida).
4. Esso Middle East (headquartered in New York), which handled Middle East upstream.
5. Exxon International Company (based in Florham Park, New Jersey), which was responsible for services such as global supply and transportation.

With the reorganization, these operations were consolidated into the Exxon Company International (ECI) headquarters office in New Jersey. The 21 international affiliates thus report directly to the ECI management committee, which consists of the ECI president and four others (one focusing on upstream and another on downstream operations). All five ECI management committee members have portfolios as the contact executive for two or more of the 21 international affiliates.

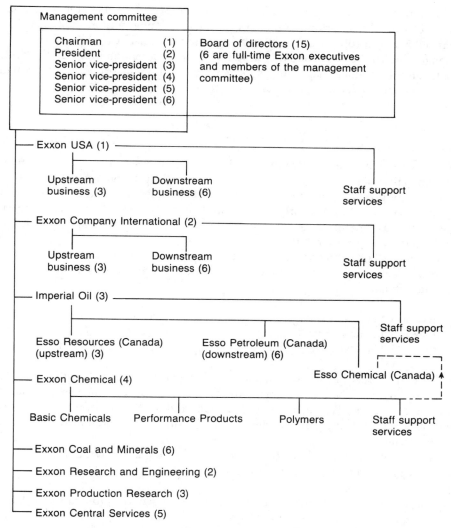

Note: ( ) = Corporate executive team liaison roles.

Figure 6.7   Exxon Corporation organogram, 1991 (with management committee executive contact designations)

Exxon's international affiliates have an integrated responsibility for whatever upstream as well as downstream operations are located within their borders. Country general managers (entitled presidents) have profit-and-loss responsibility for all Exxon oil activities and represent Exxon in all corporate interests, including not only Exxon oil but also chemical and other interests. Most affiliates have, in addition to their country general manager, a senior executive in charge of upstream, one in charge of marketing, and one in charge of refining, and in the larger ones a financial manager too. These senior executives are responsible to the country general manager and to their functional colleagues in the ECI headquarters. Both the area heads and the functional contact persons play a major role in performance appraisals and career postings and promotions.

Exxon Chemical

Exxon Chemical has undergone a series of changes which have shaped its development since its creation in the 1950s as a marketing organization for the chemical by-products of the oil company. The chemical-related manufacturing operations were split off from petroleum and added to Exxon Chemical in the late 1960s. It was organized by area until 1973, when the company introduced a product-and-geography matrix.

From 1973 to 1986 Exxon Chemical was organized by product into ten product line groups, each with a product line vice-president. By area it was divided into three regional affiliates:

1. Exxon Chemicals Americas.
2. Exxon Chemicals Europe.
3. Exxon Chemicals Asia/Pacific.

Each of these was headed by a regional president, assisted by product line vice-presidents who worked closely with the world-wide product line vice-presidents. The country general managers, in whom profit-and-loss responsibility was focused, were responsible principally to the regional heads, and secondarily for product development and strategy.

The 1986-reorganized Exxon Chemical consolidated the ten chemical product divisions into three chemical 'business' groups:

1. Basic Chemicals (formerly based in Brussels, moved to Houston in 1991).
2. Polymers (formerly based in Darien, now in Houston).
3. Performance Products (formerly based in Darien, now in Houston).

The new arrangement, as intended, unbalanced the matrix by clearly placing the responsibility for strategy and operations on the 'business groups'. Two regional offices retained coordinating roles: Exxon Chemical Americas (based in Houston) remained responsible for the USA and Latin America; Exxon Chemical International (based in Brussels) combined the responsibilities of Exxon Chemical Europe and Exxon Chemical Asia/Pacific. Each of the three chemical business groups developed technical, marketing and manufacturing sections to work closely with the national affiliates, which were organized into three units to correspond to the three chemical business groups. Under the 1986 plan, the country (or area) general manager initially was operationally responsible for the technical and support services, but had only an administrative coordinating role regarding the three business units, whose heads reported operationally to their Exxon Chemical International business group head.

Two years after the 1986 reorganization, Exxon Chemical modified the matrix to encourage area coordination. Since those designated as country (or area) general managers had insufficient 'clout' to secure cooperation among the local business units, senior persons (such as Exxon Chemical International business heads) were given additional responsibilities as country/area heads with some administrative as well as representative head functions. In this revised arrangement, the country business unit heads continued to report primarily to their respective Exxon Chemical International business group heads. In some cases the two 'boss' roles are filled by the same person.

In 1991–2, Exxon Chemical began a further modification of its organization. The move of its Basic Chemicals head office to Houston and the separation of the post of European senior executive and the Basic Chemicals headship were the initial phase of this effort.

Separate staff recruitment, training and posting

Exxon Corporation's staffing policies and practices have several features which transcend its divisions. Exxon management staffing stresses recruiting top engineering graduates directly off campus, extensive on-the-job training and development, and annual appraisals. The accent on recruiting those with outstanding academic records has fostered a sense of self-confidence and pride.

Exxon Corporation emphasizes the importance of human resources development by focusing the responsibility for the annual reviews on 'compensation and executive development committees', composed of the same senior executives who comprise the management committees, which are replicated at each level of the organization. At each level a manager meets formally with his or her area and functional/product contact persons three times a year: once to set business objectives, once to review performance vs. plan, and once to discuss people development. Management staff are regularly reviewed for performance and potential. High-flyers are identified early and moved quickly; their assignments are arranged and assessed with special care. The quality of the management staff combined with the stimulus of the annual reviews has generated a spirit of competitiveness which pervades Exxon, and may facilitate interdivisional and intercompany postings at the higher levels.

For decades Exxon Company International has developed host country nationals to manage its affiliates. Prior to the 1980s retrenchment, Exxon balanced this effort by developing and supporting an international corps of Americans who were posted to overseas assignments of several years duration. More recently, Exxon has begun to re-exert its efforts to develop and sustain a cadre of Americans for specific overseas posts and has begun to post non-Americans to headquarters assignments in the USA, in order to develop an international corps with shared appreciation of corporate goals. The net impact has been that the management staff of most oil affiliates are primarily host country nationals, with Americans serving mainly in finance and upstream posts. With the increasing integration of the EC countries there may well be more third country nationals.

Having noted the commonalities, however, one also notes the extent to which the Exxon companies recruit separately, conduct their training programmes separately, and orchestrate the careers of their managers separately. Most Exxon managers have spent their entire careers in one of the companies. While in the past those engineers who have made their career in the world of rigs, platforms, refineries and pipelines, whose Exxon heartland has been the southwest USA, have been more likely to make it to the corporate-wide posts (Sampson, 1988:203, 270), there have been increasing efforts not only to move more especially promising managers from company to company but also to promote them to corporate-wide posts.

Different styles and approaches

The Exxon companies recognize that they operate in a constantly changing political and business environment and as a consequence must continually adapt their ways of doing business. The differences in the conditions facing the older oil business and the newer and faster-changing chemicals businesses have generated different organizational approaches. While Exxon has divided its oil operations geographically, the chemicals side has subdivided itself by product. Separate recruitment, separate staff development and different conditions have led to the Exxon Chemical staff identifying with Exxon Chemical, not with Exxon as a whole. Many of the Exxon Chemical staff believe that the highly competitive nature of the chemicals business has driven them to promote empowerment and teams far more than the oil businesses, which they believe are more tradition-bound and hierarchy-conscious. Thus in working with the Exxon top management, as one Exxon Chemical senior manager has expressed it, 'we must work a bit harder to assure that the value differences do not become a source of friction and disruption' (interview, Peter Ham, 2 May 1990).

Global product divisions manage international operations

Mobil: business-separated international operations

Mobil has organized its major overseas divisions around its principal businesses (upstream oil, downstream oil and chemicals). In 1990 Mobil created a new London-based Mobil Europe Center of Operations to coordinate its European marketing and refining (downstream) affiliates, in an effort to 'improve efficiency and take full advantage of the opportunities associated with a single European market in 1992' (Mobil press release, 23 August 1990).

Crisis and change

Mobil Corporation traces its origins to the 1866 founding of the Vacuum Oil Company. In 1879 the Standard Oil Company, headed by John D. Rockefeller, purchased a 75 per cent interest in Vacuum, and in 1882 Rockefeller merged it into the Standard Oil Trust. Following five years of antitrust litigation, in 1911 the US Supreme Court ordered the Trust to be broken into more than 30 smaller companies; Vacuum and Standard Oil Company of New York (Socony) were two of these. In the next two decades, to develop their capacity to compete, both companies acquired several oil companies. In 1931, Socony acquired Vacuum, whose refining and marketing strength complemented Socony's production strength.

Socony-Vacuum developed substantial interests abroad before World War II. In 1933 it merged its Far East facilities with those of Standard Oil (New Jersey) to form the 50–50 owned Standard Vacuum Oil Company (Stan Vac), with integrated operations in 50 countries. By World War II Socony-Vacuum had also developed a network of affiliates in Europe with two refineries.

By 1950 Socony-Vacuum had redeveloped its overseas operations far beyond its prewar capacity. In 1955 the company took advantage of its widely recognized brand name by changing the corporate name to Socony Mobil Oil Company (in 1966 the name was again changed, to Mobil Oil Corporation). The 1956–7 Suez crisis critically affected the company's earnings (along with those of most international oil companies) and led to its retrenchment and reorganization. Several domestic subsidiaries were merged into the parent company, which divided itself into two major divisions: the Mobil Oil Company for the USA and Canada, and Mobil International Oil Company for the rest of the world (except for the area served by Stan Vac, until its 1962 split between the two parent companies). In 1960 the Mobil Chemical company was formed as the corporation began to expand into petrochemicals, principally by acquiring chemical companies. Later, Mobil's Mining and Minerals Company was separated from Mobil Chemical.

In 1970 the company established Mobil Oil Estates Ltd, now named the Mobil Land Development Corporation. In 1974 Mobil diversified even further by acquiring Montgomery Ward (the American general merchandise retailer) and Container Corporation of America – moves which led to the creation of Mobil Corporation as a holding company embracing Mobil Oil Corporation and the two newly acquired non-oil businesses. The dramatic 1970s' expansion of Mobil Oil's efforts and earnings led to a reorganization of its petroleum operations. The company redivided its operations by establishing a world-wide Exploration and Production Division with responsibility for all company upstream activities related to crude oil, natural gas, gas liquids, coal and minerals, and a world-wide Marketing and Refining Division consolidating the operations of the US and International downstream units.

The changing conditions of the 1980s led to major consolidating efforts. These included the sale of Container Corporation of America, Montgomery Ward and other assets that no longer fitted with the company's long-term plans, and the purchase of Superior Oil in 1984 for $5.7 billion. In 1990 the company moved from its New York headquarters to Fairfax, Virginia, outside the American capital. Thus, Mobil's story has been one of repeated change – generally in response to crises, sometimes revolutionary, more often gradual.

Two major divisions and three lesser ones

Mobil's seventeen-member, all-American board includes its chairman, its president (who heads Mobil Oil, the major part of Mobil), two executive vice-presidents (of upstream and downstream oil), the financial vice-president and three other vice-presidents. Mobil Oil continues to divide itself into two major divisions: exploration and producing (the upstream) and marketing and refining (the downstream). Organized under one vice-president are Mobil Chemical and two smaller businesses: Mobil Mining and Minerals and Mobil Solar Synergy (see Figure 6.8). Upstream and downstream oil are both divided by area: upstream has affiliates in each of the countries in which it is exploring or producing; downstream has affiliates in each of the countries in which there are refining and retail operations.

In 1990, Mobil's marketing and refining division established a new Mobil Europe Center of Operations, located in London. It has Europe-wide responsibility for the marketing and refining operations of the sixteen European affiliates, which have interests in seven refineries and a service station network in thirteen European and thirteen African countries. The new centre comprises two units, one for marketing and one for refining and supply; with this change the company has implemented a common integrated information and accounting system for its European marketing and refining operations. This change involved transferring the president of Mobil Europe (the service company based in Fairfax, Virginia, outside Washington, DC) to London to head the new centre.

Mobil Chemical, now also located in Fairfax, Virginia, comprises four product divisions – chemical products (which in 1991 absorbed consumer products), films, petrochemicals and plastic packaging – as well as a staff support unit, and a semi-autonomous trading company. All divisions, and some of their subdivisions, have their own set of international affiliates. The Petrochemical Division, for example, has an international affiliate (Mobil Petrochemicals International, Ltd.) headquartered in Brussels, Belgium. While its administration is centralized in Brussels, sales and marketing are basically decentralized, with over twenty overseas sales offices and a regional office located in Singapore. Although Mobil Petrochemicals International, Ltd. has no manufacturing facilities of its own, it does exercise effective control over 50 per cent of the production of a petrochemicals plant in Saudi Arabia, which is 50 per cent Mobil owned. Due primarily to the diversity in products and customers, there has been little attempt to coordinate Mobil's oil and chemical business operations or even the efforts of the

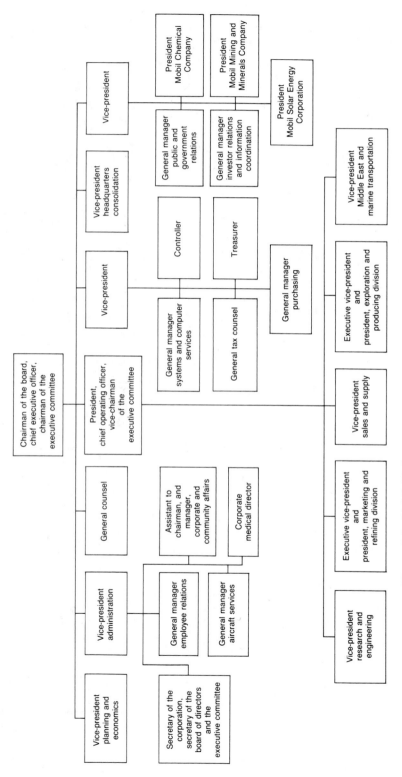

Figure 6.8 Mobil Oil Corporation organogram, 1991 (Source: Mobil Oil)

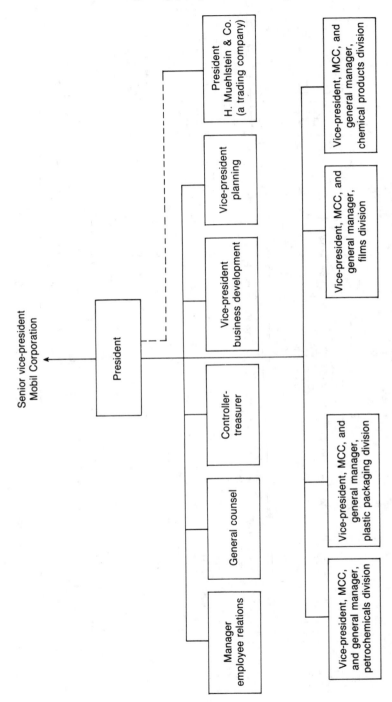

Figure 6.9 Mobil Chemical Company (MCC) organogram, 1991 (Source: Mobil Oil)

various Mobil chemical units in any country or continent (see Figure 6.9). The various units work in virtual isolation from one another with no company efforts to cooperate regarding public affairs, staffing or other issues.

Separate staffing and shared values

The upstream, downstream, chemical and other businesses generally recruit, post, promote, and handle management development separately. The corporate offices assist the operating companies in coordinating their recruitment efforts, facilitate the movement of especially promising financial, information and other functional senior managers among companies, and help in developing training programmes; but the responsibility rests essentially with the companies. Although this pattern is changing, most management careers are spent essentially in one company and often in one division. The companies have relied increasingly on host country employees. In the more mature refining and marketing affiliates, the management staff have, since the late 1960s, tended to be almost wholly host country nationals with relatively few Americans. In the more recently developed chemical affiliates, Americans continue to dominate the senior management posts. While most of those on international assignments have tended to be Americans, recently a few of the international affiliate staff have been posted for short-term assignments at Mobil Chemical in the United States.

Mobile contrasted with Exxon

Mobil differs from Exxon in a number of respects. First, each of Mobil's major parts – upstream oil, downstream oil, chemicals, and even mining and minerals – has its own overseas affiliates. Only downstream oil has developed an overseas centre – the new London-based Mobil Europe Center of Operations – to coordinate some of its overseas affiliates. Within each country the affiliates operate autonomously – with no effort, unlike Exxon, to assign one officer as the senior person to represent Mobil's corporate-wide interests.

General Electric (GE): from repeated restructuring to 'shared management practices'

Towards the dream of a 'boundaryless company'

General Electric (GE), the world's seventh largest industrial corporation and one of the more diversified, combines what were once more than 300 companies. Its corporate executive team stresses that: 'While our seemingly diverse businesses range from a television network to financial services, from plastics to jet engines, there is a unique common thread – *shared management practices* – that binds them together and creates what we call integrated diversity' (*Annual Report* 1989:4). The statement calls attention not only to GE's efforts to create common bonds but also to the extent of GE's diversification and how very little its businesses have in common.

Over several decades, continuing efforts to improve GE's profits and management effectiveness have led successive General Electric CEOs to introduce dramatic reorganizations. Those in the 1950s 'decentralized with a vengeance' (Pascale, 1990:177), introducing divisions as self-contained 'businesses'. Those in the 1960s changed the basis on which the divisions were organized; those in the 1970s introduced strategic business units (SBUs) (which were widely studied and copied); those in the 1980s radically reduced the layers of management and simplified the corporate structure. GE's organizational 'dream for the 90s is a boundaryless company, a company where we knock down the walls that separate us [...] an admittedly grand vision, requiring unprecedented cultural change' (*Annual Report* 1989:5). While these changes 'have at times done "violence" to the organization' (Pascale, 1990:177), GE's strategy appears to have been enhanced by these strong initiatives.

Each of the various GE components has developed its own networks of national affiliates. But GE has introduced a distinctive feature: an international division which promotes new business development, coordinates efforts among the various GE affiliates in a country, and provides administrative support to the smaller overseas offices.

Repeated restructuring led by strong CEOs

GE traces its beginning to the company Thomas Edison created in 1877 to manufacture and market his electric inventions (see Passer, 1953, for general history). In 1892, a group led by Charles Coffin merged the Edison firm with another to form General Electric. GE and Westinghouse, which formed a patent pool in 1896, soon dominated the American electrical industry. By the early 1900s General Electric and Westinghouse, working closely with European first-movers Siemens & Halske and Allgemeine Elektrizitäts-Gesellschaft (AEG), had become the leaders of a global oligopoly that was to remain little changed until well after World War II (Chandler, 1990:69). Under Coffin and his successor, Gerald Swope, GE diversified rapidly. 'The number of GE's product lines (lines in which the operating results were accounted for separately) rose from 10 in 1900, to 30 in 1910, to 85 in 1920, to 193 in 1930, and to 281 in 1940. By World War II it had developed one of the most diversified product lines of any industrial enterprise in the world' (Chandler, 1990:221).

GE began to expand abroad early in the twentieth century. GE licensed its technology throughout Europe, China, Japan and Latin America in return for positions in those areas' electrical companies. 'In Japan, as early as 1905 it acquired a controlling interest in Tokyo Electric; and five years later it purchased a minority interest in Shibaura Electric' (Chandler, 1990:217). Later these Japanese concerns merged as Tokyo Shibaura Electric, today known as Toshiba (Abegglen and Stalk, 1958:224). By the 1920s GE's international subsidiary, 1919-formed International General Electric Company (IGEC), had already developed national affiliates in France, Belgium, Switzerland, Italy, Sweden and Britain (Chandler, 1990:351-3). By 1929, IGEC possessed a significant interest in the newly merged Associated Electrical Industries, Britain's leading electrical enterprise, and maintained a minor stake in General Electric Ltd, Britain's second largest electrical company. In 1929 GE also acquired a substantial minority holding in Allgemeine Elektrizitäts-Gesellschaft (AEG), thus re-establishing its previous connections (Wilkins, 1974: 67). 'By 1935 GE owned 29% of Siemens, and 10% of Philips and had joint ventures in China and Japan and throughout Latin America' (Pascale, 1990:181).

Wartime losses and postwar antitrust actions forced GE to sell many of its foreign holdings, hence abruptly ending GE's overseas development:

> as a consequence [...] top management at General Electric had lost enthusiasm for foreign investment; General Electric's international business empire that had been developed since the 1880's and that Gerald Swope and Owen Young had so carefully constructed during the 1920's had been torn asunder. Only majority-owned subsidiaries (mainly in Latin America and Canada) were left untouched in the aftermath of the court decisions and subsequent reparations by General Electric. These were not the heart of the business. The empire was in shambles. When in the 1960's General Electric would begin to rebuild, it had to start almost from scratch. (Wilkins, 1974:295)

Charles Watson, who became CEO in 1940, served until 1952, with breaks for government service during World War II. The growth of GE during World War II, combined perhaps with Watson's absence, forced the company to reorganize in the 1950s. Following the pre-World War II example of Du Pont, Exxon and GM, General Electric, now led by Ralph Cordiner, dramatically decentralized – creating a series of self-contained businesses with a specific product-market scope and their own marketing, engineering, manufacturing, finance and employee relations functions. This decentralization effort was accompanied by the introduction of 'management by objective' and a stress on each unit achieving financial 'hurdle rates', as well as the utilization of the now-famous GE logo to enhance brand identity (Pascale, 1990:184–5). As GE continued to grow, and to face threats to the corporate profit margins, this postwar reorganization was followed by several more over the following decades (Aguilar and Hamermesh, 1981a, 1981b; Springer and Hofer, 1984: see Table 6.5).

In 1963 GE, under Fred Borch who succeeded Cordiner, changed the top management structures by reorganizing the company's various groups and divisions around similar markets, customers and distribution systems, rather than on the basis of similarity of products, technologies and manufacturing processes as had earlier been the case. As a result of this change and also because of the increased size of the

Table 6.5 Some General Electric organizational evolution benchmarks

Date (CEO)	Sales ($ billions)	Employees	Sectors	Groups	Divisions	Subdivisions	SBU	Departments
1954 (Cordiner)	3.3	244 000		5	20			7
1958 (Cordiner)	5.2	290 000		5	20			±12
1968 (Borch)	8.4	396 000	10	10	48			±17
1972 (Borch)	10.2	369 000	10	10	48		43	17
1978 (Jones)	22.5	405 000	6	9	49		49	17
1990 (Welch)	58.4	298 000			13	40		

Source: Aguilar and Hamermesh 1981a, 1981b; Springer and Hofer, 1984.

company, the number of divisions was increased from 20 to 29 and the number of departments from fewer than 80 to 120.

In 1968 a further change was made with the establishment of a five-man Office of the President. To reduce the growing management load on general managers at the group, division and department level, the then existing five groups were divided into ten groups, the 29 divisions into 48, and the 123 departments into 170. In the process:

> Some businesses were fragmented among the new departments and doing planning for these multi-department businesses became increasingly difficult. Hence, the original concept of a department as being not only a profit center, but also a self-contained, independent business was, in many cases, lost and a business identification problem emerged that was similar to the one faced in the late 1940's. (Springer and Hofer, 1984:750)

The continuing challenge of profitless growth led GE in 1969 to commission McKinsey & Co. to study GE corporate planning and control systems. Following submission of their study in 1970, GE introduced the now famous concept of strategic business units (SBUs). An SBU was a department, a division or even a whole group with a unique set of competitors, a unique business mission, and an ability to control the variables crucial to the success of business. GE management superimposed the SBU structure on to the existing line reporting structure. For ongoing operations, SBU managers reported within the structure of 48 divisions and 175 departments. However, the 43 units designated as SBUs prepared strategic plans for which they were responsible directly to the CEO (Aguilar and Hamermesh, 1981a:4). Of the 43 initial SBUs, 4 were groups, 21 were divisions and 18 departments. The SBU concept, which was widely heralded and studied, helped to strengthen GE's competitive positions and to improve profits. But it also led to the Balkanization of the company, leading observers to note that 'GE appeared to be moving in the direction of becoming a holding company' (Aguilar and Hamermesh, 1981a:8).

In 1977, Reginald Jones, GE's then CEO, announced the intention of revising GE's strategic planning system and establishing a sector organization structure as the pivotal concept for the redesign effort. To increase the importance and the visibility of foreign operations, GE set up a separate international unit to prepare a sector plan for GE's overseas affiliates and to foster and integrate international business for General Electric as a whole. The sectors, though, continued to have the profit-and-loss responsibility for their product lines throughout the world.

From 1981, John F. Welch, GE's new CEO, in the effort to strengthen the organization and provide more cohesiveness, sold, traded, closed or combined many of the businesses, and simplified the structure by eliminating the sectors and the groups and reducing the layers of management from ten to four. The line activities were organized into fourteen divisions. In 1990 two of the divisions were consolidated, leaving thirteen of what are now called 'businesses', all of which report directly to the corporate executive office.

GE's sales revenue grew from $22,500 million in 1979 to $55,500 million in 1989, while GE not only added through acquisitions and internally generated growth but also pruned many units – ones which, although they had generated 25 per cent of the 1980 sales did not meet the test of being 'No. 1 or No. 2'. GE's $17 billion in acquisitions in the 1980s included the 1986 $6.1 billion purchase of RCA, Borg Warner Chemicals, Montgomery Ward Credit and Ridder, Peabody, Cie Generale de Radiologie, and 50 per cent plus one share equity in Tungsram, the Hungarian lighting company. It also included joint ventures with General Electric Company of England, FUNAC of Japan, and the state-owned Italian industrial holding company, IRI.

Present structure

The GE corporate executive office, consisting in late 1992 of the chairman/CEO, vice-chairman who coordinates operations, a vice-chairman who heads international operations and an executive vice-president, oversee the thirteen GE 'businesses'. The self-contained businesses have their own functional departments; many of their subdivisions have their own international affiliates. By their very nature, some of the businesses have long been international. In the 1980s several 'businesses' significantly expanded their international efforts:

- GE Aircraft Engines' 50–50 joint venture with SNECMA of France (CFM International) dates back to 1974 and now manufactures a range of commercial jet engines (see Lewis, 1990:184–5; 243–5; 247–8). It has also teamed up with GEC-Ruston.
- GE Plastics has had a major factory in the Netherlands since 1969, and cooperates with Nagase, Mitsui and Toshiba in longstanding ventures in the Far East. In 1988 GE Plastics announced the acquisition of Borg Warner's chemical business and a $1.7 billion investment in a new plant in Spain, as well as plans for a new facility in Korea in collaboration with Lucky Corporation.
- GE Power Systems has a network of manufacturing associates in Europe, Japan, China and India to service local markets for gas turbines.
- GE Electrical Distribution Control now includes GE Fanuc, a GE joint venture of GE and Fanuc for industrial automation products. It also distributes a range of products in the Middle East and South East Asia together with Japan's Fuji Electric, and has a European joint venture with GEC of the United Kingdom.
- GE Medical Systems, by acquiring control of Yokogawa Medical Systems of Japan and Compagnie Générale Radiologie (CGR) of France.
- GE Motors has joint ventures with Hyundai and Daewoo in Korea, and with Bosch of Germany to produce small motors in Tennessee.
- GE Lighting operates two joint ventures with Tungsram and Thorn of Korea, and has an alliance with Toshiba of Japan.
- GE Appliances has a joint partnership with GEC of England.
- GE Information Services, a subdivision of GE Communications and Services, is one of the longest-established GE operations in Europe.

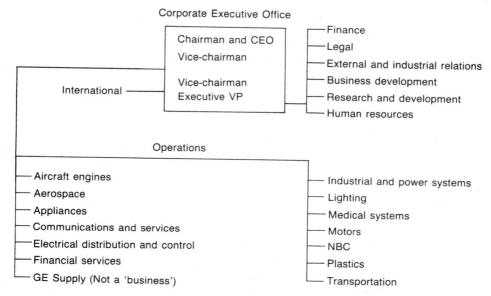

Figure 6.10 General Electric organogram, 1992 (Source: General Electric)

As a consequence of these globalization efforts, by 1989 40 per cent of GE sales were generated from outside the USA. And yet GE made no coordinated effort to build a global corporate image. Thus 'any GE business with international ambitions had to bear the burden of establishing its creditability and credentials in the new markets alone. Not surprisingly some once strong GE businesses opted out of the difficult task of building a global brand position' (Hamel and Prahalad, 1989:74).

GE International has an approximately 70-person staff unit headed by Paolo Fresco (an Italian who was appointed a board member in 1990 and in August 1992 a board vice-chairman, and one of the four-member corporate executive office). It works with the thirteen 'businesses' to promote their global competitiveness in four principal ways: first, it represents GE interests with governments and major corporations throughout the world; second, it assists 'businesses' in negotiating alliances, partnerships and acquisitions; third, it recruits and develops managers with ability to operate effectively in an international environment; and fourth, it advises on the deployment of resources to the advantage of emerging opportunities. With regional offices in London, Riyadh, Hong-Kong, Tokyo, Singapore and Mexico City, GE International works with a network of 'national executives' in key countries. In countries in which GE businesses have already developed affiliates, GE International selects a senior executive to handle this national presence responsibility as a part-time assignment. Generally, the person selected is a national of the country with well-developed local connections and is associated with one of the long-established affiliates in that country. In countries in which GE is primarily promoting development, GE International has appointed a full-time person responsible for developing business there. GE International thus facilitates development and coordination of the GE activities in specific countries.

Tempering division-driven staffing with 'global brains'

With regard to staffing, the various components of the GE businesses have functioned autonomously. Most GE managers have spent their career within one component and expect to continue in it. Except at senior levels, few persons have transferred from one component to another. When transfer has occurred, it has generally been the individual who has requested the transfer. GE employees who have sought assignment to another division apply and have been considered along with other non-GE applicants. The efforts to achieve a 'boundaryless company' are only beginning to change this pattern.

As GE has developed its affiliates overseas, it has replaced Americans with non-Americans. But few of GE's top executives have had international experience. General Electric Information Services – the oldest and most developed of the GE businesses in Europe – is, for example, almost entirely staffed by Europeans in Europe. In other parts of GE, Americans occupy the top posts. GE is taking steps to develop talent globally to change this. The efforts to extend the GE management and culture to its newly acquired overseas affiliates have not been without problems. As noted in Chapter 4, the GE takeover of CGR has been especially troubled.

In order to facilitate the development of an international cadre of managers who can move from business to business and country to country, GE International has introduced a 'global brains' effort. The initial purpose was to recruit particularly promising graduates from leading international business schools, as well as from various components of the company, to provide them with a few years' experience in GE International and then facilitate their posting to a business unit. The effort has been extended to select primary young executives from throughout GE and provide them with experience in a variety of divisions as preparation for senior management posts.

Unifying GE through 'shared management practices'

John Welch's change efforts began with simplifying the structure and reducing the bureaucratic layers from as many as 29 to as few as four. However, faced with a boundary-conscious organization driven by its vast structure and complex systems, he recognized that just moving or eliminating organizational boxes and head-count was not enough to energize the company. Welch recognized that to develop a more globally competitive company demanded not only structural but also 'unprecedented cultural' change. To help with this he brought in Noel Tichy, a noted University of Michigan organizational development expert, to advise and assist in this effort. The result has been a decade-long 'Work-out' programme to drive corporate cultural change throughout the company in the 1990s.

Welch's dream is a boundaryless company which will remove barriers between 'engineering, manufacturing, marketing, sales, and customer service' and recognize no distinctions between domestic and foreign operations. To achieve this admittedly grand vision does indeed require unprecedented cultural change. 'Work-out' is a principal element in GE's effort to achieve this change. As Dr Eurfyl ap Gwilym, an International Division spokesman, has stressed:

> An impetus behind Work-out was the realization that whilst delayering the company had brought many benefits including pushing responsibility down the line, liberating individuals and reducing cost, many people had been left overburdened with work and that a positive response was needed. An important element of Work-Out is that it is a structured approach to removing unnecessary work and tasks so as to let staff concentrate on what is important and valuable to the company and, at the same time, making better use of people's skills and talents. This is a key element in achieving continuing productivity improvements (letter, 21 July 1990).

To implement 'Work-out' GE has brought together staff from cross-sections of the business and around the globe to express their ideas and join efforts on tasks. Teamwork and partnering are concepts which the meetings stress. Understanding the importance of personally directing the impact of his programme, Welch has spoken directly to the hundreds of managers who have passed through GE's management training institute at Crotonville, New York which provides executive development programmes for 6,000 employees a year.

> At work-outs, people who often have no occasion to speak to one another during the day – hourly workers, salaried managers and union leaders – are summoned to the corporate equivalent of a New England town meeting. The pioneering 'work-outs' quickly developed into savage attacks on the worst examples of corporate bureaucracy, such as ten signatures on a minor requisition and artificial dress codes. Managers were encouraged by corporate head office to eradicate such excesses at the 'work-outs', not to refer them to committees or put them through proper channels. This ploy was supposed to increase confidence in the system. It did. Once employees are satisfied that 'work-outs' are not mere talking shops, they are eager to suggest ways their jobs can be done better. GE welders, for instance, won permission to select and order machines they use – purchasing decisions once reserved for the company's white-collared engineers. (*Economist*, 1991c:59)

Globally, GE recognizes that it has yet to tailor itself to achieve its goals. The 'global best-practices' programme has been an effort to look to other companies for practices which GE can adopt to improve its performance. GE has looked to Hewlett Packard for ideas on partnership with suppliers and quality improvement, to Digital Equipment for ideas on asset management, to American Express for ideas on customer satisfaction and to Honda for ideas on product development (*Economist* 1991c: 60).

The third weapon Welch and his lieutenants have developed to improve management performance is 'process mapping'. This is a continuing effort to manage processes better by reviewing how departments work together as products move from one to another. In these efforts, GE is relying on 'process champions'.

GE's challenge is to develop an 'integrated diversity' throughout not only the thirteen 'businesses' but also the affiliates spread throughout the world. Welch's aim is to create a company which knows no boundaries and which is unified by unwritten but shared management practices – quite a challenge for a global company which is so diversified. GE believes that developing and emphasizing these practices among its 'businesses' and national affiliates is one way to achieve world-wide leadership. What the GE teams learn on their expeditions forms part of the curriculum at Crotonville, the GE management development school.

Creating a boundaryless company

For decades GE's reorganization efforts have focused on breaking the company into self-contained SBUs, an effort which led to the walled-off syndrome that Jack Welch's efforts are now trying to minimize. GE's efforts to create a boundaryless company have been energetic. They have included simplifying the structure, facilitating interdivisional transfers and promoting corporate-wide values. The extent to which these pioneering efforts will succeed in transforming an American conglomerate into a border-transcending, multicontinental, multi-industry enterprise may depend on the extent to which Welch internationalizes the board and top management in order to increase their global-mindedness.

Continental organizations concert international operations

E.I. Du Pont de Nemours (Du Pont): abolishing the international division

Du Pont, founded almost two centuries ago, is one of the oldest multinationals. It was one of the first corporations to develop a product-divided, multidivisional organization. In 1990 it eliminated its international department, so that the Du Pont product divisions now manage their fast-growing international businesses with continent groups serving as support contingents.

Gunpowder origins

Du Pont traces its origins to 1802, when a young French Huguenot immigrant with family backing set up a gunpowder business and within three years was exporting back to Europe (Dutton, 1949:25–40). In 1902 three young Du Pont cousins took over the family enterprise, and the next year began to reorganize and rationalize the American explosives industry through merger and acquisition (Dutton, 1949:104). An antitrust decision in 1912 forced Du Pont to spin off its explosives companies, Hercules Powder and Atlas Powder (Dutton, 1949:197–8). Following the divestiture, Du Pont developed and diversified into chemicals through internal growth and acquisitions (including Grasselli Chemical in 1928 and Roessler & Hasslacher Chemicals in 1930): (Chandler, 1990:76, 174–92, especially 176).

In the 1920s Du Pont developed its interests overseas by purchasing stakes in two German chemical firms, which in 1925 became part of the newly merged I.G. Farben; as a consequence Du Pont became a small holder of stock in I.G. Farben (under 1 per cent). When, in 1926, Britain's most important chemical company, Imperial Chemical Industries, was organized, Du Pont became a small minority stock holder by virtue of its decades-long-held stake in Nobel Industries. In July 1929, 'Du Pont and ICI made a comprehensive agreement by which Du Pont granted ICI exclusive rights for patent and processes for the British Empire (except Canada) and ICI gave Du Pont the same rights for North America (except Canada). In Canada and Latin America, they developed a number of joint ventures' (Wilkins, 1974:78, 90). In 1921 Du Pont, along with General Motors with which it was closely associated, pioneered the multidivisional, product-divided company. A major feature of Du Pont's reorganization was the creation of an executive committee, whose members were freed of operational responsibilities in order to oversee the corporation (Chandler, 1962:52–113).

Following the 1952 break-up (as a consequence of antitrust litigation) of a decades-long alliance with ICI, Du Pont began to expand vigorously into Europe (Wilkins, 1974:293). It set up its first European affiliate in the United Kingdom in 1956 and its first overseas manufacturing plant in Belgium in 1959. In 1981 Du Pont acquired Houston-based Conoco, then the ninth-largest American oil company. The $6.9 billion deal, in which Du Pont outbid Seagram, gave Seagram 22.6 per cent of the Du Pont shares, marginally more than the Du Pont family members control. Seagram nominees, including three Bronfman family members, hold five of the eighteen seats on the Du Pont board of directors, and may have displaced the Du Pont family as the focus of power on the board. By 1989, six of Du Pont's ten businesses manufactured in North America, Latin America, Europe and Asia/Pacific, and nine had plants in Europe as well as in the USA. In 1990, Du Pont employed almost 144,000 employees and generated nearly $40 billion in sales.

During the 1980s, Du Pont took several steps to reduce costs. In 1985 it encouraged 11,500 (about 7 per cent) of its employees to take an early retirement option. It has sold or closed underperforming operations, with $3 billion in sales, including the Orlon operation. In 1991, the new CEO took Du Pont pharmaceutical assets – most still in development – and cut a deal with Merck & Co. to establish the Du Pont–Merck pharmaceutical company, with $700 million in sales and the potential to turn immediate profit. This was followed by a 1992 swap of its acrylic business (and some cash) for ICI's nylon business. These efforts accompanied a $1 billion reduction in fixed costs, 'in order to make our business more competitive in the world market place' (memo, 25 July 1991). Most of the reduction came from the support services for US chemicals and specialties, a step that would require thousands of people taking early retirement or being laid off.

Restructuring from 1921 to 1990

The executive committee that was organized as a major feature of the 1921 reorganization and continued with only minor modifications until 1990 was described as follows in 1980:

> The president has no power not derived from this committee, and on it he has only one vote. The vice-presidents have no authority on their own, and they are not vice-presidents-in-charge-of anything. Their collective function is to think; their chief field of action is policy-making [...] This radical form of committee management was initiated in Irénée Du Pont's term as president in 1921 to meet the needs of Du Pont's swiftly diversifying business. [...] Basically, though not functionally, it is a military form of organization, in which sharp separation is made between staff and line. The Executive committee is the general staff, along with a powerful, interlinked, nine-man Finance Committee, which holds the purse strings. Ten separate industrial operating departments form the field or line commands, each as big as many an important corporation, each headed by a general manager charged with an investment and maximum authority to run the business. Attached to staff and line are fourteen auxiliary departments carrying on such company-wide functions as purchasing, traffic engineering, and long-range research. (Lessing, 1980:110)

For its international operations, each product business relied upon managing directors located in each of the continents in which it was doing business.

In Europe in 1988, several businesses had their own continental heads who also doubled as country general managers (for example, the managing director for agricultural products doubled as managing director of France, and the managing director of Imaging Systems also served as managing director of Germany). On the other hand, several less well-established businesses shared a managing director. By the 1980s, the matrix-like arrangement was one in which the principal lines of command flowed through the product heads, but the continental product heads also reported to continental geographic heads, who reported to an international vice-president.

The Conoco Oil and the Consolidation Coal operations operated separately from the other Du Pont businesses. The Conoco upstream oil operations were divided into North American exploration and production, international exploration and production, and world-wide exploration. The downstream operations were divided between North America and Europe, with Europe subdivided into countries.

With the 1990 reorganization, the Executive Committee was replaced by an Office of the Chairman composed of the chairman/CEO, a vice-chairman (who oversees the chemical operations), the Conoco president (who was appointed a vice-chairman in 1991) and the two senior vice-presidents (one for finance and the other for human resources and corporate planning). The chairman and two vice-chairmen sit on the all-North-American board of directors. Working closely with the Office of the Chairman is an operating group composed of all the senior vice-presidents, including those heading major line operations of Du Pont and Conoco and those heading staff units.

In the 1991 reorganization the international department was dissolved and its operations decentralized. The regional vice-presidents now report directly to selected members of the operating committee (who thus have a regional portfolio in addition to their principal one): the vice-chairman/Conoco president oversees Europe, and others oversee Asia/Pacific, South America/Mexico and Canada. Thus what once was an international department coordinating all overseas activities has been dissolved into territorial support operations. The country affiliates have, in effect, become umbrellas embracing a number of product-division-directed line activities and continental-headquarters-directed staff support efforts, with the head of one of these activities having an additional role as the representative-head-type country general manager.

Spotting and developing well-rounded managers

Du Pont has long hired its management and professional corps in early career, and devoted considerable energy to spotting talent and moving it up and around. As one observer noted more than a decade ago:

> Likely managerial timber is spotted in its early thirties, usually after about ten years' service and at the assistant-director-of-a-division level, and it is closely followed by age groups. Periodically, a 'skimmer' chart is run on each department, plotting salaries by ages. If too many top-bracket salaries bunch up at the aging end of the curve, the department head is asked quietly but pointedly: 'Where are your good men?'
> Picked young men are deliberately moved about, across functional lines (from research to production or sales and vice versa), across departmental lines (from stable to expanding divisions), to develop rounded executives and get a steady transfer of ideas.
> (Lessing, 1980: 12)

Du Pont's aim has been to provide training, internal and external, based on an individual's needs and interests. Training programmes range from basic skill development to courses on coaching and counselling of subordinates for managers and professionals; they are available for employees at all levels and may involve on-the-job training, special assignments and, in some cases, formalized training programmes inside or outside the company. Du Pont provides cultural and language training to employees transferred outside the United States in order to support Du Pont's corporate vision of becoming a more global company. To do so, it builds on the strength of its diverse, world-wide workforce.

Shifting corporate culture

Two forces have long shaped Du Pont's culture. One has been the Huguenot, socially concerned culture of the Du Pont family, which continued to have a plurality equity in the company until the 1981 Conoco acquisition that brought the Bronfmans into the company. The other has been its Wilmington base, which promoted a strong home-city networking and value-sharing among its senior officers and Du Pont family board members – a factor which promoted a family-style cohesiveness. It may also have bred an inclusiveness, which may in part be responsible for the fact that a multinational whose most rapidly expanding operations have been international had never appointed an international vice-president who had lived abroad, and did not include non-US citizens until the Canadian multinational Seagrams appointed a Canadian to the board in 1981.

A number of factors appear to have shifted the emphasis in Du Pont's culture. One has been the increasing competitiveness of the 1980s, another the more aggressive business style of the Bronfmans, who now have most of the equity in Du Pont. With them has come a more hard-headed willingness to cut costs and job-actions that has profoundly affected the sense of family identity and loyalty that has long pervaded Du Pont.

Abolishing the international department

Du Pont's move to abolish its international department, which stemmed in part from it cost-cutting efforts, reflects the American corporate trend towards globalization of its product divisions. The move has simplified operations by eliminating the matrix-like arrangements on which international operations had previously run. As a consequence, though, Du Pont no longer has the coherent capacity it once had at the country level to coordinate its disparate product efforts, and to represent its corporate-wide interests effectively.

International Business Machines (IBM): the company many Japanese multinationals consider a model

With its focus on computers, IBM is the largest major multinational in the world that has continued to be essentially a single-industry company. Unlike most American multinationals (but like Japanese ones), IBM has several distinctive organization features: a strong corporate-wide culture, and a staffing policy which stresses not only hiring young and promoting from within but also hiring host country nationals for its national affiliates. IBM has achieved what many others have strived for: a home country run enterprise with a world-unifying corporate culture and host country staffed international affiliates which are generally accepted as local companies throughout the world. Many Japanese multinationals have consciously used IBM as an organizational model.

Moved by declining profits, IBM reorganized in 1988 and 1992. The 1988 reorganization clearly established six businesses. The 1992 'redefinition' which was followed and accompanied by a series of cutbacks, was aimed at making 'the lines of business' even more independent and accountable than the 1988 one, and giving the corporate headquarters a more limited role. The 'redefinition' has many of the objectives of the multidivisional reorganization initiated by Du Pont, GM and Exxon in the 1920s and widely copied by others since then, but the proposed IBM plan would continue to separate marketing and service from manufacturing and product development, just as Japanese firms do.

A Watson father-and-son dominated history

In 1914 Thomas Watson (later to be called Thomas Watson, Senior) became the chief executive of the Computer-Tabulating-Recording Corporation, a company which had been formed in 1910 as a merger of three companies. From NCR, his previous employer, Watson brought an approach to sales and motivation which included an accent on slogans, such as 'Read-Listen-Discuss-Observe-Think'. In 1924 Watson changed the company name to International Business Machines, after first using the name for the Canadian and Latin American affiliates. IBM built its first manufacturing plants in Europe during the interwar years (Chandler, 1990:201). By 1939 IBM had developed an undisputed lead in what even then was recognized as a major growth industry: office machines. It had already developed national affiliates in many European, Asian and Latin American countries (Sobel, 1981:58, 92, 135).

In 1949, Watson divided the rapidly growing IBM empire into two unequal parts. The parent company, IBM, ran the US business which continued to be the primary market for its machines and services. The rest of the globe was handled by IBM World Trade Corporation, an entity that would later be split into three parts, one for Europe, one for Asia/Pacific and one for Latin America.

In Europe, which has long been its primary international market, IBM in the late 1940s and early 1950s developed a way for IBM affiliates to have their own free trade across international borders. Each factory made parts not only for the country in which it was situated but also for export. In shipping these parts, IBM earned foreign-exchange credits which were used to import other parts. Because tariff barriers were so high, IBM shipped finished machines only to the smaller countries where it had no plants, and few IBM machines were 100 per cent manufactured in the country where they were finally assembled. Thus, has noted, IBM developed a 'kind of common market ten years before the real one existed [. . .] This trading around allowed us to operate on a much larger scale, and far more efficiently than any company that was bound to a single country' (Watson and Petre, 1990:185–6).

In 1956 Tom Watson, Jr., succeeded his father as IBM's CEO. Within a year he led an effort to reform the company so that the decision-making was less focused on the CEO than it had been under his father's vest-pocket management style. Recognizing that by the mid-1950s most major US corporations had adopted a multidivisional system with line and staff functions clearly differentiated, Watson introduced a more product-driven type of organization. He clearly defined and granted more autonomy to the product divisions established a few years earlier. A six-man corporate management committee was created to oversee plans and major decisions; this committee included, in addition to the new CEO, the head of the world trade corporation (Arthur Watson, Tom's younger brother), the chief of staff (and finance), the manufacturing head and the sales head. Supporting this was a corporate staff with expertise in finance, personnel and communications. With this plan IBM encouraged a check-and-balance scheme that eventually became famous as the IBM system of 'contention management'. IBM's pervasive culture, its promotion from within, and the salary and stock options were dynamics that made the system work (Watson and Petre, 1990:305–11).

Before the 1950s, IBM was still less than a fifth of the size of General Electric. During that decade, IBM focused on computers and forged its long lead, so long that IBM has fought protracted antitrust actions in the United States, the latest of which was not dismissed until 1982. By 1990 IBM had developed a wide range of products for the computer and office machines industry including mainframe computers, mid-range systems, minicomputers, personal computers, graphics systems, typewriters, systems and application software, and other business equipment. In constructing its business around the world IBM has relationships with

> more than 10,000 joint marketers, systems integrators, and Business Partners who reach and support the majority of our Application System/400 and Personal System/2 customers [. . .] IBM has established more than 75 equity alliances world-wide [. . .] Our partners [range] from large well-established companies such as Sears and Siemens to small entrepreneurial ventures. (IBM *Annual Report*, 1989:3)

The years since 1986, when John Akers became chief executive of IBM, have been turbulent ones for the computer industry and stressful for IBM. Given its continuing disappointing earnings, Aker's purported remarks that the company's business was 'in crisis' and that 'everyone is too damn comfortable', and the hints of further reductions in the workforce (already down 11 per cent in three years) have focused attention not only on the problems facing IBM but also on those of many other computer companies.

But even as IBM was beset by headlines of gloom (in 1991, it lost $3 billion), it has continued to make bold moves to boost sales and counter competition. It has entered into a strategic agreement to sell computer hardware to Wang. It has followed this up with unprecedented alliances with Apple and Motorola to collaborate on personal computer technology. It has also concluded agreements with Siemens to collaborate in producing the world's most advanced memory chips, and with Bull to sell a broad array of computer hardware and services to Bull's customers in Europe. These linkages illustrate IBM's continuing determination to find new opportunities for growth, to prevent Japanese competitors from increasing their dominance in critical areas of the electronics industry, and to spread the huge costs of developing the most advanced technologies.

One of the world's five largest multinationals, IBM operates in more than 100 countries, and in 1990 employed over 370,000 people and grossed more than $69 billion. Approximately 60 per cent of its operations are outside the USA.

Managing an undiversified company

A mostly American IBM board of directors includes two of the senior IBM officers and three retired senior officers of the corporation. (One non-American is chairman of two Swiss companies, the other is CEO of a German corporation.) The management committee, composed of the chairman/CEO, president and two or more senior vice-presidents, directs the affairs of the corporation. Each management committee member oversees a number of units; one oversees the international activities. (see Figure 6.11).

The management committee is assisted by a number of senior vice-presidents and vice-presidents with specific responsibilities. Four country general managers – the Canadian, Japanese, German and Italian – have been elected as IBM vice-presidents, a move designed to enhance the global image of IBM as well as to increase the representativeness of the regional perspective. In the mid-1980s IBM separated the US organization from the corporate offices in order to strengthen the focus on the American market.

In 1988, in a major part of a series of efforts to strengthen its operations and 'move more resources and authority closer to customers', IBM reorganized by establishing six (later seven and by 1992 nine) lines of businesses. These divisions have been responsible for US manufacturing and 'developing product and service solutions for customers ranging from individuals using personal systems to large enterprises with world-wide networks' (IBM *Annual Report*, 1989:7). Although the responsibility of these businesses has been world-wide, they reported to IBM's United States general manager. The planned move for IBM's communications systems headquarters to suburban London may bring an end to the anomaly. In the

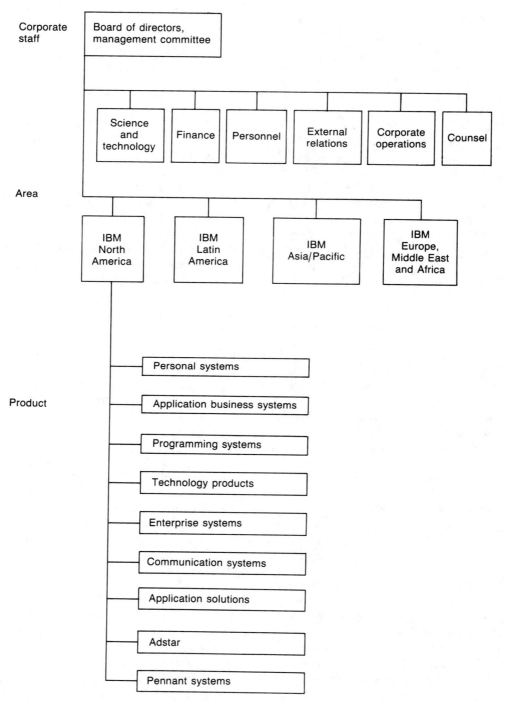

Figure 6.11 IBM's blueprint for growth, 1991 (Source: Kirkpatrick, 1992:113, 120)

process of its reorganization effort some operations, such as the $2.3 billion office products unit that were not part of IBM's core business of computing and communication have been sold or spun off.

Akers intends that the 1991-announced restructuring plan will lead to a fundamental redefinition of how IBM does business by allowing its business units more autonomy and dismantling the intricate, matrix-like management structure that has long pervaded this business empire. The plan envisages IBM becoming a group of production (that is, manufacturing and product development) companies, each focusing on one of its businesses, supported by IBM's geographically organized marketing, sales and services companies (see Figure 6.11). In addition, IBM's corporate office will remove itself from operational responsibilities. 'Each member of the new "federation of companies" is now essentially autonomous,' says Akers (Kirkpatrick, 1992: 113). By eliminating layers of management, IBM hopes to speed decision-making, shorten product development cycles and concentrate each product group's energies on becoming the lowest cost manufacturer of state-of-the-art information systems. The hope is that product managers, freed of internal politics and bureaucracy, will be able to focus energy on beating the competition (Kehoe, 1991). The key question is whether IBM can provide its independent computer businesses with enough independence without losing the opportunities or without forfeiting the means by which to achieve synergy among the parts.

Four continental offices are now responsible for the marketing and service operations: IBM North America created in 1992 by combining IBM US and IBM Canada; IBM Europe/Middle East/Africa, with its headquarters in Paris; IBM Asia/Pacific, with headquarters in Tokyo and Hong Kong; and IBM Latin America, headquartered in Tarrytown, New York. Each has a 'board' consisting of about one-half Americans and one-half non-Americans. About half of these regional boards members are IBM executives – either serving in the region (Americans and non-Americans) or US-based.

These continental offices coordinate the marketing activities of the national affiliates and direct the manufacturing activities on their continents. The continental office management teams make the decisions regarding manufacturing, volumes, pricing, planning, location, employment, investments and strategy. Since the early 1960s, manufacturing has been rationalized on a continental basis, so that there is no longer a duplication of products manufactured within a continental area. Thus, within Europe, each manufacturing location is responsible for manufacturing a given product or product part. The role of the continental offices is, however, in a state of flux. The very size of several of the national affiliates, coupled with the concern not to generate costs which do not have a value-added validity, may lead IBM to consider separating IBM Japan from IBM Asia/Pacific.

While IBM has traditionally served Europe on a country-by-country basis, IBM Europe has now delegated some business responsibilities to 'lead countries' responsible for coordinating one of the product areas. As a consequence, IBM has moved the management responsibility for mainframes to the German affiliate, that for mid-range computers to the Italian affiliate, and that for finance marketing to the UK affiliate, with a newly appointed European director general to oversee the implementation of these efforts. The Italian affiliate has been charged with the responsibility for the smaller national affiliates in southern Europe and northern Africa (what used to be the South European division). IBM France has become responsible for 'central Europe', and IBM Germany for efforts in eastern Europe. In further moves, Spain has been separated from the tutelage of Italy. The Scandinavian affiliates have been merged into one multicountry affiliate, and Belgium, the Netherlands and Ireland have similarly been merged, in an arrangement in which the support services are consolidated but the marketing operations remain organized by country.

The national affiliates which report to one of the continental affiliates are essentially marketing entities, but they also have administrative coordination responsibilities for any manufacturing facilities in the country. The national affiliates are responsible for all functional support activities such as finance and human resources; for example, the IBM Europe finance and personnel officers do not direct their German counterparts – they may only advise. National affiliates have their own board of directors and may have the following senior country-based officers: a country general manager, a head of market operations, a head of customer services and support, three staff officers (finance and planning, management services, and legal counsel), and perhaps a manufacturing head (if there are plants located in that country; but such a manufacturing manager would be operationally responsible to continental headquarters). The other senior colleagues of the country general manager report operationally and primarily to the CGM, but they maintain a technical relationship with their counterpart in European headquarters.

Host country affiliate staffing

IBM hires host country nationals for their national affiliates and promotes from within. Thus, with rare exceptions, the senior managers including the CGM of a national affiliate of IBM are host country nationals. IBM believes host country CGMs not only better appreciate the local environment, including the tax, social security, and other legal requirements and the local customs, but also are more likely to develop close rapport with local employees, customers and host country institutions.

Since IBM Europe attempts as much as possible to harmonize its European operations, the senior managers of every affiliate generally have at least two to three years' experience in continental or corporate headquarters. This helps develop the broader perspective senior managers need to balance the global objectives of IBM with the country requirements. Senior affiliate managers are generally in their 40s and have a university education. They have been with IBM for all or almost all of their careers. IBM's philosophy of having its affiliates hire only country nationals is viewed as a major factor in its success as a marketing company. An executive of one large Japanese publishing company, when asked which firm had written his firm's software, said it chose a Japanese company – IBM Japan (*Economist*, 24 June 1989a:75).

IBM stresses the continuing education of its employees. Its training centres in the United States, Europe and Asia provide an opportunity for constant improvement of competence and for socialization not only of the staff of various IBM affiliates but also of IBM business partners and many customers. According to a recently retired country general manager: 'The availability of education is a fantastic motivator. It's good business' (interview, De Meyer, 18 August 1990). In 1991, in Europe, every employee spent (on average) almost 12 days in education or training. As part of the late 1980s' reorganization efforts, more than 80,000 IBMers were retrained and reassigned to new jobs in an effort to reduce overhead positions and shift the emphasis even more to marketing (IBM *Annual Report*, 1989:19).

More recently, in a move to meet the requirements of the new organizations better and to have all field employees with the right skills, major efforts have been devoted to defining the 'New professions' of the field force, and to build accordingly a formal 'Skills Development Process' where every employee is empowered to identify and plan his or her own development, including formal education (letter, De Potter, 17 January 1992). Based on formal business and performance requirements, the training programmes on offer are considered as a major contributor to IBM's success. IBM selects its instructors from among its more experienced and accomplished practitioners; such assignments are generally from 24 to 36 months, to ensure up-to-date experience. It also calls outside experts and consultants from universities, and even started considering common curricula with outside organizations.

IBM has generally moved its fast-track professionals and managers into new assignments every two to three years, only recently extending some assignments to five years to increase the opportunity to develop more continuity in customer relations. (In fact, many IBMers remark that IBM stands for 'I've been moved.') The aim is to provide the professionals with an opportunity to appreciate a variety of perspectives so that they can interact effectively with those in different positions. The rotation practice is an integral aspect of the IBM philosophy of development and part of each individual IBMer's personal development.

IBM is committed to full employment. While IBM does not lay off employees for economic reasons, it does dismiss (or assign to dead-end positions) for poor performance. When a change is necessary, IBM will relocate and retrain employees, offering them an equal position when reductions in certain areas are required. Early retirement has also been used successfully to achieve reductions. This was a major means of reducing the total workforce by 37,000 from 1985 to 1990, thus returning to the 1981 level – a move which was accomplished while maintaining high morale and commitment to IBM (Pascale, 1990:29).

A Watson-formulated, well-articulated corporate culture

From the beginning IBM has had a strong corporate culture. The ideas of Thomas

Watson, Sr., were reinforced by his son, Thomas Watson, Jr. IBM has developed a set of basic beliefs which stresses the following principles:

- The individual must be respected.
- The customer must be given the best possible service.
- Excellence and superior performance must be pursued.

The staffing and training policies and practices are an integral part of IBM's culture. No one becomes a manager unless he or she has been to IBM Management School, whose courses last from two to six weeks. The emphasis is on *IBM* management and practices. There is a consistency in office decor and ways of doing things which extends around the world.

IBM attempts to maintain a totally sales-oriented environment in which everyone is sales-conscious. The IBM sales-oriented culture manifests itself in its slogans. One of the many mottoes at the company is that 'IBM sells solutions, not products.' Another is that 'Selling and Service are synonymous at IBM', and 'The Customer is at the top of the IBM Hierarchy.' One of the foremost rules is that 'No IBMer should ever disparage any competitor. Selling must be done on the merit of the product and services.' Another is 'IBM expects every employee to act, in every instance, according to the highest standards of business conduct.' These themes repeat themselves throughout IBM literature.

IBM believes that every action should be influenced by these policies. To stress the importance of its code of ethics, these policies are articulated to every employee in a variety of different ways, and repeated often. Failure to follow the code of ethics is grounds for dismissal. The effort to establish a common culture goes beyond ethics and extends to conservative appearance. As Thomas Watson, Jr explained:

> Of course it is true a conservative appearance had always been the custom at IBM. A whole folklore grew up about IBM conformity – the white shirts and dark suits. But there was a reason for it. In one way or another we were all salesmen in IBM, individually and collectively, and nothing distracts from a sale like an outlandish appearance. Conservative dress made sense as a marketing tool, just like a plant tour, an education program for customers, or a reputation for excellence. It showed we took our work seriously. (Watson and Petre, 1990:326)

By now the tradition is well trenched.

The company long copied by Japanese multinationals may now be about to copy them

'Our model is IBM': so Takeshi Matari, president of Canon Europe, concluded an interview discussing Canon strategic organization objectives (interview, 11 July 1989). Several features of IBM lead many Japanese multinationals to view IBM as a model for the development of the global organization. Through its culture, IBM has developed a cohesive organization which is effective in a world-wide market. With the accent on function and country, the organization allows for flexibility and autonomy for individual markets. It also allows the managers closest to the market, those who understand it best, to respond in the quickest and most efficient manner possible. IBM staffs marketing and manufacturing affiliates with host country nationals to ensure that the employees who know the most about their geographic region are able to service them. This policy has helped IBM stay on top of the market despite fierce competition in a rapidly changing environment.

An irony of the present reorganizational initiatives is that by granting the production divisions more autonomy and continuing the split of the geographically organized sales units from the production groups, IBM will take steps that may lead to it more closely resembling the Japanese companies that have long followed IBM's lead.

CHAPTER 7
European groups: globalizing product perspectives

From 'daughter' companies to global product divisions

During the high tariff years of the first half of the twentieth century, those European industrial firms that expanded internationally developed multicountry groups of omnibus 'daughter' companies, over which the parent company exerted an overlord role. Since World War II a number of factors have led most European multinationals to globalize their product divisions. These factors have included World War II disruption, diversification that was often government supported and the more recent impact of economic integration.

Several European firms survived World War II with sufficient multinational infrastructure to continue the prewar omnibus 'daughter company' tradition. Among these were six major European multinationals that survived World War II sufficiently well to rank in the Global 50 by the 1950s. They were the two British–Netherlands binationals, Unilever and Royal Dutch/Shell; two British-based multinationals, British Petroleum (BP) and Imperial Chemical Industries (ICI); and two small-country-based multinationals, Swiss-based Nestlé and Netherlands-based Philips. Unilever, Royal Dutch/Shell and Nestlé have continued this decentralized approach into the 1990s. Prodded by disappointing profits, ICI, BP and Philips had, however, already begun their moves towards global product sector management of international operations by the late 1980s, and their stepped-up organization efforts in the late 1980s and early 1990s were accompanied by significant reductions in workforce.

A second factor shaping the postwar organizational evolution of the European multinationals has been the extent to which diversification was integral to their decades-long development efforts. As they expanded and diversified multinationals such as Bayer, Philips, BP and ICI began to globalize their product groups. Bayer began its move to develop *ad hoc* affiliates into global product groups in the 1970s. On the other hand, BP, ICI and Philips, whose miniature, replica, 'daughter' companies were long established, moved more slowly to wear down their autonomy, first by developing matrix-like arrangements, and later by creating global product groups. In the Fiat, Daimler-Benz, Asea Brown Boveri and

CGE/Alcatel Alsthom cases, major mergers or acquisitions have forced sweeping reorganizational efforts.

A few interrelated factors have more recently propelled European multinationals to develop the global role of the product groups. The growing economic integration of Europe, the increasing intercontinental competition, decreased profits, and the desire to develop more streamlined organizations abetted the Philips, ICI and BP reorganizations.

Country-by-country comparison

Shaping the European multinationals throughout their evolution has been the nature of their home country political-economic environment and its governmental support. The national environments have been sufficiently distinctive for the European Global 50 multinationals to be considered on a country-by-country basis.

As the Nestlé profile that follows shows, Nestlé considers the small size of its domestic market to be the major reason that it developed itself into 'the most multinational of multinationals'. During World War II Nestlé managed its non-European operations from the US. Today Nestlé operates essentially as a holding company, managing more than 200 operating companies whose headquarters are based throughout the world. The other Swiss Global 50 company, Asea Brown Boveri (ABB), which was formed by a 1988 merger of Swedish-based Asea and Swiss-based Brown Boveri Company, presents itself as 'essentially a federation of national companies' which uses a matrix structure grouping its world-wide business activities 'into eight Business Segments comprising 50 Business Areas. Each carries responsibility for global strategic business plans, allocation of manufacturing responsibilities and product development' (ABB Annual Report, 1989:3). The country managers are responsible for operations in each country in line with the global strategies of the 'Business Area'. The decentralized operation is run from a headquarters staffed by fewer than 100 people.

The two British–Netherlands binationals, Unilever and Royal Dutch/Shell, have long ranked among the nine largest-by-assets British companies (see Table 7.1). Unilever was formed in 1930 by a joining of forces of the British 'soap-making' enterprise Lever Brothers and the Netherlands-based Margarine Unie. Its two parent companies entered into a series of agreements which provide for maximum commercial cooperation in managing the 500 product-specific operating companies which operate with a good deal of autonomy under their umbrella. Royal Dutch/Shell, as the profile that follows shows, has developed a superstructure of headquarters-located service companies to support its national operating companies, on which the group continues to depend. Thus both have continued a tradition of decentralized country-focused operations.

The two British-based companies, ICI and BP, have both been assisted in their development by the British government. It invested sufficient equity in BP's predecessor to acquire half ownership at the outset of World War I, a stake it maintained for almost seven decades. It also encouraged the 1926 merger that

Table 7.1 The largest industrial enterprises in Great Britain: by assets, 1919–91

Ranking	1919	1930	1948	1969	1991
1.	Burmah Oil	Unilever	Imperial Tobacco	Royal Dutch/Shell	Royal Dutch/Shell
2.	J&P Coats	Imperial Tobacco	Anglo-Iranian Oil[3]	BP	BP
3.	Anglo-Persian Oil	Royal Dutch/Shell	ICI	ICI	Hanson[4]
4.	Lever Brothers[1]	ICI	Unilever	Unilever	Unilever
5.	Imperial Tobacco	Anglo-Persian Oil[3]	Royal Dutch/Shell	British Steel	ICI
6.	Vickers	Courtaulds	Distillers	GEC	British Aerospace
7.	Guinness	J&P Coats	Guinness	British Leyland	Grand Metropolitan
8.	Brunner, Mond[2]	Distillers	Courtaulds	British Coal Board	BTR
9.	Royal Dutch/Shell	Guinness	Burmah Oil	British-American Tobacco (BAT)[4]	British Steel

Note: Five companies, or their predecessors, have been ranked among the top nine companies (by assets) in each of the benchmark years; they are Shell, BP, BAT, Unilever and ICI. While Royal Dutch/Shell and Unilever are British–Netherlands groups, their total bi-national assets have been the basis for the ranking.

1. Merged with Unie in 1929 to form Unilever.
2. Merged to form Imperial Chemical Industries (ICI) in 1926.
3. Anglo-Persian Oil changed its name to Anglo-Iranian in 1935, and to British Petroleum (BP) in 1955.
4. A descendant of Imperial Tobacco.
Source: Chandler, 1990: Appendices B, C; *Fortune*, 1970b:43; 1992:55–7.

created ICI, to compete with the German combine I.G. Farben. Not until the early 1990s did either of these companies move resolutely to end the matrix-like arrangement each had gradually developed to reconcile its product divisions and long-established national fiefdoms. When they did, as the profiles show, they clearly established product-division-driven organizations.

Of the seven German 1990 Global 50 multinationals, three are chemical companies, which from 1925 to 1945 were combined in I.G. Farben (see Table 7.2). Bayer, as the profile that follows shows, has developed global product groups which have enveloped the product-and-function specific affiliates. The other four German 1990 Global 50 companies – the two automakers, Daimler-Benz and Volkswagen, the electronics firm Siemens; and the steel company Thyssen – have similarly developed product-divided enterprises. As the Daimler-Benz profile that follows shows, the German banks have long played an instrumental role in governing as well as funding German companies.

The Italian government, in its efforts to spur economic development, has strongly supported not only the state-owned companies but also private ones. Two state-owned Italian holding companies rank in the 1990 Global 50. One is ENI (Ente Nazionale Idrocarburi), an agglomeration of 278 petroleum, natural gas, mineral engineering, manufacturing and services companies. The other is IRI (Istituto per la Ricostruzione Industriale), whose assortment of 400 companies includes banks, Alitalia, an aerospace group, a steel group and STET – a telecommunications and electronics conglomerate which is IRI's largest and most profitable subsidiary. The Fiat profile that follows shows how the government has supported Fiat, and other large family dynastic concerns such as Olivetti and Ferruzzi Financiari.

The French government, too, has not only championed but also protected French companies, especially the government-owned ones. Elf Aquitaine was formed in 1976 as a French state majority-owned oil and gas group in what was one of the biggest reshuffles of French state industry (before the 1992 formation of Thomson CEA Industries as a conglomerate with businesses ranging from electronics to nuclear energy). France also has a minority equity in the other Global 50 French oil company, Total, once named Compagnie Française des Pétroles, which only in 1991 eliminated these words from its name. Renault, which has received repeated infusions of government capital has developed an alliance with Volvo, the Swedish car manufacturer. The French government, which owns 80 per cent of Renault, has consented to Volvo increasing its equity shareholding to 25 per cent and to considering a merger – possibly one under which a majority French-government-owned holding company would control both groups, a step Volvo leadership has hinted it would accept. Another major French multinational, Alcatel Alsthom (once CGE), was, as described in the profile that follows, nationalized and then denationalized in the course of the 1980s. Peugeot (PSA) combines what were once two French automobile firms, Peugeot and Citroën; the merger was undertaken with government encouragement to strengthen the French car industry.

Philips, the only wholly Dutch 1990 Global 50 multinational (which reduced its wartime losses by moving its headquarters off continent during World War II),

Table 7.2 The largest industrial enterprises in Germany: ranked by assets, 1913–91

Ranking	1913	1929	1953	1969	1991
1.	Krupp	Vereinigte StahlWerke	Mannesmann	BASF	Daimler-Benz
2.	AEC	IG Farben Industrie[2]	Bayer	Bayer	Volkswagen
3.	Siemens-Schuckert Werke[1]	AEG	Hoesch	Hoechst	Siemens
4.	Deutsche Luxemburgische	Krupp	BASF	Siemens	Bayer
5.	Phoenix Gummiwerke	Siemens-Schuckert Werke[1]	Dortmund-Hörder	Volkswagen	BASF
6.	Siemens & Halske	Kali-Industrie	Siemens & Halske	August Thyssen	Hoechst
7.	Gutehoff	Siemens & Halske	Hoechst	Krupp	RuhrKohle
8.	BASF	Rhenania-Ossag, Mineralölwerk	Hüttenwerke Phönix	AEG	BMW
9.	Bayer	Mannesmann	AEG	Daimler-Benz	Robert Bosch

Note: Three companies or their predecessors have ranked in the top nine (by assets) in each of the five benchmark years; these are Siemens, Bayer and BASF.

1. Siemens & Schuckert was controlled by Siemens & Halske and Schuckert by 1953, a subsidiary of Siemens & Halske.
2. I. G. Farben was formed by the confederation of Bayer, BASF, Hoechst and other firms in 1916, merged in 1925, and split after World War II.
Source: Chandler, 1990; Appendix C4, 722–33; *Fortune*, 1970b:43; 1992:55–7.

had moved gradually before the late 1980s to increase the global role of its product divisions by changing the role of once sister-like national organizations to develop a more matrix-like structure. Not until the late 1980s did it clearly establish the global product groups as the profit-and-loss entities and convert the once semi-autonomous sister companies into confederate-like entities embracing the national units of the product groups.

The increased size, diversity, and complexity of European firms has meant that they can no longer rely on staffing with longtime associates as the major means of managing international operations. By the beginning of the 1990s, there was a wider range of organizational arrangements. Roughly they may be considered in three groups: the first are those adopted by firms such as Uniliver and ABB, as well as Royal Dutch/Shell and Nestlé, that have essentially continued a more decentralized arrangement which depends on relatively autonomous operating companies. The second are those adopted by firms such as Bayer, Fiat and Philips, which have taken a global product-group approach. And the third are those adopted by firms such as BP and ICI that have taken a global product-group approach but with continental support groups.

With the shift in organizational arrangements there also came increased reliance upon structures and systems and other American management methodology. The more cost-conscious era of the early 1990s forced many European companies, including Philips, BP, ICI, Siemens, Olivetti and Renault, to break their traditions of security by cutting their workforce by thousands.

'Operating' companies manage international operations

Nestlé Group: a holding company of globally dispersed operating companies

Nestlé, the Swiss-based food group, has long considered itself 'the most multinational of multinationals'. Its international origins, continued acquisition of globally dispersed companies,

> [the] diminutive size of its country of origin and [...] the customs barriers which have forced it to establish plants throughout the world [...] help explain why only 2% of its turnover is in Switzerland, quite a different situation from many other multinational companies which do a large part, if not the major part of their business in their domestic market. (Maucher, 1985:13)

The Nestlé Group, rapidly expanding by acquisition, operates a holding company of more than 200 operating companies, such as Lilly, Rowntree, Carnation, Chambourcy, and Crosse and Blackwell, which have long pre-Nestlé-acquisition traditions and reputations, and many of the brand names have continued. Nestlé's multinationalism is reflected in the cosmopolitanism of its board and corporate executive team, which includes a German as its chairman and CEO. The company succeeds in looking 'British in Britain, American in America, and German in Germany' (Sampson, 1982:380).

In its efforts to continue to strengthen its global organization Nestlé has not only gone on acquiring companies, but also has begun to integrate country management and strengthened its corporate headquarters by developing strategic business units to complement its long-established 'geographically based management structure' (Heer, 1991:455).

An acquisition- and diversification-marked history

Nestlé traces its history from 1866 when Anglo-Swiss Condensed Milk Co. was organized in Cham, Switzerland, by two American brothers, George and Charles Page (Franko, 1976:77; Heer, 1991:62–3), and from 1867 when Henri Nestlé formed Farine Lactée Henri Nestlé. In 1905 these two Swiss-based competitors (in milk and cereals) merged on a 50–50 basis as the Nestlé & Anglo-Swiss Condensed Milk Company.

Both companies brought to the newly merged enterprise an international infrastructure. Charles Page had headed the sales side of Anglo-Swiss Condensed Milk from London. In the 1870s Anglo-Swiss opened factories in the United Kingdom, and in 1872 in the USA. In 1883 Nestlé had established a London branch to distribute its products in Great Britain and overseas. It opened its first non-Swiss factory in Norway in 1898, and one in the United States in 1900. By 1919 the Nestlé and Anglo-Swiss Condensed Milk Company had affiliates in eight countries (Franko, 1976:9). World War I, by cutting off many markets from their supply sources, forced Nestlé to increase its local production capacity in many countries, notably Australia and the United States (Heer, 1991:116).

The interwar years marked the beginning of Nestlé's diversification. In 1929, it merged with Les Chocolats Peter-Cailler-Kohler (PCK), a company with which it had long had an alliance whereby PCK manufactured and Nestlé marketed chocolates. In 1938, Nestlé developed a new product, Nescafé, that was to become a major source of revenue (Heer, 1991:170–2). 'By 1936 the industrial and commercial activity of Nestlé and Anglo-Swiss Condensed Milk Company was very limited in comparison with the considerable interests it had acquired in companies manufacturing or selling its products. There were more than twenty such companies around the world at this time' (Heer, 1991:173), in Australia, North and South America, Asia and Europe. The company's policy of decentralization and the geographical dispersion of its activities combined with the prospects of another world war, led to a major reorganization in 1936. A Swiss company was established to carry out the domestic manufacturing and marketing activities previously performed by the parent company, and to hold the corporate trade marks. The parent company was transformed into a holding company, Nestlé & Anglo-Swiss Holding Company Ltd. A second holding company, Unilac, was created for a number of Nestlé's overseas affiliates.

With the outbreak of World War II, the Nestlé operations were split, with the CEO and some of the senior executives moving to an international headquarters in Stamford, Connecticut, from where they ran the Unilac part of Nestlé, while continental Europe continued to be run from Switzerland. The post-World War II years were marked by a series of mergers and acquisitions beginning in 1947 (see Figure 7.1) with Alimentana SA (Potages Jules Maggi) which added soups to the Nestlé range of products. The major acquisition of Crosse & Blackwell added food products in 1960, that of Locatelli cheese in 1961, that of Findus frozen foods in 1962, that of Libby canned goods in 1970, that of Ursina-Franck milk products in 1971, that of Stouffer frozen foods as well as restaurants and hotels in 1973 (which significantly strengthened its American base), that of L'Oréal cosmetics (a minority stake) in 1974, that of Alcon pharmaceuticals in 1977, and that of Chambourcy yogurt in 1978. More recent mergers and acquisitions have included Hill Brothers Coffee in 1985, Carnation milk in 1985, Buitoni-Perugini pasta and Rowntree chocolates in 1988, and Curtiss Brands chocolates and Superior Brands pet accessories in 1990.

The 1992 Nestlé acquisition of a majority stake in Perrier, won after a protracted battle with the Agnelli family, significantly strengthened its mineral water business and its French-based operations. Though traditionally averse to alliances, in the early 1990s Nestlé also formed two joint ventures: one with General Mills to develop the world-wide market for breakfast cereals and the other with Coca-Cola for canned coffee and tea. As a consequence not only of these mergers, acquisitions and alliances but also of its internally generated growth, the Nestlé Group's products, most of which are food related, included the following:

- Drinks.
- Dairy products.
- Chocolate and confectionery.
- Culinary products.
- Frozen food and ice cream.
- Food service products.
- Hotels and restaurants.
- Instant food and dietetic products.
- Pet foods.
- Pharmaceutical products and cosmetics.
- Refrigerated products.

In 1991, the 200 companies of the Nestlé Group employed almost 200,000 persons (about 3,000 of whom are located at its administrative and technical headquarters as well as its basic research and product development units in Switzerland). It operated more than 420 factories in more than 60 countries on five continents, and generated more than $33 billion in sales, of which about one-half was in Europe and about one-quarter in North America.

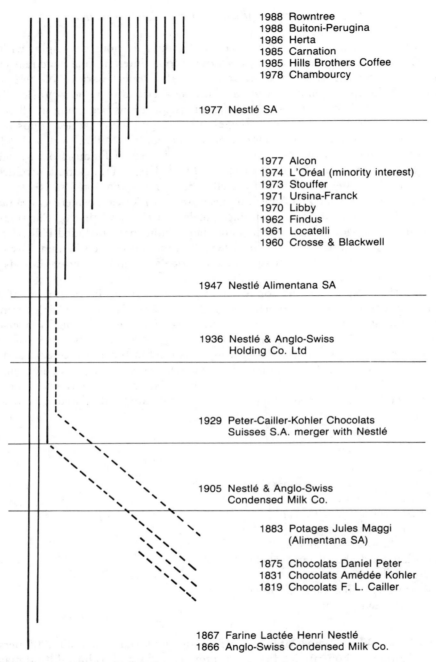

1988 Rowntree
1988 Buitoni-Perugina
1986 Herta
1985 Carnation
1985 Hills Brothers Coffee
1978 Chambourcy

1977 Nestlé SA

1977 Alcon
1974 L'Oréal (minority interest)
1973 Stouffer
1971 Ursina-Franck
1970 Libby
1962 Findus
1961 Locatelli
1960 Crosse & Blackwell

1947 Nestlé Alimentana SA

1936 Nestlé & Anglo-Swiss
Holding Co. Ltd

1929 Peter-Cailler-Kohler Chocolats
Suisses S.A. merger with Nestlé

1905 Nestlé & Anglo-Swiss
Condensed Milk Co.

1883 Potages Jules Maggi
(Alimentana SA)

1875 Chocolats Daniel Peter
1831 Chocolats Amédée Kohler
1819 Chocolats F. L. Cailler

1867 Farine Lactée Henri Nestlé
1866 Anglo-Swiss Condensed Milk Co.

Note: Subsequent additions include Curtiss Brands and Superior Brands in 1988
and majority control of Perrier in 1992.

Figure 7.1 Nestlé growth (Source: Nestlé *Annual Report,* 1990:31)

Holding company structure

Nestlé governs its far-flung group with a board of directors and group management; its chairman/CEO heads both. The 1990 board included five nationalities (American, Spanish, French and German as well as Swiss). The 1990 ten-member corporate team included a German (the CEO), two Spaniards, two British, and an Italian. (In 1991, the Italian retired and two Austrians were appointed.) Each of the corporate executive team members have portfolios. In 1990, six corporate executive team members had geographic portfolios, overseeing the six regional managements (US, Canada, Asia/Oceania, Europe, Latin America, Africa/Middle East). Four had functional portfolios (finance/administration management, R&D, technical and marketing). Three had product portfolios (chocolate and confectionery, pharmaceutical and other products). In 1993, Ramon Masap, Spanish head of Nestlé European operations, will become chief operating officer – a step that more clearly focuses responsibility in what has long been described as a 'team with a leader' (Maucher, 1988:9).

The Nestlé headquarters perceives itself performing essentially an 'arms length' role in its highly decentralized structure. Nestlé has perceived its organizational approach as:

> exactly the opposite of the policy pursued by big American companies whose most important operations are generally located within the U.S. where their state-of-the-art factories and top executives are located, and where they make most of their profits. These executives have a natural tendency, of course, to want to export their methods, applying them to all their foreign subsidiaries. (Heer, 1991:295–6)

With this decentralized structure, Nestlé's executive director-type affiliate heads have served as the linchpins binding global management and the locally based companies. Heer notes that in Nestlé's history 'the cohesion of the group depended primarily on such relationships' (Heer, 1991:296) between the affiliate heads and holding company executives. In 1989, the rapid expansion of Nestlé, through acquisitions and internally generated growth, led Nestlé to develop a subsidiary with the responsibility 'to create and develop technology in all areas of the food industry ... for passing on its marketing, organizational, management, and personnel training skills to the companies which manufacture and sell Nestlé products all over the world' (Maucher, 1985:11). The subsidiary, Nestec Ltd., thus separates the coordination of manufacturing and marketing advice and assistance from the controlling management of the affiliates, which remains focused on Nestlé.

In 1990, in order to achieve greater efficiencies, the Nestlé Group initiated two sets of steps. The first involved combining operations at the country level in the USA and the United Kingdom. Previously, Nestlé's fifteen US-based food and beverage companies – including Stouffer Foods, Carnation and Nestlé/Hills Coffee – operated autonomously. With the reorganization the US operations have been formed into six expanded business units: beverages, foods, frozen and refrigerated foods, food service, hotels, and wine. Nestlé has followed this up by more closely coordinating its UK operations, by merging them (including Rowntree) into a single organization. The other major set of changes has been to organize at headquarters two strategic business groups (one for technical and one for marketing) and seven strategic business units (SBUs). Each of the seven SBUs is responsible for a major sector of the Nestlé product span; their responsibilities will complement that of the regional managements.

Decentralized and internationalized staffing

The Nestlé Group operating companies largely manage their own internal staffing and are encouraged to develop their own local managers. In making senior management appointments in the operating companies, Nestlé takes a pragmatic approach: promoting from within whenever possible, or assigning persons from other operating companies or headquarters (interview, B. Link, 7 February 1990). The Nestlé Group management staffing reflects the international character of the company. It seeks and draws upon 'talent not only from Switzerland but also from as many markets as possible' (Maucher, 1988:11). Nestlé, with its policy of international career-long employment, 'tries to fill its leading posts by internal promotion' (Maucher, 1985:10) rather than external recruitment. Many of the headquarters staff (within which more than 50 nationalities are represented) have been assigned from the operating companies to develop an overall Nestlé perspective.

The Nestlé Group promotes management development not only by encouraging its operating companies to develop their own programmes, but also by providing some corporate-wide programmes. The operating companies stress on-the-job training as a means by which experienced employees pass on their knowledge. Most of the firms encourage their employees to follow courses of further training, either at local special institutes or their own residential training centres. In addition, senior staff in operating companies are encouraged to broaden their perspectives by working for specific periods of time in different Nestlé companies outside their own countries. Furthermore the Nestlé Group's international training centre, run by Nestec, provides corporate-wide programmes for managers and senior staff. For its managers, Nestlé has also long relied upon IMEDE, which it founded; it merged in 1989 with IMI to become IMD, one of the two most prestigious graduate management programmes in Europe.

Nestlé has developed an international corps whose role is to fill competency voids in operating companies, especially those companies in development phases. Those assigned from the international corps to the operating companies are expected to pass on their know-how to local personnel in these companies. For the corps, Nestlé recruits young persons with specific expertise such as economics, finances, sales and engineering, as well as knowledge of at least one appropriate foreign language. Nestlé assigns members of the corps to a company depending on its specific needs. Once a mission is completed, corps members are reassigned to another company needing their services. Personal requirements include maximum mobility, an open and inquiring mind, and the ability to adapt.

In the late 1980s the total number of expatriate assignments was 600. Many were those from smaller operating companies who were transferred to Switzerland or larger companies to gain experience and later return to their country of origin to take up new responsibilities. Such international postings are a means not only of developing staff, but also of promoting Group 'cohesion and team spirit'.

Promoting the 'Nestlé spirit'

The Nestlé Group promotes a 'Nestlé Spirit' throughout the operating companies. When new companies are acquired, the task of promoting this Nestlé spirit among them has required special attention. As Nestlé points out, such integration

> is not only a matter of developing new knowledge and new skills within the Group, and of giving concrete form to the desired synergistic effects, but also of ensuring the perpetuation and enhancement of the 'Nestlé Spirit', sometimes called the 'corporate culture', which is essential ... to achieve the team spirit, so vital to the Group's success. (Nestlé *Annual Report*, 1988:8)

The changing food industry

The Nestlé Group's decentralized organizational strategy has long suited an industrial environment characterized by diversity in consumer tastes and national regulations – and by insufficient economies of scale to warrant large-scale rationalization of R&D, production and marketing. Whereas consumer tastes in petroleum products, chemicals, electronics and automobiles have converged internationally, not only have national eating habits continued to differ significantly but also despite falling trade barriers in the EC, country-specific regulations continue to affect the food industry. The need to adapt to regional tastes and utilize local resources impeded the centralization of manufacturing. The increasing overlapping of tastes, the homogenization of regulations, and the development of global brands is, however, gradually changing the environment. The rapid development of global firms such as Philip Morris and P&G with the more integrated organizational strategies has led Nestlé to strengthen its oversight.

Royal Dutch/Shell: headquarters service companies assist national companies

A unifying international cadre and global culture

The Royal Dutch/Shell Group continues to adhere to an organizational strategy stressing territorial integration of activities – an approach from which the other petroleum multinationals have moved. The Shell Group has balanced this emphasis on autonomous international affiliates with a unifying corporate culture and a world-wide senior management staffing policy. The managing directors of Royal Dutch/Shell grant 'as much autonomy as possible to the operating companies'. In explaining that the committee of managing directors does not tell the operating companies what to do, a former Shell vice-chairman has said, 'Partly we're a friendly merchant bank, but we've also got the experts on tap for any Shell company that wants it' (Sampson, 1988:340). The operating companies are expected to use the expertise and are held accountable for the results. Shell's international cadre and global culture add important elements in providing global cohesion to its decentralized structure.

Over the decades the Royal Dutch/Shell group has developed several distinctive organizational features. First, because of its binational Dutch–British heritage, its central offices were split between The Hague and London. Second, by 1990 it was the largest non-American multinational and the largest oil company. The increasing diversity as well as the size of the Shell Group's operations and the need to coordinate globally has forced the development of a complex central office superstructure with nine service companies. Third, Shell has continued to allow its national operating companies significant autonomy. To manage these coherently Shell relies on a carefully selected and developed world-wide cadre of managers and a distinctive global culture.

A *binational heritage*

The Royal Dutch/Shell Group of Companies grew out of a confederation formed in 1907 between two parent holding companies: the Netherlands-based Royal Dutch Petroleum and the British-based 'Shell' Transport and Trading. By the terms of their agreement, each company kept a separate identity but merged interests (Sampson, 1988:64–7). The Dutch have been the senior partners (owning 60 per cent of the equity) in the combined enterprise, largely because it was the Dutch concern's head, Henri Deterding, who initiated the merger and directed the company until shortly before his death in 1939.

Under Deterding's direction the company grew rapidly; but, like many founding fathers, he so focused decision-making on himself that little was done to build an effective corporate structure. Until 1959, the two parent companies, with two sets of central offices, managed its affiliates throughout the world by performing a coordinating role, providing policy recommendations and monitoring their activities. Each parent had its

> own geographic spheres of interest and specialist functional
> responsibilities, although there was some duplication. The group's
> growing interest in petrochemicals was treated as a functional area
> engaged in the production and distribution of oil by-products. The
> growing complexities of rapid post-war expansion and the subsequent

organizational confusion initially remained hidden by a complacency born of a seller's market where mere possession of oil almost ensured profits. (Channon, 1973:115)

By 1959 growing world competition had made the organizational problems more evident. On the advice of McKinsey and Company, Royal Dutch/Shell restructured the central headquarters operations:

> Four new central service companies were created out of the original two holding companies. Regional boundaries were redrawn and control was decentralized to geographic regions which were to operate autonomously within broad lines of central policy and budgets, and subject to the advice of a newly appointed set of regional coordinators. Chemicals were divorced from oil operations, and a separate chemical division was set up with its own central service functions. The seven group managing directors were each given both functional and area responsibilities to ensure that each part of the world received the attention of a managing director, who at the same time maintained a global view by the supervision of a functional area. (Channon, 1973:115)

This structure has generally persisted and the autonomy of the operating companies continued even through the oil crises of the 1970s and 1980s (see Senge, 1990:178–81, for a description of how the Shell Group Planning staff helped prepare the operating companies for the crisis which in other companies led to greater centralization). But with the addition of five more service companies and a sophisticated information system, the headquarters structure has become far more complex. The operating companies continue, nevertheless, to exert a significant degree of autonomy. Shell began its chemical operations as early as 1928. Unlike the other oil companies, which have separated chemicals into a separate product sector with its own national affiliates, the unified management of these omnibus operating companies continues to direct the local chemical operations. Royal Dutch/Shell expanded into mining and metals in the 1970s. In 1991 the Group employed more than 130,000 people world-wide and its total sales of $103 billion ranked it second internationally behind General Motors.

A federation of national organizations

As shown in Figure 7.2, the two parent companies share control of the Royal Dutch/Shell Group; Royal Dutch has 60 per cent and 'Shell' Transport and Trading has 40 per cent interest in the Group, whose principal components are three group holding companies – Shell Petroleum NV (Netherlands), The Shell Petroleum Company Limited (United Kingdom) and Shell Petroleum Inc. (United States), for which in 1985 the parent companies paid $5.7 billion for the outstanding equity in order to achieve 100 per cent ownership. The parent companies appoint the directors of these holding companies and receive income in the form of dividends.

Structure of the Group

The Royal Dutch/Shell Group of Companies has grown out of an alliance made in 1907 between Royal Dutch Petroleum Company and The 'Shell' Transport and Trading Company, plc, by which the two companies agreed to merge their interests on a 60:40 basis while keeping their separate identities. Today the title describes a group of companies engaged in the oil, natural gas, chemicals, coal and metals businesses throughout the greater part of the world.

Parent companies

As parent companies, Royal Dutch Petroleum Company and The 'Shell' Transport and Trading Company, plc, do not themselves directly engage in operational activities. They are public companies, one domiciled in the Netherlands, the other in the United Kingdom.

The parent companies directly or indirectly own the shares in the Group holding companies but are not themselves part of the Group. They appoint directors to the boards of the group holding companies, from which they receive income in the form of dividends.

Royal Dutch/Shell Group of companies

Service companies

Shell Internationale Petroleum Maatschappij BV
Shell Internationale Chemie Maatschappij BV
Shell International Petroleum Company Limited
Shell International Chemical Company Limited
Billiton International Metals BV
Shell International Marine Limited
Shell Internationale Research Maatschappij BV
Shell International Gas Limited
Shell Coal International Limited.

The main business of the service companies is to provide advice and services to other Group and associated companies, excluding Shell Petroleum Inc. and its subsidiaries. The service companies are variously located in the Netherlands or the United Kingdom.

Shareholdings

There are some 400,000 shareholders of Royal Dutch and some 300,000 of Shell Transport. Shares of one or both companies are listed and traded on stock exchanges in eight European countries and in the USA.

The estimated geographical distribution of shareholdings at the end of 1988 was:

	Royal Dutch %	Shell Transport %	Combined %
United Kingdom	2	96	40
Netherlands	37	*	22
USA	32	3	20
Switzerland	18	*	11
France	6	1	4
West Germany	3	*	2
Belgium	1	*	1
Luxembourg	1	*	*
Others	*	*	*

*Less than 1%

Group holding companies

Shell Petroleum NV and The Shell Petroleum Company Limited between them hold all the shares in the service companies and, directly or indirectly, all Group interests in the operating companies other than those held by Shell Petroleum Inc.

* Shell Petroleum NV holds equity shares in Shell Petroleum Inc. which are non-controlling but entitle it to the dividend flow from that company.

Operating companies

Operating companies are engaged in various branches of the oil and natural gas, chemicals, coal, metals and other businesses in many countries. The management of each operating company is responsible for the performance and long-term viability of its own operations, but can draw on the experience of the service companies and, through them, of other operating companies.

Diagram boxes: Individuals and institutions | Individuals and institutions → Royal Dutch Petroleum Company (Netherlands 60%) | The 'Shell' Transport and Trading Company, plc (United Kingdom 40%) → Shell Petroleum NV* (Netherlands) | The Shell Petroleum Company Limited (United Kingdom) | Shell Petroleum Inc.* (USA) → Service companies → Operating companies in more than 100 countries (other than Shell Oil Company and its subsidiaries) | Shell Oil Company (USA)

Legend:
— Shareholding relationships
— Advice and services
— Shareholding relationship — Advice and services

Figure 7.2 Royal Dutch/Shell organogram (Source: Royal Dutch/Shell Group of Companies *Annual Report*, 1988:21)

The British-based and Netherlands-based holding companies hold all the shares in the service companies and, directly or indirectly, all Group interests in the several hundred operating companies, other than those held by Shell Petroleum Inc.

The Shell Group is managed by a six-member committee of managing directors (CMD), individually known as group managing directors. In 1990 this committee comprised three British members and three Dutch ones and was headed by a Dutch chairman, Lodewijk van Wachom, and a British vice-chairman, Sir Peter Holmes. This committee, whose key planning and personnel decisions must be unanimous, 'considers, develops and decides upon overall objectives and long term plans to be recommended to operating companies' (Royal Dutch/Shell, 1988:3). Each committee member oversees a sphere of interest which generally includes one continental region, one or more functions and one or more business product sectors. Except for the chairman and vice-chairman, each member serves as a director of two to four of the service companies. Thus, each of the heads of the corporate staff functions, the product business sectors and the regional offices reports to one of the six managing directors who work together and make decisions on a consensus basis (see Figure 7.3).

The nine service companies support the efforts of the operating companies by providing three types of expert advice and assistance:

1. Business product expertise.
2. Functional expertise.
3. Regional coordination.

The service companies which focus on the more technical activities, such as exploration, production, manufacturing and research, are located in The Hague. The service companies with primarily commercial/marketing roles are located in London. Most service companies focus on the affairs of a business 'sector'. Since petroleum is the major business, the petroleum companies are the largest service companies. They house most of the functional and regional coordination support.

Each of the regions has a regional coordinator whose responsibility it is to represent the shareholders' interest in the management of the operating companies. The regional coordinators, who are organizationally located in the downstream oil service company in London, are assisted by small staffs. With their assistance, the regional coordinators keep the committee of managing directors informed and ensure the provision of expert advice and assistance from the service companies.

Divided as the central organization is between London and The Hague, and comprised of nine service companies, many staff support units and the regional operations, it is as complex as the operating companies are integrated.

The operating companies

Within each country one affiliate has a comprehensive embracing role for all, or almost all, of the Royal Dutch/Shell activities there. The management committee of

```
Regions
United Kingdom and Ireland      (1)  (3)
Europe                          (1)  (3)
Africa and South Asia           (1)  (3)
East and Australasia            (1)  (3)
Middle East                     (1)  (3)
Caribbean, Central and
South America                   (1)  (3)
Eastern Europe                  (1)  (3)
```

```
Countries
Canada                          (1)  (3)
United States
```

```
Functional services
   Finance and computing   (3)
   Legal                   (3)
   Materials               (1)
   Organization            (3)
   Personnel               (1&3)
   Planning                (1&3)
   Public affairs          (3)
   Research                (7)
Toxicology, health, safety
and environmental conservation  (1)
```

```
Business sectors
○ Upstream oil and gas   (1)  (3)
○ Downstream oil         (1)  (3)
○ Marine                 (6)
○ Natural gas            (8)
○ Chemicals              (4)
○ Coal                   (9)
○ Metals                 (5)
```

```
Service companies
1. Shell Internationale Petroleum Maatschappij BV
2. Shell Internationale Chemie Maatschappij BV
3. Shell International Petroleum Company Limited
4. Shell International Chemical Company Limited
5. Billiton International Metals BV
6. Shell International Marine Limited
7. Shell Internationale Research Maatschappij BV
8. Shell International Gas Limited
9. Shell Coal International Limited
```

```
The main business of the service companies is
to provide advice and services to other Group
and associated companies, excluding Shell
Petroleum and its subsidiaries. The service
companies are variously located in the
Netherlands or the United Kingdom.
```

Note: Numbers refer to the service company in which these function, sector and regional staff are housed.

Figure 7.3 Royal Dutch/Shell three-dimensional support matrix (Source: Courtesy of Royal Dutch/Shell)

this omnibus affiliate is headed by a country general manager and may include managers of marketing, distribution and supply, chemicals, production, finance, and human resources. The country general manager with his or her management team is directly responsible for the other Shell affiliates in the country (with a few exceptions such as a Shell research laboratory). The management committee always includes a mixture of host country nationals and those assigned from the Shell international cadre. The integrated Shell affiliates obtain advice from the service companies to ensure that in making decisions they have the full range of expertise within the Group, but assert autonomy, and generally achieve credibility as local companies.

International corps

To manage its complex global operations Shell has developed an international corps whose members are recruited throughout the world for career-long Shell employment. The Group recruits globally and the local operating companies recruit locally. Individuals wanting an international career apply directly to the Group headquarters, and individuals who prefer to remain in their home country apply directly to the local company. Regardless of where an individual is hired, the intent in Shell is to hire and promote managers who can adapt to different conditions and constantly changing circumstances. Even those who are hired by local operating companies are given the opportunity to gain experience outside their own discipline and outside their own country. In this way potential high-flyers are exposed to a succession of new challenges and unfamiliar environments, and develop business, area and functional expertise.

Top management devotes considerable attention to executive development. Periodically, the committee of managing directors examines the progress of identified people in various jobs – jobs which are selected to provide appropriate experiences and challenges for each individual. In some cases promising people 'burn out' as they progress. Others are 'late bloomers'. The periodic assessment provides an opportunity to adjust development paths and reassign mentors depending on the revised expectation.

Shell encourages international cross-posting of its managers. All senior managers have had work experience in different foreign countries and also in different functional areas. It is not unusual for a country affiliate manager with 21 years of service with Shell to have already had seven postings, including experience in line and staff posts in four different countries, in corporate and regional headquarters, and in three operating companies. Shell believes that multiple perspectives increase mental and behavioural flexibility – an essential characteristic for Shell managers.

Shell attempts to manage its staff development policy so that every member of each affiliate management team has at least one out-of-country assignment and so that each team includes at least one expatriate. As one country manager phrased it,

Shell believes that diversity of experience increases the ability of senior managers to appreciate another management perspective. Shell also recognizes that mutual interests improve teamwork among the diverse parts of Shell, and relieve the 'benign tension' that can develop between affiliates and headquarters.

Local people recruited through international headquarters are placed in an international corps and may spend their entire career working outside their own country. Rapid movement through various jobs and frequent management training and meetings, which are hallmarks of a Shell career, tend to develop unifying values and a loyalty to the parent company. Some international employees may have little sense of identification with their home country other than their pension fund, which is normally vested in their home country.

Shell recognizes that not all people want extensive international careers, and provides challenging, diverse experiences in its local companies as well. Local people recruited locally are assigned to different jobs throughout their career but within their home country. Should those hired locally change their mind about an international career, they may apply to the international headquarters.

Two groups within Shell have especially promising careers there. Graduate engineers from a top technical university appear to have an advantage within the more technical parts of Shell. (The three Dutch group managing directors are graduates of Delft.) On the other hand, graduates of such elite universities as Cambridge appear to have an advantage in the commercial areas. (Two of the three recent British group managing directors are Cambridge graduates.) Shell was one of the few mega-multinationals whose executives voiced concern over the shrinking number of 20–30-year-olds from which to recruit in the 1990s and the effect this would have on Shell's future.

The world-wide family

Shell's strong corporate culture appears to be a major factor providing its organizational cohesion. It has a long history of autonomous country affiliates and many of these are managed by people who adapt well to the local environment as well as identifying with the parent company and sharing a pride and self-confidence that stems from association with the Group. While Shell employees feel part of a world-wide family, they take pride in their local company. This global feeling has been fostered by posting personnel from country to country, but the local *esprit de corps* manifests itself in the rapidity with which even those on expatriate assignments come to think of the local company as 'we'.

The Shell culture, by encouraging the 'we' identification with the national operating company, fosters national pride and the feeling that the company cares about national interests and conditions. The fact that some local employees believe that the local company can operate counter to the wishes of headquarters while perceiving themselves as members of one corporate-wide family may highlight one of the dynamics fostering Shell's cohesion. The Shell Group appreciation of cultural diversity may well stem from its binational origins.

What next?

Shell's heritage as a binational company has facilitated its development as a multi-local enterprise. Its international cadre and culture provide unity to what remains a federation of country units. Its financial success may have tempered its will to tamper with the existing organizational structure. Shell leadership has stressed its intention to proceed cautiously and slowly, not rushing into organizational change for change's sake. Shell thus remains the only major oil company that organizes its international activities principally by area. The country integration of the oil and chemical business enhances intracountry efficiencies, but hinders cross-border efficiencies. Since the integration of Europe will reduce the advantages of such a geography-divided organization, Shell may in time be forced to shift to a more product-driven organization – despite the high costs of such a transformation.

Global product divisions manage international operations

Bayer: from function-driven to product-driven in three stages

Prompted by the need to organize its rapidly growing and increasingly diversified international businesses more competitively, Bayer has since 1965 undertaken three major reorganizations (see Figure 7.4). The cumulative impact of these efforts has been the transformation of Bayer from a functionally divided company concerned principally with its domestic management into one whose product groups have world-wide responsibility. As a consequence of its organizational efforts, Bayer has earned a reputation as the best organized of the three major German chemical companies (Seifert, 1991).

Three successive major reorganizations

The company that F. Bayer and J.F. Wescott founded in 1863 was a maker of synthetic dyes. As early as 1870, Bayer established foreign offices in Vienna and New York. In 1876, it organized a dye operation in Moscow, and in 1882 developed a plant in Rensselar, New York (Chandler, 1990:179). In 1881, Bayer organized as a shareholding corporation. By the 1890s Bayer was producing pharmaceuticals; it introduced aspirin in 1899 and began producing photographic supplies in the early 1900s. Because Bayer and the other major German dye firms (Hoechst and BASF) had grown large by exploiting economies of scope, they had become by 1900 as diversified as any industrial firm in the world (Chandler, 1990:474–80).

As a consequence of World War I, Bayer's overseas properties were confiscated (Sterling Drug grew initially through the acquisition of Bayer's American

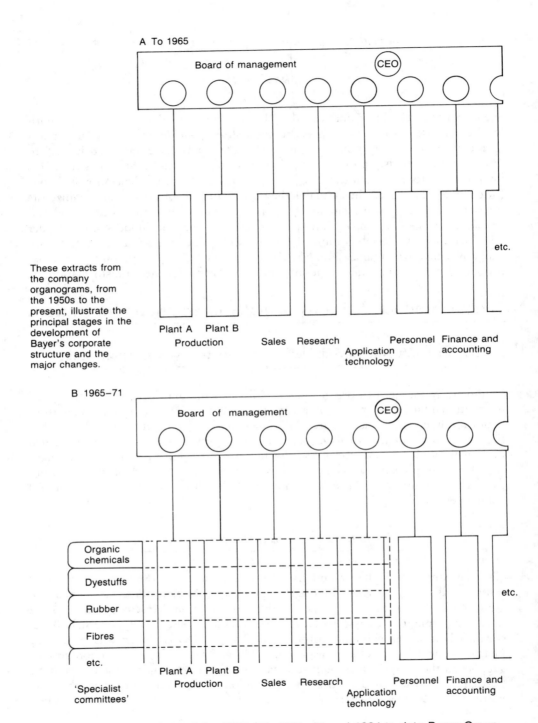

These extracts from the company organograms, from the 1950s to the present, illustrate the principal stages in the development of Bayer's corporate structure and the major changes.

A To 1965

Board of management   CEO

Plant A   Plant B
Production   Sales   Research   Personnel   Finance and
                           Application   accounting
                           technology

etc.

B 1965–71

Board of management   CEO

Organic chemicals

Dyestuffs

Rubber

Fibres

etc.

'Specialist committees'

Plant A   Plant B
Production   Sales   Research   Personnel   Finance and
                           Application   accounting
                           technology

etc.

Figure 7.4 The impact of the 1965–71, 1971–84 and 1984 to date Bayer Group reorganizations (Source: Vossberg, 1984:52–3)

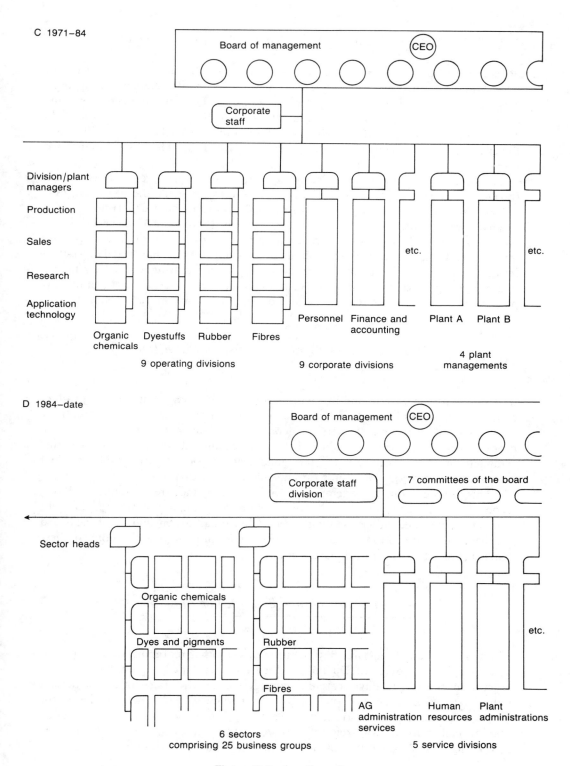

C 1971–84

Board of management — CEO

Corporate staff

Division/plant managers

Production

Sales

Research

Application technology

Organic chemicals — Dyestuffs — Rubber — Fibres

9 operating divisions

Personnel — Finance and accounting

etc.

9 corporate divisions

Plant A — Plant B

etc.

4 plant managements

D 1984–date

Board of management — CEO

Corporate staff division

7 committees of the board

Sector heads

Organic chemicals

Dyes and pigments

Rubber

Fibres

AG administration services

Human resources

Plant administrations

etc.

6 sectors comprising 25 business groups

5 service divisions

Figure 7.4 (continued)

properties): Chandler, 1990:164). In 1925 Bayer, Hoechst and BASF, which since 1904 had been allied and in 1916 had formed a consortium, merged into a single corporation, I.G. Farben (Chandler, 1990:564–87). The merged company developed synthetic rubber, sulfonamide and colour film (Agfa), among others. In 1945, with the defeat of Germany, the Allies confiscated I.G. Farben. In 1951, Bayer AG and two of Bayer's major competitors, BASF and Hoechst, were formed from I.G. Farben.

Since 1951 Bayer has expanded its operations in a variety of business fields, through aggressive product innovations, acquisitions, mergers and joint ventures. Before 1965, Bayer's organization was divided into functional departments, each headed by a member of the board of management ('*Vorstand*') whose head (the CEO) was vested with sole decision-making authority. Until 1965, Bayer's international activities developed randomly. Over the years, as Bayer had diversified into related areas and expanded internationally, manufacturing and sales affiliates had been created whenever and wherever a market or production opportunity was perceived. The stage was set for the first of three reorganizations.

1965: creating product-focused committees

In 1965, with its first major postwar reorganization, Bayer introduced product coordinating committees that overlaid what continued to be the essentially functional structure. The functional departments remained dominant while the product decisions were coordinated by the product committees. Under this arrangement each member of the management board undertook a dual responsibility, directing one function and one product division.

This organization arrangement proved to be a short-term solution. Bayer recognized that, first, the coordinating committees did not ensure a sufficient product perspective, and, secondly, the direct divisional responsibilities of the board members handicapped the board in its efforts to develop an objective point of view that benefited the corporation as a whole.

1971: introducing the product division

Within a few years, therefore, Bayer, undertook another reorganization. This time Bayer sought the advice of Du Pont, which had developed a multidivisionalized structure in the 1920s. Bayer carefully considered the advantages of this structure, with an international division such as Du Pont had developed. The study led to the adoption of a divisional structure – but the Du Pont model of a separate international division was rejected. Therefore the product divisional structure introduced in 1971 assigned to each division world-wide product profit-and-loss responsibility and direct control over its international operations. As Heinrich Vossberg, Bayer's principal organizational strategist, has stressed:

> Bayer preferred to have each division responsible for its own international affairs, rather than an international division. This facilitates communication and allows the company to acquire international management expertise and knowledge in all the product divisions rather than one department. Bayer sees this approach as essential to its corporate culture and corporate direction (interview, Vossberg, 18 July 1989).

This reorganization also relieved the *Vorstand* members of direct operating responsibilities by delegating these duties to a second tier. Thus, with the introduction of product divisions, the board members were freed from direct responsibility for a functional department or a product group. The change facilitated the board's making decisions on an objective basis and avoided power struggles when divisional issues were brought to it.

The power structure of the board members also changed as a result of a change in German corporate law. The position of CEO was changed from that of a 'one-above-others' leader ('*Führerprinzip*') – whose vote was the only one that counted – to that of '*primus inter pares*' who must have the support of at least one half of the board members for a major decision. This new organization provided Bayer with a multidivisional corporate structure.

1984: integrating, clarifying and creating sectors

Thirteen years later Bayer again reorganized. This time the heads of the supervisory board and the management board set up a three-man team led by the *Vorstand* member who was already designated (but not publicly) as the next CEO. The reorganization that this team recommended divided the nine divisions into 24 'business groups', gradually reduced the *Vorstand* from fourteen to nine members, and created six sectors with each sector containing from two to five 'business groups' (Seifert, 1991:152). To quote from the internal Bayer magazine, *Bayer Reports*:

- The management emphasis has been shifted from the parent company to Bayer World by integrating Bayer's foreign activities and those of the subsidiaries more closely in the organization.
- The various business areas had been regrouped and restructured, and responsibilities more clearly defined, in order to increase the Company's efficiency and flexibility on the world market.
- Certain duties previously performed by the Board of Management have been delegated to lower management levels so that the Board can concentrate more on corporate policy and on defining objectives for the Company as a whole. (Vossberg, 1984)

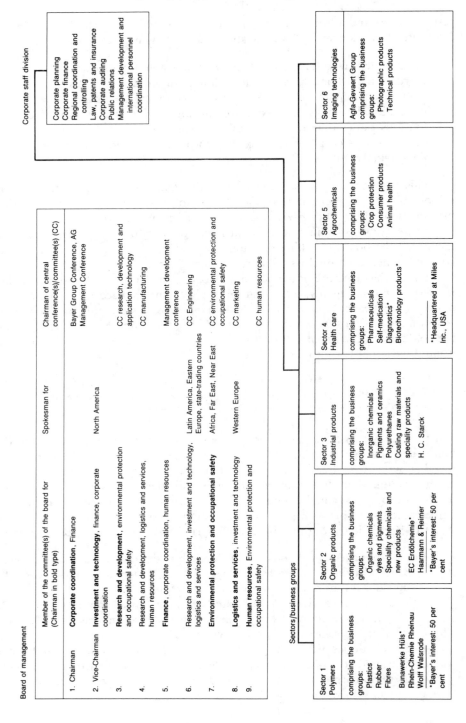

Board of management

Corporate staff division

	Corporate planning
	Corporate finance
	Regional coordination and controlling
	Law, patents and insurance
	Corporate auditing
	Public relations
	Management development and international personnel coordination

	Member of the committee(s) of the board for (Chairman in bold type)	Spokesman for	Chairman of central conference(s)/committee(s) (CC)
1. Chairman	**Corporate coordination**, Finance		Bayer Group Conference, AG Management Conference
2. Vice-Chairman	**Investment and technology**, finance, corporate coordination	North America	
3.	**Research and development**, environmental protection and occupational safety		CC research, development and application technology
4.	Research and development, logistics and services, human resources		CC manufacturing
5.	**Finance**, corporate coordination, human resources		Management development conference
6.	Research and development, investment and technology, logistics and services	Latin America, Eastern Europe, state-trading countries	CC Engineering
7.	**Environmental protection and occupational safety**	Africa, Far East, Near East	CC environmental protection and occupational safety
8.	**Logistics and services**, investment and technology	Western Europe	CC marketing
9.	**Human resources**, Environmental protection and occupational safety		CC human resources

Sectors/business groups

Sector 1 Polymers	Sector 2 Organic products	Sector 3 Industrial products	Sector 4 Health care	Sector 5 Agrochemicals	Sector 6 Imaging technologies
comprising the business groups:	comprising the business groups:	comprising the business groups:	comprising the business groups:	comprising the business groups:	Agfa-Gevaert Group comprising the business groups:
Plastics	Organic chemicals	Inorganic chemicals	Pharmaceuticals	Crop protection	Photographic products
Rubber	dyes and pigments	Pigments and ceramics	Self-medication	Consumer products	Technical products
Fibres	Speciality chemicals and new products	Polyurethanes	Diagnostics*	Animal health	
		Coating raw materials and speciality products	Biotechnology products*		
Bunawerke Hüls*	EC Erdölchemie*				
Rhein-Chemie Rheinau	Haarmann & Reimer	H. C. Starck			
Wolff Walsrode	*Bayer's interest: 50 per cent		*Headquartered at Miles Inc., USA		
*Bayer's interest: 50 per cent					

Service divisions					
AG administration services	Human resources	Plant administration, environmental protection and occupational safety	Central research and development	Central engineering	
Purchasing	Personnel policy	Plant administration, Leverkusen	Chemical research	Project engineering	
Traffic and distribution services	Personnel, Leverkusen	Plant administration, Dormagen	Technical development and applied physics	Plant safety and technical inspection	
Advertising	Social matters, Leverkusen	Plant administration, Uerdingen	Research and development services	Utilities	
Accounting	Training, Leverkusen	Plant administration, Elberfeld		Process control systems	
Information systems	Personnel department, Dormagen	Plant administration, Brunsbüttel		Central workshops	
	Personnel department, Uerdingen	Environmental protection			
	Personnel department, Elberfeld				
	Personnel department, managerial employees				
	Pension insurance department				

Figure 7.5 Bayer organogram, 1989 (Source: Bayer *Annual Report*, 1988:116–17)

In 1990 the Bayer Group, the world's fourth largest chemical company, generated more than $26 billion in sales. Through internal efforts as well as through acquisitions Bayer had diversified internationally into a number of chemical-related areas. Overall, the Bayer Group, with its 25 business groups, comprises 400 companies in over 60 countries, and generates 65 per cent of its sales outside Germany and over 30 per cent outside Europe.

Supervisory board and management board

As required by German law, Bayer has a supervisory board (*Aufsichtsrat*). The board is composed entirely of outsiders. Half of the members are shareholder representatives, the other half labour union and employee representatives. Its primary responsibility is to select and supervise the Bayer board of management (*Vorstand*). Since most small shareholders in Germany give their shareholder voting rights to their banks, the banks, along with the unions, have a significant influence on German corporate management.

The board of management consists of nine members, each of whom has one or more portfolios (see Figure 7.5). Until the 1990 appointment of a Belgian, the members of the board of management were also all German. Each board member chairs one or more board committees such as marketing, manufacturing, research and development, finance, human resources, investment, and environmental protection. Four board members serve as the spokespeople for the regions: North America, Western Europe, Asia and Africa, and Latin America combined with East Europe. These spokespeople provide advice and counsel, but the primary reporting relationship is through the business groups. The board of management members remain freed from its day-to-day business responsibilities. Decisions and analysis are prepared for the board by committees, each comprising members of the board, line executives and staff specialists.

The business group heads, while directly responsible for operational results to the board, work closely with the sector heads, 'who function as strategy controllers' (Seifert, 1991:152). A sector head has no formal authority but has longstanding corporate experience; his or her advice is therefore important to the group heads and to the board. There are two types of sector head: one is the younger and promising division head understudying a position, the other the experienced older manager approaching retirement.

Each business group holds world-wide business responsibility and has its own headquarters. While most of the group head offices are at the corporate headquarters of Bayer in Leverkusen, Germany, some are located in other German cities and some outside Germany. The Miles Corporation, for example, was integrated into Bayer as the diagnostics business group and biotechnological business group, with both groups having their world-wide headquarters in the USA. Six of Bayer's 25 business groups are headed by non-Germans. These business groups are split into over 100 business units, but these exist only conceptually for business planning. In spite of its sector/group structure, Bayer has maintained centralized human resource and administration departments.

The organization of the Bayer national affiliates is similar to that of its corporate structure. In several countries, a single umbrella-like national affiliate has been created as the legal entity embracing the individual business units, which report directly back to their respective group head offices (see Figure 7.6). Within this umbrella-like arrangement several business unit heads may constitute a management board with its head designated as national spokesperson, who deals with local issues and external affairs affecting general Bayer interests, conferring with the board member designated as regional spokesperson.

The two largest foreign groupings are those in the USA and Japan. As of 1988, all of Bayer's activities in the USA were consolidated under Bayer USA Inc., its management holding company. Its operating companies include Mobay Corporation, Miles Inc., Haarmann & Reimer Corporation, Deerfield Urethane, Inc., Wyrough and Loser, Inc., NRC Inc., and Hermann C. Starck, Inc., as well as the newly formed Agfa Corporation. The Bayer Group in Japan comprises twelve companies with over 3,000 employees.

Cross-divisional German-oriented staffing

Bayer manages this complex organization with a staffing policy which stresses diversity of experience. Employees must have cross-divisional experience before moving to the fourth (out of seven) management level in the hierarchy. To advance to the fifth layer, employees must have extensive international experience. The company strongly encourages its managers to take cross-divisional and international assignments to develop into well-rounded managers. With only a few exceptions (for highly specialized posts), Bayer hires young university graduates and develops the more qualified ones with cross-divisional and international assignments. Non-German employees with high potential are also given assignments early in their careers at a headquarters location, typically in Leverkusen. Since speaking German is essential for upward mobility and promotion for all employees of Bayer throughout the world, during the German assignment promising managers are expected to become fluent in the language.

Bayer does not believe in hiring people trained in 'management'. In Bayer's understanding, management is the individual capacity of coordinating and is acquired by knowledge and experience. Bayer's managers have generally earned their degree in the sciences and are frequently chemists with doctorates. At the directors' level, more than 60 per cent hold doctorates, and almost 10 per cent are listed in the corporate report with the designation 'Professor'.

German-based corporate culture

The German-based corporate culture has sometimes conflicted with the country

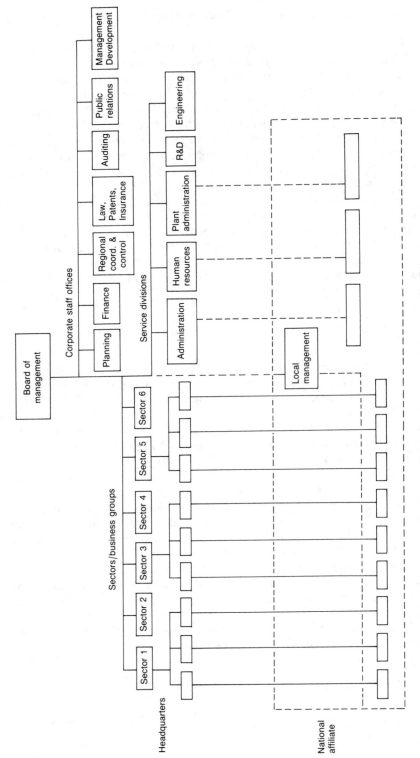

Figure 7.6 The Bayer organization and affiliates

culture of the national affiliates. Bayer managers point out that in comparison with the USA, German employees expect less direct supervision and less detailed specification of target objectives. People are perceived as working with shared assumptions and prefer general goals rather than specific directives (interview, Vossberg, 18 July 1989).

An important societal force shaping the corporate culture of Bayer is the extensive public concern for the environment. Bayer prides itself on having been concerned with the environment long before it became a public issue. The company makes extensive investments in order to be a 'good corporate citizen'.

A postwar-developed company

As a company that rebuilt its foreign affiliates after World War II, Bayer did not face the challenge of integrating well-developed autonomous affiliates into its operations. Bayer undertook the shift from a function-driven to a world-wide product-driven company in a three-stage, twenty-year incremental effort. Its major challenge may be how to reconcile its distinctive German-stressed staffing and culture with the staffing needs and cultures in non-German countries.

Daimler-Benz: bank-led rapid diversification and growth

Daimler-Benz has long been the major star in the Deutsche Bank constellation. Deutsche Bank played a significant role in initiating the rapid diversification by acquisition which Daimler-Benz began in 1985. One aim has been to expand Daimler-Benz from a motor vehicle company to one whose scope embraces road, train and air transport, with the high-technology core required to remain on the cutting edge. Another aim has been to develop its American and Asian presence. The challenge facing Daimler-Benz is to develop the structures, staffing arrangements and shared corporate vision and values which will allow it to achieve the desired synergies that have motivated its diversification drive. One of the key strategic issues Daimler-Benz will have to face in its efforts to globalize will be whether to develop motor vehicle manufacturing capacity overseas, and if so, how to assure the same high standard that has gained Mercedes-Benz its reputation for quality.

From cars to conglomerate

Karl Benz founded Benz & Co. in 1883; Daimler was founded seven years later. In 1909, both the Benz and Daimler companies began building aircraft engines. In 1926, the two companies merged as Daimler-Benz (Chandler, 1990:528–9). In 1946 the Stuttgart-based company began rebuilding its destroyed plant facilities;

in 1948 it resumed the development and production of motor vehicles; and by 1950 it was exporting its products to 50 countries.

Since 1985, with the stimulus of Deutsche Bank and the lead of Edzard Reuter, initially as finance director and since 1987 as CEO, Daimler-Benz has diversified rapidly into defence and electronics, principally by acquisitions. Daimler-Benz took control of AEG (Allgemeine Elektrizitäts-Gesellschaft, which from the 1890s to the 1940s was, along with GE, Westinghouse and Siemens, one of the global industry's 'Big Four') and Dornier in 1985, MTU (Motoren & Turbinen Union GmbH) in 1986, and MBB (Messerschmitt-Boelkow-Blohm GmbH) in 1989. (The latter provided Daimler-Benz with a share in the Airbus Industry consortium.) It followed up these acquisitions with a number of alliances announced in 1990 and 1991. MTU has combined its jet engine operations with the Pratt and Whitney unit of United Technologies. MBB has formed a joint venture with the French aerospace group, Aerospatiale SA, linking their helicopter businesses. In 1991 Daimler-Benz acquired a 34 per cent stake in Cap Gemini Sogeti SA, Europe's largest computer services company, and an option to take majority control. The 1990-announced alliance with the Mitsubishi grouping presents a range of opportunities for Daimler-Benz to continue its globalization efforts by developing strategic major motor, electronic and aerospace ventures. The rationale for the alliance was described by Hanns Glatz, a Daimler-Benz spokesman, as follows: 'To do business in Japan you must go into business with the Japanese' (interview, 16 January 1991). To continue the Daimler-Benz global expansion, Reuter also 'has in mind further acquisitions of yet un-named companies in the United States' (Olins, 1989:138).

A Deutsche-Bank-controlled company

Deutsche Bank owns 28 per cent of Daimler-Benz stock (and votes the shares of many others). The Deutsche Bank CEO, who is the supervisory board chairman of Daimler-Benz, oversees not only the direction of Germany's largest bank but also the destiny of a network of German companies by virtue of the bank's extensive holdings (see Table 7.3) and of the fact that 'the twelve directors of Deutsche Bank sit on more than 100 boards' of German companies (*International Management*, November 1989:8). Representatives of Deutsche Bank have headed Daimler-Benz's supervisory board virtually without a break since 1926, when the bank organized the merger of Daimler and Benz to surmount the economic crisis then facing both companies. Since 1955, five successive Deutsche Bank CEOs have served as chairman of the Daimler-Benz supervisory board. (In 1975 the Deutsche Bank bought from the Flick group its 29 per cent share of Daimler-Benz, to prevent its sale to Iran, and subsequently sold most of this stake to 'friendly' institutions.) It was Alfred Herrhausen, the Deutsche Bank CEO from 1985 until his terrorist slaying in 1989, who engineered the replacement of the former Daimler-Benz CEO with Edzard Reuter in 1987. In addition to the Deutsche-Bank-nominated chairman, the supervisory board includes ten labour representatives, another

Table 7.3 Deutsche Bank's non-bank holdings of 10 per cent or more

Company	Holding (%)	Activities
Daimler-Benz, Stuttgart	28.37	Vehicles, aerospace
Philipp Holzmann, Frankfurt am Main	30.00	Building
Hutschenreuther, Selb	25.09	Porcelain
Karstadt, Essen	25.26	Retailing
Klöckner-Humboldt-Deutz, Cologne	41.14	Engineering
NINO, Nordhorn	23.93	Textiles
Allianz Holding, Munich	10.00	Insurance
Fuchs Petrolub, Mannheim	10.00	Oil, chemicals
Hapag-Lloyd, Hamburg	12.50	Transport, tourism
Heidelberger Zement, Heidelberg	10.00	Cement
Leifheit, Nassau/Lahn	10.00	Household electricals
Linde, Wiesbaden	10.00	Engineering
Münchener Rückversicherung, Munich	10.00	Reinsurance
Phoenix, Hamburg	10.00	Rubber
Salamander, Kornwestheim	10.00	Shoes
Südzucker Mannheim/Ochsenfurt, Mannheim	16.90	Sugar
Vereinigte Seidenwebereien, Krefeld	10.00	Silk weaving
Josef Vögele, Mannheim	10.00	Construction machinery

Deutsche Bank representative, three representatives of other banks and the CEOs of Bayer and Deutsche Shell.

The Daimler-Benz board of management comprises the chairman, the Mercedes-Benz CEO (who is the board vice-chairman), the Mercedes-Benz vice-chairman, the AEG CEO, the Deutsche Aerospace CEO, the Daimler-Benz Inter Services (Debis) CEO, and the heads of the finance, human resources/employment, and research and technology support divisions. The executive board composition reflects the fact that Daimler-Benz operates as an executive holding company with overall responsibility for the four major operating divisions, coordinating, controlling and monitoring them in strategic matters which include finance, research and development, and initiating new efforts.

The diversification efforts have led Daimler-Benz to organize itself first into three and then into four major sectors, each of which operates with its own identity and logo. Mercedes-Benz, the principal part, comprises what until only a few years ago was the entire Daimler-Benz company. It consists of two sectors: passenger cars and commercial vehicles. The board of the Mercedes-Benz part has reflected its bifurcated character: it has included the CEO, the deputy CEO (who heads, together with another board member, the commercial vehicle sector) and one board member for the car sector, as well as two sets (one for cars and one for commercial vehicles) of junior board members: two sales directors, two manufacturing directors and two research and development directors. Mercedes-Benz – with sales distribution and service affiliates in 21 countries – is the division with the most fully developed set of foreign operations. The Mercedes-Benz division has not located any of its car manufacturing sites in other countries because, according to many car analysts, the 'Made in Germany' label has been one of the company's valuable sales features. (Trucks are manufactured in Brazil and the USA, but in the USA trucks carry the brand name Freightliner.)

The AEG management board consists of the AEG CEO plus the heads of several functional services. AEG has reorganized the array of its divisions into six 'fields of activity': automation systems, office and communication systems, electrotechnical systems and components, consumer products, microelectronics, and transportation systems. The aerospace and defence unit, Telefunken System-Technik, was transferred to Deutsche Aerospace as of January 1989.

The Deutsche Aerospace sector was created as an umbrella for four operating companies: MTU, Dornier, Telefunken System-Technik (TST) and MBB. A 1990 restructuring regrouped the activities of the companies into four activity areas: space, aviation, defence and propulsion, with each area having specific product subareas. The four operating companies will not remain separate legal entities within Deutsche Aerospace, but brand names will continue to be used. Each of the four activity areas is represented by one member on Deutsche Aerospace's expanded eight-member board, which includes the Deutsche Aerospace CEO and three other officials with functional support portfolios.

The fourth major part of Daimler-Benz was created in July 1990. It comprises several services such as a software house, finance services, insurance, and trading and marketing services. Initially the new division has relied primarily on the other divisions as customers, but it has begun to develop outside customers.

To foster the high-technology synergy among the divisions, Daimler-Benz has organized its research and technology under a common overseer, but the operations are divided into four research institutes attached to the four main operating divisions, with each of the institute managers assigned a global corporate task transcending the divisional boundaries operating (Jonquières, 1991).

Staffing: the 'Stuttgart old-boy network'

'In the "old" Daimler-Benz organization, one was born in Stuttgart, one started work with Daimler, one was employed for one's whole career with Daimler, one's relatives and friends worked for Daimler, one took pride in this company, and one died in Stuttgart,' a senior Daimler-Benz official has wryly remarked in pointing out the staffing challenge facing the newly diversified Daimler-Benz. The 'Stuttgart old-boy network' worked well for decades, generating not only the corporate top executives but also the managers of the foreign affiliates whose ability and compatibility had been well tested in the Stuttgart-based Daimler-Benz environment. The addition of AEG, which is Frankfurt-based, and of the other acquired companies will add to the complexity of mind-sets.

It is still too early to determine the extent to which Daimler-Benz will coordinate executive development among its four divisions. The Daimler-Benz corporate management perceives the value in encouraging movement among the divisions and assignments abroad. Steps have been taken to extend the Daimler-Benz staff development programme to the entire group and to encourage transfers between the corporate parts. Daimler-Benz has developed new leadership training programmes for senior managerial staff, intended to bind the various units more closely together. The newly diversified Daimler-Benz is also recruiting more widely, bringing in more non-Stuttgart people – and even a few non-Germans (principally Austrians, Belgians, Spanish, Americans and Dutch) – into senior posts.

Extending a common vision and values

Daimler-Benz, recently diversified by acquisition, does not yet have a common set of corporate values. For decades, pride in the quality of its Mercedes product has been the basis of the Daimler-Benz corporate culture. The long-established Daimler-Benz support of sports, cultural and environmental efforts has added a 'corporate citizen' *esprit* and shared values. Edzard Reuter has announced the goal of extending the traditional corporate stress on citizenship and quality throughout the newly acquired parts of Daimler-Benz. This is reflected in the corporate image which its advertising presents. As already noted, training programmes have been instituted to accelerate the efforts to achieve this goal.

Integrating diversity

The diversification effort, which was intended to strengthen Daimler-Benz, has presented major organizational challenges. The initial indigestion problems have led some observers to question whether Daimler's move into other businesses may have been too bold, especially when contrasted with the performance of its arch-rival Bayerische Motoren Werke (BMW), a company that has stuck steadfastly to making cars. It has already taken steps to rationalize its newly diversified structure. It recognizes the task ahead in developing top management with a Daimler-Benz corporate-wide perspective and extending its concern for quality through the newly acquired parts. The Deutsche Bank's salient role in the Daimler-Benz network provides the stimulus for continued organizational development. Its alliance with Mitsubishi provides a source of speculation regarding future developments.

Fiat: dynasty-led, government-fed rapid diversification and growth

The Fiat Group is the largest private-sector corporation in Italy and the world's sixth largest corporation whose principal business is motor vehicles. While the Fiat Group remains principally a motor vehicle company (with more than half of its 1990 sales and profit coming from Fiat Auto and more than 75 per cent from motor-vehicle and motor-vehicle-related businesses), the Group's businesses also include trains, aviation, robotics, bio-engineering, publishing, thermomechanics and insurance.

The Fiat Group is the centrepiece of an Agnelli-led business empire, whose interests include banks, mutual funds, insurance, food and department stores, advertising and tourism. By the late 1980s, following Fiat's rapid growth in the 1970s and 1980s, the Agnelli family (who own 39.4 per cent of Fiat) 'controlled nearly a quarter of the [Italian] Stock Exchange [...] and in the view of critics made free use of the clout it derived from 569 subsidiaries and 190 associated companies [...] in 50 countries' (Friedman, 1989:90–1).

Fiat's rapid growth, driven by a desire to become a European-based global company, has posed major structural, staffing and corporate cultural challenges. To meet this challenge Giovanni Agnelli and Cesare Romiti, Fiat's managing director, have asserted firmer headquarters control, focusing more resolutely on motor vehicles and developing strategic alliances. The Alcatel Alsthom alliance and swap of businesses facilitates the meeting of these objectives.

The Agnelli dynasty and the network of Italian power

The Turin-based Agnelli empire has developed from the automobile company Fabbrica Italiana di Automobili Torino (or F.I.A.T.) founded in 1899 by Giovanni Agnelli, grandfather of the present chairman. The bonanza of orders accompanying World War I enabled the company to diversify from cars and trucks to guns and airplane engines, thus jumping from the thirtieth to the third-largest industrial company in Italy. During the interwar period (when the company diversified into civil engineering) and the World War II years, the senior Agnelli through his connections facilitated the company's continuous development; upon his death in 1945 his fortune was estimated at $1 billion. After the founder's death, Professor Vittorio Valletta, the trusted steward of the founder since the 1930s, led Fiat for two decades of postwar reindustrialization and expansion (see Bairati, 1983). By 1966, when grandson Giovanni (known as Gianni) Agnelli took leadership of the company, Fiat produced 75 per cent of cars sold in Italy, controlled key civil engineering and cement interests, owned a merchant fleet and ran a major Italian newspaper (see Pochna, 1989). Fiat had become 'the linch-pin of Italy's post-war economic growth [... and wielded] tremendous influence along the corridors of power in Rome' (Friedman, 1989:56).

In the early 1970s, Fiat's stagnating automobile market and its consequent fiscal crises led the company to diversify further by engaging in high-technology fields such as biomedicine and telecommunications. By the mid-1970s the corporate conglomerate included a headquarters holding company and ten subsidiary companies which controlled over 100 divisions and yet had never produced a set of consolidated financial accounts. In 1976, to consolidate and manage Fiat, Gianni Agnelli recruited Carlo De Benedetti to replace his brother Umberto as managing director. De Benedetti lasted less than 100 days. As one Fiat executive who lived through the brief interregnum puts it: 'He was rejected by the Fiat culture. He wanted to dominate. He came on too strong, too fast. He just was not accepted by anyone' (interview, Rossetti, 10 September 1990). De Benedetti has since gone on to control a substantial CIR- and Olivetti-based empire of his own.

Following De Benedetti's departure, the Agnellis appointed Cesare Romiti as managing director. With Agnelli backing, he pursued a strategy of diversifying into military equipment, banking, publishing, and a number of other sectors. Romiti imposed financial order and discipline at Fiat after the slack divisional autonomy of the 1970s and further strengthened his command of operations in 1988 when he forced the resignation of the longtime head of Fiat Auto (which then accounted for two-thirds of the Fiat Group's operating profits). He then took on the managing directorship of Fiat Auto as well as the managing directorship of the Fiat Group. He also pruned the workforce from 360,000 to less than 290,000.

In the 1980s, Fiat and Ford discussed the possibility of merging their European operations, but the negotiations floundered in 1989 on the issue of 'who would hold the reins' (interview, Rossetti, 9 January 1992). In 1990 Fiat took several steps which strengthened its motor vehicle businesses and trimmed the non-vehicle-related businesses. These included merging the Fiat and Ford truck businesses into a Fiat-controlled joint venture, and their tractor businesses into another Fiat-controlled joint venture; winning control of Enasa, the Spanish truck maker; and granting controlling interest in its telecommunications and rail equipment businesses to CGE (now Alcatel Alsthom) in return for gaining control of CGE's battery subsidiary, in a deal in which Fiat secured 6 per cent of CGE shares and CGE 3 per cent of Fiat shares. Fiat also discussed a range of agreements with Chrysler but these were broken off in November 1990 (*International Management*, 1990:66).

The rapid growth of Fiat from sales of $2.3 billion in 1970 to over $47 billion in 1989 has been facilitated by Agnelli's influence in the capital markets and access to significant funding from private and public sources (Porter, 1990:436). In commenting upon the Fiat exercise of power, Italy's then deputy prime minister has said: 'The country's structure is like that of a great pyramid with Fiat on the top [. . .] Fiat has grown powerful in great part as a result of political help. [. . .] In Italy [. . .] all of the big groups are owned by a handful of families' (Friedman, 1989:157), whose dynasties are interrelated in a web-like maze (see Figure 7.7). Fiat's ability to negotiate subsidies and loans has been facilitated not only by Agnelli's power as Italy's leading tycoon, but also by Fiat's role as the leading private-sector employer throughout Italy. For example, a 1991 planned $3 billion subsidy, which is being investigated by the EC, would support the development of factories, research and training in less-developed southern Italy. One of the effects of Fiat's rapid government-supported growth has been the extent to which Fiat activities have been Italy-based, and its products have depended upon Italian sales; 56 per cent of Fiat's 1990 sales were Italian (and more than 90 per cent were European).

Corporate structure

Fiat is run by a triumvirate of Giovanni Agnelli as its chairman, his younger (by

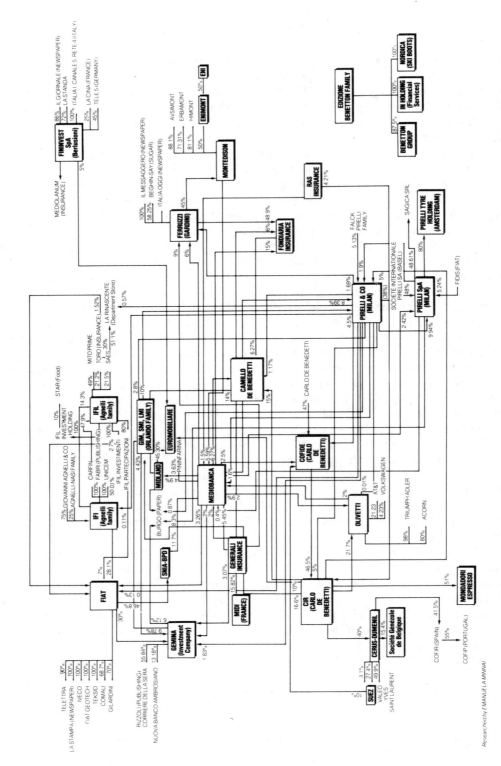

Figure 7.7 Italy's private-sector dynasties' network of power (Source: Reproduced by permission of the *Financial Times*)

Researched by EMANUELA MINNAI

fourteen years) brother Umberto as its vice-chairman (and designated successor as chairman), and Cesare Romiti as managing director. The fifteen other board members include a Belgian, a Dutchman and a German. In a 1991 restructuring Romiti appointed two deputy managing directors, one to oversee the vehicle and vehicle-related sectors and one to oversee the non-vehicle-related sectors.

The principal sector, Fiat Auto, produces not only Fiat but also Lancia, Autobianchi, Innocenti, Maserati, Ferrari and Alfa-Romeo cars. Alfa-Romeo was purchased from IRI in 1986 in a deal which displayed Agnelli's political connections and persuasive power (see Friedman, 1989). Other motor vehicle sectors include:

- Commercial vehicles (Iveco), which includes the British-based Iveco-Ford truck joint venture and Enasa, the Spanish truck maker whose control was won in late 1990.
- Farm construction equipment (Geotech) – Ford and Fiat agreed in 1990 that Fiat should create a London-based joint venture, merging Ford-New Holland tractor and earth-moving operations with Geotech to form a $5 billion joint venture, which Fiat manages and of which it holds 80 per cent controlling interest.

Vehicle-related sectors include:

- Automotive components (Magneti-Marelli). The agreement with Alcatel Alsthom adds CEAC (Compagnie Européenne d'Accumulateurs) to make it into Europe's leading supplier of lead acid car batteries; and the agreement with Toyota's Nippon Censo for the joint production of car air conditioners and heaters further strengthens its position.
- Industrial components (Gilardini).
- Production systems (Comau).
- Metallurgical products (Teksid).

The non-vehicle-related sectors include:

- Civil engineering (which includes Fiat Impresit-Cogefar).
- Aviation (Fiat Avio).
- Publishing and communications (Itedi).
- SNIA BPD, which comprises defence and space, fibres, chemicals, textiles, bio-engineering and other activities.
- Insurance (Toro Assicurazioni).
- Financial and real estate (Fidis and Fiat Finance Europe).
- Rolling stock and railway systems (Fiat Ferroviaria), of which in 1990 CGE (now Alcatel Alsthom) acquired 51 per cent control.
- La Rinascente, purchased in 1990, which adds a retailing segment to Fiat.
- Telecommunications (Telettra) (which in 1990 was merged with Alcatel-Face, CGE's Italian affiliate to create Alcatel Italia which was initially owned 75 per cent by Alcatel Alsthom and 25 per cent by Fiat.

These sectors operate in 52 countries through more than 950 subsidiaries and affiliate companies, 'each enjoying extensive management autonomy within the strategic guidelines agreed with Fiat S.P.A. the Group Parent' (Fiat, *Consolidated Financial Statements*, 1988:11).

Several Fiat sectors, and especially Fiat Auto, have their own sets of foreign affiliates. Major foreign operations have been located in France (engine plates), Germany (trucks), the United States (robotics), the United Kingdom, Spain, Argentina, and Brazil, Poland, what was Yugoslavia, Hungary and the former Soviet Union. About 22 per cent of Fiat employees work outside Italy.

With the aid of several associates whom he brought with him from Rome, Cesare Romiti has begun steps to reconcentrate power within what has been the sprawling Fiat agglomeration. Fiat has not only concentrated power in the Turin headquarters; in each of the countries (France, Germany, the USA, United Kingdom, Spain, Argentina and Brazil) in which there are significant operations it has established service companies whose head oversees the financial, personnel and other functional support activities of all Fiat affiliates in the country, and who represents Fiat's political and public interests. These administrative-coordinative-type country general managers are Italians who have long been associated with Fiat and have developed good working relations with its top executives. They work closely in their countries with the commercial product affiliates, most of which are headed by host country nationals.

Turin-based staffing

When Fiat was smaller, more focused on cars and more concentrated in Turin, there was more unity. As Fiat rapidly diversified, the various companies comprising the network largely developed and staffed their own management. Most managers have spent their whole career in one sector. Even with the rapid diversification, only about 10–12 per cent have been brought in from the outside. The exception has been in top management. The Agnellis and Romiti have identified persons – outside and inside the Fiat organization – in whom they have confidence, assigned them major responsibilities, and reassigned them from sector to sector. The affiliates are led by people in whom headquarters has developed confidence. Most of them are local people who have developed within the company.

Fiat has focused the responsibility for managerial development and organizational change for all Fiat companies in its subsidiary, ISVOR (the acronym of its Italian title, which translates as 'institute for organizational development'), which traces its origins to 1922. Fiat has long stressed intensive training and education as crucial to corporate success, and has taken a lead in the emphasis on courses designed to improve general management effectiveness. University graduates joining the Fiat Group undergo at entry a five-month basic programme designed to make them operational faster and to enable them to have an open-minded vision of their role in the Group. With each promotion and each international assignment, managers undergo additional programmes. More than 15,000 middle managers and

4,000 senior managers go through corporate-wide programmes, which are designed to foster employee participation, an effort in which central management is encouraging decentralized management. The management courses' emphasis on effective communication and intercultural competence as well as professional know-how is designed to develop the global vision of Fiat managers and therefore their effectiveness. ISVOR also offers courses in English, and intensive seminars for non-Italian top managers to improve their knowledge of the Italian language and culture and of Fiat.

An Agnelli-based culture

'The internationally successful Italian companies frequently have this sense of an extended family and are often led by a founder or a descendent of the founder' (Porter, 1990:436). The Fiat culture may in fact be described as a blend of the Italian *joie de vivre*, the Turin-based network of extended family and friends, an Agnelli-inspired *esprit de corps* exuberance, and even yet a trace of the Professor Valetta sense of 'How Fiat does things'. Fiat has used its power base to promote a corporate image, *esprit de corps* and sense of social responsibility by sponsoring sports facilities and cultural activities.

Working for Fiat has been a family tradition for many employees. Their parents and other relatives worked for Fiat; many expect their children to work for the company too. Fiat has tried to expand this family sense as it has expanded its facilities throughout Italy and other countries. The Fiat culture generates high expectation levels – a sense which was reflected in the reaction of many Alfa-Romeo employees when they became part of Fiat: 'Now we must work, we are part of Fiat' (interview with Rossetti, 6 June 1990). And indeed, the productivity and profitability of Fiat rose dramatically following the takeover. While the rapid growth into a highly diversified agglomeration of companies was accompanied by a loss of a unifying sense of how things are done at Fiat, recent structure, staffing and training efforts are reviving a sense of Fiat unity.

Threats

'For years Fiat has faced the twin challenge of converting its agglomeration into a unified company whose parts provide synergy for one another, and transforming itself from a very Italian company into a truly European-based global one' (interview, Rossetti, 6 June 1990). These challenges are particularly demanding. The decline in European car sales, the increasing threat from American and Asian manufacturers – especially from their European-based facilities – and thus the decline in sales and profit for most European vehicle manufacturers has magnified the importance of the challenge. Fiat has long depended on a protected domestic market which as recently as 1986 accounted for more than 66 per cent of its sales. With the integration of the European market, this market share has slipped to

47 per cent in 1991. This slippage threatens the long-term success of the company. The 1990 deals, which focused on motor vehicle businesses and forged long-term strategic alliances, may facilitate the meeting of this challenge.

Alcatel Alsthom: integrating the ITT acquisition

The French Alcatel Alsthom – until 1991 the Compagnie Générale d'Electricité (CGE) – like the Netherlands-based Philips, Japanese-based Matsushita and NEC, German-based AEG, British-based General Electric Company and US-based General Electric, is a major multinational which has diversified beyond its original electrical products base. Alcatel Alsthom may be described as a holding company whose activities embrace telecommunications, energy and transport, energy storage, nuclear power and publishing. Just before its denationalization in 1987 CGE acquired ITT's telecommunication and related businesses (long ITT's core). It merged this acquisition into CGE's principal subsidiary, Alcatel, thereby creating the world's leading producer of telecommunications equipment. In 1990 CGE entered into an agreement with Fiat in which CGE traded controlling interests in its battery subsidiary to Fiat and gained control of Fiat's telecommunication business (Telettra) for Alcatel and of the rail equipment for CGE Alsthom, and both groups cemented a strategic alliance by swapping shares.

In 1991 Alcatel purchased Rockwell International Corporation's network Transmission Systems in the USA, and Nornada's, Canada Cable and Wire, thus strengthening its North American position. It also purchased the cable unit of Daimler-Benz's AEG.

Nationalization, denationalization and internationalization

CGE was formed in 1898. While initially its focus was the production and distribution of electric current, it later developed cables, electric machinery, telecommunications and engineering businesses. The French government nationalized CGE in 1982. In 1987, following the socialist loss of control of Parliament, CGE was denationalized. Even before the denationalization, CGE had begun an aggressive expansion, most notably by the acquisition of ITT's telecommunications business, which was merged into Alcatel in January 1987. Also in 1987 CGE purchased Générale Occidentale (which owns *L'Express*). In a later move CGE entered into a joint venture with the British-based General Electric Company (GEC), establishing GEC Alsthom as a major multinational power technology and rail transport joint venture. The 1990-announced change of name from CGE to Alcatel Alsthom accompanied efforts to increase name recognition as well as to rationalize its organization along product lines.

In 1990 Alcatel Alsthom grossed more than $26 billion and employed more than 200,000 people in 110 countries: 37 per cent in France, 41 per cent in other

European countries, 6 per cent in North America and 16 per cent in the rest of the world.

A decentralized holding company structure

While Alcatel Alsthom has taken steps to simplify and consolidate its complex operational structure by absorbing the capital of three of its subsidiary holding companies, Compagnie Financière, Alcatel Alsthom and Générale Occidentale, the structure remains complex as well as decentralized (see Figure 7.8). The parts operate with minimal control exerted by a small headquarters staff of about 300 people. Many subsidiary senior executives have little if any contact with Alcatel Alsthom headquarters.

Not only does each of the product-driven major subsidiaries act separately in developing its businesses and affiliates, but so do several of the international affiliates of the subsidiaries. As a holding company, Alcatel Alsthom leadership has developed a decentralized approach with each part possessing considerable autonomy in determining its own operations and support arrangements. The Alcatel Alsthom style is therefore more decentralized than that of many other European firms. This subsidiary autonomy manifests itself in the fact that Alcatel and GEC Alsthom advertise separately – and are far better known publicly than was CGE, whose name was not generally recognized outside France.

Alcatel, which since June 1990 (when ITT reduced its share from 37 per cent) has been 68.5 per cent held by Alcatel Alsthom, 30 per cent by ITT (with the CEO of ITT as the non-executive chairman of Alcatel), and 1.5 per cent by Crédit Lyonnais, is the principal Alcatel Alsthom subsidiary, accounting for more than 60 per cent of its staff and sales. (In 1992, ITT sold its remaining equity in Alcatel. As part of the transaction ITT received newly issued shares in Alcatel Alsthom, giving the US conglomerate a 7 per cent stake in the French conglomerate. At this time, Rand Araskog, the ITT CEO, relinquished his non-executive chairmanship of Alcatel and was elected to the board of Alcatel Alsthom.) Alcatel's principal businesses are telecommunications, business systems and cables (equipment for public telecommunication operators, other carriers and defence operations). Fiat's telecommunication business has been added to Alcatel as a result of the 1990 Fiat–CGE swap.

GEC Alsthom, the 50 per cent owned subsidiary formed by the joint venture with GEC, accounts for 18 per cent of Alcatel Alsthom revenue. The product of this merged operation includes nuclear turbo-alternators, gas turbines, robotics, and engines for the TGV high-speed trains, as well as vessels. This subsidiary now has control of Fiat's rail equipment business as a result of the 1990 Fiat–CGE swap.

CEGELEC, which is 78 per cent owned, accounts for about 9 per cent of CGE revenue. It focuses on electrical contracting and industrial process control. It embraces what until 1988 had been CGEE Alsthom and two GEC units which were added as a related aspect of the agreement with GEC which created GEC Alsthom.

Framatome, which accounts for about 5 per cent of Alcatel revenue, is a joint

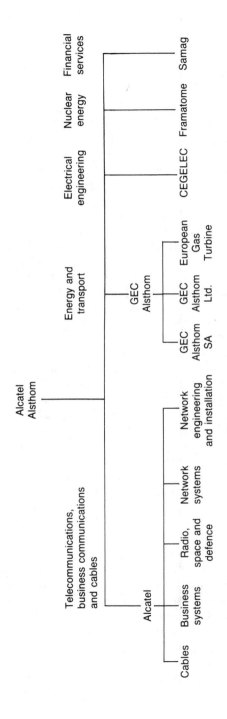

Figure 7.8 Alcatel Alsthom organogram, 1991

Note: The chart does not show components comprising these groupings/subsidiaries and minor activities such as Générale Occidentale, Groupe Express, etc.

venture with the French government. Its business is nuclear engineering and nuclear boiler construction. After lengthy negotiations over which partner would run and exercise controlling interests, Alcatel Alsthom was forced to agree to let management control of the nuclear plant building pass into government hands.

Through a holding company Alcatel Alsthom also has interests in two battery companies; as noted earlier, controlling interests in these were traded to Fiat in 1990. Alcatel Alsthom interests also include a number of diverse activities, one of which is a publishing company, Générale Occidentale. Together the battery companies and other diverse interests account for less than 7 per cent of the enterprise's revenue.

While the conglomerate's businesses have long focused on electronics, telecommunications, energy and energy-related services, the 1,000 related and competing affiliates and subsidiaries have represented an agglomeration of units whose products did not carry the CGE name. Only with the change of the corporate name and accompanying structural changes has the enterprise developed some sense of corporate unity.

Alcatel

Alcatel comprises principally two types of company. Most of the pre-ITT merger, French-based ones focused on one business – for example, CIT focused on public telecommunications, Telec/Opus on business systems, and Câbles de Lyon on cables. In contrast, the former ITT companies were national ones that handled telecommunications and other businesses. In organizing the conglomerate, Pierre Suard, CEO of Alcatel as well as Alcatel Alsthom, and his management committee faced the challenge which ITT struggled with for so long: how to balance national and product interests.

Under ITT the country heads had long presided over their national fiefdoms like zealous feudal lords. Harold Geneen, the longtime ITT CEO, asserted control by requiring regular reports and meetings and using product line managers to work directly with the product sections within each national company. But stronger country general managers resisted the pressure, relying on national pride and the rapport with their governments and PTT (post, telephone, and telegraph) public corporations, which had long been their major sources of business. Some executives were more successful than others in maintaining their operational independence. The matrix-like structure allowed for shifts in emphases over the years (Sampson, 1973).

Pierre Suard has taken steps to rationalize this conglomeration of companies, with the creation of five product groups whose responsibilities cut matrix-like through the national organizations. These are as follows:

1. *Cables*, with Câbles de Lyon as its lead unit (and its head the product sector head).
2. *Business Systems*, with Telec Alcatel as its lead unit (and its head the product sector head).

3. *Radio, Space and Defence* (called transmission until 1990), with several French-based units and German-based SEL as its lead units.
4. *Network Systems*, with Alcatel's Belgian-based Bell Telephone, Spanish-based Alcatel Standard Electrico, and German-based Alcatel SEL, and the public switching and line transmission parts of Alcatel CIT as major units (the Network Systems head sits on the Alcatel board).
5. *Network Engineering and Installation*, with Italian-based Face as its major unit (and its head the product sector head). This is the product sector which now controls what was once Fiat's Telettra, the Italian telecommunications company (which as the result of the 1990 Fiat–CGE swap is now controlled by Alcatel now renamed Alcatel Italia).

Three of these groups are headquartered in the Paris area, as is the Alcatel corporate management headquarters, where most of the staff offices are located (Alcatel also has 20 persons in its official corporate office in Amsterdam). The Network Engineering and Installation is based in Milan. The Network Systems Group is based with the Advanced Manufacturing Technology Centre in Zaventem, Belgium.

The five groups have varying degrees of profit-and-loss responsibility, depending principally on the extent to which they must implement a global strategy as soon as possible. By 1990, Alcatel had given full profit-and-loss responsibility to the Cables Group and had significantly increased the responsibility given to the Business Systems Group; in both cases the products are basically the same throughout the world. At the opposite extreme is the public switching systems part of the Network Systems Group, whose products (switches) frequently need to be significantly adapted to national markets but whose generic core (System 12) is common to all. In between is the Radio, Space, and Defence Group. All product groups are responsible for the optimization of the consolidated profit-and-loss of the companies concerned, while these companies are responsible for their own profit-and-loss. As the head of Radio, Space and Defence explains: 'We still experience the strong pressure of national responsibility because we require a lot of network know-how. What we are trying to do is to rationalize R&D, organize full transfer of technological know-how (except for defense) and integrate all our capability for export markets' (*Alcatel Link*: Spring 1990:11). In implementing this, many managers in this product group combine line responsibility for a particular product unit in one company with staff coordination responsibility for that product throughout the entire group.

Separate subsidiary staffing

Staff-wise, the major parts of the Alcatel Alsthom agglomeration operate separately and face different challenges. The major issue for GEC-Alsthom has been to reconcile the French and British staffs and cultures. For Framatome, this issue has been one of reconciling public and private control. Alcatel, with its goal of being international, that is a European-based company operating world-wide, faces the challenge of exploiting the advantages of having a workforce in many countries. To this end it has established an international mobility programme to facilitate mobility throughout Alcatel and to develop an international *esprit de corps*.

Within Alcatel, international mobility programmes already exist in various forms and in various ways. At present there are more than 300 mobility positions identified in Alcatel. On the management level, the exchange of managers takes place between companies and the headquarters, or product group staffs. The staffing process for headquarters' positions includes seeking internal candidates before an outside search is begun. Two- to three-year transfers are organized so that the employee remains tied to his or her home unit during the assignment, while the host company arranges for all local needs. The contractual conditions are standardized by headquarters which also provides the units with the information needed to compensate different living costs in various countries.

The Alcatel Way

Alcatel presents a case study of the merger of corporate cultures: the French-driven Alcatel one and the American-driven ITT one. The adoption of English as the Alcatel language has facilitated the transition to, as well as emphasized the stress on, becoming an international company. To facilitate cultivation of a common culture further, Alcatel has undertaken a number of steps to promote 'the Alcatel Way'.

The effort to define and develop the Alcatel Way began in 1989 with an initial report by an *ad hoc* committee that broadly set out the culture which could be said to exemplify Alcatel. This was followed by the holding of a series of management seminars to achieve further amplification and corporate-wide involvement. As Yves Reale, Alcatel's director of management resources, explains:

> The Alcatel Way is much more than simply a corporate culture. It involves defining both where we are going – corporate strategy – and how we are going to get there with issues relating to organization, management of human resources, and communication. One of the most wonderful aspects of the seminars [which Alcatel has undertaken] was its spirit of co-operation and how much our own notions, among those of us who initiated Alcatel Way, were expanded and improved through interaction with the 280 participants. (*Alcatel Way* 5: 90: 2)

Alcatel is an example of a successful transcontinental merger. Its success is due in large part to the extent to which a dynamic CEO has taken the lead in rationalizing the structure, optimizing R&D resources, creating common transitional products, developing a cadre of managers with transnational perspectives, and initiating efforts to develop and cultivate a common culture for a transcontinentally merged organization – whose principal parent was only recently a state-owned corporation.

Philips: metamorphosis to a more focused, product-split company

Philips is one of the world's largest electronics firms, along with IBM, GE and AT&T in the USA, Hitachi, Matsushita, Toshiba and NEC in Japan, and Siemens and Alcatel in Europe. Philips began the development of its network of international affiliates shortly after World War I. The exigencies of the interwar period fostered the development of these affiliates as relatively autonomous members of a Philips group of national companies. From the late 1940s through to the 1980s, Philips product divisions operated in a matrix-like arrangement with the national organizations, with the emphasis gradually shifting to the product divisions.

The European integration momentum, the Japanese marketing invasion and the decline in profits accelerated the final phase of Philips's metamorphosis from a group of national organizations into a global multinational organization whose more focused product divisions are now responsible for international operations.

From light bulbs to electronics

Philips began in 1891 as a manufacturer of incandescent light bulbs in Eindhoven, the Netherlands. Not until May 1991 was the official name of Philips changed from Philips Gloeilampen fabrieken to Philips Electronics. The two Philips brothers complemented each other: Gerard, who founded the company, was a technical genius; his younger brother Anton, who joined the company later, was the entrepreneurial manager and salesman. Its organizational structure long reflected the split of the technical side of the business from the commercial.

By the early 1900s, the company was exporting products internationally. After World War I, Philips began to diversify from lighting products and to develop a series of foreign affiliates. From 1919 to 1930, Philips organized eighteen European affiliates. By 1933 it had organized its US affiliate, now the second largest Philips organization (the Netherlands one remaining the largest). This international expansion was accomplished principally through the acquisition of manufacturing companies. Perceived cultural differences between countries and the need to avoid protectionist legislation accented the autonomous role of the national affiliates from their inception. As a result, the products produced in each country developed characteristics specific to each national environment. During World War II and the German occupation of the Netherlands, the international affiliates developed even more autonomy (Philips, 1978:157–81).

Following World War II, as Philips started to diversify, its product divisions began to develop matrix-like relationships with the national organizations. The national organizations negotiated with the product divisions for the technical know-how and resource support for manufacturing and marketing the products in their countries. The advent of the European Common Market facilitated Europe-wide competition and fostered Philips's efforts in the 1960s and 1970s to standardize its products and establish international production centres, thus rationalizing its manufacturing. In 1972, Philips formally established a matrix organization (see Figure 7.9). While continuing to hold the national organizations responsible for realizing profits through sales and service, the product divisions were made clearly responsible for corporate-wide product marketing, manufacturing, research and technical development strategies – and thus for the creation of profit potential.

In the 1980s, Philips expanded in the United States by acquiring lighting and consumer electronic businesses, including part of Westinghouse. In 1987, Philips increased its equity in its principal American affiliate to 100 per cent. By the end of the 1980s Philips had established affiliates in more than 60 countries, with 60 per cent of its sales in Europe (6 per cent in the Netherlands), 24 per cent in North America, 8 per cent in Asia/Oceania, 6 per cent in Latin America and 2 per cent in Africa. In the late 1980s, the increased onslaught of Asian and American competition significantly reduced profit margins and accelerated the pace of change. Philips streamlined its organization by narrowing the range of business to focus on the more profitable ones. In the process the workforce was reduced by 20 per cent. This, combined with the restructuring costs, led to a 1990 net loss.

An international structure

The international character of Philips is reflected in the fact that both its supervisory board and its group management committee (GMC) include several foreigners. In 1990 Philips added a Swede (the recently retired Volvo CEO), a German (the Hoechst Chairman) and an American (a former Exxon senior vice-president) to its supervisory board, which already included two Americans, a German, a Frenchman, a Belgian and an Englishman, thus increasing the international representatives to a majority on this oversight body.

In 1990, as a consequence of normal retirements and some earlier-than-expected departures (including that of the CEO) stemming from the continuing lag in profitability, there was a substantial turnover in the GMC: which included a new CEO (Jan Timmer) who had been a sector head (consumer electronics). Four of the new GMC members are non-Dutch. Two were promoted from within Philips in 1990: one a Swiss national and the former head of Philips France, another is a Norwegian. In a break from its promote-from-within tradition, two more were appointed from outside Philips: in May 1991 an American was recruited from Hewlett Packard to head technology, and in 1992 a Briton was recruited from British Aerospace to head finance.

While until the early 1980s almost all GMC members focused on functional responsibilities, as of 1990 two members had area responsibilities, two had functional responsibilities (research and technology and finance) and four headed product sectors. With the new appointments by 1993, Philips expects to have focused the overall management responsibility for Philips in a four-member board of managers (including the finance and technology heads) which will serve as the core of GMC.

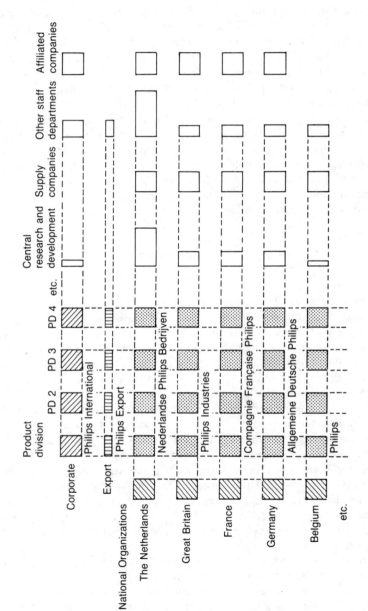

Figure 7.9 Philips's transnational, matrix-like organization, c. 1988 (Courtesy of Philips Electronics)

In the effort to develop a more globally competitive organization, since 1987 Philips has accelerated its efforts to shift to a more product-driven structure and spin off several units which no longer fit. The defence division was sold to Thomson, most of the major appliance division to Whirlpool, and in 1991 most of the computer systems division to Digital Equipment Corporation. In the process, Philips has reduced the number of employees from 380,000 to 250,000, mainly through rationalization and deconsolidation.

Philips's eight product divisions focus on product lines on which Philips intends to concentrate (see Figure 7.10). These are as follows:

1. *Lighting* (Philips's original business and still its most profitable one), which has been given a more autonomous position within Philips so that it may have more clear-cut control of its activities in order to achieve maximum results. This unit has considerable US interests.
2. *Components*, a major part of which is located in the USA.
3. *Consumer electronics*, which includes Polygram (a London-based subsidiary owned 80 per cent by Philips).
4. *Domestic appliances and personal care* (DAP).
5. *Medical systems*.
6. *Industrial and Electric Acoustic systems*.
7. *Information systems*.
8. *Communication systems*.

For reporting purposes, medical, industrial. information, and communication systems are grouped into a professional systems sector, and consumer electronics, and domestic appliances and personal care are grouped into a consumer products sector.

The eight product divisions are responsible for Philips's participation in a number of companies, some of which are joint ventures; these include not only Polygram but also Marantz Japan (50 per cent) and a number of others in which it has majority or minority equity. Philips also has a number of general industrial supply companies which fall outside the scope of the production divisions, including glass, the engineering works, and the plastics and metalware factories.

The eight product divisions divide into approximately 60 subdivisions ('business units' or 'product groups'), each of which manages a homogeneous packet of products. Approximately 25 per cent of these product subdivisions now locate their headquarters outside the Netherlands, at the source of product (manufacturing/ marketing) strength. Philips is developing these product subdivisions as global strategic units with responsibility for production facilities and the promotion of their products. They now have profit-and-loss accountability – a dramatic change from the earlier years, when Philips was a confederation of independent national organizations that cut across product lines. This transition to a product-driven organization has facilitated phase-ins of new products. In the pre-reorganization arrangements, country affiliates were not keen to take losses related to the phase-in

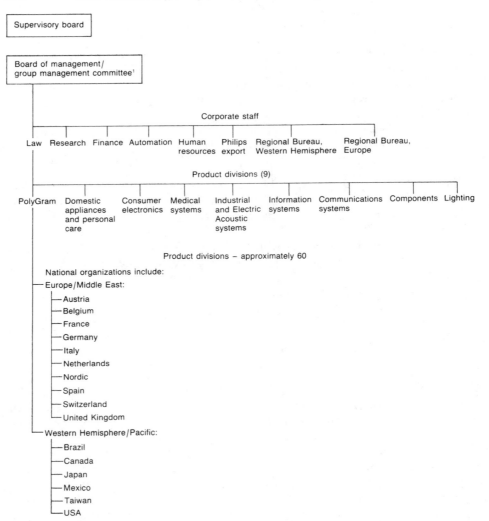

Note: 1. Includes CEO/chairman, two vice-chairmen (one for Europe and Middle East, one for America and Asia), one member for finance, one member for research and technology, and four members heading up sectors.

Figure 7.10   Philips organogram, 1991

development of a new product. In the new organizational arrangement, it is the responsibility of the product division to absorb any losses in the phase-in.

The product divisions have established 'councils' where the marketing and sales offices of that division meet and determine a transnational strategy and local tactics. The product divisions are continuing to rationalize manufacturing so that industrial plants focus on one product for continent-wide markets, rather than produce a complete or near-complete line of products for one-country markets. In the process

150 smaller manufacturing facilities have been closed as production has been continentalized – the product subdivisions rather than the individual national affiliates becoming the major focus of Philips.

This enhancement of the responsibility of the product divisions and the product managers has significantly modified the role of the country manager. The new organizational arrangement provides for three types of country organizations. In so-called 'key countries' – the United States, the United Kingdom, the Netherlands, France, Italy, Germany and Japan, where product divisions have manufacturing as well as sales affiliates – the product divisions manage their own marketing and manufacturing. In this arrangement the country's general manager and his or her management team are responsible for general corporate representation and common management responsibilities. In so-called 'local business' countries – such as Nigeria, Tunisia, Peru, Portugal and India – the national organizations function as integrated sales affiliates which import products from the product divisions; whatever manufacturing it does is generally for the local market. In the so-called 'large countries' – Austria, Belgium, Brazil, Canada, Mexico, Nordic (Scandinavia), Spain, Switzerland and Taiwan, which have more extensive local production – Philips uses a hybrid arrangement, the specifics of which depend on the situation. In several of the 'large' as well as the 'key' countries, Philips has located international production centres, which are basically steered by the product divisions.

The country general managers in the 'key' and 'large' countries represent the Philips' corporate interests, interfacing with the government and other major corporations and coordinating for common corporate legal, fiscal and human resources. But since the heads of the product units now report directly into the product divisions (where the profit-and-loss responsibility is now focused), the country 'chairmen' are clearly no longer executive directors. Their positions are ones of significant prestige and influence but they do not possess the power of command. These country general managers report to the two Philips vice-chairmen (those in Europe and the Middle East to one and those in the Western Hemisphere and the Pacific Rim to the other); each of these vice-chairmen is assisted by a regional bureau. The product divisions and the national affiliates continue to interact together in a matrix-like configuration, but the focus of responsibility has shifted substantially from area to product.

Shifting from the 'old-boy network'

Philips hires by product divisions in each of the countries in which it operates. More than 85 per cent of middle and higher managers have spent their career entirely within Philips, more than 70 per cent within one product division. The product divisions, in consultation with national managements, post most expatriates. A few managers are 'housed' and posted from the Philips International Division. The GMC selects the country general managers and financial officers of the national organizations. In 1990, Philips had about 1,200 persons on expatriate assignment:

700 Dutch and 500 non-Dutch. The expatriate assignments were considered a reward, as well as essential experience, for career-oriented managers. General knowledge of Philips culture and particular knowledge about business and technology are considered indispensable for successful careers. Several criteria affect the prospects of achieving a high managerial post: personality, beyond average ability, self-confidence, varied experience including international assignments, an insight into Philips culture, and well-developed corporate connections.

Before 1990, employees were seldom laid off. The cutback of 55,000 employees and the consequent perception that positions are no longer as secure has shocked employees and affected corporate loyalty. To accompany the radical change in the Philips organization, the new CEO has introduced a sweeping educational programme known as Operation Centurion, designed to focus managers' minds on the reorganizational goals and profits.

The Philips informal organization may be more powerful than the formal one, especially in normal, day-to-day activities. Project decisions are made in informal meetings, working arrangements are made through an informal network. Contacts in previous postings (and the Eindhoven golf club) foster the development of informal networks, strengthening career-long and sometimes lifelong ties.

Philips' shared values

Philips does not articulate a corporate culture; nevertheless, it has a strong one. There is nothing written, there is no formal training, but employees learn it. As one Philips manager has noted, 'The ability to learn and adapt to the Philips culture in the shortest possible time is one of the determining elements of career advancement' (interview, Dennis Igbarra, 13 June 1990). The network of contacts and shared culture facilitates coping with its complicated and bureaucratic structure. Gentlemen's agreements are obligations. In everyday communication, criticism and complaints are made verbally. The employees are motivated by autonomy in their job, self-fulfilment, setting their own goals, exercising responsibility and the enjoyment of the challenge, as long as they stay within the rules. The position of the boundaries can often only be discovered by crossing them. The complexities of such an organization are seldom learned in less than two to five years.

One of the great strengths of Philips as a company is its power to invest in new developments, research and production facilities. The choice of good technical solutions and decisions to follow innovative development paths has transformed the working environment. This pride in their product fosters strong employee identification with the company name. The effort to extend the corporate identification throughout its affiliates led to replacing local brand names such as Valvo in Germany, RTC in France and Mullard in the United Kingdom by the common name Philips.

The shock of change

Philips has long stressed technological excellence. It may have – relatively speaking – paid less attention to marketing, to changing competitive conditions and to the customer. It has also been said that it has taken Philips too long to bring new products onto the market. By some this may be perceived as the arrogance of the engineering approach. As a consequence of its historical development, Philips has been late in recognizing that the 1950s' and 1960s' sellers' market turned into a buyers' market, with especially strong new competitors.

Increased world-wide competition has hastened Philips's efforts to transform its organization from a country-divided one into a more product-driven one. Transition, accompanied as it has been by reduced profits and severe staff reductions, has generated trauma. By early 1992 Philips's efforts to cut up to 55,000 jobs from its mid-1989 total of 300,000 – along with its other loss-cutting initiatives – had appeared to have returned the company to profitability. What, if any further efforts are needed, and how long will be required for the reorganizational efforts to pay off fully, are questions which have been uppermost in the minds of many. What is clear is that Philips courageously reorganized – taking steps that exacerbated the short-term losses – in order to be prepared for competing more vigorously in the changing global market. Its return to profitable status in 1991, at a time of industry-wide difficulties, was a remarkable corporate turnaround that rewarded the drastic reorganizational efforts.

Continental organizations represent corporate interests

Imperial Chemical Industries (ICI): strengthening the business groups and dismantling affiliates

In February 1991, Imperial Chemical Industries (ICI) began a major reorganization to consolidate its business groups and strengthen their global role. In July 1992, ICI followed this up by stating its intention to split itself in two – with the drug and agrochemical operations becoming a separate company known as ICI Bio.

The initial 1991 reorganization plan transferred the sales responsibilities of the European affiliates to the business groups and transferred their affiliates' support services responsibilities to a redeveloped ICI Europe and newly created, multicountry regional support centres. A 1992 modification, which ICI announced as 'the second stage in the process of rationalizing ICI's operations in Europe' in order to manage its Western European (including UK) operations 'as a single market' (ICI memo, 13 January 1992), gave their business groups the full multifunctional responsibility for their operations in Western Europe, but retained the cost-effective support services provided by the regional centres. A network of 'national managers' will combine a major business group role with an additional role 'providing a corporate presence in each country'. (ICI memo, 15 January 1992). The unanticipated January 1992 announcement disbanded the only recently strengthened ICI Europe, and left in doubt what steps might be taken to coordinate the national managers and provide a corporate continent-wide presence.

Cumulatively, these organizational changes, which were designed to sharpen ICI's marketing focus on its corporate customers, were its most recent transitions shifting its organizational strategy from one that relied heavily on integrated national affiliates to one that relies on global business groups. The moves were intended to transform the ICI organization from a three-dimensional arrangement 'in due course to a two dimensional organizational structure comprising the International Business operations supported by Functional Services' (ICI memo, 15 January 1992). While the 1991-initiated reforms began before Hanson acquired a 2.8 per cent stake in May 1991, the threat of a takeover bid intensified ICI's efforts to carry out the reorganization and achieve the increased profitability that were the aim of the $500 million reorganization. Splitting the company in two is intended to enhance the capacity to raise funds to develop the drug and agrochemical businesses.

Long-time alliance with Du Pont

ICI traces its origins to 1926 when Nobel Industries, Brunner Mond (the product of a 1918 merger) and two other British chemical companies were merged into one giant industrial company to compete more effectively with I.G. Farben (Reader, 1975). In 1929, under the leadership of Lord McGowan (who did not retire until 1950), ICI strengthened its relations with Du Pont (whose alliance and participation in numerous joint ventures with Nobel Industries and its predecessors dated from 1907), by signing an agreement calling for 'A full exchange of technical information [... and the allocation of] major markets between them' (Chandler, 1990:274, 358–65, specifically 363; see also Wilkins, 1974:79).

In its association with Du Pont, ICI developed overseas activities principally in Commonwealth countries and Latin America. No major investments were made in the United States, as a result of the agreement with Du Pont. Another agreement with I.G. Farben was partially responsible for ICI's strictly limited investment in Western Europe. When antitrust action against Du Pont (in the United States) caused the transatlantic relationship to be broken up in 1952, ICI essentially took over the operations in the Commonwealth and British colonial territories, while Du Pont held those in Latin America (Channon, 1973:143).

Since then, ICI has expanded not only by internal growth but also by acquisitions of technology-related companies that diversified its product lines and expanded its territorial base primarily in North America, Europe and Asia/Pacific. The development of its American market continued into the 1980s with the acquisition of US-based companies, including Beatrice Chemical Company in 1985, the Glidden Group in 1986, Stauffer Chemicals in 1987, the Conti Seed Division of Continental Grain and KSH, Inc., in 1989. These acquisitions have increased ICI's US presence to such an extent that by 1990 US sales accounted for about 30 per cent of ICI's world-wide sales, compared to 22 per cent in the United Kingdom, 25 per cent in continental Europe and 18 per cent in Asia/Pacific. By 1990 ICI's sales exceeded $23 billion, it employed more than 132,000 people on six continents, it sold in over 150 countries and it manufactured in over 40. By swopping its nylon business for Du Pont's acrylic business ICI will further strengthen its core operations.

Successive organizational transitions

With its formation in 1926, ICI developed the organization that it essentially continued with until 1962. Under the leadership of Lord McGowan, who ran the company in an autocratic fashion until his retirement as chairman in 1950 at the age of 76, ICI divided the domestic manufacturing operations into production groups (each with its own chairman and board of directors), placed domestic selling operations under the control of one of the central service departments, and developed overseas affiliates that handled local manufacturing as well as sales. Most of the full-time members of the board of directors were responsible for a service department and a manufacturing group.

Not until the 1962 reorganization was responsibility focused in single division heads by making the chairman of each division individually responsible for his division's affairs. The 1962 reform retained the full range of service departments with corporate-wide coordination for each function, and established a series of board-level coordinating committees to deal with interdivisional and international issues (Channon, 1973:143–4). In 1966 ICI followed up these changes by creating ICI Europe, to coordinate the continental sales affiliates, whose manufacturing responsibilities were lost to the product divisions.

The next major reorganization came between 1983 and 1985. To simplify the cumbersome structure, the number of divisions was reduced, the number of full-time board members halved from eighteen to nine and the role of committees drastically curtailed. To meet the transcontinental needs of an increasing number of clients, such as those in the aerospace or automotive industries, ICI began to create globally organized businesses. A world-wide pharmaceutical division was set up in 1983 and a global agrochemicals one organized in 1984. In the succeeding years, an increasing number of ICI's operations were reorganized to operate on a global scale.

Under the new arrangement, the product divisions increased their responsibility for overseas manufacturing and marketing strategy. The geographically based units – which for all but a few countries (such as the USA, Canada and India) were grouped into the six territories – continued to be responsible for sales but in only a few cases for manufacturing. The 1991-initiated reorganization strengthened and clarified the primacy of the businesses in determining their strategies and their accountability for their performance. The reorganization thus marked a major transition affecting the role of the geographic entities.

The reorganization stems from ICI's desire to appreciate more fully the market conditions affecting its products, many of which are basic ones which enter manufacturing processes at an early stage. The recognition that in the rapidly integrating economic environment of Europe the purely national focus will not disappear but will prove less important has led ICI to shape an organization designed to be responsive and flexible. Thus the new organization is expected to be capable of handling the needs of the more national-market-oriented agrochemical and pharmaceutical businesses, and also of those businesses which are rapidly becoming more transnational.

ICI foresaw that the reorganization effort would involve the development of an ICI-wide compatible information system, not only to foster corporate-wide communication and planning but also to facilitate future reorganization. The development of such a cross-border enabling information system has accounted for a significant share of the expected $500 million reorganization cost.

The new global organization

'ICI's organization culture is complex: it could not be otherwise for a company that operates around the world in businesses that extend from basic chemicals to the most complex areas of science' (*ICI World Data*, 1990:27): (see Figure 7.11). Heading the complex group is the board of directors, comprising eight insider executives and eight outsiders (the latter include two Germans and two Americans). The eight insider directors constitute an executive team which meets once a week to deal with strategic policy issues, capital spending, acquisitions, divestments and senior appointments. With the exception of the chairman/CEO and the COO (a post created in 1991), each of the executive directors has specific functional or territorial responsibilities for different aspects of the business. Two are territorial directors: one for the Western Hemisphere, which includes the Americas, Europe and Turkey and one for the Eastern Hemisphere, which includes the Middle East, the Indian subcontinent, Asia/Pacific, Australasia and Africa. The other four divide the functional responsibilities: one handles group personnel, another group finance, another group research and technology, and the fourth group safety, health and the environment. As part of the efforts to streamline and tighten the organization, since December 1991 the chief executive officers of the seven ICI business groups report directly to the chief operating officer, and consequently board members no longer have additional portfolios overseeing the business groups.

The reorganization established a senior management body known as the performance and policy committee, comprising the eight members of the executive team plus the seven chief executive officers of the business groups and the finance general manager, to monitor individual business and territorial performance, corporate thinking and policy formation. This committee consults regularly with the

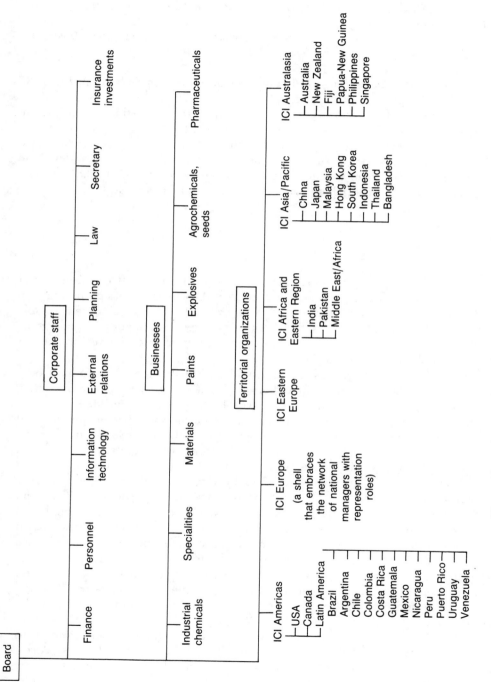

Figure 7.11 Imperial Chemical Industries organogram, 1992

heads of the functional staff departments and the chairmen of the territorial administrations.

In its reorganization, ICI has sorted its businesses into seven global businesses as follows:

1. *Industrial chemicals*. This is the bulk chemical group initially formed in 1987 as ICI Chemicals and Polymers.
2. *Specialities*. This group, as a key aspect of the reorganization was formed in January 1991. It includes colours and fine chemicals.
3. *Materials*. This group, formed in March 1991, includes advanced materials, (headquartered in the United States), polyurethanes (headquartered in Belgium), fibres and acrylics (which was separated from ICI Chemical and Polymers) and films (which had been a stand-alone business).
4. *Explosives*.
5. *Paints*.
6. *Agrochemicals/seeds*.
7. *Pharmaceuticals*.

In the process of reorganization, Sir Denys Henderson, the ICI chairman, has pledged to scrutinize every business and let go of those that are less promising, and thus narrow the span of businesses. All or much of advanced materials may be sold (one part has already been sold to Kawaski Steel); specialities is undergoing reorganization; and ICI may be looking for an acquisition or a joint-venture partner to develop its pharmaceutical business.

While the business groups' global, multifunctional responsibilities have been broadened to include the research and development, manufacturing and marketing of their products throughout most of the world, a few affiliates outside Europe and North America continue to manage 'regional businesses'. The major regional businesses are petrochemicals, plastics, general chemicals and fertilizers in Australia, nitrogen products in Canada, chlor-alkali and fertilizers in Malaysia, fertilizers and fibres in India, fibres and general chemicals in Pakistan, and polyvinyl chloride in Argentina. The 1991 reorganization initially established three major territorial administrations to provide such area-based functional support as required and agreed upon. A pre-existing European one was redeveloped and strengthened in 1991 before it was abolished in 1992. The regional support centres that in Europe had developed in 1991 were left in place to function under the tutelage of the corporate staff offices as well as the business groups. An American one was created to embrace not only the United States but also Canada and Latin America (but a coordinator for Latin America continues to operate from the ICI corporate headquarters). A third major territorial administration was created for Asia/Pacific.

Outside the major territories, a few other territorial administrations continue to exist: Australasia (a 63 per cent owned entity that embraces several affiliates), Africa and Eastern Region (which is headed by a headquarters-based executive and consists of three parts), and Eastern Europe.

Shift to more international staff and interdivisional assignments

ICI management and professional staffing has attempted to increase overseas university recruitment, decrease dependence upon British personnel for filling world-wide senior posts and promote cross-border assignments. ICI has long recruited heavily from British universities. In other countries, where ICI has been less well known and university recruitment thus less relied upon, ICI has stepped up its recruitment efforts by more aggressive promotion efforts. As part of its stepped-up university recruitment effort, it now offers twenty university students a year a two-month summer internship at an ICI site outside their home country.

At present, ICI has about 900 staff on international postings. The number reflects ICI's recognition that its global enterprise needs as much cultural mix and diversity and experience as possible. ICI's executives ranks were predominantly British twenty years ago; by 1992 less than half of the company's top 150 executives world-wide were British. This has reflected the long-standing ICI goal of moving towards a more international senior cadre. In the past, most ICI employees have tended to spend much of their career in one ICI business, territory or function. Beginning in the late 1980s, though, there was a shift towards an effort to move people, especially particularly promising ones, across products, territories and functions to stretch their development. A major concern of senior management has been to review the progress of promising managers, and assess what additional experience would add to their potential in order for them to be prepared for senior posts as the opportunities arise. A corollary goal has been to provide the international assignments that ensure a broader experience.

In its recruitment and career planning, ICI aims to accommodate three different career aspirations as regards international experience; some recruits prefer to remain in their home country, some appreciate an international experience of limited duration (three years), and a few welcome extensive international postings. While corporate headquarters determines the required outcomes of basic training and runs the senior management courses, the ICI businesses have the primary responsibility for training of staff, which includes enhancing their professional skills, appreciating the challenges affecting their business, and developing their personal effectiveness and skills in managing people.

The Future

In its effort to develop an organization which enhances its capacity to be flexibly responsive, ICI has developed one that many ICIers proudly believe and many analysts suspect is ahead of the pack. If there is a danger, it may be that ICI is ahead of its customers in considering all of Western Europe as one integrated domestic market.

A major reorganization aim has been to achieve a better allocation of common resources and a better use of common information bases employed by the various parts of the multinational mosaic, thus facilitating more effectiveness in working across borders, more synergy, more flexibility and more capacity in making future organizational changes – and so to become more competitive. What remains is a disparate organizational approach to what it now considers its home market (all of Western Europe), its other more mature markets such as North America and Australasia, and its developing markets.

The stated rationale of the proposed corporate split has been to allow the two companies to seize opportunities for global expansion from a firmer financial base. The demerger will discourage takeover efforts – a major concern when it was first conceived in December 1991. It remains to be seen if the advantages of demerger outweigh the loss of advantages of corporate-wide size, scale and synergy.

British Petroleum (BP): transforming an 11×70 matrix into a streamlined 4×3 one

From 11×70 to 4×3

British Petroleum (BP), in launching Project 1990, undertook 'Not only [...] a radical streamlining of the company's structure, and its management processes, but also of its cultures' (Lorenz, 1990a:20). The 1990 corporate reorganization, launched by BP's new chairman Robert Horton, followed a BP divestment programme which by the late 1980s had reduced eleven business 'streams' to four: exploration, oil refining and marketing, chemicals and nutrition. The reorganization, not only by focusing on four streams but also by developing regional management in Europe, the Americas and Asia/Pacific, as Horton puts it, transformed the 11×70 matrix into a 4×3 one. The extent of the metamorphosis belies Horton's claim that 'This is not a reorganization [...] and I'm not restructuring BP [...] After ten years, organizations build up an accretion of barnacles on their hull and need a jolly good scrape' (Butler, *Financial Times*, 20 March 1990:22). The reorganization initiatives led by Horton included staff reductions and efforts to transform the corporate culture. Continuing concern regarding the financial prospects of the company on the part of the outside directors led the board in June 1992 to replace Horton with Lord Ashburton, a long-time outside director, as chairman and with David Simon, who had been COO, as CEO.

From Anglo-Persian Oil Company to BP

BP traces its origins to the Anglo-Persian Oil Company (APOC) founded in 1909 to exploit the first Middle East oil discovery, in southwest Persia. In 1914, at the outset of World War I, the British government (led by Churchill as head of the Admiralty), in a *mariage de convenance* to guarantee itself the control of a long term of supply, not only signed a long-term contract for fuel for the Royal Navy but also invested about £2 million in the company, thereby gaining majority ownership (see British Petroleum, 1977:535–49; Chandler 1990:298–9; Ferrier, 1982: 97–201; Sampson, 1988:70–6 for early history).

In 1917 APOC purchased what had been the UK marketing affiliate (named British Petroleum) of the German oil multinational Europäische Petroleum Union (EPU), which the British government had confiscated with the outbreak of World War I (Ferrier, 1982:217–19). From 1917 to 1929, APOC significantly expanded its refining and marketing activities in Europe and Australia. In 1920 it coestablished an Australian company and acquired a shareholding in Norsk Braendselolje. In the following year it formed a Danish and a French company (British Petroleum, 1977:540). In 1924 APOC purchased what had been EPU's Austrian and Swiss marketing affiliates. From 1926 to 1931 it substantially strengthened its position in Germany by acquiring control of Deutsche Petroleum (EPU's descendant) and Deutsche Erdol, whose war-related loss of properties in Britain, Poland and Rumania doomed their efforts to regain their prewar rank as 'third and fourth in the global oligopoly (behind Jersey Standard and Royal Dutch/Shell)' (Chandler, 1990:519–20; Ferrier, 1982:494). In 1935, when the Iranian government asked foreign governments to use 'Iran' as the name of the country instead of 'Persia', the company changed its name to the Anglo-Iranian Oil Company.

In 1951 the Iranian government nationalized the company's Iran-based oil fields and major (Abadan) refinery, a move that by cutting off its upstream strength profoundly affected the company. With the help of the British and American governments, the Anglo-Iranian Oil Company re-established its interests in Iran, but only as part of a consortium, in which it received a 40 per cent share (British Petroleum, 1977:542–3). In 1955, as a consequence of the nationalization of the company's Iranian base, the company renamed itself British Petroleum (taking the name of the marketing affiliate that had been expropriated in World War I) Chandler 1990:209, 298–300). As a result of the Iranian action, British Petroleum (BP) rapidly developed refining capacity near its main markets of Western Europe and eagerly sought new sources of oil. In the 1950s BP discovered major new sources in the Persian Gulf, giving the company the largest proven crude reserves of any company. In 1965 BP discovered natural gas in the North Sea and by 1975 had 'landed' oil from its 'Forties' field. In 1969 BP struck oil in Alaska.

While the company had spread its geographic area of activity after World War II, it lacked a downstream position in the lucrative US market, a lack made more poignant by the development of major North-American-based upstream resources. In 1968 BP acquired that part of Sinclair Oil not merged into Atlantic-Richfield (now ARCO). In 1969 it purchased an equity share in Standard Oil Company of Ohio (Sohio), thereby expanding its American network for the sale of its copious upstream supplies (Sampson, 1988:190–1). In 1978, BP gained a majority interest in the Sohio operation. Later BP acquired that part of the Gulf downstream operations not merged into Chevron.

Following the oil crisis of the 1970s, BP diversified. In 1980, it purchased Union Carbide's European operations, thus expanding the chemical business it had begun with the acquisition of the Distillers chemical business in 1965 and separated into a separate subsidiary in 1967 (Channon, 1973:117). In 1980 BP also acquired the international mining company Selection Trust. The following year Sohio bought Kennecott Copper, the largest American copper company (then one of the 150 largest US international corporations). BP also acquired coal mines (Sampson, 1988:334). In 1987 BP acquired the remaining outstanding shares in Sohio: the Cleveland headquarters of Sohio became the North American headquarters of BP, and BP signs began to replace the Sohio and Gulf signs on BP's US service stations. In the same year, the British government sold its equity interest in BP, thus ending its status as a semi-government-owned corporation.

In 1990 BP generated almost $60 billion in sales, employed more than 110,000 persons scattered over five continents, and was the world's third-largest oil company.

Successive restructuring

In 1918 the company organized with a management committee of five, two of whom were government appointed. Each member headed one of the following activities: oil fields, pipelines and refineries; commerce, engineering and administration; shipping; finance; and governmental affairs and concessions. The arrangement was a hybrid that incorporated features from German and American practices, the German ones via the organization that Deutsche Bank had put in place for British Petroleum (Ferrier, 1982:299). Structurally the company maintained this functional organization for decades. By the 1960s there were seven managing directors, six of whom held responsibility for key functions. 'The functional groups were internally divided on a regional basis, and the only formal coordinating body in BP was at the main board level' (Channon, 1973:117).

In 1970 BP instituted a major structural change by shifting the line responsibilities to an area-division basis.

> A new committee, the B.P. Trading Executive Committee, was set up to serve as a permanent formal body for coordinating functional and regional activities worldwide. Four regional directors were appointed to provide the line of authority between the B.P. Trading Board and the trading companies, with the regional directors responsible for the

performance of companies within their region. Four functional directors remained responsible for 'operations', such as crude oil sales and shipping for which the regional directors were not responsible, 'finance and planning', 'technical', and 'administration'. (Channon, 1973:117)

BP was thus beginning to move away from the multicountry system.

Robert Horton's predecessor, Sir Peter Walters, reorganized shortly after his accession in 1981. His development of checks and balances both across BP and up and down its hierarchy moved the company to become increasingly diversified. The basic elements of the structure Walters introduced were:

> Clearly separated international business streams (divisions) with their own boards and negotiated financial relationships at all levels across the business streams and between them and the head office [. . .] Yet as the 1980's progressed, bureaucracy grew as committee was piled on committee [. . .] and the head office involved itself with operational issues in addition to strategic and financial ones. (Lorenz, 1990a:20)

As the 1980s progressed, BP formed eleven 'business streams': upstream oil, downstream oil, shipping, coal, minerals, detergents, chemical, nutrition, electronics/computers, finance and new ventures. These worked with affiliates in 70 countries: the BP head office's corporate, services and regional advisory units (such as Shell has) provided an additional overlay in this complex, matrix-like structural configuration.

By 1988 BP had divested itself of many of its businesses and had organized itself into four business streams; but it continued with the bureaucracy developed to handle the 11×70 matrix. In 1989 a BP survey of its top 150 BP managers indicated the extent of disappointment and concern that BP's structure impeded both its operational flexibility and collaboration between different businesses. Following this, Horton, upon his appointment as deputy chairman and obvious successor to Walters, secured BP board agreement to commission Project 1990 – a research and consultation project which prepared the organizational revolution eight months before Walters' retirement in early 1990 – even before Horton had officially been confirmed as Walters' heir apparent.

Project 1990

The Project 1990 reform incorporated several major elements. First BP revised the role of headquarters. The managing directors throughout the 1980s had formed a top layer exerting both control and executive authority, with each director holding two or more portfolios. In 1989, of the seven insider (or executive) board members, four chaired the boards directing the various business streams; four held the responsibility for a major region; and four headed a major function such as public affairs, human resources, research and development, finance and information systems.

While the portfolio arrangement continues, Horton has redistributed the power: two have hemisphere portfolios, the others have functional ones. The four business groups now report through the 1990-established post of deputy chairman/COO. The seven managing directors (who sit on the sixteen-member board of directors, whose outside members include an American, an Irishman and a German) continue to exert a supervisory role, but their ability to exert executive power has been diluted by removing many of the supporting staff (the headquarters complement of 540 has been reduced to 160, and 70 of the 86 head office committees have been eliminated). The corporate staff has been organized into teams, each reporting directly to Horton, chief operating officer David Simon, or one of the other executive board members. 'Information services, a huge central facility in many corporations, has been broken up and put entirely in the hands of the four divisions' (Nulty, 1990b:22).

Second, BP strengthened not only the global role of the four business streams but also the role of the major divisions within these streams. Thus the principal chain of command goes down from the head of BP Oil to the head of BP Oil Refining division, and then to the regional heads, before going to the local heads. Similarly, the person responsible for polymers (in BP Chemicals) in a particular area reports up principally through a regional polymers 'boss', back to the London-based polymers 'boss', who reports to the head of BP Chemicals. BP Nutrition, based in Antwerp, is essentially a holding company whose parts (one of which is Purina Mills in the US) operate almost autonomously, not only from the other BP streams but also from one another; many BP operations are hardly aware of the presence of nearby BP Nutrition units. (There are some reports that BP Nutrition may be 'for sale'.) This increased stress on the product perspective has had a profound impact not only on the role of the Europe, America and Asia/Pacific regional heads, but also on the role of the regional product heads of BP Exploration, BP Oil and BP Chemicals and on the roles of the BP country heads.

Third, BP created three regional *alter egos* to serve as the board's regional presence in developing strategies reinforcing corporate-wide issues, and in representing corporate interests in the American, European and Asia/Pacific territories. One is located in Cleveland (the former Sohio headquarters), one in Brussels and one in Singapore. In America, this has meant downsizing the Cleveland headquarters operations by transferring the responsibility for most support services to the regional product entities (BP Exploration, BP Oil and BP Chemicals). In Europe, this has meant moving part of the BP headquarters contingent to Brussels to form a new office. In Singapore, it has meant posting a number of executives to begin the task of coordinating Asia/Pacific efforts. The role of the American regional head, who chairs BP America and is responsible for the Western Hemisphere and Africa, has been enhanced by the fact that he has been one of the seven managing directors. The executive responsible for Asia/Pacific has also been one of the BP managing directors. (The Europe regional head has not been a BP managing director; the BP chief operating officer has represented the European interests on the board.) These *alter egos* work with the regional heads of BP Oil, and to a lesser extent with the heads of the other business streams. They have a government and public relations unit reporting to them, as do the national heads within their territory.

The fourth major change has been the role of the national companies, some of whose heads once played such a potent role in the BP matrix-like arrangement that they were often referred to as the 'barons'. 'It used to be infuriating to deal with BP Germany,' said a BP executive once, because its head 'treated [...] the heads of the group's international businesses as his juniors'. With BP's carefully engineered shift in power towards international 'business streams over the [1980s], that's virtually all changed' (Lorenz, 1990b:12). The former head of Deutsche BP now heads BP Oil Europe. Even the head of BP America (which manages more BP assets than exist in the United Kingdom) has derived his power and influence more from his status as a BP managing director than as the regional *alter ego*.

Segmented staffing

Potential recruits are interviewed by representatives of various BP business groups before the initial assignment to slot into one of the business groups. BP has recruited primarily by area, and most of its managers have made their career in one business group. Most training has been intragroup and generally intracountry. One of Horton's Project 1990 goals is:

> To shatter the company's bureaucracy and replace it with teams that will, he hopes, respond quickly to changing conditions and make the company a desirable place to work.
>
> [Horton says] 'We want a more flexible organization that works on trust and openness and teamwork rather than on hierarchy. If the Eighties were a time of change, the Nineties will be a decade of surprise.'
>
> Horton expects it will take two to five years to penetrate to all of BP's far flung extremities [...] Payroll cuts and reassignments are accomplishing most of the shrinkage in corporate staff. The diminished group will move from a giant and sooty modern office tower into a gracious old building that was the company's headquarters in the 1920s ... (Nulty, 1990b:158)

BP's acquisition of Sohio has hastened the process of international mingling. Several BP executives, including Horton, led the effort to integrate Sohio into BP; and former Sohio executives now hold seven posts at BP headquarters. Horton has vowed that a non-Briton can get to the top.

Changing vision and values

BP recognizes that to make the reorganization work will require a fundamental change in the mandate and mode of managing. For managers who have got to the middle or the top by behaving for years like stereotype military commanders who are always controlling and checking subordinates, it is different to start delegating real power and trusting the recipient to use it well. The company has begun the process by issuing a three-page 'Vision and Values' statement which commits the company to creating a trusting internal environment. But the challenge of 'Walk as we Talk' is a stern test for everyone who has struggled to the top of BP over the past twenty years by practising precisely the values which Horton and his colleagues are now trying to change. Horton himself, who was considered by many to be the epitome of the old guard 'Theory-X type' manager, could espouse but could not set a rolemodel for the more participative style that is essential for the success of the new organizational arrangements. In management, says one BP executive, 'there is always a contradiction between control and support, direction and participation. The key is to vary them. It is a matter of ambiguity and paradox' (Lorenz, 1990c: 20).

Creating a European continental office

BP has taken a lead among European multinationals in establishing continental coordinating offices in North America, Asia/Pacific and Western Europe. The decision to locate the European continental office in Belgium, not Britain – a step that distinguishes it from other multinationals – may reflect BP's recognition of its off-continent insularity. It may be that this insularity, which has been reflected in the United Kingdom's ambivalence regarding the European Community, has allowed BP to appreciate more fully the value of a tricontinental organizational approach that does not so readily view other continental concerns through a home continent and a home country prism.

CHAPTER 8

Asian *keiretsu* and *chaebol*: globalizing functional perspectives

From trading companies to function-specific affiliates

The collective evolution of the largest Asian industrial corporations provides a third point of view – a final point of triangulation – for comparing the international organizational development of leading multinationals. Wartime destruction, post-war trauma and decades-long, government-orchestrated growth has transformed the economy and shaped the features of Japanese and South Korean industrial organizations. While many of the salient features of Japanese business had their roots in the years before World War II, the trauma of the war and postwar years so affected the Japanese and South Korean economies that essentially today's leading Asian multinationals may be considered to have been reborn in the postwar years.

While all the leading multinationals have grown remarkably in recent decades, the growth of Asian ones has been spectacular. While the sales generated by the ten leading American multinationals multiplied by six from 1969 to 1991 and the ten leading European ones' sales multiplied by thirteen, those of the ten leading Asian ones multiplied by twenty (see Table 8.1).

In Japan, the legacy of the prewar family-owned holding companies (*zaibatsu*), which were dissolved under the occupation, shaped the emergence of the postwar, cross-held-equity groupings. The way that, with government orchestration, they organized their global growth affected such significant features as reliance on trading companies and other marketing-specific entities. The leading Japanese multinationals have continued to attract the elite and enact an almost fanatic corporate work ethic that has been reinforced by career-long employment and continuous management development.

The South Korean *chaebol*, which did not enter the world stage until after their recovery from the Korean War, have been even more government encouraged, more motivated by national pride, and as capable of attracting the elite and exacting their corporate allegiance. They have continued to operate as diversified conglomerates under unified direction.

273

Table 8.1 Comparison of sales growth of top ten American, European and Asian multinationals, 1969–91

1969 leaders	Sales ($bn)	1991 leaders	Sales ($bn)
AMERICAN			
GM	24	GM	124
Standard Oil	15	Exxon	104
Ford	15	Ford	89
GE	9	IBM	65
IBM	7	GE	60
Chrysler	7	Mobil	57
Mobil	7	Philip Morris	48
Texaco	6	Du Pont	38
ITT	6	Texaco	38
Gulf	6	Chevron	37
Total	*102*		*659*
EUROPEAN			
Royal Dutch/Shell	10	Royal Dutch/Shell	104
Unilever	6	IRI	64
Philips	4	BP	58
Volkswagen	4	Daimler-Benz	57
BP	3	Fiat	47
ICI	3	Volkswagen	46
British Steel	3	Siemens	45
Montecate Edison	2	ENI	41
Siemens	2	Unilever	41
British Leyland	2	Nestlé	36
Total	*39*		*539*
ASIAN			
Hitachi	3	Toyota Motor	78
Toyota Motors	2	Hitachi	56
Toshiba	2	Matsushita Electric	49
Mitsubishi Heavy Ind.	2	Samsung	44
Matsushita Electric	2	Nissan Motor	43
Nissan Motor	2	Toshiba	33
Yawata Iron & Steel	2	Honda	31
Nippon Kokan	2	NEC	27
Fuji Iron & Steel	2	Sony	27
Sumitomo Metal Ind.	1	Daewoo	25
Total	*20*		*413*

Source: *Fortune*, 1970a,b, 1992.

This introduction focuses on the evolution and distinguishing characters of Japanese multinationals.

From zaibatsu to keiretsu

For several decades before World War II a few combines, known as *zaibatsu*, dominated the Japanese economy: 'Groups like Mitsubishi, Yasuda, Sumitomo or

Mitsui, having started advantageously, continued to benefit from government influence in, for example, the allocation of technology. They also gained immeasurably from their privileged access to capital' (Clark, 1979:42: see Allen, 1990, for one of a number of descriptions of prewar *zaibatsu*). Each *zaibatsu* had at its core a holding company controlled by the founder family. Such a holding company owned a substantial percentage of each of a number of core companies, including a bank, a trading company, a trust company and an insurance company, as well as a number of manufacturing companies. Each of the core companies would own a further percentage of many of the other core companies, so that the *zaibatsu* as a group would control 40–100 per cent of the capital of each of the major members (Hadley, 1970:62–7). Since the core companies tended to have subsidiaries of their own, the whole *zaibatsu* appeared as a vast constellation of related companies extending over a range of industries:

> There was a great measure of central management co-ordination with the officers of the holding company holding presidencies and directorships in the core companies. The member firms did business together, making particular use of the group trading companies as agents and to some extent initiators of new business. So great was their collective power and so wide were their interests that the *zaibatsu* had some pretention to economic self-sufficiency. (Clark, 1979:42–3)

The emergence of the prewar *zaibatsu* reflected the evolution of internalized markets for resources such as capital, technology, trained labour and managerial talent that are especially scarce in rapidly developing countries:

> Without waiting for uncertain developments in the external and open markets for the resources, the pre-war *zaibatsu* structure enabled its affiliate firms to share scarce resources and rapidly to diffuse technological and managerial innovations among themselves. The division of manufacturing, mercantile, and financial tasks among the same *zaibatsu* group permitted it to grow rapidly by pursuing economies of scale of the group organization as well as a joint entry in new industrial fields. This kind of 'group capitalism' shaped much of pre-war Japan. (Tsurumi, 1990:10)

Each *zaibatsu* contained a bank and an insurance company to provide funds and financial services, and a trading company to buy and sell goods on behalf of the member firms. By the advent of World War II the four leading *zaibatsu* so dominated the Japanese economy that they controlled almost one third of the national investment in heavy industry and almost one half of Japan's banking resources (Hadley, 1970:45–57).

The post-World War II occupation significantly reshaped the industrial structure and corporate behaviour of prewar Japan not only by dismantling the *zaibatsu* but also by purging their senior executives. The dissolution of the *zaibatsu* severed hundreds of former *zaibatsu*-affiliated firms from the control of their holding companies, creating smaller independent firms. The purging of those in executive positions put younger managers in charge of rebuilding these war-affected offspring of the old *zaibatsu* (Tsurumi, 1990:9). The prospect of any central super-company re-emerging was undercut by the US-imposed, 1947-enacted antimonopoly law which made such holding companies illegal, and limited the stake that a bank might have in any company to 5 per cent. In addition, the new entrepreneurial executives – those starting new companies as well as those restarting older ones – were far too independent to concede their autonomy to any central body.

The emergence of the postwar business groups and groupings in the 1950s and early 1960s may be traced in part to the redeveloping companies' need for capital and other resources:

> Government loans and subsidies were channeled through a few large commercial banks which were held responsible for a rigorous economic evaluation of investment projects of shipyards and shipping firms. Since many fiscal incentives and allocation of scarce foreign exchange were tied to the export performances of shipyards and other manufacturing firms, general trading firms became indispensable. Once in place, this clustering of trading and manufacturing firms around a select number of large commercial banks subsequently enabled the government to allocate resources to targeted growth industries. (Tsurumi, 1990:10)

The government played a big role, in part through the Ministry of Finance and the Ministry of International Trade and Industry (MITI), in orchestrating economic development.

> MITI officials gave orders directly in the years 1951–55, kept a tight rein on investment money [...] in the years 1955–60, and from 1961 onwards they allowed the individual firms to set their own investment programs through what was called 'voluntary adjustment'. In practice MITI's non-legal sanctions, such as threatening a cut in allocated quotas of still scarce commodities, were effective. In 1970, MITI achieved a long-standing ambition by merging Yawata Steel and Fuji Steel, which had been split under the occupation, into Nippon Steel. (Horsley and Buckley, 1990:59)

Six major groupings

By the 1970s six major groupings of companies had emerged and gathered into their orbit many of the leading firms. Each grouping clustered around and became popularly identified by the name of its member commercial bank: Mitsubishi, Mitsui, Sumitomo, Fuyo (Fuji Bank), Daiichi-Kangyo and Sanwa. (Fuji Bank was once Yasuda Bank, the core of the prewar Yasuda *zaibatsu*; Daiichi-Kangyo Bank was formed by a merger of the Daiichi and Kangyo banks in the 1960s. Mitsui Bank merged with the Taiyo Kobe Bank on 1 April 1990 to form the Mitsui Taiyo Kobe bank. The merged bank changed its name to Sakura Bank on 1 April 1992.)

The sheer size of these groupings is staggering. For example, the three largest Mitsubishi member corporations – Mitsubishi Electric, Mitsubishi Heavy Industries and Mitsubishi Motors – individually ranked in 1991 among the world's 63 largest in revenue. Eleven Mitsubishi companies rank among the Global 500 largest industrial corporations (*Fortune*, 1992). Members of these groupings own shares in one another, rely upon grouping banks and insurance companies, and do business with one another, often through their trading company. The member companies of each grouping work together through regular meetings of their Presidents' Club and their senior managing directors' conference to manage and to discuss joint research activities and programmes, to avoid gaps and overlaps in their efforts, and to develop 'common plans for the management of the new joint ventures' (Young, 1979:49). Their more specialized committees plan common sponsorship of cultural events and social activities. Participation in some social efforts may include companies such as Sony that do not belong to the grouping. (For example, Sony participates in some Mitsui social efforts but does not belong to the Mitsui grouping.)

Employees tend to identify with and share pride in belonging to their grouping as well as their company. The members of the three groupings that share the strongest sense of a common *zaibatsu* heritage – Mitsubishi, Mitsui and Sumitomo – have developed closer linkages than those in the other three groupings – Fuyo, Daiichi-Kangyo and Sanwa (even though the Fuyo grouping includes the lead bank and other former companies in the former Yasuda *zaibatsu* and several companies of the former Nissan combine, the most powerful 'new *zaibatsu*' of the twentieth century, which embraced Hitachi, Nippon Mining and Nissan Motors) (Roberts, 1989:311). The strong sense of common interest and closer association of the Mitsubishi, Mitsui and Sumitomo groupings is reflected in the extent of cross-holdings (Sumitomo 26 per cent, Mitsubishi 24 per cent, and Mitsui 15 per cent). It is also reflected in the wider use of the common name and image: 17 of the 19 Sumitomo core companies are named Sumitomo; 22 of the 28 Mitsubishi core companies are named Mitsubishi and use the Mitsubishi logo; and 14 of the 26 Mitsui core companies use Mitsui in their title (*Diamond*, 1991, and direct corporate sources). But by comparison with their prewar progenitors, all the postwar groupings are loose affiliations in which member companies not only cooperate, but also compete, and frequently do business with companies that compete with other members of their grouping.

With regard to their association in groupings, the major Japanese multinationals may be considered in a spectrum: those that are associated with the three more tightly knit *zaibatsu*-descended groupings; those that are associated with three looser groupings; and those that have remained unassociated, or associated with one of the smaller associations, such as the Todai one (see Table 8.2). All of these groupings have four or more members in the 1990 Global 200; in comparison only nine countries – the United States, Germany, Britain, France, Italy, South Korea, Switzerland, Sweden and of course Japan – have four or more.

Such major multinationals as Mitsubishi Electric and Mitsubishi Motors, Toshiba and Toyota (albeit only as an observer), and NEC and Sumitomo

Table 8.2   Japan's leading corporations: by industry and by major groupings, 1990

Six major groupings	Mitsubishi	Mitsui	Sumitomo	Fuyo	Daiichi-Kangyo	Sanwa	Non-associated
(Number of core companies in groupings)*	(28)	(26)	(19)	(28)	(44)	(40)	
SERVICES							
Banks							
Daiichi-Kangyo					×		
Mitsui Taiyo Kobe/Sakura[s]		×					
Sumitomo			×				
Fuji				×			
Mitsubishi	×						
Sanwa						×	
Industrial Bank of Japan							×
Tokai							×
Bank of Tokyo							×
Mitsubishi Trust Company	×						
Norinchukin							×
Trading							
Sumitomo			×				
C. Itoh					×		
Mitsui & Co.		×					
Marubeni				×			
Mitsubishi	×						
Nissho Iwai						×	
Tomen		×					
Nichimen						×	
Kanematsu					×		
Insurance							
Nippon Life						×	
Daiichi Mutual Life					×		
Sumitomo Mutual Life			×				
Asahi Mutual Life					×		
Mitsui Mutual Life		×					
Yasuda Mutual Life				×			
INDUSTRIAL							
Food/Tobacco							
Taiyo Fisheries							×
Japan Tobacco							×
Chemical/rubber/plastics							
Bridgestone							×
Asahi Glass	×						
Asahi Chemical Industry							×
Mitsubishi Kasei	×						
Sumitomo Chemical				×			
Petroleum refining							
Nippon Oil							×
Idemitsu Kosan							×
Showa Shell Sekiyo					×		
Cosmo Oil						×	
Metals/metal products							
Nippon Steel							×
Sumitomo Metal Industries			×				
NKK				×			
Kobe Steel[j]					×	×	
Kawasaki Steel						×	
Sumitomo Electric Industries			×				

Table 8.2   (continued)

Six major groupings	Mitsubishi	Mitsui	Sumitomo	Fuyo	Daiichi-Kangyo	Sanwa	Non-associated
Electronics/computers/ Scientific and photographic							
Hitachi[j]				×	×	×	
Matsushita Electric Industrial							×
Toshiba		×					
NEC			×				
Mitsubishi Electric	×						
Sony							×
Fujitsu					×		
Canon				×			
Sanyo Electric							×
Fuji Photo Film		×[m]					
Sharp						×	
Matsushita Electric Works							×
Industrial and farm equipment							
Mitsubishi Heavy Industry	×						
Motor vehicles							
Toyota		×[o]					
Nissan				×			
Honda							×
Mazda			×				
Mitsubishi Motor	×						
Nippondenso		×[m]					
Isuzu Motors					×		
Suzuki Motors							×
Publishing/printing							
Dai Nippon Printing							×
Toppan Printing							×

Notes: The table lists banks with assets exceeding $200 billion, trading companies with sales exceeding $15 billion, insurance companies with premium annual income exceeding $10 billion, and industrial companies with sales exceeding $6,180 billion in 1990 (that is, those ranking in sales among the 200 largest industrial corporations in the world in 1990); rankings of individual firms are those provided by *Fortune*, 1991a,b. Firms have been grouped in six major groupings.

Nine countries had four or more of their industrial corporations ranked among the world's 200 largest in 1990 by sales; they were the USA (68), Japan (40), Germany (31), Britain (14), France (12), Italy (6), Switzerland (5), South Korea (6) and Sweden (4) (*Fortune*, 1991a,b).

*Number of core companies (that is, firms represented at monthly meetings of groupings) as reported by *Diamond*, 1991.
[o] Observer status
[m] Company with a *keiretsu* tie with one of the Mitsui principal members.
[j] Corporation affiliated with more than one grouping.
[s] Name changed from Mitsui Taiyo Kobe Bank to Sakura Bank on 1 April 1992.

Metal Industries belong to one of the more tightly knit groupings. Nissan and Canon, Isuzu and Fujitsu, Sharp and Kobe Steel, and Hitachi (which participates in all three) are associated with looser groupings. Such leading firms as Nippon Steel, Matsushita Electric Industries, Honda and Sony have continued essentially unassociated with any of these six major groupings.

Pluralism, specialization, elitism and trading company-led internationalization

With the death of the *zaibatsu*, several features have marked Japanese multinationals. The first is pluralism; not only are Japanese multinationals free from holding-company control but also the larger Japanese multinationals have developed as the core of a group of product/function specialized companies, many of which exercise considerable operational autonomy. The second is specialization; Japanese firms have tended to focus on fewer product lines and even when they have diversified they have tended to organize relatively autonomous divisions or even separate companies for the newer lines. Third is the trading-company-led internationalism; Japanese companies have tended to rely on trading companies to handle their international markets. The fourth is elitism; the core companies of the Japanese multinationals have maintained a sense of *esprit de corps* and *élan* that enables them to select, motivate and retain the fittest survivors of the Japanese educational system. While the *zaibatsu* are gone, some of their traditions have continued to affect the organizations and operations of Japanese business.

The larger Japanese firms have assembled around them a multitude of related companies which together comprise a group. The larger multinationals embrace hundreds of subsidiaries: Hitachi has 688, Mitsui & Co. 513, Mitsubishi Corporation 459, Marubeni 378, Honda 352, Matsushita 340, Sumitomo Corporation 287 and Toshiba 215 (*Economist*, 1991d:58). Such firms produce related products, supply component parts, sell these products or provide organizational support services. Some of the firms comprising these complexes may be spun-off divisions, others may be acquisitions. In addition to the wholly owned or partially owned subsidiaries there are many other suppliers and distributors that have developed close, continuing relationships.

> each large core manufacturing firm has developed a cluster of related supplier firms so that the division of tasks can be exploited to the greatest advantage of the group. By sharing long-term production goals and necessary technical know-how between supplier plants and custom plants, the group synchronizes production scheduling for support-member firms. This system lies behind the famed 'just in time delivery system' (*kanban*) where supplier plants deliver necessary supplies to appropriate sections of the customer plant's production processes 'just in time' for production. Rather than the unit prices of supplies, zero-defect quality and timely delivery are the two overriding variables which are considered by industrial customers in their selection of suppliers.
> (Tsurumi, 1990:10)

Many distributors are similarly associated. While the core companies may control their related firms through the ownership of shares and the selection of their top executives (sometimes 'parachuting' those who retire early or do not make the final promotion in the core company), the technological interdependence and purchase and sale agreements provide the even more important bonding in these pluralistic arrangements.

The specialization of Japanese firms has been a feature concomitant with their pluralism. The traditional division of tasks among many firms has generated function-specific companies, later further divided into product-specific manufacturing and market-specific sales companies. Over the decades as Matsushita Electric spun off a number of its manufacturing divisions as separate subsidiaries, it was the corporate domestic sales arm that continued to be responsible for their domestic marketing and its long-autonomous trading company that handled international marketing. Similarly, as Hitachi developed its agglomeration of companies, it established one sales company to handle consumer sales and a corporate international division to handle industrial products, with each consisting of two halves, one for domestic business and one for overseas business.

Among the important concomitant features of the specialization, one has been the homogeneity of a specific company's workforce. 'Those who work for it are more likely to have common views, common knowledge, and common backgrounds than – to make the contrast extreme – a western conglomerate selling cars, writing insurance and making chemicals. It is rather easier for the specialized company to create a team spirit and even a sense of community' (Clark, 1979:63). Another consequence of specialization has been to lessen the emphasis on financial management as the overall rubric uniting the firm; focusing on managing a well-defined core competence rather than a portfolio facilitates developing shared values that go beyond quarterly bottom lines. Also, the extent of specialization generates interdependence among the companies. To increase their economies of scale, Japanese companies have avoided unrelated diversification, preferring to invest their energies in developing overseas, and in diversifying from a well-developed technological core as NEC, Hitachi, Mitsubishi Electric, Matsushita and Sony have done (Kono, 1984:102–16, 342–3: also see Kobayashi, 1991:81–7; Prahalad and Hamel, 1990, for a discussion of the development of a core competence by NEC).

A third attribute of the Japanese multinationals has been their initial dependence on international trading companies for the development of their overseas business, and the subsequent function-divided development of Japanese multinational overseas operations. Because Japan was initially 'so isolated, physically, psychologically and linguistically, dealing with foreigners was inordinately painful for most Japanese businessmen' (Halberstam, 1986:292; interview, Schmuckli, 29 May 1991), Japanese firms relied largely upon trading companies (*sogo shosha*) to handle overseas purchasing, sales and new venture development. 'It was the trading companies of these groups that first built the logistical and sales channels for exports, and which organized and took equity positions in early overseas investment' (Abegglen and Stalk, 1985:248). And because the development of overseas business was so crucial to the development of Japanese business the trading companies had a particularly valued role, especially compared to the traditional American international division, whose sales were an addendum to their company's domestic sales.

For those Japanese companies long associated with groupings – and for those who became associated with a grouping in order to take advantage of its banking, international trading and other resources – it was the trading companies that initially led the overseas development effort. Those unassociated with a grouping developed their own international entity: Matsushita developed its own trading company and Sony an international division. These international entities at first tended to develop distributorships. Later, when and where advantageous, some replaced these distributorships with sales affiliates – sometimes, as Nissan has experienced in the United Kingdom, with significant trauma. The trading companies also initiated production ventures (either alone or on a joint basis).

As the corporate profiles that follow show, only a few Japanese multinationals have made decisive steps towards establishing an overall continental coordinating presence in Europe or America. Hitachi has established only a public affairs and relations office. While Matsushita and Mitsubishi Electric have broadened the role of their continental sales organizations to exert a limited liaison role, the production operations still report essentially to their Japan-located production headquarters. Sony and Nissan have gone further by establishing continental organizational arrangements that tie in the continental sales organizations with the continental production arms of the corporate production divisions.

The fourth attribute of Japanese multinationals has been the powerful sense of *esprit de corps* and elitism that pervades major companies. There has been a strong correlation between the size of the company, the level of wages it pays, the number of university graduates it recruits, career-long employment, advantageous rate of interest on its loans, and the social prestige and pride generated by association with the company, all of which contribute to a sense of elitism. The differentiation between the major and lesser companies that has been called 'industrial dualism', or *yasuda*, and 'industrial gradation' (Clark, 1979:64–73) has enabled the leading Japanese companies to recruit what they have considered the best students from the best universities, to invest in indoctrinating and developing them as company-specific (that is, Mitsubishi, Mitsui, Hitachi, Nissan or Sony) men with a strong corporate loyalty and work ethic, to promote corporate loyalty with rites and songs, and to expect to secure this corporation-above-all devotion throughout their career and retain the 'best', despite promotion and pay policies that generally continue to be geared principally to seniority. While international job-hopping has increased among Japanese executives, especially those who have worked overseas, career-long employment with one Japanese firm remains the norm.

In Japan more than elsewhere, the country's corporate policies of hiring the best from the best university, promoting wholly from within, and using training to emphasize and enhance the corporate *esprit de corps* ensure an elitist sense of commitment to a corporate 'we'. Under these circumstances, it is little wonder that a Japanese company is a way of life as well as a style of management. It facilitates Japanese management communication and eases the need for overt control, but it presents problems of working with those of other cultures. But while, seen from a foreign viewpoint, Japanese multinationals have many points in common, when viewing them close up they differ remarkably. As the profiles that follow show, even those in the same industry differ significantly. For example, while some have considered Matsushita Electric to be the 'paragon' of Japanese-style corporation

(Horsley and Buckley, 1990:66), Sony has been considered the maverick. And while many consider Mitsui & Co. and Mitsubishi Corporation as indistinguishable, a closer look demonstrates significant differences between these historic adversaries.

The Japanese corporations' stress on shared values as the bond that provides their organizational coherency has strengthened the corporate commitment, facilitated the efforts of many corporations to provide varied experiences, and fostered communication and coordination that have traversed corporate boundaries. Japanese firms have stressed staffing, but the critical element shaping staffing has been the development of the corporate – Mitsui, Mitsubishi, Matsushita, etc. – man. Japanese firms have been concerned with structure – witness Mitsubishi's early development of the production division. But the concern for shared values has been the cohesive force that has affected the success of these arrangements. It is curious that Sony, the maverick and the most Westernized of Japanese companies, which has long neither published nor apparently felt the need for an organizational chart, has been the most pioneering in developing cross-functional American and European organizations and in integrating non-Japanese into top management posts.

Trading company develops international operations

Samsung Group: a nation-encouraged, extremely diversified conglomerate

The Samsung Group, South Korea's largest enterprise, is the largest multinational in a 'newly industrialized country'. Samsung, and a few other highly diversified South Korean conglomerates (*chaebol*), dominate their country's economy. The 1990 sales of the 30 largest conglomerates totalled almost 90 per cent of Korean gross national product. The top four *chaebol* alone – Daewoo, Hyundai and Lucky-Goldstar as well as Samsung – represented more than 30 per cent of Korea's 1990 exports.

The South Korean government has encouraged and supported the growth of these family-owned *chaebol* as a means of triggering Korea's rapid industrialization:

> The *chaebol* have been favored and heavily supported by the South Korea government. They command the capital and clout to make huge investments in industries such as shipbuilding and semi-conductors. Each is prone to enter every important Korean industry, especially if one of the others does so [. . .] It has led to firms that are widely diversified in unrelated fields but still managed with a high degree of central control. It is important not to confuse the Korea *chaebol* with the Japanese *keiretsu* whose members have informal ties and partial interlocking ownership but are managed with great independence. (Porter, 1990:472)

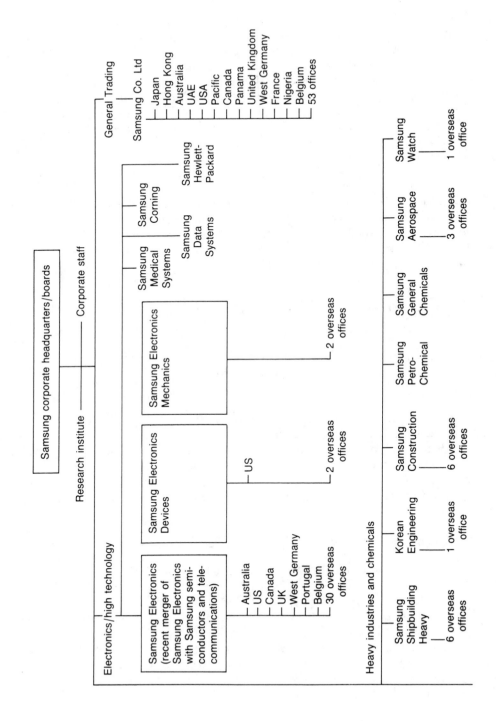

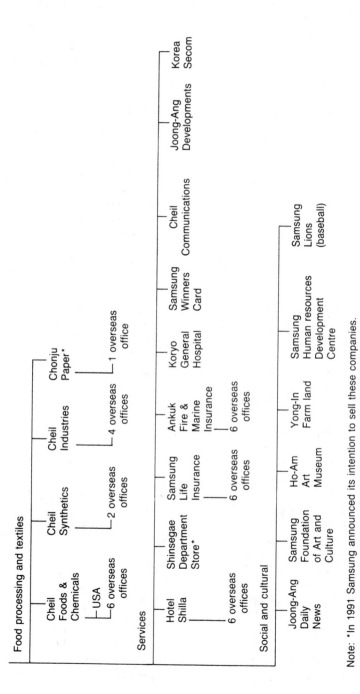

Figure 8.1   Samsung Group organogram, 1991

Note: *In 1991 Samsung announced its intention to sell these companies.

The *chaebol* have engaged in such a wide range of disparate businesses 'partly to insure against the risk that the government may restrict entry to a new industry, [and] partly to satisfy the founder's vanity' (*Economist*, 1990:18). Not until 1991 did the South Korea *chaebol* begin to focus their efforts – and then only under orders from the Korean government that they must choose three industries on which they would concentrate and that only for those areas would they henceforth be eligible for loans from the government-owned Bank of Korea.

Samsung alone accounted for 15 per cent of South Korea's gross national product in 1988 (*Newsweek*, 20 November, 1989:26). Its rapid growth since its refounding in 1953 to become the world 24th-largest industrial company has been spectacular. While the principal manufacturing and technological strength of the Samsung Group focuses on electronics, it is an extremely diversified conglomerate with interests ranging from aerospace and shipbuilding, chemicals and textiles, to a hotel and a hospital, a newspaper and insurance, and an art museum. Samsung leadership recognizes it faces major challenges in transforming its existing monocultural and highly nationalized corporate entity into a multicultural business entity.

Founder-led for five decades

B.C. Lee, who founded Samsung General Store in 1938, remained at the helm of the Samsung conglomerate until his death in November 1987. By 1950 Samsung had grown into Korea's largest trading company. In 1953, after the Korean War during which the business was largely destroyed, Samsung began redeveloping by establishing overseas branches and building Korea's first industrial plant, a sugar refinery. During the 1950s and 1960s Samsung, spurred on by South Korea's military government and its Economic Plan, devoted most of its resources to establishing a diversity of industries such as life insurance, department stores, paper manufacturing, such services activities as the Samsung Foundation of Art and Culture, the Koryo (Korean) General Hospital, and several manufacturing companies. In the early 1970s Samsung moved aggressively into electronics by establishing companies for picture tubes, electronic components, telecommunication exchanges and semiconductors. In the late 1970s it diversified into shipbuilding, heavy equipment, power plants and chemicals. In the 1980s Samsung continued to diversify into high-technology industries.

Thus in less than four decades Samsung grew into a $45 billion conglomerate consisting of more than twenty major companies that employ more than 180,000 people engaged in several categories of activities, including electronics, heavy and chemical industries, consumer manufacturing, service enterprises and a general trading company (see Figure 8.1). It is this extremely diversified conglomerate for which Kun-Hee Lee (the founder-chairman's third son, who became chairman upon the death of his father in 1987) has set the goal of 'glocalization'. He faces the challenge not only of transforming an agglomeration of disparate companies into a more globally developed and industry-focused one, but also of undertaking this effort with an organization that is no longer a founder-based autocracy and must develop and depend upon more collegial management style.

Korean law, like Japanese law, forbids holding companies; thus, like the Japanese *zaibatsu*-descended groups, the Samsung Group companies (and those within each of the other major South Korean conglomerates) are tied together through interlocking ownership. Unlike the case with the Japanese groupings such as Mitsui and Mitsubishi, though, there is an overall Samsung Group board, which consists of the Samsung Group chairman, several vice-chairmen (each of whom heads one of the major groups into which the conglomerate is divided), and the president of each of the companies. Under the new chairman the presidents of each company have been given more responsibility. 'The chairman's power today is only a fraction of what his father's was a decade ago' (interview, Young Chang, 13 June 1990). The president of Samsung's research institute, Lim Dong Sung, has gone further, stating that the new chairman's power 'is probably only 10% of what his father's was' (*Economist*, 1990:9).

The Samsung Group corporate headquarters executive staff assists the Samsung Group chairman/CEO in overseeing the activities of all the companies, by coordinating the planning, financing, and research and development. The executive staff includes many high-flyers assigned for three to five years from the various companies (interview, Soung-Hoon Shin, Manager Overseas Planning Division, 18 April 1989).

Samsung Co. Ltd., the trading company, plays the role closest to that of the mother company in the conglomerate. The trading company has pioneered the diversification efforts by its development of new businesses before they were spun off as separate companies. It has led the globalization efforts by establishing affiliates throughout the world to market Samsung Group products and by paving the way for a few of the individual product companies to organize their own affiliates. When and where these companies, such as Samsung Electronics, have set up their own affiliates, they are (generally) located adjacent to the Samsung Co. offices. In a foreign country the head of the trading company affiliate may be considered the 'senior' person representing the Samsung Group interests. In 1989 Samsung Co. Ltd. organized major regional offices: one in New York for America, one in London for Europe (Africa and the Middle East), one in Hong Kong for Asia, and one in Tokyo just for Japan. The trading company affiliates and offices report through these regional offices.

Monocultural staffing

The Samsung Group stresses the importance of developing the 'Samsung man' in its recruitment, training and promotions. The Samsung Group recruits management staff on behalf of all the management companies. Almost without exception they are Korean, and they are recruited directly from the top universities in South Korea. Those selected are chosen by means of a Samsung written and oral examination system, in which the Samsung Group founder/chairman was often personally involved. Once when asked why he spent his precious time in this activity, he is reported to have replied, 'Because hiring our future leaders is the most important way I can spend my time' (interview, Young Chang, 13 June 1990). After an initial three to six months of a rigorous indoctrination and education programme, the trainees select the company with which they wish to spend their career; transfers are rare, but do occur. The emphasis on education and training continues through an employee's career. Even the overseas Korean staff must return once a year for 'spiritual renewal'.

The Samsung Group companies invest a major share of their resources in upgrading the technical and job-related abilities and skills of their employees. At each level in a manager's career, he or she is required to spend a certain designated amount of time on the job and in education at the Samsung Human Resource Development Centre. They are also required to pass a series of examinations to qualify for further promotions. High-flyers, as already noted, are posted to corporate headquarters at an early stage of their career.

As Samsung pursues its 'glocalization' effort, its major staffing challenge is how to accommodate the monocultural tradition and highly nationalistic corporate culture to the need to become accepted throughout the world. Samsung recognizes the need to develop host country nationals as executives, but has not determined how this can be accomplished within such a monocultural system.

A *highly nationalistic culture*

'The commitment of personnel to the company, and the willingness to risk everything to preserve it, is distinctive in Korea with the possible exception of Italy' (Porter, 1990:472). Several factors drive this commitment. One is the highly competitive nature of the *chaebol*. Another is the sense of patriotic zeal to build Korea through building the company. A third is the corporate sense of family which *chaebol* leadership manages to cultivate throughout the organization.

Samsung states and restates three basic management principles. The first translates as 'We do business for the sake of nation-building', a statement that reflects the Samsung determination to increase the Korean standard of living as well as the strong nationalism which drives its *esprit de corps*. The second is its stress on the human factor, as reflected in its personnel policies and practices. The third is the effort to improve its management effectiveness and efficiency through modern, rational practices.

The management of Samsung recognizes that as the Korean economy develops rapidly and the standard of living and education of the workers rise sharply, the company will have to operate in a very different social environment, one in which it will be difficult for rigid, centralized, unified management policies and operations to survive and remain as the dominant mode of operation. Samsung must find ways to combine the traditional emphasis on cohesiveness based on patriotic nationalism and uniformity, together with a more humanitarian approach based on internationalism and pluralism. Finding ways to meet the dilemma of reconciling nationalism with globalism – attempting to present a distinctive image while maintaining a diversity so similar to that of other South Korean conglomerates – poses a major challenge for Samsung as it pursues its goal of 'glocalization'.

The next phase

All Korean multinationals face the same challenge as Samsung: how to sustain their move into international markets. The strategy of low-cost mass production, which sustained Korea's rapid development from the 1960s, is no longer viable, as increasing wage levels and a meagre export growth of 3 per cent in 1989 and 1990 demonstrate. To meet the challenge of improved technology, the *chaebol* are increasing their R&D and capital expenditures. But securing the necessary capital has been increasingly difficult, for capital has become scarcer, government support has waned and interest rates have soared. The 1991-initiated government policy limiting government support to three of their numerous business spheres, which was aimed at creating greater focus among Korea's giants in world industry, has strained Korea's traditionally close government–business relations. Not only are the *chaebol* reluctant to part with any of their carefully nurtured parts, but they also see their diversified companies as providing revenues and reducing risks inherent in supporting their efforts to develop their core businesses. Samsung has responded by shedding two units, Chonju Paper Manufacturing Co. and Shinsegae Department Store Company, by selling on the stock market the shares held by members of the Lee family and other Group companies.

The fact that all four of the leading Korean *chaebol* have reacted to the government policy by choosing to focus on electronics, three (including Samsung) on petrochemicals and two (including Samsung) on heavy industrial shipbuilding, demonstrates the competitive nature of the challenge they are facing. 'Korean companies cannot pursue a policy where market diversification replaces increasing product quality,' says Dr Koo Bohn Young, economic secretary at the presidential office, 'but diversification will help supply the revenues necessary for investment in new equipment and productivity' (Ridding, 1991:iv).

Mitsui & Co.: global trading and developing

Mitsui & Co., lead member of the Mitsui grouping, is one of the six major Japanese trading and development companies, each of which is a lead member of one of the six major groupings of Japanese corporations. While Mitsui & Co. is not an industrial corporation, a description of its activities and organization has been included in this comparative book because the role of the trading companies has been so vital to the development of Japanese multinationals overseas. Until the mid-1970s, Mitsui & Co. and other trading companies were virtually the only Japanese multinational presence overseas. Since then they have continued to play a key role in developing new markets and joint venture operations, but many Japanese industrial corporations have also developed significant overseas presence.

In 1990 Mitsui & Co. reorganized its European operations by strengthening the role of Mitsui & Co. (Europe) as the integrator of the activities of its fifteen European affiliates.

More than 300 years of tradition

Mitsui & Company, and the Mitsui grouping of which it is a lead member, traces its origins to the early 1600s when a family business was begun and expanded into a chain of dry goods stores. In 1683 the family opened several exchange offices which became the foundations of Mitsui Bank, whose role ever since has paralleled and complemented that of other Mitsui enterprises (Roberts, 1989). In 1876, Mitsui & Co. (Mitsui Bussan Kaisha) and Mitsui Bank were founded as separate corporate entities. Mitsui & Co. opened its first offices outside Japan in Shanghai and London in 1877 and in Hong Kong, New York and Paris in 1878.

Before World War II, the Mitsui *zaibatsu* was one of the world's largest business organizations. Its family-dominated *honsha* controlled more than twenty major subsidiary corporations, the largest of which was Mitsui & Co. The twenty corporations in turn controlled almost 300 sub-subsidiaries – Mitsui & Co. alone had more than 121. Together the *zaibatsu* employed as many as 1.8 million people in Japan and 1 million overseas. The Mitsui *zaibatsu* controlled 15 per cent of the nation's paid-up capital and 30 per cent of its overseas investments (Roberts, 1989:50).

Following the war, the Allied occupation broke the Mitsui and other *zaibatsu* up into many companies (see Figure 8.2). Later, Mitsui & Co., with Mitsui Bank and Mitsui Real Estate, took the lead in pulling together the many Mitsui descendants into a Mitsui grouping of companies (see Table 8.3). The trading company, the bank and the real estate firm have served as the coordinating hubs of the Mitsui 'group of groups' (Roberts, 1989:492–5). The Mitsui Bank, the financial hub, has provided 25–30 per cent of the Mitsui Group borrowing; its 1990 merger with Taiyo Kobe Bank makes the merged company (now the Sakura Bank) one of the largest banks in the world (along with the lead banks of the other major Japanese groupings). Mitsui Real Estate has been the property hub of the alliance. Mitsui & Co., the trading hub, has handled about 20 per cent of the total sales of the leading Mitsui Group companies. The CEOs of these three companies lead 'the Presidents Club' (*Nimokukai*) which meets monthly and comprises the chairmen and presidents of the major members of the grouping. The executive directors of all Mitsui companies also meet monthly. These two meetings promote cooperative efforts among all the companies in the grouping, providing ideas for joint projects and coordinating Group activities of the joint Public Relations Committee, the Information Systems Conference and the Interbusiness Research Institute which was established in 1978 as a 'think tank' for its efforts (Roberts, 1989:494–6). The Mitsui Grouping also sponsors joint special clubs.

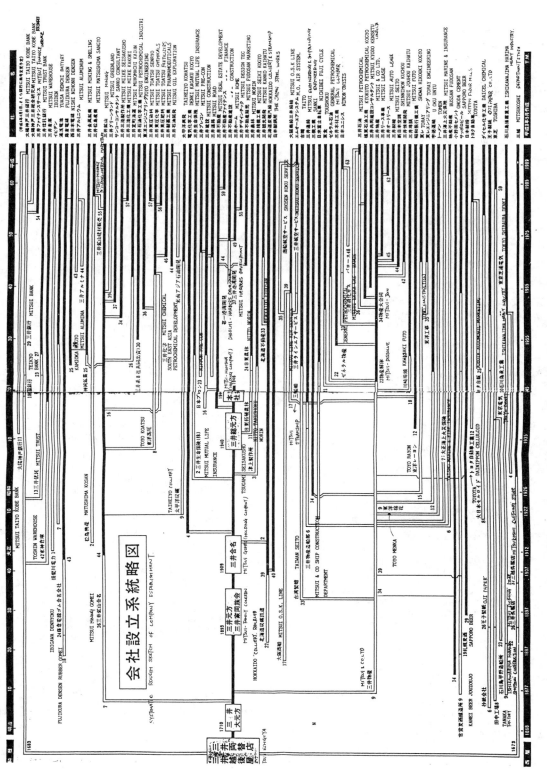

Figure 8.2 Mitsui Group evolution (Courtesy of Mitsui)

Table 8.3   Major companies in Mitsui grouping, 1991

Cement
  Mitsui Precon Co. Ltd
  Onoda Cement Co. Ltd*

Chemicals
  Daicel Chemical Industries Ltd
  Denki Kagaku Kogyo Kabushiki Kaisha*
  Mitsui Petrochemical Industries Ltd*
  Mitsui Pharmaceuticals Inc.
  Mitsui Toatsu Chemicals Inc.*
  Mitsui Toatsu Dyes Ltd
  Mitsui Toatsu Fertilizers Inc.

Commerce
  Hokkaido Colliery & Steamship Co. Ltd*
  Mitsui & Co. Ltd*
  Mitsui Matsushima Co. Ltd
  Mitsukoshi Ltd*
  Nihon Unisys Ltd
  Toshoku Ltd
  Tomen Corporation

Construction
  Mitsui Construction Co. Ltd*
  Mitsui Harbour and Urban Construction Co. Ltd
  Mitsui Home Co. Ltd
  Mitsui Designtec Co. Ltd
  Mitsui Wood Products Inc.
  Mitsui Road Co. Ltd
  Sanki Engineering Co. Ltd*
  Shin-Nippon Air Conditioning Engineering Co. Ltd

Energy
  General Sekiyu Kabushiki Kaisha
  Kyokuto Petroleum Industries Ltd
  Mitsui Oil & Gas Co. Ltd
  Mitsui Oil Exploration Co. Ltd

Engineering
  Mitsui Consultants Co. Ltd
  Toray Engineering Co. Ltd
  Toyo Engineering Corporation

Finance and Insurance
  The Mitsui Taiyo Kobe Bank Ltd*①
  Mitsui Leasing & Development Ltd
  Mitsui Mutual Life Insurance Company*
  The Mitsui Trust and Banking Co. Ltd*
  Mitsui Marine & Fire Insurance Co. Ltd*
  Mitsui Auto Leasing Ltd
  Mitsui Finance Service Co. Ltd
  Mitsui Fudosan Finance Kabushiki Kaisha

Food
  Mitsui Norin Co. Ltd
  Mitsui Sugar Co. Ltd
  Nippon Flour Mills Co. Ltd*
  Taito Co. Ltd

Machinery
  Ibiden Co. Ltd
  Ishikawajima-Harima Heavy Industries Co. Ltd*
  Mitsui Engineering & Shipbuilding Co. Ltd*
  Mitsui Miike Engineering Corporation
  Mitsui Miike Machinery Co. Ltd
  Mitsui Seiki Kogyo Co. Ltd
  Showa Aircraft Industry Co. Ltd
  Toshiba Corporation*
  Toyota Motor Corporation (Observer)*
  Yuasa Battery Co. Ltd
  Nichibei Fuji Cycle Co. Ltd

Mining
  Mitsui Mining Company Limited*
  Suncoh Consultants Co. Ltd
  Nippon Mining Co. Ltd

Nonferrous Metals
  Fujikura Ltd
  Mitsui Aluminium Co. Ltd
  Mitsui Mining & Smelting Co. Ltd*
  Nishi Nippon Electric Wire & Cable Co. Ltd

Paper
  Oji Paper Co. Ltd*

Real Estate
  Mitsui Real Estate Development Co. Ltd*
  Mitsui Real Estate Sales Co. Ltd
  Taiheiyo Kouhatsu Inc.
  Bussan Real Estate Development Co. Ltd
  Mitsui Greenland Company Limited

Steel
  The Japan Steel Works Ltd*

Synthetic Fibers and Plastics
  Toray Industries Inc.*

Transportation
  Mitsui O.S.K. Lines Ltd*
  Utoku Express Co. Ltd
  Mitsui Muromachi Shipping Co. Ltd

Warehousing
  The Mitsui Warehouse Co. Ltd*
  Mitsui Wharf Co. Ltd

Other Services
  M.O. Air System Inc.
  Mitsui Kanko Development Co. Ltd
  Mitsui Knowledge Industry Co. Ltd

① Name changed to Sakura Bank 1992
*Principal members of Mitsui Group whose chairmen and presidents comprise the Nimoku-kai (Second Thursday Conference), or the Presidents' Club
Source: Adapted from Mitsui and Co. Annual Report 1991:70

Several of the Mitsui member companies form the core of large groups (*keiretsu*) of companies. Toyota, an 'observer' member, leads a constellation of companies, and has ties with Mitsui dating from 1899 that have been strengthened through marriage, financial investment and executive moves since then. Toshiba, whose 1991 sales exceeded $33 billion, is one of the world's 30 largest multinationals. Toray Industries and Oji Paper gross more than $6 billion and $4 billion respectively. While Mitsui companies tend to rely on Mitsui & Co. for their overseas trading (marketing and purchasing), Toyota and Toshiba have developed their own overseas networks in major markets; but they continue to rely on Mitsui in minor markets.

Mitsui & Co. is a huge, complex group in its own right. It 'invests and dispatches managerial personnel to about 940 companies. Of its subsidiaries and affiliates about 620 are based in Japan and more than 300 are located outside Japan [...] These companies and Mitsui & Co. together employ about 60,000 personnel' (*Mitsui Trade News*, March/April 1989:2). The company not only trades but also undertakes business development. Toray Industries and Mitsui Engineering and Shipbuilding are enterprises which began as development projects of Mitsui & Co., and were later spun off as separate companies. In Japan, Mitsui & Co. subsidiaries manufacture and/or sell in such diverse businesses as steel and metal products, machine tools and office equipment, petroleum and chemicals, textiles, lumber and housing, foodstuffs and Coca-Cola. In the United States, Mitsui & Co. affiliates develop and sell iron ore, and sell machine tools and tubing, phosphates and fertilizers, gram and canned goods, petroleum and electronics. Mitsui & Co. affiliates and joint ventures also develop and sell iron ore and coal in Australia, and sell Yamaha products in Germany and the United Kingdom, Toyotas in Chile, Subarus in Belgium, fertilizers and coffee in Brazil, canned goods in the Netherlands, fabrics in Indonesia and textiles in Taiwan. The majority of its overseas manufacturing investments are concentrated in South East Asia.

Structure

The principal structural elements of Mitsui & Co. include the headquarters staff divisions, the operating divisions, and the area offices in Japan and overseas. The overall structure is a matrix-like arrangement coordinated by a board of approximately 50 members, including the heads of major component groups. The board is headed by a corporate management committee consisting of the chairman, the vice-chairman, the president, four executive vice-presidents (one of whom heads European operations) and four senior executive managing directors.

Mitsui has nine operating sectors as well as a headquarters administrative staff. In 1991, the sectors were as follows:

1. Iron and steel.
2. Machinery and information industries.
3. Chemicals.

4. Food.
5. Construction.
6. Energy.
7. General Merchandise.
8. Textiles.
9. Transportation.

The nine operating sectors contain 21 business units, each headed by a member of the Mitsui & Co. board of directors. In 1991, Mitsui launched its 'Long-term Corporate Strategy Action Plan', which introduced new 'business units' or 'superdivisions' that will be, as the Mitsui CEO has stated, able to 'engage in long-range investment activities on the basis of enlarged scales and develop further integrated strategies from a global viewpoint' (speech, Nashika Kumaga, 4 July 1991). 'The plan will enable the business divisions to engage in longer-range investment with deeper pockets. At the same time, these business units will be delegated with decision-making on virtually any scale, with the sole exception of investments of corporate-wide importance' (interview, Yoshida, 22 November 1991).

The 165 overseas offices located in 88 countries report directly to the corporate management committee. Since 1974 the overseas operations have been organized into regions, each of which is headed by officers with board member status (Young, 1979:185). For the most part, these regional heads have dual roles as country heads and regional coordinators. For example, the chairman and managing director of Mitsui & Co. (Australia) also serves as chairman of Mitsui & Co. (New Zealand); the head of Mitsui & Co. (Middle East) not only heads the Bahrein office but also oversees twenty more in the Middle East; and the CEO of Mitsui & Co. (USA) also coordinates all the other Mitsui & Co. affiliates in North, Central and South America.

The integration of Europe has led to a reorganization so that the chairman and managing director of Mitsui & Co. (Europe) and the chairman and managing director of Mitsui & Co. (UK) are no longer the same person. As part of the reorganization, Mitsui & Co. (Europe) now owns about 60 per cent of the equity of each of the European affiliates (which had previously been wholly owned by the parent company) and each affiliate has been given lead responsibility for one or more of the products. For example, the Brussels-based affiliate has lead responsibility for basic chemicals and dairy products (interview Yoshida, 22 November 1991). Country general managers (who generally carry the title of president) have profit-and-loss responsibilities for the Mitsui operations in their country and have strong coordinating roles. A Mitsui & Co. affiliate is principally a trading company but is also responsible for the oversight of whatever other Mitsui & Co. operations are in the country.

A typical Mitsui & Co. country affiliate is led by a president, an administrative officer and several product managers (one or more of whom may be vice-presidents). The product managers report primarily to the country general manager, but also to senior product heads in headquarters, who have the responsibility of providing information feedback to the group manufacturers (see Figure 8.3). The country administrative officer likewise reports not only to the country head but also directly to an administrative office at headquarters. If there is a locally unresolvable difference, the local product manager may appeal to the group head in Tokyo and the country head may request the support of the continental regional head; both the group head and the regional head are board members, so if necessary the issue may be resolved at that level.

In such a decision-making network, executives choose carefully the issues they wish to appeal. One country general manager, for example, has noted that he would be more likely to press his views in the chemical field – the one he knows best. The product managers would also choose issues carefully. In case of continuing tension, the country president may request a product manager's transfer. In a culture which values harmony, a country president and his or her lieutenants avoid discord (and the need for such transfer). In this matrix-like arrangement, the country ties are stronger than the product ones (in contrast to the case in Mitsubishi, where the product lines are stronger). Within the overall approved framework, the country office can proceed on most matters without specific approval. For other matters, approval must be sought via the '*ringi system*'; every involved official must sign off (interview, Tetsuro Inaji, 22 September 1989).

Career-long staffing

Mitsui & Co. recruits its Japanese executives through an exhaustive and comprehensive culling process. Most are selected from leading Japanese universities. The expectation is that the executive will stay with Mitsui & Co. for life. Mitsui & Co. rarely hires an executive in mid-career: few Mitsui & Co. executives depart for non-Mitsui positions – in part because so few Japanese firms recruit in mid-career and in part because few firms are as prestigious as Mitsui. One of the reasons given for not hiring executives in mid-career is that the Mitsui philosophy is so distinctive that newcomers would have difficulty adapting to a new culture. (One major problem envisaged in the recent Mitsui Bank merger with Taiyo Kobe Bank is the challenge of integrating corporate cultures.) This is the issue Mitsui faces when confronting the need to hire non-Japanese executives in its affiliates.

Mitsui & Co. executives begin their careers in basic training programmes designed not only to develop their competence but also to indoctrinate them in the Mitsui philosophy and spirit. Candidates are rotated throughout the company and closely monitored for five to ten years before a definite career path is set. Mitsui supports not only language training but also acquisition of an MBA, especially for those who may be posted to international assignments. Exceptionally qualified people may be sent in early or mid-career for executive development programmes abroad. A few are posted for one-year stints as 'assignment' to the senior corporate executives. Mitsui promotes according to seniority and proven ability. Pay scale is determined by rank, not by job; thus an employee may be assigned to a more responsible post, without receiving a 'promotion' or salary increase.

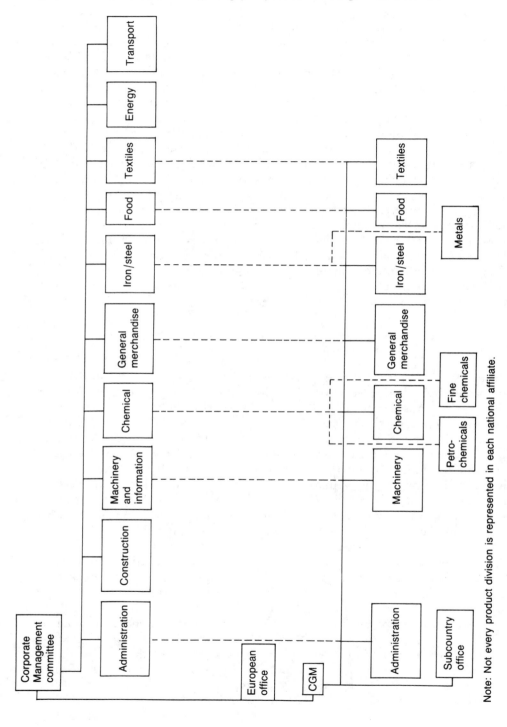

Note: Not every product division is represented in each national affiliate.

Figure 8.3 Mitsui & Co.'s relations with an affiliate

Home-based executives are thoroughly pre-tested in the Mitsui system before they are given international assignments. These tests are based on professional, personal and physical criteria. Most Japanese expatriates return to Japan after 'approximately' four to five years, but there is no clear rule except for certain areas of 'hardship' with a maximum three-year limit. Thus the period of overseas assignment is very flexible and varies in individual cases. In the 1960s, the average used to be about three years, in the 1970s it was four years; and now it is about five years. The general policy is to pull executives back to headquarters regularly to make sure they do not lose touch with how things are done at Mitsui and to make certain they continue to feel part of the mainstream. Non-Japanese senior managers occasionally attend seminars in Tokyo.

Mitsui & Co. affiliate management personnel have been almost exclusively Japanese. While Mitsui does not have an articulated policy of hiring Japanese nationals, the difficulty in recruiting non-Japanese who can work effectively in a Japanese environment has been an impediment to hiring more host country executives. While English is the official language outside Japan, Japanese is the operating language in Japan and continues as a language of convenience throughout the Mitsui systems, including some international fax messages. The distinctiveness of the Japanese culture and the homogeneity of its society, especially in its executive ranks, reinforces the difficulties in integrating non-Japanese into management posts. Another difficulty appears to be that

> most non-Japanese candidates tend to ask for promotion to senior posts
> (which would take ten or more years for their Japanese counterparts)
> after a couple of years with the company and quit when they are not
> promoted. This is a case of different business and labor practices.
> Efforts are being made to adapt corporate culture to the local situation.
> (letter, T. Inaji, 2 December 1991)

In an effort to meet these difficulties, the Benelux subsidiary was encouraged by the London-based European regional head to recruit more host country executives, and thus has a higher proportion of non-Japanese executives than other affiliates, with a mixture of Japanese and host (Dutch and Belgian) country nationals in the top management posts. The host country nationals have been assisted by young Japanese in second-level posts. Several Japanese managers are likewise assisted by host country nationals. The dual reporting relationship, one to the country head and the other to Tokyo product head, presents a difficulty when the manager is non-Japanese. One of the roles of the Japanese assistant managers is to assist the host country national in helping him or her understand the home office philosophy and practices and to explain to Tokyo the conditions in Europe. The host country nationals are encouraged to visit Japan and become familiar with headquarters operations and culture.

Pride in heritage

Mitsui has a few noteworthy features in its corporate culture which distinguish it from that of other Japanese corporations. Pride in the long and distinguished Mitsui history continues to underpin the Mitsui *esprit de corps*. Mitsui executives emphasize that the extent of their delegated autonomy, which encourages initiatives and bottom-up management, distinguishes Mitsui from other Japanese firms, many of which have a more elaborate system for clearing and approval of contracts initiated by the affiliates. Mitsui managers also point with pride to their determination to identify the customers' specific needs, and to take whatever steps are necessary to assure that their needs are met.

Mitsui & Co. as a parent

Mitsui & Co., like the other major Japanese trading companies, has had a profound impact on the rapid growth and overseas expansion of Japanese companies. First, Mitsui & Co. has identified new opportunities not only for trade but also for developing industrial enterprises – opportunities which it has proceeded to take, often in alliance with other companies. Second, Mitsui & Co. has opened up new overseas markets for other Japanese companies – not only those in the Mitsui grouping such as Toyota, but also many outside the grouping. And third, Mitsui & Co. has facilitated the provision of financial support provided by Mitsui grouping banks and other banks, which has been essential for their rapid growth. Trading companies have been a major factor in the success of Japan, Inc.

Global functional systems manage international operations

Toyota: Toyota Motor Corporation, Toyota Group and the Mitsui grouping

Toyota Motor Corporation, the largest Asian multinational in sales, assets and profits, is the core company of the Toyota Group (*keiretsu*) of companies and a participant in the Mitsui grouping. Toyota's ties with Mitsui date from 1899 when Mitsui signed a ten-year agreement with Sakichi Toyoda, the founder of what is now known as the Toyota Group, to produce and sell his looms. Since then the ties have been strengthened by bonds of marriage, equity holdings and the appointment of Mitsui executives as Toyota executives (Toyota Motor Corporation, 1988: 27–8).

Toyota has long exemplified the split between sales and manufacturing that pervades Japanese industry. In Toyota's case, a separate (not a subsidiary) corporation, Toyota Motor Sales, managed Toyota's sales from 1950 to 1982. Since 1982, the sales sides of the company has continued to operate with significant autonomy. Although the Toyoda family now owns only a minute percentage of the corporate equity, its chairman and president, as well as one of the four executive vice-presidents, are Toyoda family members. While the family name is Toyoda, a variation of this was chosen as the corporate name.

Toyoda Automatic Loom founded, Mitsui Group funded

Toyota Motor Corporation traces its origins to the automobile department that Kiichirō Toyoda and his brother-in-law (and brother by adoption) organized in 1933 within Toyoda Automatic Loom Works (Toyota Motor Corporation, 1988:47). Toyoda Automatic Loom Works was by then the major concern in a group of companies organized around a core that included Toyoda Spinning and Weaving. Kiichirō's father, Sakichi, a loom inventor and entrepreneur, 'having learned from his two previous failures' (Toyota Motor Corporation, 1988:31), founded Toyoda Spinning and Weaving with financial backing from Mitsui in 1918. In 1926, he spun off the loom manufacturing department as a separate (and soon major) concern as Toyoda Automatic Loom, and appointed as its president his adopted son Raisburö, who was also his son-in-law and a younger brother of the head of a Mitsui branch office. Before his death in 1930, Sakichi encouraged his son Kiichirō to enter the automobile business and provided the initial funding. When the Japanese government passed legislation in 1936 that required Japan-based automobile companies to be at least 50 per cent owned and managed by Japanese nationals, the brightened prospects for the enterprise led to the decision to expand operations. The 1937 incorporation of the Toyota Motor Company facilitated the attraction of the investment necessary to construct an automobile plant. The Mitsui Group provided half of the funding (Cusumano, 1985:56–60).

Initially, Toyota Motor Company consisted of seven departments: 'the Administration Department, Sales Department, Manufacturing Department, Engineering Department, Technical Department, Total Vehicle Engineering Administrative Department, and Research Department' (Toyota Motor Corporation, 1988:67). Kiichirō personally headed the last two. In 1941, by which time Toyota Motor had already become the nucleus of the Toyota Group, Raisburö became chairman, Kiichirō president, and a Mitsui director was recruited as the executive vice-president. The new president reformed the organization of the company by setting up a 'Planning Council as a liaison group between TMC and Toyoda Steel Works, Toyoda Machine Works and Toyoda Automatic Loom Works as the first step toward strengthening the company's planning capabilities' (Toyota Motor Corporation, 1988:78).

The initial postwar years were extremely difficult ones for Japan and Toyota. With industrial capacity in ruins, the economy showing no signs of recovery and the family holding company dissolved, Toyota started from scratch. Several of Toyota's affiliated companies changed their names: for example, Toyota Steel Works became Aichi Steel Works. The manufacturing capacity had to be rebuilt and the sales network re-established.

In 1949, with a combination of strikes and low sales, Toyota ran up a large inventory backlog of unsold vehicles and an ominous operating deficit. The financial difficulties led to the Bank of Japan organizing a consortium of banks, led by the Mitsui Bank, which provided funds to rescue Toyota on three conditions: that Toyota incorporate the sales department as a separate company (in which Toyota

Motor Company was prohibited from investing), limit its production to orders from the sales company and discharge surplus employees. Kiichirō Toyoda, who had tried desperately to honour the family no lay-off tradition and had promised not to let go of any employees, resigned as president and the bank chose his successor (Halberstam, 1986:129).

The reorganization led to closer ties with the Mitsui Bank. Fukio Nakagawa was sent from Mitsui to Toyota to monitor the company's financial reorganization; he became executive vice-president in 1953 and president in 1961. During the 1950s Mitsui and several other banks became the largest shareholders in Toyota, replacing Toyoda Automatic Loom and Toyoda Industries (the Toyoda family holding company) as the major investor (Cusumano, 1985:75–6). Toyota's ties with Mitsui were further strengthened by the 1953 marriage of Hiroka Mitsui to Kiichirō's son, Shoichiro, who became Toyota Motor Sales president in 1981, and Toyota Motor Corporation's president in 1982 (*Who's Who in the World, 1991–2*:1100).

The separate existence of Toyota Motor Sales enhanced its ability to focus on marketing. Toyota Motor Sales cooperated closely with Toyota Motors in all areas of operations, especially in product development. The Korean War and the consequent market for military vehicles restored viability to the Japanese automobile industry in the early 1950s. In its competition with Nissan, Toyota was able to develop a small but consistent lead in the domestic market due to a combination of manufacturing, product development and marketing factors. This performance was all the more extraordinary, given that Toyota, unlike Nissan, never allied itself with a foreign automobile concern – even though General Motors (to comply with the 1936 legislation) initiated negotiations in 1936, and negotiations were held with Ford in 1938 (which were terminated with the outbreak of war in Europe) and in postwar years. While going without foreign assistance meant that initially the quality of Toyota vehicles was poorer than Nissan ones,

> nothing was more important than the experience Toyota engineers accumulated designing their own vehicles and accommodating design changes in manufacturing [. . .] By the mid-1950s, not even Nissan engineers could find any differences in quality or performance between Nissan and Toyota vehicles. Toyota actually had an advantage in that it used more universal machine tools, which made it easier to modify outdated or faulty designs and to introduce new features. (Cusumano, 1985:112–13, 117)

A second advantage that Toyota gained was a formal structure to coordinate product development. In Toyoda Automatic Loom's automobile departments, Kiichirō created 'a staff office for "supervision and improvement" to solve problems in manufacturing and product designs, manage relations with dealers, gather technical information or feedback from customers, settle claims and advise parts suppliers. After 1937 this became part of Toyota's staff organization' (Cusumano, 1985:117) The office was re-established during the late 1940s, and it continued to play an important role in product development, working in conjunction with Toyota Motor Sales when it was created as a separate company in 1950, and became the research department of the Toyota Motor Corporation when the two companies were merged in 1982.

A third advantage that Toyota developed was its marketing organization. In 1935, Shotaro Kamiya, who had once worked for Mitsui and had risen to head of marketing for GM Japan, joined Toyota as head of marketing. In the 1930s, Kamiya developed Toyota's sales network by recruiting many GM and Ford dealers who 'were unhappy with the way the American subsidiaries treated them' (Cusumano, 1985:123). Following the war, Kamiya also recruited many prewar Nissan and Isuzu dealers to join Toyota and appointed a former Nissan dealer as the first chairman of the newly created dealers' organization to assure them a welcome. (Toyota Motor Corporation, 1988:98–9). When Toyota Motor Sales was organized as a separate company in 1950, Kamiya became its president.

When the demand for automobiles began to expand rapidly in the 1950s, due in part to the Korean War, Japanese automakers faced a choice: make more components themselves, found additional subsidiaries, or recruit more suppliers from existing firms, such as the former aircraft industry (Cusumano, 1985:241). Despite the fact that during the 1930s Toyota, like Nissan, had adopted the vertical integration approach which Ford Motor Company had pioneered, Toyota, again like Nissan, adopted the external sourcing approach, increasing their dependence for components on firms over which they had little or no financial control. They took this approach because it required less capital and provided a faster way to build up a parts network. By investing more time than money to help their suppliers, Toyota and Nissan learned how to control firms, sometimes without investing in them directly: by dispatching executives, providing technical assistance and loans of equipment or money, and arranging purchases of all or nearly all a company's output for extended periods of time. In this way, increased levels of externally sourced manufacturing led to lower costs and higher productivity (Cusumano, 1985:241–2).

In the aftermath of the Korean War, motivated in part by the desire to increase economies of scale, Toyota began to plan to export their motor vehicles. Toyota, and Nissan as well, studied Volkswagen's successful marketing strategies, dealer relations, and decision to establish fully owned affiliates. In 1957, Toyota began exporting cars abroad and established an American sales affiliate that year (Toyota Motor Corporation, 1988:165–7). Not until 1964, though, when Toyota developed automobiles which could withstand prolonged high-speed driving, did the American affiliate become operational (Rae, 1982:15–18). By 1976 Toyota and other Japanese car manufacturers accounted for more than 10 per cent of US sales and more than 50 per cent of its imports; by 1980 they accounted for more than 20 per cent of US sales and more than 67 per cent of the imports (Cusumano, 1985:391). By then Japan, under pressure from the United States, no longer had legislation protecting its automobile industry and had adopted 'voluntary' limitations on the number of automobiles that would be exported to the US.

In 1982, Toyota merged Toyota Motor Sales into Toyota Motor Corporation. From 1950 to 1982 their separate existence had allowed one select group of executives to concentrate on product engineering and another on building the largest dealer network in Japan. By 1982, though, growth had slowed and Toyota resolved to merge the two companies in order to eliminate having two sets of executives, to reduce redundancies in market research and to simplify the process of information gathering and analysis.

> Absorbing Toyota Motor Sales as an in-house division also rationalized vehicle distribution, ending the practice whereby Toyota sold its output to Toyota Motor Sales, which then resold the vehicles to dealers. Furthermore, the merger made it easier for Toyota to manufacture overseas or enter into joint ventures. Toyota Motor Sales used to handle sales abroad, but Toyota's directors considered this arrangement undesirable if they were to begin producing cars outside of Japan. These 'merits' outweighed several potential drawbacks or problems: the loss of Toyota Motor Sales as a distinct organ for market analysis, personnel difficulties caused by joining the two firms; and opposition from Toyota dealers. (Cusumano, 1985:135–6)

By the mid-1980s Toyota operated, and owned in whole or in part, automobile assembly or manufacturing plants in Brazil (1958), Peru (1966), Portugal (1972), Australia (1971), Indonesia (1971), New Zealand (1977), Thailand (1962) and India (1984). Plants were added in Canada and Taiwan in 1986, the Philippines in 1988 and Venezuela in 1989. In North America, Toyota joined with General Motors in 1984 to form a joint venture: New United Motor Manufacturing, Inc. (NUMMI) in California. It followed this up with the establishment of its own manufacturing facility in Kentucky in 1988. Within a few years, Toyota had multiplied its overseas manufacturing capacity (see Figure 8.4). In 1992, it opened in the United Kingdom a passenger car plant to provide automobiles for the European market.

Toyota's initial moves into Europe focused on the Scandinavian countries; it opened a European office in Copenhagen in 1963. The move of Toyota Motor Europe to Brussels in 1969 reflected the success of its efforts to set up distributorships throughout Europe. In 1989 Toyota Motor Marketing Services Europe was also established, alongside Toyota Motor Europe in Brussels. In 1990 the two organizations were merged into Toyota Motor Europe, Marketing and Engineering (TMME).

The combined organization which reports to the overseas business office in Tokyo is responsible for the wholesale marketing to distributors of vehicles such as Lexus, Hilux and 4-Runner (which are manufactured in Japan), the purchasing and wholesale marketing of spare parts and accessories procured in Europe, aftersale servicing of industrial vehicles, technical development and general administration. With regard to models such as Carina, Celica and Corolla, Toyota Motor Corporation offices in Japan continue to work directly with the distributors. Toyota Motor Europe does not have responsibility for manufacturing operations in which Toyota is involved in Europe, such as a 73 per cent locally owned Portuguese assembly operation and joint production with Volkswagen of pick-up trucks; nor is it responsible for the passenger car plant and engine plant opened in the United Kingdom in late 1992.

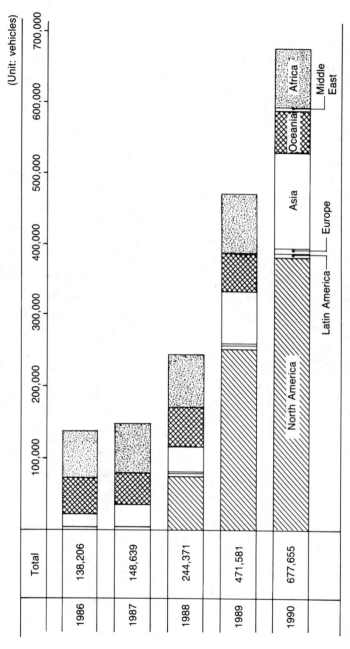

Figure 8.4 Toyota's production outside Japan (Source: Toyota Motor Corporation, 1991:9)

Note: An automobile is considered foreign-made when less than 60 per cent of the completed vehicle's FOB price is accounted for by parts shipped from Japan.

	Total
1986	138,206
1987	148,639
1988	244,371
1989	471,581
1990	677,655

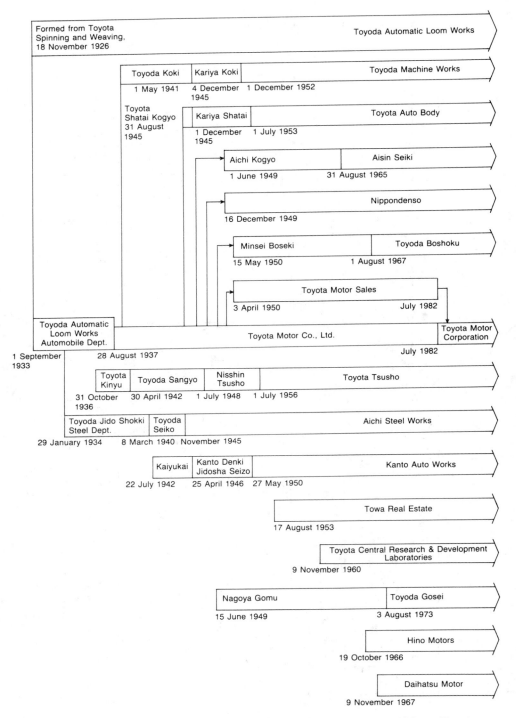

Figure 8.5 Creation of Toyota Group companies (Source: Adapted from Toyota Motor Corporation, 1991:142)

By 1990, Toyota Motor sales exceeded $64 billion, of which its US sales accounted for 27 per cent, European sales 11 per cent, and other overseas sales 11 per cent. Five decades after its founding, the company had transformed itself from the department of a larger company into not only the largest (in sales, profits and assets) Japanese company but also the head of a much larger group.

The Toyota Group and Toyota Motor Corporation

The Toyota Group includes fourteen additional companies considered as the principal Toyota Group members. Of these Toyota Automatic Loom, Nippondenso and Aisin Seiki are Global 500 manufacturing companies and Toyota Tsusho is Japan's tenth-largest trading company (with sales exceeding $13 billion annually). As shown in Figure 8.5, most of these firms were formerly divisions of the

> automaker, or in some cases, of Toyota's historical parent, Toyoda
> Automatic Loom Works. In essence, these companies enjoy a *keiretsu*
> relationship based on a parent–child relationship. In addition, a number
> of other Toyota group companies were created through capital
> investments by the automaker. In general all of these equity-affiliated
> companies are called Toyota Group companies or Toyota *keiretsu*
> companies. (Toyota Motor Corporation, 1991:191)

Toyota Motor Corporation exerts influence not only through equity participation – in many cases enhanced by Mitsui Group equity – but also by appointing its directors to the boards of their companies and assigning or transferring its staff to management parts of these companies (see Figure 8.6). The parent company may also transfer technology and facilities to assist the *keiretsu* associated companies. Such suppliers may be expected not only to manufacture the component parts but also to invest in designing and developing the components in close collaboration with the parent company. In this way, Toyota, like many other Japanese companies, has organized its major suppliers 'into its business culture' (Toyota Motor Corporation, 1991:139). Outside this *keiretsu* system exists a number of independent Toyota Group suppliers that have been organized into cooperative associations called *kyohokai*.

The Toyota Motor Corporation itself is run by a 50-member board of directors, all of whom are Japanese and all of whom are Toyota executives. Until a September 1992 change the senior executives included the chairman (Eiji Toyoda, Kiichirō's cousin), the president (Shoichiro Toyoda, Kiichirō's son) and four executive vice-presidents. One of the executive vice-presidents oversees administration, finance and domestic sales; another oversees research and development; another (a former MITI official who joined Toyota as an 'advisor' in 1984) oversees external relations; and the fourth (Tatsuro Toyoda, also the son of Kiichiro, who worked for Toyota Motor Sales from 1953 to the 1982 merger) oversees production, logistics and international sales (Toyota Motor Corporation, 1991:75). In September 1992 Tatsuro succeeded his brother as president when Shoichiro became chairman. The twelve-member executive committee includes six senior managing

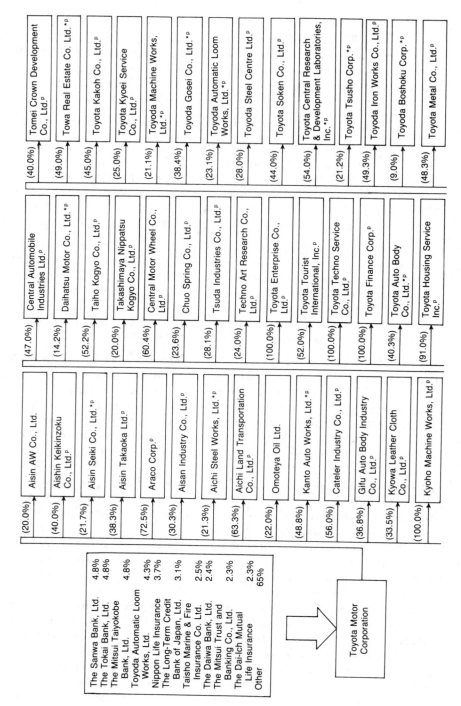

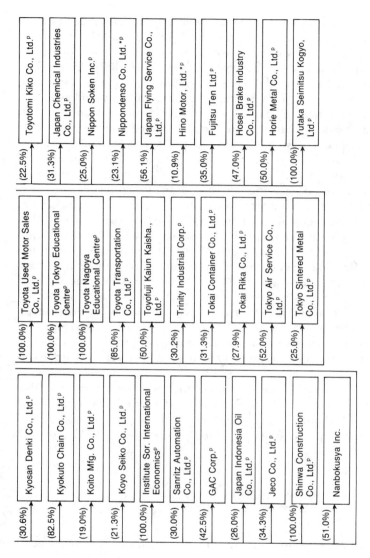

Figure 8.6   Toyota Motor Corporation's relations with Group companies' (Source: Toyo Keizai, Inc., 1990:143)

Notes: [p] Company's management includes former or present Toyota Motor managers/directors.
* One of the major Group members.

directors, of whom two focus on R&D, one on finance and accounting, one on production, one on personnel and one on overseas marketing and sales.

Toyota Motor Corporation has organized itself into 'classes', each of which consists of a number of departments or divisions (see Figure 8.7). Like other Japanese companies, Toyota has divided the R&D, production, and marketing and sales activities into separate classes. This functional integration even applies to the design, production and marketing of Lexus, the new luxury-class automobile that Toyota advertises as a distinct product. This functional separation carries over to overseas operations. The overseas affiliates division manages international marketing operations. The production control and distribution division directs the international production operations. On each continent the production and sales units cooperate, but there are no institutionalized coordinative mechanisms.

On the American continent, Toyota Sales, a wholly owned affiliate, manages US sales through locally owned regional distributors; the manufacturing and R&D companies operate separately. In Canada, the sales company is 50–50 owned with Mitsui & Co.; there are also two wholly owned manufacturing companies. In addition to the manufacturing operations in Brazil and Peru, there are sales companies in Peru (49.1 per cent owned by Mitsui & Co.) and Venezuela.

In Europe, Toyota Motor Marketing Services Europe manages the sales through a series of country distributors, all of which are locally owned except Toyota Deutschland, the successor to the almost bankrupt distributorship that Toyota 100 per cent acquired in 1974 (Toyota Motor Corporation, 1988:166–7), and an industrial vehicle sales joint venture (which is 60 per cent owned by a Japanese oil company).

In Asia and Oceania, Toyota 100 per cent owns the sales affiliates in Australia (which also assembles vehicles) and New Zealand, and partially owns those in Indonesia (49 per cent), Thailand (59.6 per cent) and Malaysia (18 per cent), each of which is also an assembly operation (Toyota Motor Corporation, 1991:254–6).

Staffing split two ways

Toyota staffing is split two ways. Not only does Toyota separate the management of Japanese personnel from the management of non-Japanese, but also the careers of marketing and sales staff managers are seldom assigned outside sales operations, and those whose careers are in production and R&D are seldom assigned sales positions.

Toyota, like other major Japanese firms, recruits Japanese graduates directly from universities, with the new class joining the company on 1 April, at the end of their final academic year. The new recruits, whether they are destined to the sales or non-sales side (which depends primarily on whether they were engineering graduates), undergo their initial seven months' training programme together. This consists of two months of coursework focusing on Toyota origins, organization and

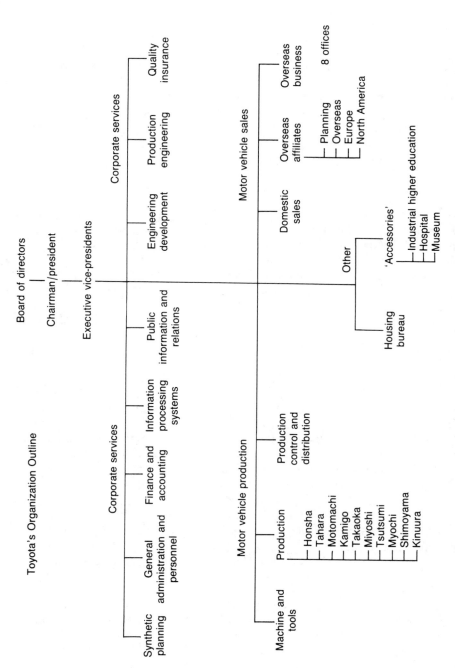

Figure 8.7 Toyota Motor Corporation organogram, 1991 (Source: Adapted from Toyota Motor Corporation, 1991:65–73)

operations, two months of work in production facilities, and three months in dealerships, selling automobiles. After this, they begin their careers in one scale or the other in Toyota. In time some may be posted temporarily or permanently to one of the Toyota Group companies.

In staffing its overseas operation, Toyota has moved many locals to senior posts, but Japanese continue to hold the top posts in the affiliates. Toyota has tended to rely more upon locals for personnel and accounting operations, and upon Japanese for production and quality control operations, which are the core of Toyota's strategic competence.

Group shared values

In 1935, the Toyoda brothers codified their father's principles and presented them as 'Toyota Precepts'. The fundamental spirit of these precepts constitutes the basic philosophy that Toyota enunciates today: 'Making society more affluent through car making' (Toyota Motor Corporation, 1988:37–8). As already noted, the Toyota principles which are cultivated in the training programmes are promoted throughout the Toyota Group by the posting of Toyota Motor Corporation-trained managers. This common corporate direction and corporate behaviour provide a glue that cements not only the various parts of Toyota Motor but also all of the Toyota companies.

From corporate department to conglomerate overseer: from Mitsui dependence to interdependence

Toyota provides a remarkable example of a case that is not atypical in the Japanese corporate environment. Within a few years, Toyota, which began as a department of another company in the 1930s, split off into a separate but subsidiary company, grew larger than its parent, and eventually became a core firm in a family of firms. Through its financial aid and expertise, Mitsui made possible Toyota survival, and with its overseas marking initiative it facilitated Toyota's international growth. Toyota, which has been sufficiently successful for it to be no longer dependent on its 'parent', has become the powerhouse that dominates the Toyota Group, is a leading participant in the Mitsui Grouping, and is Japan's largest enterprise.

Mitsubishi Electric: major member of the Mitsubishi grouping

Mitsubishi Electric, Japan's eighth-largest industrial company and one of the world's twelve largest electronics/electric/computer companies, is the largest manufacturing company included in the Mitsubishi grouping. It has recently strengthened the role of its continental affiliates. The extent of Mitsubishi Electric global spread is demonstrated by the fact that 49 per cent of its 1989 sales were generated by its North American affiliates.

The Mitsubishi grouping comprises hundreds of companies brought together by a common *zaibatsu* history and heritage, tied together with cross-shareholdings (see Table 8.4), interlocking directorates, joint ventures, long-term business relationships and monthly Presidents' Council and managing directors' meetings. At the heart of the Mitsubishi consortium are 28 'core' companies, whose heads participate in the regular Presidents' Council meetings.

The sheer magnitude of the Mitsubishi grouping is demonstrated by the fact that ten Mitsubishi industrial companies ranked in the 1990 *Fortune* Global 500; Mitsubishi Electric ($21.2 billion), Mitsubishi Heavy Industries ($16.4 billion),

Table 8.4 Companies of the Mitsubishi grouping, 1990

	Percentage equity owned by other Mitsubishi companies	Sales 1990 in $ billions of *Fortune* 500
Mitsubishi Aluminum	100	
Mitsubishi Construction	100	
Mitsubishi Plastics Industries	57	
Mitsubishi Motors	55	16.7
Mitsubishi Cable Industries	48	
Mitsubishi Oil	41	4.3
Mitsubishi Warehouse and Transportation	40	
Mitsubishi Steel Manufacturing	38	
Mitsubishi Petrochemicals	37	3.3
Mitsubishi Mining and Cement	37	2.6
Mitsubishi Kakoki	37	
Mitsubishi Corporation	32	
Mitsubishi Paper Mills	32	
Mitsubishi Trust and Banking	28	
Asahi Glass	28	8.7
Nikon Corporation	27	
Mitsubishi Bank	26	
Mitsubishi Estate	25	
Nippon Yusin	25	
Mitsubishi Rayon	25	
Tokyo Marine and Fire Insurance	24	
Mitsubishi Gas Chemical	24	
Mitsubishi Kasei	23	8.2
Mitsubishi Metal	21	5.6
Mitsubishi Heavy Industries	20	16.4
Kirin Brewery	19	5.6
Mitsubishi Electric	17	21.2
Meiyi Mutual Life Insurance	0	
	Median: 28%; Average: 35%	

Source: *Business Week International*, 24 September 1990b:39; *Fortune*, 1991a,b.

Mitsubishi Motors ($16.7 billion), Mitsubishi Kasei (chemicals – $8.2 billion), Asahi Glass ($8.7 billion), Mitsubishi Metal ($5.6 billion), Kirin Brewery ($5.6 billion), Mitsubishi Oil ($4.3 billion), Mitsubishi Petrochemicals ($3.3 billion) and Mitsubishi Mining and Cement ($2.6 billion). As a point of comparison, the only countries with more than ten Global 500 companies are the United States (167), Britain (43), Germany (32), France (29), Sweden (15), Canada (13), South Korea (11) and of course Japan (111).

Each of the 28 core companies within the Mitsubishi association operates separately from the others, issues its own annual reports, pays its own taxes, manages its own profits-and-losses and controls many subsidiaries. Mitsubishi companies are independent and are tenaciously competitive. They are also interdependent in their efforts to seek cross-company synergies and develop alliances, not only with Mitsubishi companies but also with others. For example, the joint efforts with Daimler-Benz affect several Mitsubishi companies. The fact that the Mitsubishi member company corporate headquarters are clustered together (between the Imperial Palace grounds and the Tokyo train station) fosters their cooperative efforts. Its members represent a broad cross-section of the Japanese economy, from manufacturing to trade to finance.

The rise, break-up and regathering

The Mitsubishi companies trace their origins to 1870 when Yotaro Iwasaki, the manager of a trading house, founded a shipping business which later adopted the name Mitsubishi. In the 1880s it launched two endeavours which formed the core of Mitsubishi: with the purchase of a mine it began an operation later incorporated as Mitsubishi Mining Company, and with the rental of a government-owned shipyard it began what became Mitsubishi shipbuilding, which in turn spun off Mitsubishi Motors in the 1970s.

With the formation of the trading company Mitsubishi Goshi Kaisha in 1893, Mitsubishi began to expand into Asia. The group grew rapidly, competing against the older Mitsui organization. Following World War I, the Mitsubishi *zaibatsu* continued to expand. Mitsubishi Electric, which in 1921 was separated from Mitsubishi Shipbuilding, was one of many companies established by the Mitsubishi *zaibatsu* over the decades. The various Mitsubushi companies then coordinated their efforts through regular meetings:

> To coordinate the operations of the Mitsubishi companies as a single entity the Mitsubishi Kyogikai [top management meeting], antecedent to the Kinyokai [Friday meeting – which remains in use today] was organized in 1937. Although this served as a forum, the true unifier among the Companies was a moral alliance that emphasized the original spirit of the founding of Mitsubishi and a sense of admiration for the 'fundamental faith' of Koyato Iwasaki, the fourth family member to serve as president, who led the company until his death in 1945.
> (Mitsubishi Public Affairs Committee, 1990:11–12).

Under the Allied occupation, Mitsubishi, like other Japanese *zaibatsus*, was broken up into 139 small companies. Later, many of the progeny merged into the Mitsubishi companies which today comprise the Mitsubishi grouping. Mitsubishi Corporation (the trading company) was reformed in 1954; Mitsubishi Heavy Industries, whose predecessor (Mitsubishi Shipbuilders) had spun off Mitsubishi Electric in 1921, was reformed in 1964 and spun off as Mitsubishi Motors in 1970.

Mitsubishi Electric

The all-Japanese, 26-member board of directors which heads Mitsubishi Electric Corporation includes the chairman, the president, three executive vice-presidents (one heads corporate strategic planning, another heads one of the larger product groups, and the third oversees manufacturing, engineering and R&D), three senior managing directors (one heads marketing and another heads one of the larger product groups), eight managing directors (one of whom heads international operations) and twelve directors. Thus, for the most part the senior board members hold functional, not product, portfolios.

The six major product groups are as follows:

1. Electronic Devices.
2. Electronic Products and Systems.
3. Information and Communication.
4. Consumer Products.
5. Automatic Equipment.
6. Energy and Industry Systems.

As Figure 8.8 indicates, the component parts of these divisions focus on planning, management and marketing of these products, most of which are manufactured by subsidiary companies. The International Operations Group handles all Mitsubishi Electric international activities including comprehensive planning, coordination, exporting, local production, sales, aftersales service, and technology transfers.

Mitsubishi Electric took steps in 1990 to strengthen its continental coordination efforts in both North America and Europe. In North America Mitsubishi Electric enhanced the role of Mitsubishi Electric America, Inc., the umbrella holding company, by merging its two US sales affiliates (Mitsubishi Electric Sales America Inc. and Mitsubishi Electronics America Inc.) into one sales affiliate (Mitsubishi Electric America). The role of the merged affiliate has been expanded to include administrative coordinating liason with several manufacturing subsidiaries, each of which continues to report primarily to its production division in Tokyo. The new sales affiliate has six product sales groups, each with profit-and-loss responsibility. These correspond to the six major Mitsubishi product divisions and continue to work directly with them.

The role of the Mitsubishi Electric Europe coordination centre, located in Ratingen, Germany, is less pervasive. The office now consists of a chairman (recently transferred from Tokyo), a deputy chairman (who heads the Mitsubishi

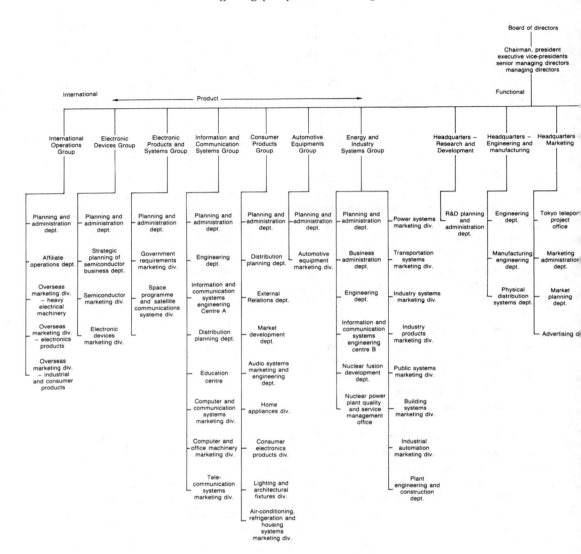

Figure 8.8 Mitsubishi Electric organogram, 1989

Electric European finance company), a planning and administrative office (for strategic planning, purchasing and standards), general affairs (including personnel and public relations) and a Brussels-based public affairs office. While its role is to provide administrative support for the various marketing affiliates and some manufacturing national affiliates, these units continue to report directly to their respective Tokyo-located divisional headquarters.

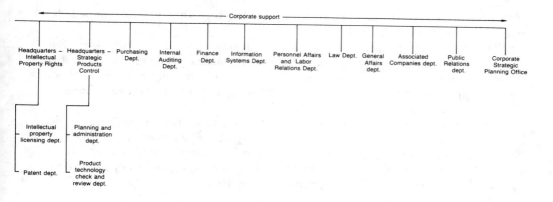

Separate Japanese/non-Japanese staffing

Mitsubishi Electric recruiting in Japan is done on the basis of recommendations from the top Japanese universities. An applicant must have received 30 top marks out of a possible 40 during his or her university career. Furthermore, he or she must be in the top percentage of his or her class, have a Certificate of Good Performance, and interview well. The hiring policy at overseas branches is not as formal as the policy at Mitsubishi, Japan. The overseas offices recruit non-Japanese mainly on the basis of interviews.

Promotions are made primarily on the basis of seniority. The system leads to promotion after the first eight years, with the next step after an additional four years, and another after three more years. As a result, one must be with the company for at least 15 years to become a managing director, after having climbed the necessary four levels of management.

The personnel policies for expatriates and nationals are not the same. For expatriates, compensation is agreed upon at headquarters, while for nationals it is determined nationally. Standards of living, hours, vacation, insurance and school for children are taken into consideration for both expatriates and nationals. Bonuses are given annually or semi-annually.

Mitsubishi Electric offers career-long employment to their employees, as do most major Japanese corporations. There is a significant amount of job rotation, both functional and geographic. This may result in an employee having to leave a post he or she thoroughly enjoys, but it also enables the employees to become familiar with a diverse set of operations and contacts.

The 'Mitsubishi Spirit'

Mitsubishi Electric and other Mitsubishi companies reflect the stereotype of the 'Mitsubishi Man'. They are disciplined and organization-minded compared with Mitsui men who are reputed to be more individualistic. Mitsubishi member companies use the Mitsubishi three-diamond logo and stress the 'Mitsubishi Spirit', whose main points are corporate responsibility to society, integrity, fairness, and international understanding through trade, by posting the points in corporate offices, repeating them in corporate brochures and propagating them in the corporate training sessions.

Mitsubishi promotes its corporate culture by staffing the top positions of its affiliates with home country nationals who instil the Mitsubishi way, as well as the Japanese way, which they believe is essential to the effectiveness of their companies.

Having your independence and interdependence too

Mitsubishi Electric provides a prime example of an organization that appears to have achieved the advantage of independence. The company is totally autonomous, setting its strategy, developing manufacturing and marketing its products. Yet through its alliance, it has the research financing and other advantages that come from interdependence.

Hitachi: diversified constellation of function-specific firms

Hitachi, whose 1990 sales of more than $50 billion compare with those of GE, manufactures a highly diversified spectrum of industrial and consumer electronic and telecommunication equipment. Hitachi has, however, remained essentially a function-divided multinational, with the sales groups organized separately from the production divisions.

The extent of Hitachi's diversification has led it not to rotate managers among divisions as extensively as many other Japanese companies. This more limited rotational policy allows its managers to develop a more specialized knowledge of the product field in which they work. The corporate stress on Hitachi philosophy and its emphasis on training has fostered a corporate-wide 'Odaira Spirit.'

Once associated with Nissan

Hitachi traces its origins to an electric repair shop established by Namihei Odaira in 1910. After World War I, Hitachi diversified into generators, water wheels, pumps and non-electrical machines. In the interwar years, Hitachi, unlike other Japanese electric companies, did not have joint venture agreements with other foreign companies, such as those Toshiba had with General Electric, NEC with ITT, Fuji Electric with Siemens, and Matsushita with Philips (Abegglen and Stalk, 1985:224). From 1928, the Nissan combine's investment fuelled Hitachi's development. With the approach of World War II, Hitachi began to produce electric wires, communication equipment, vacuum bulbs and ships. Many of these diversifications were carried out by acquisition of other companies (Kono, 1984: 83–4, 291).

The postwar occupation severed Hitachi's relations with Nissan by disbanding the *zaibatsu* (Halberstam, 1986: 134), purged Hitachi of its leadership and divested it of its wire manufacturing, shipbuilding and other businesses. To rebuild quickly, Hitachi associated itself with not only the Fuyo grouping (with which the Nissan companies associated) but also the Sanwa ones (and later also the Daiichi-Kangyo one), whose banks assisted with financing and whose trading companies helped develop overseas markets. Hitachi also secured licences to produce power generators from GE and for computer and television technology from RCA, among others.

In 1960 Hitachi divided its manufacturing into production divisions (after rearranging its production system so that each plant belonged to only one production division). By 1990, Hitachi's range of products included power systems and equipment, information and communication systems and electronic devices, industrial machinery and plants, wire and cable, metals, chemicals, and consumer products such as TVs, VCRs and household appliances. Eighty-five per cent of its sales continued to be generated in Japan.

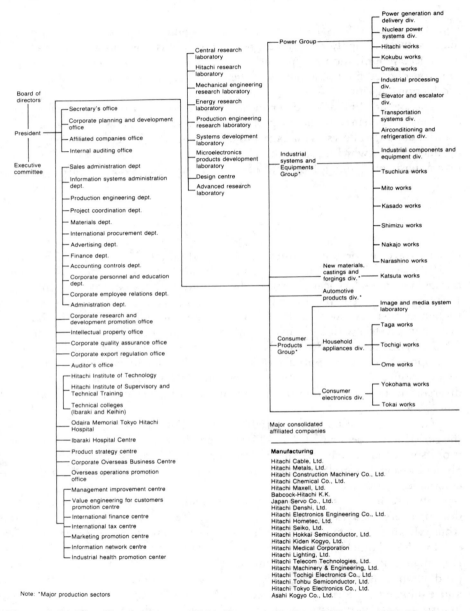

Figure 8.9 Hitachi organogram, 1991 (Source: *Outline of Hitachi*, 1991:22–3)

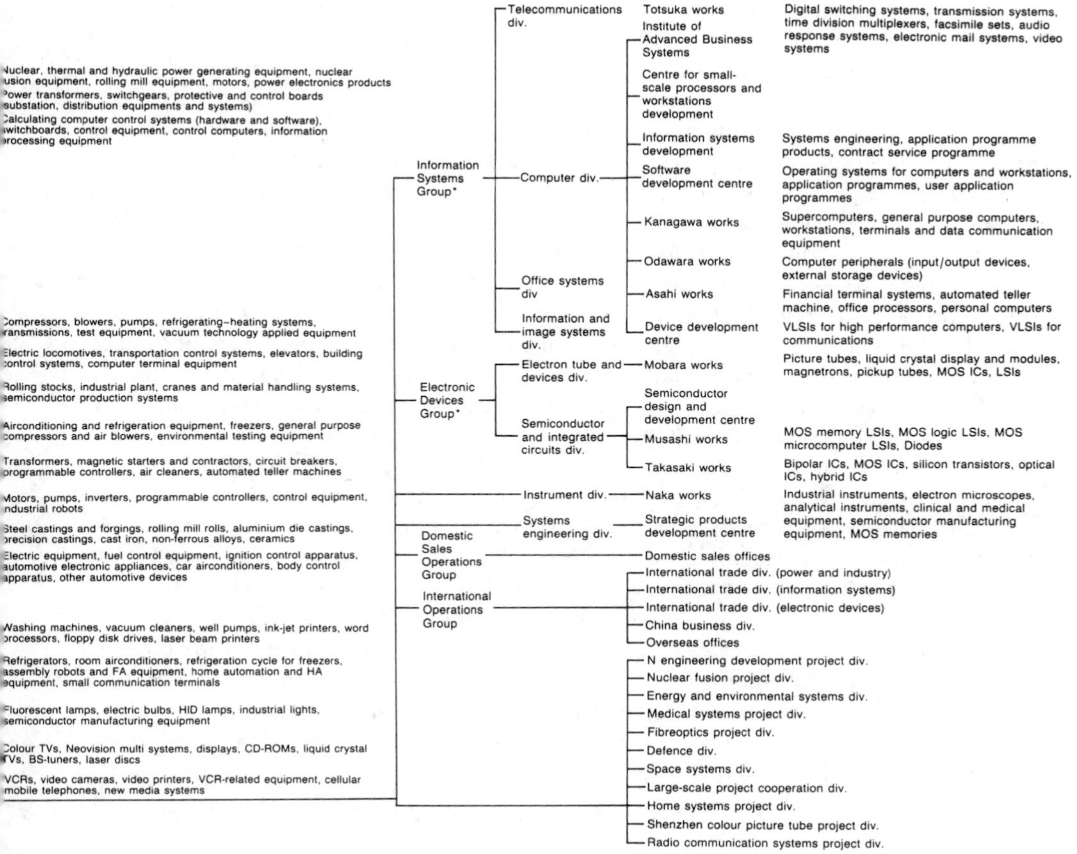
Vuclear, thermal and hydraulic power generating equipment, nuclear usion equipment, rolling mill equipment, motors, power electronics products
Power transformers, switchgears, protective and control boards substation, distribution equipments and systems)
Calculating computer control systems (hardware and software), switchboards, control equipment, control computers, information processing equipment
Compressors, blowers, pumps, refrigerating–heating systems, ransmissions, test equipment, vacuum technology applied equipment
Electric locomotives, transportation control systems, elevators, building control systems, computer terminal equipment
Rolling stocks, industrial plant, cranes and material handling systems, semiconductor production systems
Airconditioning and refrigeration equipment, freezers, general purpose compressors and air blowers, environmental testing equipment
Transformers, magnetic starters and contractors, circuit breakers, programmable controllers, air cleaners, automated teller machines
Motors, pumps, inverters, programmable controllers, control equipment, ndustrial robots
Steel castings and forgings, rolling mill rolls, aluminium die castings, precision castings, cast iron, non-ferrous alloys, ceramics
Electric equipment, fuel control equipment, ignition control apparatus, automotive electronic appliances, car airconditioners, body control apparatus, other automotive devices
Washing machines, vacuum cleaners, well pumps, ink-jet printers, word processors, floppy disk drives, laser beam printers
Refrigerators, room airconditioners, refrigeration cycle for freezers, assembly robots and FA equipment, home automation and HA equipment, small communication terminals
Fluorescent lamps, electric bulbs, HID lamps, industrial lights, semiconductor manufacturing equipment
Colour TVs, Neovision multi systems, displays, CD-ROMs, liquid crystal TVs, BS-tuners, laser discs
VCRs, video cameras, video printers, VCR-related equipment, cellular mobile telephones, new media systems
Information Systems Group*
Telecommunications div.
Computer div.
Office systems div
Information and image systems div.
Totsuka works
Digital switching systems, transmission systems, time division multiplexers, facsimile sets, audio response systems, electronic mail systems, video systems
Institute of Advanced Business Systems
Centre for small-scale processors and workstations development
Information systems development
Systems engineering, application programme products, contract service programme
Software development centre
Operating systems for computers and workstations, application programmes, user application programmes
Kanagawa works
Supercomputers, general purpose computers, workstations, terminals and data communication equipment
Odawara works
Computer peripherals (input/output devices, external storage devices)
Asahi works
Financial terminal systems, automated teller machine, office processors, personal computers
Device development centre
VLSIs for high performance computers, VLSIs for communications
Electronic Devices Group*
Electron tube and devices div.
Mobara works
Picture tubes, liquid crystal display and modules, magnetrons, pickup tubes, MOS ICs, LSIs
Semiconductor and integrated circuits div.
Semiconductor design and development centre
Musashi works
MOS memory LSIs, MOS logic LSIs, MOS microcomputer LSIs, Diodes
Takasaki works
Bipolar ICs, MOS ICs, silicon transistors, optical ICs, hybrid ICs
Instrument div.
Naka works
Industrial instruments, electron microscopes, analytical instruments, clinical and medical equipment, semiconductor manufacturing equipment, MOS memories
Systems engineering div.
Strategic products development centre
Domestic Sales Operations Group
Domestic sales offices
International Operations Group
International trade div. (power and industry)
International trade div. (information systems)
International trade div. (electronic devices)
China business div.
Overseas offices
N engineering development project div.
Nuclear fusion project div.
Energy and environmental systems div.
Medical systems project div.
Fibreoptics project div.
Defence div.
Space systems div.
Large-scale project cooperation div.
Home systems project div.
Shenzhen colour picture tube project div.
Radio communication systems project div.

Sales and service

Hitachi Transport System, Ltd.
Hitachi Information Systems, Ltd.
Hitachi Sales Corporation
Hitachi Plant Engineering & Construction Co., Ltd.
Hitachi Credit Corporation
Nissei Sangyo Co., Ltd.
Hitachi Building Systems Engineering and Service Co., Ltd.
Hitachi Electronics Service Co., Ltd.
Hitachi Software Engineering Co., Ltd.
Hitachi Air Conditioning & Refrigeration Co., Ltd.
Hitachi Mokuzai Jisho, Ltd.
Hitachi Engineering Co., Ltd.
Hitachi Techno Engineering Co., Ltd.
Hitachi Printing Co., Ltd.
Hitachi Engineering & Services Co., Ltd.
Hitachi Auto Systems Co., Ltd.
Hitachi Service & Engineering (West) Ltd.
Hitachi Service & Engineering (East) Ltd.
Chuo Shoji, Ltd.
Hitachi Welfare Service, Ltd.

Overseas

Hitachi America, Ltd.
Hitachi Semiconductor (America) Inc.
Hitachi Electronic Devices (Singapore) Pte. Ltd.
Hitachi Consumer Products (U.K.) Ltd.
Hitachi Computer Products (America), Inc.
Hitachi Automotive Products (USA), Inc.
Hitachi Consumer Products (Europe) GmbH
Hitachi Television (Taiwan) Ltd.
Hitachi Home Electronics (America), Inc.
Hitachi Computer Products (Europe) S.A.
Hitachi Consumer Products (S) Pte. Ltd.
Hitachi Semiconductor (Europe) GmbH
Hitachi Telecom (USA), Inc.
Hitachi Consumer Products (Malaysia) Sdn. Bhd.
Hitachi Europe Ltd.
Hitachi Semiconductor (Malaysia) Sdn. Bhd.
Hitachi Australia Ltd.
Hitachi Data Systems Corp.
Hitachi Asia Pte. Ltd.

The agglomeration

As shown in Figure 8.9, the Hitachi group comprises a core company, Hitachi, Ltd., and more than 50 major subsidiaries. Like most other Japanese companies, Hitachi has closely integrated into its production supply chain not only major and minor subsidiary companies but also many others that it does not own. Likewise, for its sales efforts Hitachi depends not only on its two sales operations groups but also on its autonomous subsidiary, Hitachi Sales Corporation. Hitachi Ltd.'s two sales operations groups, one for international and one for domestic sales, are responsible for most of the industrial electronic sales. The Hitachi Sales Corporation subsidiary handles the international and domestic sales of the consumer electronic products, which constitute less than 15 per cent of Hitachi's total sales volume. In addition, some autonomous Hitachi subsidiaries, such as Hitachi Chemical, Hitachi Cable and Hitachi Maxell, handle their own sales. Furthermore, for a few specialized products Hitachi divisions and subsidiaries continue to use trading companies.

The core company, Hitachi Ltd., consists of six production groups and two production divisions, plus the two operations groups concerned principally with sales, several research laboratories, a number of corporate staff departments, and several divisions concerned with intergroup coordination (see Figure 8.9). All of these entities report to one person on the 24-member executive committee of the 36-member board. The executive committee includes a chairman, a president, four executive vice-presidents who oversee the major product sectors, one executive vice-president who oversees international operations, and seventeen executive managing directors (one of whom oversees the research laboratories, and another the domestic sales operations). The eight production sectors (some of which are divided into two or more production divisions) comprise the approximately 30 plants or works departments that have long been Hitachi's profit-and-loss entities. The production divisions, to which Hitachi is considering shifting profit-and-loss accountability, coordinate the works departments and handle negotiations with the various sales entities.

As many Japanese electronic firms have long done, Hitachi continues to divide its sales operations into four unequal quadrants by splitting consumer products from industrial products, and separating international from domestic sales. The autonomous subsidiary, Hitachi Sales Corporation, which handles consumer products, consists of two major parts: domestic and international. The international part has organized sales affiliates in many countries including the USA, Canada, Panama (for Latin America), Australia, Taiwan, Thailand and nine European countries. Hitachi Sales Corporation coordinates its European operations from a London-based office. In most countries Hitachi Sales Corporation continues to rely on distributors.

For its non-consumer or industrial electronics products, Hitachi relies principally on its Domestic Sales Operations Group and the International Operations Group. The latter divides its efforts among several divisions. Four handle sales: one is responsible for electronics, one for information systems, one for power systems, industrial processes and components, and one for all Chinese business. (In 1991 the unit that plans new business development was established as a separate division.) International Operations Division includes the European and American corporate offices which are responsible for representing Hitachi public affairs and public relations interests. For the coordination of a major share of its continental sales efforts, the International Operations Group has organized Hitachi America Ltd., Hitachi Europe Ltd., Hitachi Australia, Ltd. and Hitachi Asia Pte. Ltd., and relies extensively on distributors. For some products Hitachi has organized a separate international marketing company, such as Hitachi Data Systems for computers. The Hitachi Sales and Hitachi Ltd. operations work separately from one another and from the numerous manufacturing facilities that the production divisions have developed overseas. The sales units are held accountable for their budgets and sales goals; profit-and-loss responsibility is focused on the manufacturing plants.

Pay and promotion has been seniority-based

Like that of other Japanese firms, the Hitachi stress on human resources, reflected in its slogan 'The Essence of Enterprise is People', reinforces its accent on recruitment and training, as well as its corporate culture. Hitachi hires approximately 2,000 new employees every year, among whom about 80 per cent of the university graduates are engineers.

Hitachi views the education and training of its managers as a career-long investment. Those recruited from university begin their service with Hitachi by taking a multiweek orientation programme, which indoctrinates them in the company philosophy and teaches them about the various divisions. Following this corporate-wide orientation, the management trainees are assigned to a division for continued training, which includes a few months working as a manual labourer, computer courses and, for some, language programmes.

Like other Japanese companies, Hitachi has traditionally set salaries principally by grade and made promotions mainly on seniority, but it has begun to move towards considering demonstrated ability as well. With every promotion, managers attend training programmes at the company training centres, focusing on conceptual and management skills (Kono, 1984:321). The increasing diversity among divisions and the rapid pace of change have led Hitachi to encourage specialization, which has reduced the frequency of interdivisional transfers, except for finance and other management-support professionals.

Hitachi's efforts to integrate non-Japanese into management posts in its overseas companies have been slowed by the distinctiveness of its culture. As the overseas companies have matured, Hitachi has promoted more non-Japanese to senior ranks in both its sales and manufacturing companies.

The 'Odaira Spirit'

Hitachi's philosophy, called the 'Odaira Spirit' after the corporation founder, stresses harmony, sincerity and a pioneering spirit. Its philosophy stresses national interest and technological orientation rather than the consumer and marketing orientation which characterizes Matsushita. But like that of Matsushita, the creed motivates by encouraging a group commitment to fellow human beings that transcends personal interests. The corporate philosophy has long provided direction to the corporate strategy and pervaded the corporate education efforts and promotional literature.

Overseas fragmentation

Hitachi has moved vigorously not only to improve its product technology but also to develop its overseas manufacturing base. Hitachi's vigorous growth, its diversification into multiple production divisions that have developed their own overseas manufacturing facilities, and the continued split of the overseas marketing and manufacturing operations may fragment Hitachi's efforts to develop coherent global localization strategies.

Continent-coordinated global localization

Matsushita Electric Industrial (MEI): establishing a continental management support headquarters

Matsushita Electric Industrial (MEI)'s rapid prewar growth stemmed from the organizational strategy of its founder, Konosuke Matsushita, who split his firm into three production divisions – with what he called 'autonomous management' – each focusing on a specific product or market (Matsushita, 1988:23). In the effort to spur its rapid postwar growth, Osaka-based Matsushita has diversified as well as globalized. Since the mid-1980s, Matsushita has applied its size and financial might to diversifying and to changing the emphasis of its business strategy. Although consumer electronics continue to account for over 50 per cent of its sales, the other part, including industrial and professional electronics, will be the focus of future growth.

The $6.1 billion acquisition of MCA, the American entertainment company, reflects a strategy for accelerating diversification and global development. (The price makes it the biggest takeover by a Japanese company of an American one, exceeding the purchase of Columbia Pictures by Sony and of the Rockefeller Center by the Mitsubishi group.) Matsushita has also moved to develop its overseas presence by establishing Asian, European and American regional headquarters to coordinate their marketing efforts. This move required the merging and integrating of its overseas trading company subsidiary into the main company. Despite its diversification and globalization efforts, Matsushita essentially continues its function-divided and function-driven organizational strategy.

Founder-led for 71 years

Few men have so personally dominated the development of a major multinational for so long as Konosuke Matsushita. In 1918, at the age of 23, he founded the company which in one capacity or another he led for seven decades – until his death in 1989. The company took off with its introduction of bicycle battery lamps in 1923. In the 1930s, despite the depression, with the assistance of Sumitomo Bank, he relentlessly continued the expansion of the enterprise. 'This was the period during which the company adopted a management system based on financially independent divisions for major product lines' (Matsushita, 1988:223). Matsushita has continued this strategy by spinning off the more developed operating units as separate subsidiaries. In 1935, Matsushita created a subsidiary, Matsushita Electric Trading Co. Ltd., to handle overseas trade (Matsushita, 1988:227).

Following World War II, the Allied occupation dissolved Matsushita as part of its efforts to disband the *zaibatsu* (Matsushita, 1988:244–5). In 1950 Matsushita announced a fresh start and resurrected its division system. In 1962 the first European sales office was established, in West Germany; the first European manufacturing facility, Philips Matsushita Battery Corporation, was established in conjunction with Philips in 1970. Matsushita followed up its 1960s entrance into the US market with the purchase of Motorola's consumer products in 1974; but it continued to export most of its products from Japan until the mid-1980s.

Konosuke Matsushita retired in 1973, but continued as 'executive advisor' until his death in 1989. His adopted son (and son-in-law) Masaharu Matsushita has served as chairman since 1977, but no longer chairs the boards of the subsidiary corporations as the founder did.

In the 1980s, Matsushita decided to shift the emphasis of its business away from consumer electronics and into the area of information technology. The basic product areas are information and communication, factory automation, new audiovisual products, semiconductors, household-related products and automotive electronics. Matsushita, whose brand names are National, Panasonic, Quasar and Technics, is one of the world's largest producers of consumer and industrial electronic products. Matsushita has 132 companies outside Japan (3 regional headquarters companies, 12 manufacturing and sales, 78 manufacturing, 27 sales, 7 research, 4 finance and Matsushita Corporation of America). Together they employ nearly 210,000 people, with 84,000 in 38 countries outside Japan. Their 1990 sales exceeded $43 billion, of which more than 40 per cent was outside Japan.

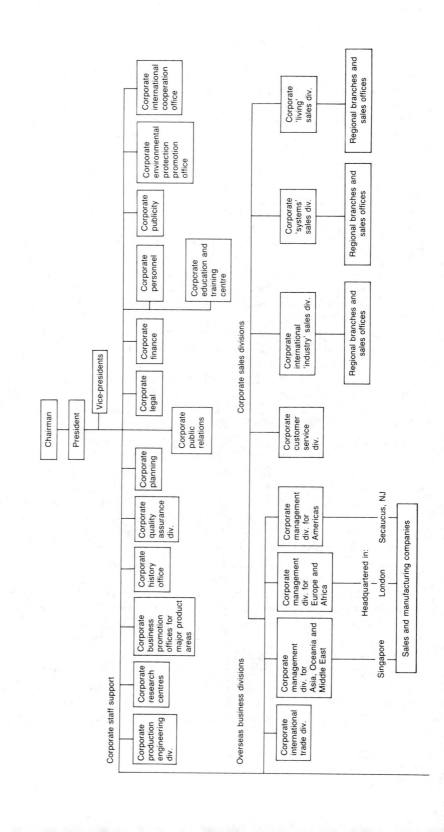

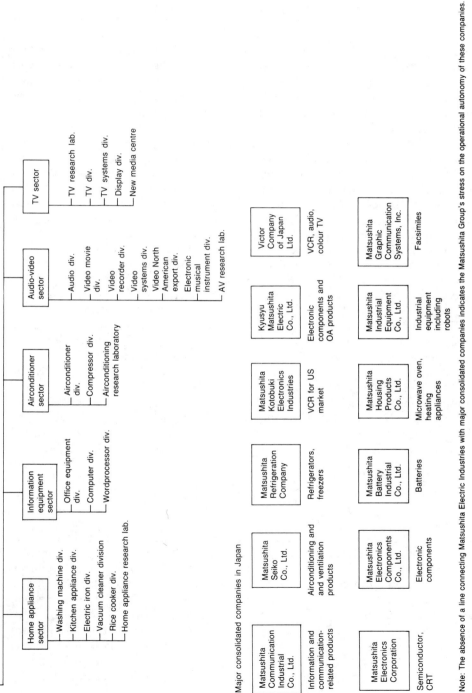

Manufacturing divisions

Home appliance sector
— Washing machine div.
— Kitchen appliance div.
— Electric iron div.
— Vacuum cleaner division
— Rice cooker div.
— Home appliance research lab.

Information equipment sector
— Office equipment div.
— Computer div.
— Wordprocessor div.

Airconditioner sector
— Airconditioner div.
— Compressor div.
— Airconditioning research laboratory

Audio-video sector
— Audio div.
— Video movie div.
— Video recorder div.
— Video systems div.
— Video North American export div.
— Electronic musical instrument div.
— AV research lab.

TV sector
— TV research lab.
— TV div.
— TV systems div.
— Display div.
— New media centre

Major consolidated companies in Japan

Matsushita Communication Industrial Co., Ltd.

Information and communication-related products

Matsushita Electronics Corporation

Semiconductor, CRT

Matsushita Seiko Co., Ltd.

Airconditioning and and ventilation products

Matsushita Electronics Components Co., Ltd.

Electronic components

Matsushita Refrigeration Company

Refrigerators, freezers

Matsushita Battery Industrial Co., Ltd.

Batteries

Matsushita Kotobuki Electronics Industries

VCR for US market

Matsushita Housing Products Co., Ltd.

Microwave oven, heating appliances

Kyusyu Matsushita Electric Co., Ltd.

Electronic components and OA products

Matsushita Industrial Equipment Co., Ltd.

Industrial equipment including robots

Victor Company of Japan Ltd.

VCR, audio, colour TV

Matsushita Graphic Communication Systems, Inc.

Facsimiles

Note: The absence of a line connecting Matsushita Electric Industries with major consolidated companies indicates the Matsushita Group's stress on the operational autonomy of these companies.

Figure 8.10 Matsushita Electric Industrial Group organogram, 1990 (Courtesy of Matsushita Electric Industries)

Integrating product and area perspectives into a functionally driven structure

Heading Matsushita Electric Industrial is a 36-person board of directors, all of whom are Japanese. All but two board members are Matsushita executives (one of the two outsiders represents the Sumitomo Bank with which Matsushita has long worked closely). A senior management team comprises the chairman, the president (with whom the Japan-based major consolidated companies work) and four vice-presidents (one focusing on marketing, one on manufacturing, one on research and technical development, and one on finance and administration). Other members of the board of directors include those responsible for the major business and manufacturing divisions and the principal corporate functional support services, and those heading the major Asian and American regional headquarters. While this arrangement stresses a shared pattern of responsibility, the manufacturing and marketing responsibilities are functionally separate, with the manufacturing activities organized by product and the sales activities organized by market.

As Figure 8.10 demonstrates, the closely integrated Matsushita complex embraces several types of entities. The major Japanese subsidiaries are structurally not integrated into Matsushita; MEI appoints their top officials, monitors their financial results and buys their products. The manufacturing divisions, to which the foreign manufacturing affiliates are responsible, are grouped into five sectors.

The corporate functional offices include personnel, finance, the corporate business promotion offices, corporate quality assurance division, corporate legal and corporate international cooperation office (to which the international liaison offices outside Japan report directly), and corporate research centres (to which the corporate research centres outside Japan report directly). Three corporate sales divisions divide responsibilities by markets served; that is, industry, systems and living. These three divisions directly supervise domestic and international sales. The continental management support offices which Matsushita has recently created support the administration of Asian, European and American sales companies.

Developing regional headquarters

'The main objective of Matsushita just now,' says Eric Bean, spokesman for Matsushita in Europe, 'is to achieve a greater degree of internationalization or what the Japanese like to call "globalization".' Thus the company has recently introduced a policy of regionalization' (speech, 4 May 1989). To initiate this policy Matsushita established an American regional headquarters in Secaucus, New Jersey, an Asian headquarters in Singapore, and a European headquarters near London.

The European headquarters, which was established in 1988, has been organized similarly to the ones in Singapore and Secaucus, New Jersey. The new company, Panasonic Europe (Headquarters) Ltd., coordinates Matsushita's sales affiliates in Western Europe, where the company has thirteen sales subsidiaries in addition to several sales agents. Panasonic Europe also supports Matsushita's sixteen manufacturing subsidiaries in Western Europe by coordinating their marketing activities. This reflects Matsushita's basic policy to operate closer to the market; by shifting their European headquarters to the U.K., the company anticipates being able to make faster management decisions for their European Operations thus further strengthening their sales and manufacturing operations.

The merger of the Matsushita Electric Trading Co. into the main company was a necessary precondition for developing the continental centres. Matsushita began strengthening the role of the regional headquarters by posting a significant number of executives from Osaka to the new continental headquarters. Under the new arrangement (see Figure 8.11), the national sales companies report to the regional management offices. The manufacturing companies, which are affiliates of the Japanese-based subsidiaries (and have a supplier–customer relationship not only with Panasonic affiliates but also with other companies which market the finished products under their own label), continue to report to their Japanese-based headquarters. Thus the creation of the regional headquarters has provided a

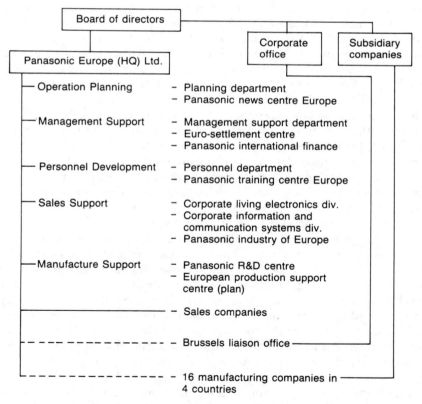

Figure 8.11 Panasonic Europe organogram, 1990 (Source: Courtesy of Panasonic Europe)

continental coordinating presence on three continents, and so added an area input to what continues to be basically a function-driven organizational strategy.

'Matsushita makes the man before the product'

The management staffing policies and practices of Matsushita reflect its basic corporate motto: 'Matsushita makes the man before the product.' This philosophy, which reflects and reinforces the Japanese corporate cultural approach, affects management, recruitment, education, training and assignments. Matsushita, like other Japanese multinationals, hires its Japanese professional employees directly from leading universities for career-long employment. It is a prerequisite for employment that applicants have obtained a degree from a top Japanese university, usually in engineering or economics. Candidates for management positions must pass the company general management exam, which includes extensive interviews. Through ongoing in-company education and job rotation through diverse parts of the company, Matsushita develops well-rounded managers for the general manager posts.

New employees go through an in-company training programme, which indoctrinates them in Matsushita business practices and company beliefs. This includes a three-week initial orientation to learn the Matsushita philosophy and history, followed by three to four months as a trainee in manufacturing, another two to three months as a trainee in marketing, and then course-work in cost accounting and marketing (Kono, 1984:320). Training is seen as a continuous process which extends throughout one's career.

Most top management positions have been filled largely by Japanese; Matsushita attributes this practice to the cultural differences between the monocultured Japanese and other nationalities. Matsushita Japanese managers generally have been rotated, with assignments serving in different line and staff positions, before obtaining their foreign assignments, which are increasingly perceived as essential for those aspiring to top level posts. Country general managers are usually 35–50 years of age.

As Matsushita has developed internationally, it has recognized the need for more non-Japanese managers. The staffing practices developed for the non-Japanese managers have differed remarkably, however, from those long established for the Japanese ones. In recruiting local managers Matsushita has tended to recruit from the market place, looking for those who have already had relevant experience. Matsushita seldom assigns non-Japanese outside the country in which they are recruited. The efforts to develop local nationals recruited directly from universities have faltered, largely because the non-Japanese were not sufficiently patient with the seniority- and age-oriented promotion policy, and left for better-paying jobs with other companies. However, the company now recognizes the importance of this problem if it is to be accepted as a genuinely integrated European company.

In the efforts to develop a more national face and to achieve 'insider status' in each country, Matsushita is taking steps to increase its reliance upon host country staff. It has stressed training for its non-Japanese staff by developing continental training centres, and has arranged for senior managers to make study visits to Osaka. They have also placed non-Japanese in many understudy positions, with the expectations that they will take over the senior posts in many of the affiliates (as has been the case in the USA where an American president works with a Japanese chairman). The most striking initiative undertaken to integrate non-Japanese into Matsushita's global workforce has been the 1991 initiative to send 100 non-Japanese employees for training and on-the-job work experience for up to one year in Japan (letter, Bean, 28 November 1991). Their working language will be English. Matsushita expects this effort 'to have a positive effect, not only on the participants, but also on their Japanese counterparts' (memo, Setsuo Mizoguchi, 25 September 1991).

As Matsushita has increased its reliance upon non-Japanese, it has increased the assignment of younger Japanese to technical assignments within the affiliates in order to facilitate technological transfer and assurance of global standards. These assignments also provide younger employees with global experience and assure the continuation of the Matsushita values in the affiliates.

Matsushita, like all other East Asian firms, faces a challenge in integrating its Japanese and non-Japanese staff. While the goal is to develop 'local' companies along the IBM model, it is difficult to accomplish this quickly while preserving the corporate cultural glue which Japanese multinationals believe has been the principal ingredient of their success; but the steps it has taken are bold ones to meet the challenge.

Founder-driven corporate culture

No other corporate founder laboured so diligently for so many decades to develop and articulate a distinctive corporate culture. Konosuke Matsushita articulated his philosophy over several decades, beginning with the formulation of a corporate code in the 1930s, founding the PHP Institution in 1946 (Matsushita, 1988:256) and continuing to write books until the 1980s. This philosophy sets forth the governing ideas that have driven Matsushita.

The corporate credo, 'Through our industrial activities, we strive to foster progress, to promote the general welfare of society and to devote ourselves to the development of world culture', which Matsushita employees recite regularly, describes the corporate sense of purpose. The corporate 'spiritual values', first set out in the corporate code, stress national service through industry, fairness, harmony and cooperation, struggle for betterment, courtesy and humility, adjustment and assimilation, and gratitude, which are promoted in the in-house training programmes and enhance the company's *esprit de corps*.

Spreading the Matsushita philosophy overseas

This spirit has contributed to the sense of dedication and self-discipline of all Matsushita staff, and especially the Japanese managers. Time is valued; tardiness and laxity are not tolerated. Loyalty to the company, even above family is expected and rewarded. As Matsushita continues its globalization, one of its major challenges is to ensure this spirit pervades its overseas affiliates – even as their management becomes more and more local.

Nissan Motor: establishing continental coordinating offices

Nissan has been one of the least diversified mega-multinationals. While it has begun to diversify, having established units for aerospace, marine, textile machinery and industrial machinery, 90 per cent of its sales are still derived from motor vehicles. The enterprise has continued to be organized essentially along functional lines with marketing, manufacturing and R&D activities organized separately at the corporate, continent and country levels. While Nissan in 1990 established Nissan North America and Nissan Europe as continental umbrella affiliates, these new organizations focus primarily on the direction of their marketing, sales and service companies on those continents, but they also provide administrative support to the manufacturing operations.

Nissan zaibatsu

What has become Nissan Motor Company traces its origins to 1933, when Yoshisuke Ayukawa founded the company as a new enterprise of the Nissan *zaibatsu*, splitting it off from Tobota Casting in 1933 (see Figure 8.12). Ayukawa, who as a young man had studied in the United States from 1905 to 1907, had formed his first company (Tobata Casting) upon his return to Japan in 1910. Its prosperity in World War I led to 'truly remarkable programs of inter-war growth, using different members of his family to push into related industries such as mining

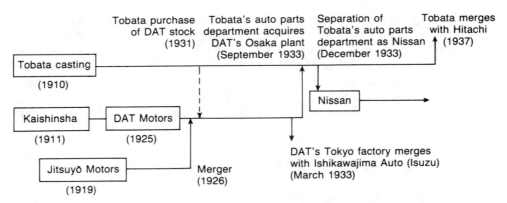

Figure 8.12 Formation of Nissan Motor (Source: Nissan Jidōsha sanjū nen shi,)

and electrical supplies' (Halberstam, 1986:135). The entry into auto and truck manufacturing was undertaken even though the more established *zaibatsu* were hesitant to compete with Ford and GM, which already shipped knocked-down units for assembling in Japan. Nissan's start was expedited first by acquiring DAT Motors' Osaka plant (hence the name of the first Nissan auto, Datsun), and then by hiring US engineers and purchasing an entire vehicle factory and its vehicle design from the US firm Graham Paige in 1936 (Cusumano, 1985:27, 47). By the late 1930s,

> the Nissan concern, most powerful of the 'new *zaibatsu*', consisted of Hitachi[...], Nippon Mining[...], Nippon Marine Products[...], Nissan Motors, [...] Nissan Chemical Industries, Manchurian Heavy Industries, and hundreds of subsidiaries, all controlled by the holding company officially called Nippon Sangyo, but known familiarly as 'Nissan'. (Roberts, 1989:31: see also Cusumano, 1985:28–30)

Following World War II, the Nissan *zaibatsu* was dismembered, Ayukawa and other Nissan leaders were imprisoned and purged, labour problems were acute and the market for automobiles in a warstricken Japan was limited. Nevertheless, Nissan resumed the production of motor vehicles in 1945. At the suggestion of MITI it concluded an agreement with Austin 'to assemble cars from imported knock-down sets for three or four years, and then switch gradually to components made in Japan' (Cusumano, 1985:8). By the mid-1950s Nissan had overcome its initial financial and labour problems with the stimulus of the Korean War and the leadership of Katsuji Kawamata, who was initially assigned from the Industrial Bank of Japan as the 'finance man', became president in 1957 and served until 1977. Like Toyota, Nissan vigorously expanded its production by developing a network of suppliers in many of which it had little if any shareholder's equity.

In the 1950s, Marubeni, the trading company of the Fuyo alliance (which includes Hitachi as well as Nissan and many others) 'pushed [Nissan] to export their cars' (Halberstam, 1986:292). Nissan first began developing the Asian market in 1957 when the company introduced assembly plants into Taiwan, and in 1960 into India. In 1976 it began manufacturing in Australia.

Nissan initially entered the US market by engaging two Japanese trading companies, Marubeni and Mitsubishi, to sell a Datsun model to American dealers (Cusumano, 1985:133). In 1960 Nissan established Nissan Motor Corporation in the United States to market its trucks and automobiles, with east-coast and west-coast offices. Nissan's initial efforts in the US were tortuous, but they paid off in their dramatic development of the American market (see Halberstam, 1986, and Rae, 1982, for a description of these years). In 1983 Nissan established a manufacturing plant in Tennessee. By 1990 the USA accounted for 28 per cent of Nissan's world-wide sales.

In the 1960s Marubeni assisted Nissan in establishing distributorships in a number of European countries. Nissan began manufacturing in 1986 in the United Kingdom. By 1988 it had wholly or partially owned affiliates managing distribution in Germany, Switzerland, the Netherlands, Italy, France and Spain. In 1990, Nissan terminated the contract with Nissan UK, long Europe's most successful distributor (but one with whom Nissan had long-running disputes that went beyond marketing). In 1991 Nissan Europe increased their equity stake in Richard Nissan SA, the French importer and distributor of Nissan motor vehicles, from 10 per cent to 82 per cent, and took management control. The Marubeni Corporation has continued to own the Belgian distributorship and, in 1991, established Nissan Norge (Norway). Local concerns have continued to own the distributorships in Sweden, Finland, Ireland, Denmark and Austria.

By the late 1980s Nissan had continentally localized its design engineering, product development and manufacturing, as well as sales and servicing activities. Thus, at the outset of the 1990s Nissan's European and North American motor vehicle manufacturing, R&D and management operations were more comprehensively developed than those of any other Japanese motor vehicle company. In 1990, when almost one half of its sales were overseas, Nissan incorporated Nissan North America and Nissan Europe to launch Nissan's 'tripolar corporate management structure', with headquarters in Japan, North America and Europe.

Nissan management structure

Following a 1991 Nissan reshuffle the Nissan Management council consisted of the chairman, the president, four executive vice-presidents and five executive managing directors. The executive vice-presidents divide responsibility for the corporate activities: one oversees corporate communication and financial accounting, one production, one overseas activities, and one purchasing and diversification planning and marketing. One of the executive managing directors heads the Americas Operations Group and serves as both president of the newly created Nissan North America and chairman of Nissan Motor Manufacturing Corporation USA, one of the firms included in the Nissan North America umbrella. One of the managing directors is head of the European Operations Group and president of the newly formed Nissan Europe. While the European manufacturing operations do not come under the Nissan Europe umbrella, the Nissan Europe president serves as both chairman of Nissan Motor Manufacturing (UK) Ltd. and a board member of Nissan's Spanish manufacturing company, and the operating heads of these manufacturing operations are Nissan Europe board members. Thus the continental marketing and manufacturing are coordinated through cross-functional management teams that include the top manager of both operations.

Nissan Europe and Nissan North America are now responsible for continental marketing decision-making responsibilities, thus enabling Nissan to implement its market-driven philosophy more effectively through quick and accurate responses to customer needs in Europe and North America. The change has involved transferring many market-related and other functions hitherto performed by the Tokyo Head Office to the continental affiliates. Both new continental affiliates include marketing, sales, service, settlement of accounts, legal matters and purchase planning. Nissan Europe, for example, includes Nissan's wholly or partially owned distributors in the

United Kingdom, Germany, the Netherlands, Switzerland, Italy and France (which previously reported directly to Tokyo), as well as four newly created Nissan service companies including the acceptance, motor parts and finance companies (see Table 8.5). North American Nissan has taken under its umbrella not only the North American sales and services companies but also the research and development, design and manufacturing companies (plus an industrial equipment company and a textile equipment company). The continentally based manufacturing facilities and technological (R&D) centres continue to report directly to Tokyo but do coordinate with the continental offices. (One Nissan executive stresses the need for close coordination at the continental level of manufacturing and R&D, as well as marketing, in order to compete as an 'insider'.) A department has been set up within the new continental offices for mapping out strategies for the entire European market.

Essentially, all long-range planning, analysis and strategic positioning will be finalized by the headquarters in Japan, with increased input from the regional office; however, the tactical component of the strategy will be the responsibility of the Nissan Europe office. Nissan Europe is also setting up an office in Brussels, Belgium, the 'capital' of the European Community, to monitor the changes taking place as a result of the 1992 open market. The information gathered by this group is essential as Nissan attempts to establish itself as a 'European company' in the coming years. This group will develop more in-depth contacts in the European Community and

Table 8.5 Profiles of Nissan continental affiliates, 1990

Continental affiliate	Shareholding	Employees	Affiliates/subsidiaries under the umbrella
Nissan Europe NV	Wholly owned by Nissan Motor Co.	160	Nissan Motor Deutschland GmbH Nissan Motor Nederland BV Nissan Motor (Schweiz) AG Nissan Italia, S.p.A Richard Nissan SA Nissan Motor Acceptance Corporation Nederland BV Nissan International Finance (Nederland) BV Nissan Motor Parts Centre (Europe) BV Nissan Distribution Service (Europe) BV
Nissan North America, Inc.	Wholly owned by Nissan Motor Co.	30	Nissan Motor Corporation in USA Nissan Motor Manufacturing Corporation USA Nissan Research & Development, Inc. Nissan Design International, Inc. Nissan Motor Acceptance Corporation Nissan Finance of America, Inc. Nissan CR Corporation Nissan Motor Corporation in Hawaii, Ltd. Nissan Industrial Equipment Co. Nissan Textile Machinery Corporation in USA

with various country governments with the goal of understanding, ahead of time, the implications of EC legislation for Nissan.

The creation of these two continental headquarters moves Nissan one stage further in the process of globalization. As shown in Figure 8.13, it began in the late 1940s with a system in which all functions were concentrated in Japan, then moved in the mid-1950s to one in which marketing was extended overseas, to one in which manufacturing overseas was begun, to one in which R&D was begun, and finally to one in which management coordination has been localized.

Blending home and host country staff

A major challenge facing Nissan Europe is the integration of the European and Japanese cultures and different management styles. The corporate philosophy of putting the customer first is considered the binding element. Nissan spends thousands of dollars annually on each European employee to ensure adequate operations skills, quality training and company identity. The concept of thinking first of the customer affects all of Nissan's employees, regardless of whether their customer is internal or external to the corporation. This includes the training of Nissan distributors' and dealers' managers.

Most Nissan Europe and Nissan North America top managers are Japanese. A few Americans and a few Europeans have been placed in vice-presidential slots in their respective continental affiliates. Filling senior positions with Europeans who combine an understanding of both Japanese ways of accomplishing things and the capability of operating effectively has been a major goal and is setting a difficult challenge. This may eventually lead to a rationalization of the staffing issues and the hiring of more European locals as Nissan develops into its new potential in Europe.

Integrating values

The current management style of the factories in the United States and the United Kingdom combines both Japanese and local styles, but with a heavy emphasis on the Japanese methods.

Nissan's overseas development strategy was initiated prior to the 1992 initiatives. Consistent with its long-term goals of customer satisfaction and local economy, Nissan recognized that it was insufficient to export only fully assembled vehicles from Japan to overseas markets, and that it was necessary to produce vehicles where they found customers. Thus, Nissan's active preparations for the expected changes in the European auto market reflect a long-term objective of increasing market share and ensuring a strong position in the European market. The basic tenet of their current activities is to establish themselves as a more European company with increased European management, more local content in the

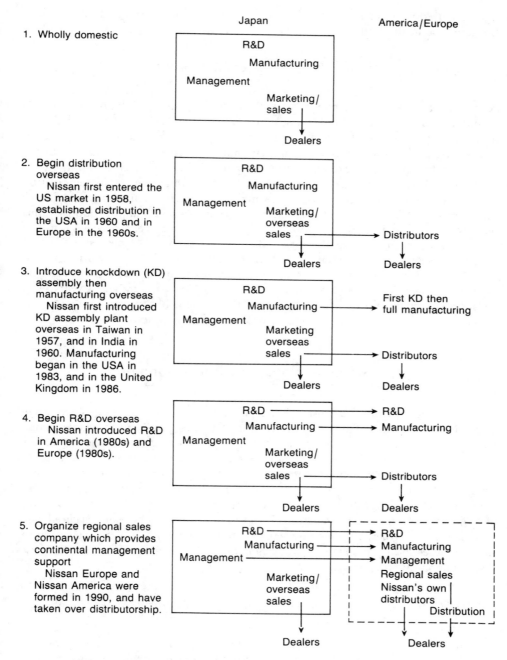

Figure 8.13 Globalization and change in Nissan's overseas functions and organization (Source: Courtesy of Osawa, 1989)

manufactured products, localized R&D activities, and more local autonomy from the Japanese headquarters.

Establishing continental footholds

Nissan has been the Japanese motor vehicle leader in terms of globally localizing its manufacturing and R&D – efforts in which Toyota and Honda have trailed. The development of its manufacturing base in the USA as well as Europe has placed it in a strong position to compete in markets that are increasingly sensitive not only to imports but also to the extent of imported parts. With the integration of the EC's internal market, the Japanese European-made cars will thus be in a stronger position to compete throughout Europe, especially in those countries such as Italy and France that have more vigorously protected their local industries with import quotas. Thus while Japanese-made cars accounted for less than 12 per cent of the European market in 1990, in an intra-European, barrier-free market Japanese and Western auto makers expect their percentage to increase after 1993. This expectation has led the EC to negotiate an agreement under which limits on market penetration by Japanese auto makers would be lifted only gradually over a number of years. The question is which auto makers will survive the crunch. Nissan, with its vigorous strategy of global localization, appears well poised to be one of the survivors.

Sony: rapid global continentalization

Sony, a company founded postwar, has in a few decades developed extensive marketing networks, major manufacturing facilities, and an enviable name recognition in America and Europe as well as Asia. By the late 1980s Sony had not only developed global businesses in video equipment, audio, television and records but also diversified into entertainment, with its acquisition of CBS Records and Columbia Pictures. From 1987 to 1991 Sony more than tripled its sales, from less than $8 to more than $26 billion, thus catapulting it into the Global 40 position. Except for its recent acquisitions in the entertainment industry, Sony secured this remarkable rate largely through internal growth in a fiercely competitive electronics and computer industry that by 1990 included five Japan-based (and two Korean-based) Global 50 corporations.

Milestones towards becoming a multicontinental company

The company now called Sony was co-founded by 25-year-old Akio Morita and 38-year-old Masaru Ibuka in 1946. The company began using the name Sony in 1955 and officially changed its name from Tokyo Tsushin Kogyo Kabushiki Kaisha (Tokyo Telecommunications Engineering Company) to Sony Corporation in 1958 because, as Morita later explained, 'The new name had the advantage of not meaning anything but "Sony" in any language; it was easy to remember, and it carried the connotations we wanted' (Morita, 1986:69–71).

For the initial development of its overseas sales Sony chose not to rely upon one of the major trading companies, as most Japanese firms have long done, but to develop its own international operations group to select and support distributors in the various countries overseas. By 1960 Sony began the development of its own overseas presence with the founding of Sony Corporation of America, as a sales and service organization for the USA and Sony Overseas SA as a means of developing its distribution network in Europe (see Figure 8.14). Morita, then Sony's executive vice-president as well as its principal owner, personally headed the United States operation from 1960 to 1966, an experience that internationalized his outlook and strengthened his determination to develop a global company with multicontinental foundations (Morita, 1986:97–129).

Sony began in the late 1960s to replace its distributorships with sales and service affiliates: in the United Kingdom in 1968, Canada in 1969 (the distributor continued as a part owner of the affiliate), Panama and Germany in 1970, France, Spain and Italy in 1973, Denmark in 1974, Saudi Arabia in 1975, Belgium in 1977, and the Netherlands, Switzerland and Austria in 1979. The European sales and service companies were initially set up as 'second-tier' affiliates owned by Sony Overseas, but by the late 1970s these became 'first-tier' affiliates working directly with Sony headquarters (Sony Overseas was converted from a holding company to a financial services company).

As early as the 1970s Sony began to build manufacturing facilities overseas, in the United States, Brazil and Wales. The efforts accelerated in the 1980s with the building of plants in Germany, France, Spain, Italy, Austria, Malaysia, Thailand,

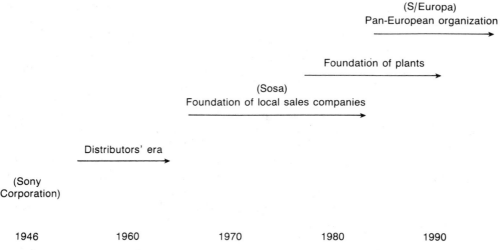

Figure 8.14 History of Sony in Europe (Source: Courtesy of Sony)

Korea and Taiwan; thirteen more facilities were added in the USA in 1990–2. In the United States, Europe and South East Asia as well as Japan (*Tokyo Business Today*, 1990:46), the continued development of these manufacturing facilities has reflected Sony's philosophy of making products where the markets are.

Like other Japanese multinationals, Sony long operated as a function-split organization. As Jack Schmuckli, once the head of Sony Deutschland, now head of Sony in Europe, recalls:

> Twice a year the 'product kings' [the representatives of the production sectors] and the 'country kings' [the heads of the sales companies] lined up across the table and negotiated a firm six months' commitment that spelled out the quantity and transfer price of the goods to be delivered. This arms'-length split lasted until the early 1980s when the oil-crisis-induced recession drastically reduced sales. Despite the sales companies' pleas to renegotiate their commitments, the production divisions continued producing inventory backlogs and forced the sales companies to accept them. In 1982, therefore, Sony broadened the role of the production divisions [renamed business groups] to include the responsibility for global marketing strategy. Initially a few of the business groups exerted their newly strengthened power forcefully, causing disruption in the sales affiliates. (interview, 29 May 1991)

In 1985 the dramatic drop in the dollar and corollary rise in the yen, combined with the impact of the Single European Act and the continued host country anti-import pressures, led Sony to rationalize its manufacturing globally. Since by the mid-1980s more than 80 per cent of Sony's sales were overseas but only 20 per cent of its manufacturing was, the dramatic shift in the exchange rates sky-rocketed the cost of Sony's Japanese manufacturing, with no way to pass the cost on to the consumer and remain competitive. Sony, therefore, accelerated the pace of its global localization and redressed the balance of power between the global product and local sales perspectives by establishing Sony Europa GmbH in 1986. Since then the various product-focused business groups have organized their own European headquarters which direct their manufacturing operations and, working in cooperation with Sony Europa, plan and implement marketing strategy and plant development.

In the late 1980s Sony also expanded its American operation – principally by acquiring CBS Records, now renamed Sony Music Entertainment, for $2 billion in 1988 and Columbia Pictures Entertainment Inc., now renamed Sony Pictures Entertainment Inc., for $3.4 billion in 1989, and thus launching Sony into a new industry. In 1989 it added two non-Japanese to its board – the first Japanese company to do so. One was Jack Schmuckli, president of Sony Europa and chairman of European operations. The other was Michael Schulhof, then president of Sony USA. In 1991 Sony added Pete Peterson, chairman of the Blackstone Group, as an outside, non-Japanese board member.

By 1991 Sony had developed globally to such an extent that 74 per cent of its sales (up from 66 per cent in 1989) were outside Japan, 29 per cent in the USA,

28 per cent in Europe, and 17 per cent in other areas. It followed up its initial marketing successes with the development of production facilities in Europe and America, thus forming a triad system including Japan. The ongoing investment in Asia, America and Europe indicates that Sony is continuing its grand strategy for developing multicontinental production as well as marketing networks.

Structure: globalization through continentalization

Sony is composed of more than 570 companies, most of which are either sales or manufacturing companies. For this agglomeration Sony has not developed an organization chart; Sony public relations explains that the organization is growing and changing too rapidly (interview, A. Ostkamp, 29 June 1991). Heading the enterprise is an eleven-member executive committee that includes the co-founder/honorary chairman (Masaru Ibuka), the co-founder/chairman (Akio Morita), the president/CEO (Norio Ohga), three deputy presidents and five senior managing directors. Of the three deputy presidents, one is Morita's brother who under Ohga heads up the American operations from the Sony USA base in Park Ridge, New Jersey; another is the COO and most likely CEO-heir apparent, who heads the electronics businesses. The five senior managing directors oversee finance, human resources, domestic sales, audio and TV. Included among the other 26 members of the board of directors are the heads of the product groups, of corporate offices and of the continental organizations, as well as longtime Sony executives who are now outside directors serving as directors of leading Japanese banks, the Bank of Tokyo and the Mitsui Taiyo Kobe Bank, and the already-noted, 1991-appointed non-Japanese outside executive.

Sony's electronic business sectors – consumer video equipment, audio equipment, television, recording media, professional products and components – are Tokyo-based. Its entertainment business is based in Los Angeles. The American operations are embraced within one umbrella-like entity entitled Sony USA (SUSA) which includes two groups (see Figure 8.15). The electronics group has been organized with three major units: SONAM (Sony Corporation of America) is the general sales company for consumer and professional products; SEMA (Sony Engineering and Manufacturing America) coordinates most of Sony's American-based production operations; and SMPGA (Sony Magnetic Products Group America) is the vertically integrated company responsible for the manufacture and sale of recording media products. The software group, established in 1991 as Sony Software with Michael Schulhof as president, includes Sony Music Entertainment, Sony Pictures Entertainment and a new Sony Electronic Publishing unit.

The European operation, which continues to manage a more heterogeneous market, works with a matrix-like arrangement (see Figure 8.16). The Sony Europa organization facilitates this by including within its extended framework the European business group heads, who are involved in its executive committee. They are responsible administratively to the head of Sony Europe and functionally, for manufacturing and marketing strategy, to their business group 'bosses' at Sony

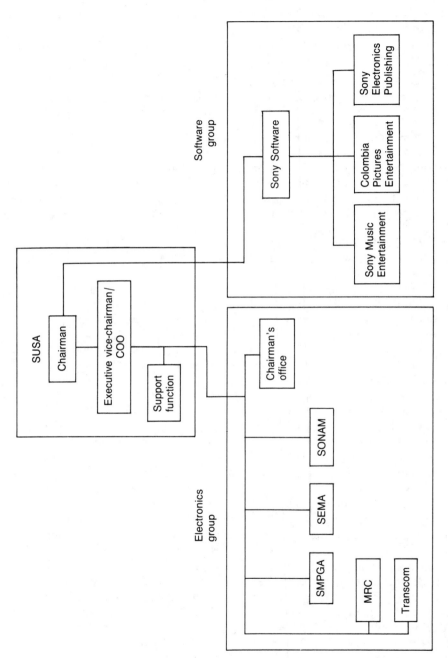

Figure 8.15 Sony in the United States

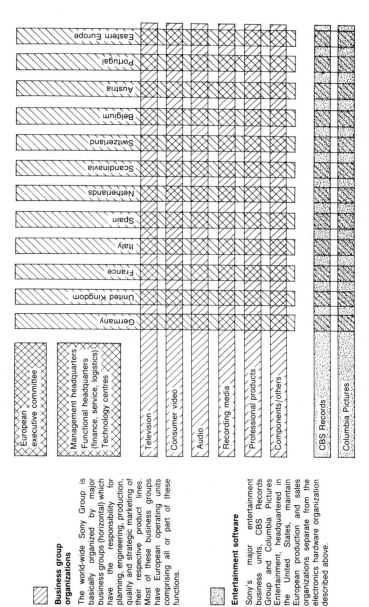

National sales and service organization

The organizational units closest to the market are Sony's national sales and service companies in each country in Western Europe (vertical). Typically, these sales organizations consist of three major units: consumer products, professional products and magnetic products. Eastern Europe is served through an international sales organization based in Frankfurt.

Business group organizations

The world-wide Sony Group is basically organized by major business groups (horizontal) which have the responsibility for planning, engineering, production, quality and strategic marketing of their respective product lines. Most of these business groups have European operating units comprising all or part of these functions.

Headquarters and support companies

Both horizontal and vertical units share common management and functional headquarters, engineering centres and support companies.

Entertainment software

Sony's major entertainment business units, CBS Records Group and Columbia Pictures Entertainment, headquartered in the United States, maintain European production and sales organizations separate from the electronics hardware organization described above.

Figure 8.16 Sony's European operations: organizational structure (Source: Courtesy of Sony)

headquarters in Tokyo. The heads of each of the sales companies and management support units are the direct responsibility of the Sony Europa head. While the business groups are divided by product, the sales companies divide their sales force by client, consumer products, professional products and magnetic products. Components and OEM (original equipment manufacture) are marketed directly, not through the sales affiliates. The software/entertainment businesses are managed directly from the USA with only loose coordination with Sony Europe.

Outside of the USA and Europe Sony's operations are not as integrated. Sony of Canada handles Canadian sales, Sony of Panama handles Central and South American sales, Sony Corporation of Hong Kong handles Hong Kong and South East Asia sales, and Sony (Australia) handles sales in Australia, New Zealand, and the Pacific Islands. The manufacturing facilities in these areas are controlled directly by their business groups.

More Westernized in its staffing

'Sony is more Westernized in its approach to staffing than any other Japanese multinational.' This statement was made not by a Sony executive, but by the European public affairs director of a major Sony competitor (interview, 16 May 1990). A number of factors contribute to this assessment besides the fact that Sony is the only Japanese multinational to include non-Japanese on its board. The most obvious is there are so few Japanese in the American and European operations. For example, of the over 18,000 Sony employees in Europe, there are only about 250 Japanese; even at the European headquarters in Cologne fewer than one-sixth of the 200 staff are Japanese – and they are not concentrated in the upper ranks. Although most of the European business group heads are still Japanese, only one of the sales affiliate heads is Japanese. A closely related factor is that Sony, unlike most Japanese firms, promotes more on the basis of merit than of seniority. The language of communication in both the European and American headquarters is English.

The language split between Japanese and English has meant that the non-Japanese managers have not been as integrated into the intensive training cycles that Sony's Japanese managers experience. Sony Europe and Sony USA have developed their own management development programmes; the 'graduation course' for Sony's European senior executives is the IMD European Executive Seminar. Complementing these efforts are short management development courses taken in Japan.

Founder-led culture

The Sony culture has been heavily influenced by the outgoing and outspoken leadership of Morita, its co-founder, long president and CEO, and now chairman, whose book *Made in Japan* has gained world-wide attention. Its employees share

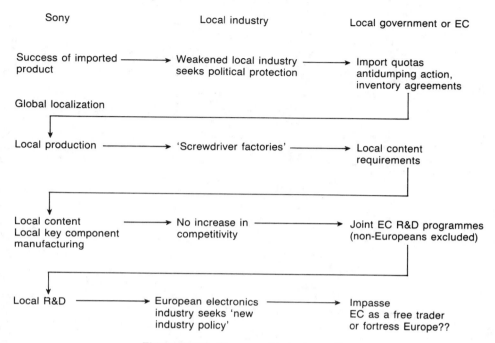

Figure 8.17   Sony and industry policy

a pride in the company's internationalism, rapid growth and reputation for innovation and quality. They appreciate its apparent rankless informality and concern for the employees. And they appear to relish what they believe is a somewhat unconventional, 'maverick' culture, neither Japanese nor Western yet combining features of both.

Successful transitions

The Sony organization prides itself on having organizationally adapted to changing conditions in order to facilitate its dramatic growth (see Figure 8.17). Sony began with successful international marketing, first through distributorships and then through its own sales affiliates. It anticipated host country protectionist efforts by establishing assembly plants. Later, it responded to changing exchange rates and anticipated 'local content' legislation by increasing the local manufacturing of key components – and followed this up by continentally localizing R&D. The combined impact of corporate intent and host country external pressure has led to the development of a tricontinental organization.

PART IV
Reorganization: for managing transcontinental enterprises

CHAPTER 9
Leading teams: for strategic corporate coherence

An agenda for a coherent organizational strategy: for managing locally world-wide

Among the few certainties in the increasingly uncertain future of multinationals are change at an increasing pace and more complexity. To strengthen their competitive advantage, successful multinationals will continue to redevelop their agendas and continue to reorganize in order to develop their global strategies and their world-wide organizations with the aim of confronting the global–local dilemma more effectively. This will require developing 'glocal' organizations throughout the world, capable of thinking globally and acting locally world-wide to mobilize diverse resources in order to secure shared goals.

In the early decades of the twentieth century, the more successful multi-nationals, as Chandler has described, were those that made a 'three-pronged investment in production, distribution and management' (Chandler, 1990:8). The collective histories of 26 of the largest enterprises on three continents, outlined in Chapters 6–8, provide evidence that in the final decades of the twentieth century, many mega-multinationals are making three sets of interdependent investments to maximize their prospects for successfully managing their increasingly complex, multidimensional mosaics. First, they are globalizing their marketing, manu-facturing, and research and product development management support service, strategies and infrastructures. Second, they are continentally localizing their activities in order to compete more effectively locally and world-wide. And third, they are increasing their capacity for strategic coherence by strengthening the cross-border linkages, with structuring, staffing and value-sharing initiatives that depend upon the corporate capacity to develop and sustain leaders capable of orchestrating cross-border coherence and change.

Towards increasing complexity

A host of forces has accelerated the urgency, the tempo and the complexity of multinational reorganizations. The quickening advances of technology and the desire to exploit them quickly, the economic integration of continental communities, increased intercontinental as well as intracontinental competition, and other global forces have transformed and complicated the global environment in which multinationals compete. Multinationals have reinforced the external forces driving change and magnifying complexity by accelerating their efforts to increase sales, profits and market shares – not only to gratify the stakeholders but also to enhance their efficiencies of scale and scope. In those industries, such as petroleum and chemicals, motor vehicles and equipment, metals and increasingly food, which require especially large investments to achieve competitive advantage, the need for growth has long been acute.

In order to expedite their growth – through internally generated development, acquisitions and mergers, and various forms of alliance – multinationals have continued expanding across industrial and territorial borders. They have continued globalizing the roles of their product(ion) divisions by continentally extending their manufacturing, technical and management support as well as marketing functions. The more a corporation has expanded, the more complex the interaction of the product, geographic and functional parts, and the greater the challenge of making their multidimensional complexity coherent.

The multidimensional organizational complexity of the leading multinationals' international operations has increased beyond the capacity of traditional global organizational strategies – whether the once-pervasive European, national-company-territory-driven approach, the American multi(product)-divisional approach (with or without an international division), or the Japanese global, function-driven approach. Multinationals face a paradox: the more they grow to maintain their competitiveness, the more complexity they must manage coherently – if they are to exploit their advantages of scale and scope. To continue growing and generating profits, successful multinationals must continue to seek more effective ways of managing their diverse parts. In order to continue to be competitive, the synergies that multinationals gain from cross-hierarchy collaboration must more than counterbalance the costs of the superstructure coordinating the diverse parts.

Since wall-like borders reduce the opportunities for realizing economies of scope and scale, the multinational needs to develop an organization whose parts share resources and work together effectively. The core of the global–local dilemma confronting the multinational is how to reconcile the global role of the operating divisions with the need for cross-divisional communication and coordination at corporate, continent and country levels. The challenge is to develop organizations whose major corporate parts have sufficient independence to respond quickly to technical and market changes, but whose corporate whole may exert sufficient interdependent coherency to enable it to refocus and leverage its human, financial, technical and other resources more strategically across operating divisions as well as country borders.

Learning from experiment and experience

The previous chapters, while sketching the multidimensional complexity of the multinational organizational challenge, have described many of the reorganizational initiatives that leading multinationals have taken to meet the global–local dilemma. This chapter draws on the experiences of these leading multinationals to present an agenda of organizational initiatives. Together they outline a modular framework intended to foster cross-border communication and coordination, and thus corporate coherency. Cumulatively they advance four themes developed throughout this comparative book. First, a multinational needs to balance and blend three sets of organizational perspectives – product, functional and territorial – to maximize and concert more effectively the use of its diverse resources. Second, a multinational requires three sets of management dynamics – structuring, staffing and sharing values – with which to mobilize its increasingly complex competing, and yet complementary, sets of perspectives. Third, in order to foster effective communication and coordination across divisions and national borders, a multinational needs to develop transdimensional networks, teams and leaders that laterally overlay the various vertical operational hierarchies. Fourth, to sustain and support the lateral overlay of teams and leaders, a multinational needs to augment significantly its efforts to develop and empower management teams and their leaders. Together these organizational themes set out an interdependent arsenal of tools whose combined strength would improve a multinational's capacity for coherently mobilizing its diversity.

The underlying issue specifically addressed is how best to relate a multinational's international parts to its product and functional parts. More and more multinationals that once regarded their international affiliates as entities distinct from their domestic businesses are globalizing their corporate divisions in order to develop global strategies more effectively. On the other hand, multinationals that once viewed international operations as mere extensions of their various domestic divisions are now looking to develop (or redevelop) their territorial organization in order to strengthen their capacity to mobilize their diverse divisional resources at country and continental levels. The issue of how to integrate international operations is an integral aspect of the larger challenge: how can multinationals create more aligned organizations, ones that can flexibly leverage resources across internal borders and can motivate cross-border teamwork to focus a multinational's collective energy on competing successfully? Since the walls dividing the more profit-and-loss-driven, SBU-type organization are especially formidable, addressing this issue is particularly poignant.

The ideas presented in this chapter focus on what structuring, staffing and value-sharing steps the leading multinationals have taken to develop transborder teams and leaders. The fast paced world of international business, which

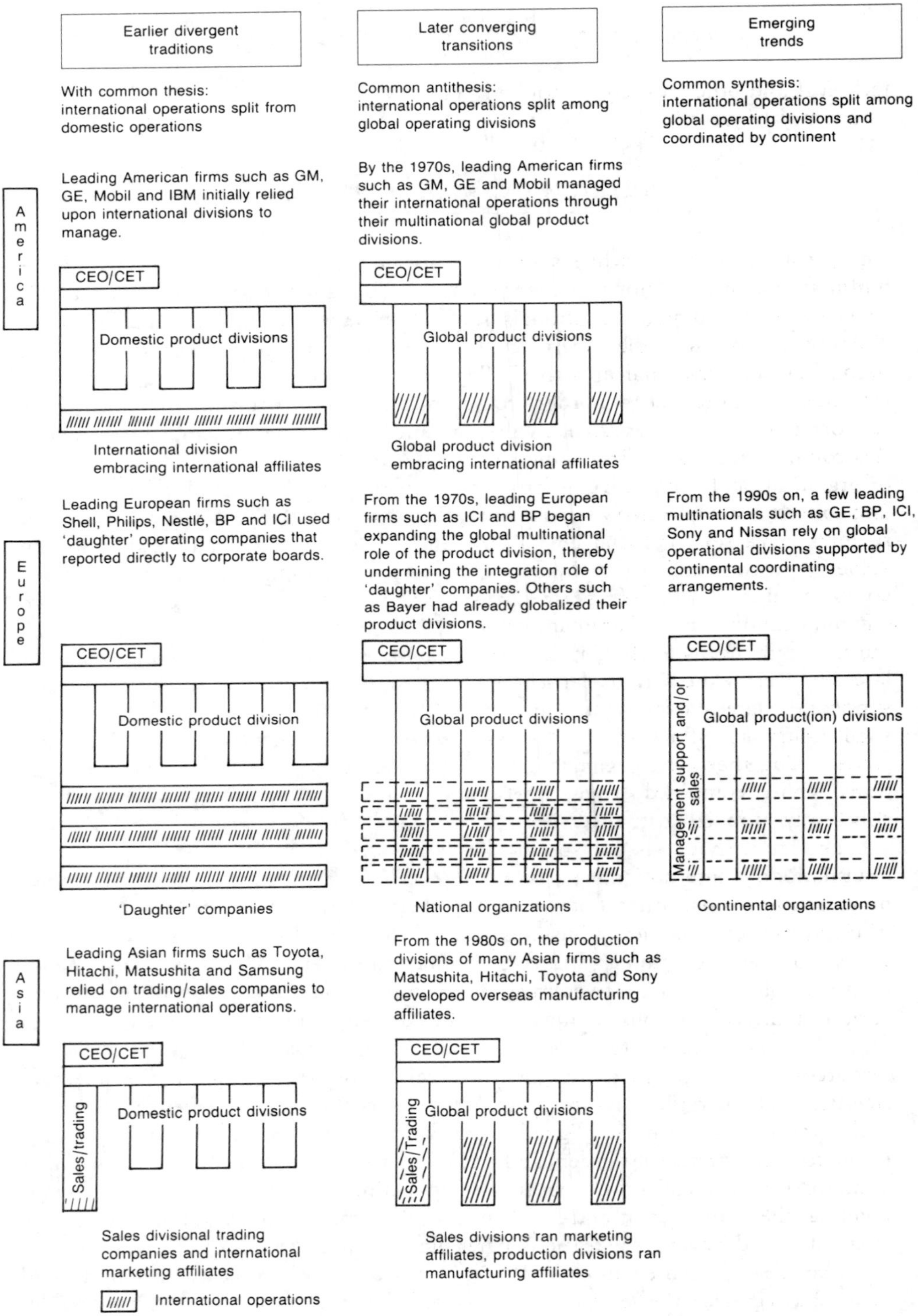

Earlier divergent traditions	Later converging transitions	Emerging trends

With common thesis: international operations split from domestic operations

Common antithesis: international operations split among global operating divisions

Common synthesis: international operations split among global operating divisions and coordinated by continent

America

Leading American firms such as GM, GE, Mobil and IBM initially relied upon international divisions to manage.

By the 1970s, leading American firms such as GM, GE and Mobil managed their international operations through their multinational global product divisions.

CEO/CET

Domestic product divisions

International division embracing international affiliates

CEO/CET

Global product divisions

Global product division embracing international affiliates

Europe

Leading European firms such as Shell, Philips, Nestlé, BP and ICI used 'daughter' operating companies that reported directly to corporate boards.

From the 1970s, leading European firms such as ICI and BP began expanding the global multinational role of the product division, thereby undermining the integration role of 'daughter' companies. Others such as Bayer had already globalized their product divisions.

From the 1990s on, a few leading multinationals such as GE, BP, ICI, Sony and Nissan rely on global operational divisions supported by continental coordinating arrangements.

CEO/CET

Domestic product division

'Daughter' companies

CEO/CET

Global product divisions

National organizations

CEO/CET

Management support and/or sales

Global product(ion) divisions

Continental organizations

Asia

Leading Asian firms such as Toyota, Hitachi, Matsushita and Samsung relied on trading/sales companies to manage international operations.

From the 1980s on, the production divisions of many Asian firms such as Matsushita, Hitachi, Toyota and Sony developed overseas manufacturing affiliates.

CEO/CET

Sales/trading

Domestic product divisions

Sales divisional trading companies and international marketing affiliates

CEO/CET

Sales/Trading

Global product divisions

Sales divisions ran marketing affiliates, production divisions ran manufacturing affiliates

///// International operations

Figure 9.1 Successive phases in the organization of international operations of prototypical leading American, European and Asian industrial corporations

Table 9.1 Successive organizational phases in confronting the global–local dilemma

	Earlier divergent traditions	Recent convergent transitions	Prospective emerging trends
Operational distance	Significant local/country autonomy	Decreasing local/country autonomy	More corporate-wide continental coordination
Driving organizational perspectives	Primarily by country	Increasing use of global operating divisions	Increasing use of continental coordinating organizations to support global divisions
Management dynamics	Stress one dynamic	Increasing use of more than one dynamic	Concerted use of structure, staffing and shared values

increasingly depends upon transborder communication and teamwork, demands the integration of these three dynamics. While the traditions of American, European and Asian multinationals have differed, the recent reorganizational transitions of many leading American, European and Asian multinationals have indicated an increasing convergence that points to a prospective synthesis of the two earlier approaches. The earlier-developed, long-dominant one stressed the split between the domestic company and foreign operations; the later-developed one has stressed the split among global operating – product or functional – divisions. The emerging one, which multinationals such as IBM, BP, Nissan and Sony have taken steps towards developing, embraces efforts to balance and blend three critical perspectives: product, function and geography (see Figure 9.1). The reorganizational initiatives driving this convergence – more cross-border enabling structures, more power-sharing, linchpin managers, and more corporate-concerting core values that foster coherent corporate direction – provide the ideas comprising the prospective emerging trends that this agenda for change outlines (see Table 9.1).

Strengthen 'our' corporate-concerting ideas: beyond cultural colonialism

Cultivate corporate-concerting ideas that strengthen 'our' enterprise-wide sense of mission, vision and style. Such advice incorporates several corollary propositions. First, who do we intend to include in 'our' multicultured (occupational as well as national) 'us'? Second, what do we intend the mission and vision of 'our' macrobusiness to be? Third, how do 'we' intend to present 'our' enterprise to ourselves and others? And fourth, what do 'we' intend our corporate-wide shared principles and practices to be?

Who do 'we' intend to include in our internationally and industrially diverse 'us'?

Who do 'we' intend to include in our internationally and industrially diverse 'us'? Who do we intend to include in 'our' ever-moving mosaic, which we intend to bind with a common structure and staffing? Defining who we are, and who we intend to be, is as difficult as it is vital. For the effort brings to the surface the organization-dividing cleavages that complicate attempts to resolve the global–local dilemma. As a multinational has diversified into more products, developed in more countries and depended on a greater variety of professionals and more 'locals', the effort has become even more challenging. To be globally effective, corporate missions, visions and principles need to embrace values that may be shared by more than the home country, the longtime major businesses and the principal professions.

Heavily country-influenced corporate cultures do not transplant easily into foreign environments – as European multinationals with their confining borders have long had to appreciate, American multinationals have been reminded and Japanese ones have only recently begun to recognize. As corporations such as General Motors and Daimler-Benz have discovered, single industry-influenced corporate cultures also do not readily transplant across industry lines. Nor are corporate cultures developed principally by one profession – whether 'upstream oil' men, 'bean-counters', marketeers or R&Ders – readily embraced by those in other professions. Cultural colonialism, whether across national or occupational frontiers – especially when these parts have differing organizational traditions – does not win the minds and hearts of those in what are so easily perceived as the lesser parts. To secure commitment requires developing a sense of 'we' which clearly embraces an extended family that includes the diversity of groups whose concerted efforts are required to maximize the enterprise's global advantage.

Just as a human extended family may embrace, with differing degrees of closeness, a few or many nuclear families, so a multinational extended family may embrace, with differing degrees of closeness, a variable number of organizational groups. Many factors have affected how widely and how closely a multinational embraces disparate groups within its multinational 'we' (see Figure 9.2). These include the extent of its diversity, the extent to which corporate leadership considers these groups vital to its fundamental purpose, and the extent to which the multinational has developed the capacity to encourage harmony or exert hegemony, or both, throughout its extended family. In their approach to this issue, American firms have long relied, and more recently European firms have increasingly relied, principally on structure to define the corporate 'we'. On the other hand, Japanese groupings and groups have relied far more upon shared ideology to extend the common sense of 'we' throughout their extended families of companies.

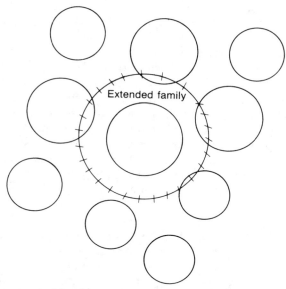

A Corporate extended family core values do not extend to all component parts.

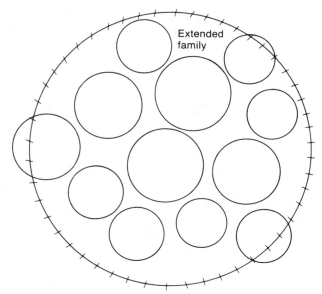

B Corporate extended family core values do extend to all component parts.

Figure 9.2 Comparison of corporate extended families

The importance of defining who 'we' intend to be, and cultivating and promoting value-sharing throughout those that the 'we' is intended to include, is indicated by a comparison of the American and Asian approaches to organizational strategy. Thus, to present what may be two extremes, whereas the GM corporate 'we' has not appeared to embrace either Hughes or Electronic Data Systems (EDS), both of which are structurally embraced within GM, a number of independent companies with no common corporate superstructure have long shared the Mitsubishi sense of extended family. Without the binding and bonding of shared values, a multinational has greater difficulty achieving sufficient corporate cohesion to justify a corporate superstructure. A multinational with parts that do not share, and have little prospects of sharing, its corporate core values may consider two alternatives. One is to set apart some or all of the disparate parts by selling or spinning them off. Another is to attempt to accommodate the disparate sets of values by redeveloping, possibly with enlarged parameters, the mission, the vision and the principles of the corporation.

Shared ideas provide the corporate sense of 'we' that binds mosaic-like structures and bonds profession-divided staff, thus enhancing their capacity for corporate coherency. Clarifying, communicating and celebrating corporate-wide core values foster the coordination of the ongoing operations of a company and vitally enhance the prospects of securing support for proposed changes in structure and systems, and staffing and skills, as well as shared beliefs and behaviour. The stronger the culture, the less companies need to rely upon commands, 'policy manuals, organization charts, or detailed procedures and rules' (Peters and Waterman, 1982:75) for achieving compliance. Clearly articulating the corporate values provides the criteria with which a company's leadership may determine in what, where, when and how to invest the corporate resources and judge its performance.

What do 'we' intend 'our' macrobusiness to be?

Successful diversified multinationals focus on their corporate purpose by defining its macrobusiness. To mobilize the disparate parts of a multinational, the corporate definition of its purpose and mission needs to be 'much more than good intentions and fine ideas. It represents a framework for the entire business, the values which drive the company and the beliefs that the company has in itself and what it can achieve' (Colin Marshall, deputy chairman and chief executive of British Airways, quoted in Campbell, Devine and Young, 1990:19). To motivate, it must go beyond exhortations to 'make a profit' or to 'serve society'.

Focusing on the multinational's macrobusiness is the vital first step in determining who comprises the corporate 'we' and developing a strategically capable organization. The extent of diversification of most mega-multinationals has magnified the task of defining a coherent macrobusiness; that is, a portfolio or cluster of businesses that gain from their mutual interdependence. This requires focusing upon what is the root of their interdependence and what core competence, comparative advantage or competitive strength pervades the enterprise, enabling the individual parts to complement one another so that the whole is competitively stronger than the sum of the parts. Focusing on the macrobusiness clarifies the priorities and facilitates the cross-border allocation and mobilization of resources. It shapes how diverse perspectives and professional skills are balanced and blended. And setting the priorities facilitates determining what processes and what component parts of the company may be more economically sourced outside the company without jeopardizing its competitive advantage (Hamel and Prahalad, 1989:74). It fosters a corporate-wide view that transcends and encompasses the narrow perspective of what have often been the not only self-contained but also self-protecting business units comprising the multinational mosaic.

Such an effort to remove intracorporate barriers does, however, threaten the autonomy so long exercised by many business units. Defining a multinational's macrobusiness may require considering not only the extent of diversification across industries but also the extent of vertical integration of suppliers and distributors. The challenge is to define the macrobusiness sufficiently broadly to allow capitalizing upon technological or marketing strengths, and yet avoid describing it so broadly that there is insufficient interdependence to provide opportunity for leveraging core competences across intracorporate frontiers.

To justify its recent rapid diversification through acquisition, Daimler-Benz has redefined itself into a transportation company whose parts benefit by their interchange of quality engineering and advanced technology. In order to avoid being trapped in what threatens to be a declining industry, Philip Morris has redefined itself from a cigarette into a consumer packaged products company. Sony expanded from transistor radios into consumer electronics by capitalizing on their competence to miniaturize. Canon expanded from cameras to office equipment by capitalizing on their reproduction competence and NEC leveraged the semiconductor competence into their C + C (computers and communication) interdependent businesses.

The advantage of focusing on the macrobusiness has long been so evident to Japanese firms that they have had a predisposition to spin off not only horizontally related businesses but also vertically related ones that were not indispensable to the core operation (as many of Hitachi's component suppliers and its chemical business have been spun off). The perils of diffusing attention over too broad an array of businesses has been sufficient to lead companies such as Ford, Mobil, BP and Philips to divest themselves of businesses that did not fit.

Defining and focusing on the corporate macrobusiness is clearly an initial step in developing a strategically coherent organization. It provides the criteria not only for determining in what businesses to invest, but more vitally for refocusing resources among businesses to enable the macrobusiness to compete more effectively world-wide. When the definition is articulated and acted upon consistently, it also provides the managers within the businesses with ground rules for determining how the businesses will interact and support one another.

What do 'we' intend our corporate macro-image to be?

With their increasing product scope and geographical spread, many diversified multinationals face the issue of presenting a focused image. When corporate parts have developed their own identities, public image and brands, corporations have hesitated to discard the diffused, multiple approach. On the other hand, when a corporation serves overlapping product and geographical markets (and the more focused the macrobusiness the more likely it is that the markets will overlap), a coherent corporate image strengthens the identity and expedites the development of new markets. A corporate brand identity makes more effective use of the advertising budget through leveraging across products and countries. And it allows for the development of a consistent, coherent corporate message. For example, Bayer consistently plays the theme 'expertise and responsibility'.

Many organizations have corporate parts or associated companies with different last names but sharing the common first name – for example, Exxon Chemical and Mitsubishi Electric – or common first initials – for example, IBM Japan and GE Information Services. Labelling all products with the corporate logo not only endorses the product but also promotes the corporate identity. Corporations may combine the advantages of the multiple and the monolithic approaches by adopting this 'endorsed' or 'dual name' strategy.

Together, a shared global corporate brand and a shared core competence provide the cement binding the corporate mosaic. Lacking this cement, a multinational's parts are loose tiles – easily losing out to global competitors that steadily invest in and develop their core competences and exploit their corporate brand image (Hamel and Prahalad, 1989:79).

What do 'we' intend our corporate shared principles and practices to be?

Corporate-wide beliefs and behaviours help transcend the walls isolating the various product, professional and national turfs, and thus produce a common *esprit de corps*. Shared values support efforts to empower the workforce, especially its managers, whose cross-border leadership is essential for creating a coherent organization.

An effective multi-industry, multicontinental culture appreciates and embraces a variety of subcultural ways of doing things. It nurtures and 'celebrates' them (Hickman and Silva, 1987:216–240). An effective supraculture appreciates the wise old dictum 'In all things essential, unity; in other things, diversity' by stressing strategic themes which transcend the corporate mosaic. It encourages the various divisions and affiliates to develop their own subcultures, which not only complement the supraculture but also identify the distinctiveness of the various parts of the enterprise. This enables the individuals to identify with and share pride in a smaller unit, much as a regiment or a ship in the military develops a pride in its part of the total organization.

To cultivate border-transcending beliefs and behaviours requires clarifying which values would bind the organization together, communicating these values throughout the multinational mosaic and celebrating them through role-modelling. The first requires stressing principles and practices that not only reflect the multinational's ethos but are also compatible with and cultivable within the enterprise. The second and even more difficult part, infusing these values throughout the system, requires continuous investments in staff education and training, and development and orchestrated distribution by 'culture carriers'. The third requires the consistent application of these values by corporate leaders who not only preach but also practise the beliefs and behaviours they advance. Such consistent cultivation of shared principles and practices throughout the extended family fosters compliance with corporate objectives; it may help to secure commitment.

Promoting value-sharing throughout the organization depends upon three additional critical factors. One is the development of a structure that not only does not insulate divisions and affiliates from one another but in fact enables transborder collegiality. The second is the development of staff processes that generate cross-divisional and cross-national assignments – thus developing cross-border 'culture carriers' and the consequent cross-pollenization among the pieces comprising the multinational mosaic. The third is the proactive promotion of core values by top management. All three are vital to the development of an organization capable of strategic corporate coherency, which requires as a start distinguishing between the global management responsibilities and local management ones.

Globalize corporate governance: beyond myopic-mindedness

Multinational efforts to resolve, or accommodate, the global–local dilemma confront the basic structural issue of distributing management power by defining the roles and responsibilities of the corporate board and the corporate executive team, the major corporate divisions and the corporate functional support services – and the local operating units.

In attempting to resolve the global–local issue, multinational leaders face the strategic questions of what and how much to delegate. Successful multinational leaders have endeavoured to push operational decisions down as far as possible and increase the responsibility of the on-site management, but they have retained control of the vital strategic concerns affecting the corporation. As earlier stressed, a critical element of the corporate leadership role involves the cultivating of the governing ideas guiding the development of corporate grand strategy. Another element involves aligning and coordinating the major corporate parts. A third critical element is stewardship of the organization's vital, generally scarce, common resources such as investment capital, proprietary technology and innovative techniques, and corporate reputation. But the most important one is developing the capabilities and the commitment of its people.

Successful multinational initiatives to restructure corporate operations to meet these concerns have affected global governance as well as local general management and coordination. A number of multinationals have taken steps that enhance their corporate capacity to view issues with a more intercontinental outlook. These include separating the global and home country headquarters, internationalizing the corporate board, developing a more internationally representative corporate team, creating a non-executive board chair post, siting the headquarters of major operating divisions at their points of competitive advantage, and focusing on the strategic stewardship of common resources. These steps enable corporate leadership to overcome the myopic preoccupation with home country, major division or principal profession concerns that affects many multinationals.

Separate the global and home country headquarters

Separating the global headquarters from the headquarters of the home country organization reduces the temptation for leaders to be so preoccupied with domestic issues that they are myopic regarding international ones. A number of multi-nationals have organized the domestic operations as a separate national organization, more or less comparable to the non-domestic affiliates. Royal Dutch/Shell, in part because of its binationalism, has long treated its UK and Netherlands affiliates like its other international affiliates. Nestlé and Philips have also separated their domestic companies from the parent company. While IBM separated its world headquarters from its US headquarters in the 1980s, it was not until the 1992 reorganization that the corporate production divisions were freed from the oversight of the US affiliate. Matsushita has likewise moved in this direction by merging its international trading company into the overall organization.

When global management doubles as home country management, the preoccupation with the pressing domestic matters fosters viewing global matters as an extension of domestic ones. Separating the domestic and world-wide management clarifies the point that the domestic company is one of the international affiliates, perhaps the major one, but not the one whose perspective frames the whole picture.

Internationalize the board of directors

Internationalizing the board of directors with a more internationally representative cross-section of members enhances the global image and ability to appreciate the rapidly changing nuances of international issues. A few multinationals have gone beyond adding a token international member. BP has a German, an Irishman and an American. Of ICI's eight outside directors, two are American and two are German (one was Japanese until 1990). Nestlé's board includes French, Spanish, German and American nationals. Philips's supervisory board has seven nationalities represented (Belgian, British, American, Italian, Swedish and German, as well as

Dutch). The ABB board includes two Swiss, two Swedes, two Germans, one American and one Luxembourger.

Comparatively few American companies, such as Philip Morris Exxon and Du Pont, have non-US, 'outsider' board members. In some cases, these board members represent major shareholders or strategic alliances. Sony is the only major Japanese multinational with a foreign 'outsider' on its board. As multinationals continue to expand across national and continental borders, such board internationalization helps counterbalance the home country mind-set which continues to limit the international vision of many multinationals. One does not have to decide whether an effective global operation requires 'a genuine equidistance of perspective' (Ohmae, 1989b:152; 1990) or 'the competitive advantage' of the home country in a particular industry (Porter, 1990) to recognize the advantages of more internationalized boards.

A significant obstacle to expanding board membership to include more international representations has been that many boards are already large – and filled with members who represent interest/stakes that cannot be ignored. American socio-political mores have pressed American corporations to include ethnic minorities and women; German firms by law fill half of their 'supervisory' board posts with representatives of labour; and Japanese and South Korean boards are (almost) totally composed of top management. But the need to include more international members is too important to ignore.

Create a non-executive board chair post

Creating a non-executive board chair post would strengthen the capacity of the board of directors to exert its trusteeship role of monitoring corporate progress and top executive performance. Most of the world's leading corporations combine the roles of board chairperson and CEO, thus allowing the CEO to set the agenda of the board and otherwise control the discussion of the body which is meant to be monitoring his or her performance. The presence of an 'outsider' as non-executive chairperson helps focus the board's attention on its trustee responsibilities and enhances its capacity to intervene when necessary. Selecting a non-executive as the executive committee chairman, as GM's board did in early 1992, provides an alternative approach to the issue of sustaining outsider leadership.

Having a body composed wholly of outsiders, as the Daimler-Benz, Bayer and Philips boards are, enables their boards to focus even more resolutely on their primary mission: to serve as the central organ for review and appraisal of the enterprise objectives and its top management. The existence of a separate 'supervisory' board facilitated the replacement of the Daimler-Benz CEO in 1987 and the Philips one in 1990. The insider domination of GM's board would appear to have been a major factor inhibiting the outsiders' capacity to intervene – as they finally did in the 1992 coups that forced the resignation of the CEO chairman and a few other top GM executives and split the CEO chairman post, appointing a non-executive to the chair. The 1992 ousting of the BP CEO/chairman led to the separation of the responsibilities of the board chair from those of the CEO – a move designed to enhance the board oversight role.

Develop an internationally representative and experienced corporate executive team

Developing a more globally minded corporate executive team also fosters globalization. No one person possesses the necessary talents, perspectives and experience to run a mega-multinational without the advice and assistance of a team of peers who complement and have confidence in one another. Those multinationals that wish to ensure the necessary cross-section of international perspectives would gain by including in the executive team individuals who have multiple insights gained from a variety of job experiences. Including product, functional and area responsibilities among team members' portfolios ensures that these perspectives can be represented and reconciled from the top down.

A number of major European multinationals – especially those whose small domestic base has made them dependent on international markets – has made greater progress than Americans or Asians in internationalizing their corporate executive teams. Nestlé's eleven-member management board, which is headed by a non-Swiss, includes five nationalities: Swiss, Spanish, American, Austrian and German. The Philips group management committee includes a Norwegian, a Swiss and an American (the last of these recruited from outside Philips), who were added to the committee in the course of the 1991 major management reshuffle. P&G, eight of whose twenty-five corporate officers were born and bred outside the United States, has been one of the few American multinationals to have made significant progress in internationalizing its top executive ranks, Philip Morris is another. Sony, which promoted an American and a German to its board in 1990, is the only major Asian multinational to have made a start.

Many multinationals have internationalized the top management global outlook not only by including more foreign-born nationals in the senior ranks at country or continental and corporate levels, but also by placing a high premium on significant international experience. As will be noted later, multinationals have done this by posting promising management to a variety of international assignments and by making such international experience a prerequisite for consideration for promotion to senior levels.

Locate major divisional headquarters at the point of 'competitive advantage'

Several multinationals have improved the ability of their major operating divisions to compete by locating divisional headquarters near the major source of sales, the focus of manufacturing, or the locus of the principal competitors. This is the location that provides the maximum 'competitive advantage of area' (see Porter,

1990, for the concept of 'the competitive advantage of nations'), which derives from the stimulus of more immediate contact with changing conditions and changing strategies.

Instant communication and rapid transportation have reduced the need for proximity between the corporate headquarters and the headquarters of the major businesses. Such an organizational relocalization enables multinationals to be more truly multinational, by locating the headquarters of one or more of their businesses overseas. The headquarters of two Bayer group companies (those constituting Miles, Inc.) are in the USA. GE's international division headquarters is in London. IBM has moved the headquarters of its communication system division to the United Kingdom. The headquarters of Sony's recently acquired entertainment business has remained in the USA. The operating divisions of several multinationals, including GM, Mobil, BP and Sony, have created continental centres for coordinating their operations by continent.

Develop the strategic stewardship of common resources

The development and stewardship of a multinational's most valuable resource – its people – are too important to be left to its component parts. Capable and committed staff are too scarce for any corporation to undercut its capacity to move persons across intercorporate borders to posts where their skills are most in demand, their potential is stretched, and their opportunities for appreciating corporate diversity improved. Appreciating an organization's multidimensional complexity as a total system, and the internal and external forces driving corporate complexity and change, cannot be left to the corporate parts. To be coherent, a corporation requires a corporate-led, comprehensive approach to the management of the learning process of the organization whereby managers throughout the organization come to understand their trends and forces (see Senge, 1990:299). This requires a centralized approach not only to management education but also to recruitment, postings and promotions.

The major Asian multinationals have long stressed the holistic, recruitment-to-retirement development of the corporate man. Several European firms such as Fiat and Bayer, whose corporate-wide institutions for managing learning predated the development of their multidivisional organizations, have continued to rely on these centralized institutions. In the United States, IBM has long been notable for its corporate-wide staff development efforts. GE has become more so. But others, such as Ford and GM, have severely cut back the few interdivisional efforts they once made. The extent and focus of these staff development efforts is a concern that this chapter addresses later.

Localize lateral coordination: beyond hierarchies

A significant structural initiative that multinationals have taken to make their international operations more competitive has been the development of continental organizations that facilitate and foster cross-hierarchy collaboration. Such organizational initiatives have shaped the role and responsibilities of a continental organization, affected the role and relationships of the international affiliates, and led to efforts to develop systems that are multidimensionally compatible.

Develop and clarify the role of continental centres

Developing and clarifying the cross-hierarchy, concerting role of continental organizations enhance a multinational's territorial capacity to harmonize and rationalize its multiple corporate efforts. Western Europe and North America have become increasingly economically integrated economies, in which efforts to reduce custom and other national barriers have generally been more successful than the GATT-orchestrated, world-wide ones. Asian/Pacific countries have begun to follow their example. The EC progress toward economic and political unity has led many multinationals to establish or strengthen continent-wide coordinating organizations. The more progress continental neighbours make toward achieving economic integration, the greater the need for such continent-wide coordination. American multinationals such as IBM and 3M have long depended upon continental organizations. BP and Sony are examples of multinationals which have more recently developed such centres. Such continental entities serve to link the global operating divisions with the local affiliates, to rationalize their manufacturing, to enhance their R&D, and to augment their human resources, public affairs and other management support efforts on a continent-wide basis.

The responsibilities of multinational continental centres have varied depending upon their role. The IBM continental organization manages the sales-focused country affiliates and coordinates the continent-rationalized manufacturing facilities. The Sony continental organization manages the country sales affiliates and supports the continental efforts of Sony's production-focused business groups. Du Pont's continental organizations are essentially comprehensive staff support centres. BP's provide a regional corporate presence. The more diversified the multinational's businesses, the more difficult to develop continental organizations with a comprehensive coordinative role.

Several factors will affect the development of the continental centres. These include the extent of expertise required to support national operations and the extent of economic integration of the countries. Many continental and sub-continental centres may more closely manage smaller country operations which cannot support more specialized expertise. Many multinationals may continue to organize the marketing of some products (that is, industrial ones) by continent, and the marketing of others (that is, the more general consumer ones) by country. Other multinationals may wish to adopt a somewhat incremental, *ad hoc* approach to testing the adjustment of its continental/national mix. Thus, many diversified multinationals may require a continental coordination centre with maximum flexibility, capable of providing a high degree of support to some national affiliates for some products while providing more opportunities for local initiatives and local variations to others.

Some multinationals may find it useful to create regional (or multicountry) offices as BP and IBM have done. Such offices provide the opportunity to focus on the particular needs of a subcontinent or region (such as Eastern Europe, Latin America or South Asia). They also provide a means to group smaller countries so that they can be handled more effectively and economically. The development of regional teams may erode the need for fully staffed country offices in smaller countries.

Support country corporate coherency

Maintaining and sustaining, within each country in which a multinational operates, a corporate presence capable of orchestrating corporate-wide hierarchy coordination would enhance concerted usage of common resources and coordinated focus on local customers, and thus improved corporate coherency at the local level. While intercontinental and intracontinental economic integration have shaped continental organizations, so has transnationalization reshaped the role, responsibilities and relationships of the country affiliates. The omnibus country affiliate with unified management, which so dominated the first half of the twentieth century, has become rarer and rarer – preserved only by a few multinationals such as Royal Dutch/Shell.

The globalization of the corporate operating divisions has fractured or fragmented country corporate operations, and the enlargement of the role of many continental organizations to include the rationalization of manufacturing and the direction of industrial and professional marketing – as well as the coordination of country consumer marketing – has changed the concept of the country affiliate. As a consequence, relatively few multinationals have the capacity at the country level to concert their divided resources upon ongoing operations or emerging opportunities.

The role of national affiliates will continue to be affected not only by the degree to which their national economies have become integrated into a larger inter-dependent community, but also by the size and significance of the national economy of which they are part, and the extent to which the multinational has developed its markets and facilities in that country. What is evident, though, is that nation-states will retain some political and economic autonomy, and that their residents will retain distinct customs and tastes for decades to come. The concept of nationalism, while only a few centuries old, is so fundamentally established that no supranational power will overpower it in the foreseeable future. The EC and other suprasovereign institutions, along with the multinationals, will erode the concept of sovereignty, but they will not eradicate long-established national pride and preferences. The need for a coherent national presence will continue. A strategically capable country presence would appreciate country customs and local conditions and provide a focal point of contact for national interests. At a minimum, a multinational would benefit by having a Mr/Ms GE or Mr/Ms Exxon, a Mr/Ms Philips or Mr/Ms Shell, a Mr/Ms Mitsui or a Mr/Ms Samsung in every country in which it does business.

An effective way to ensure the consideration of a country perspective and present a coherent face at the country level is to include all of a multinational's country operations within a single organizational framework. Such a national organization might be a loose agglomeration led by senior managers designated as national executives (the GE model), a confederation led by a team with a spokesperson (the Bayer model), the more closely associated Philips model, the federated 3M model, or the unified Shell model.

Selecting a model requires careful consideration of just what needs to be synchronized at the country level and which support services, such as human resources, finance, information services and public affairs, can be advantageously shared among the business units. At a minimum, there needs to be country representation which ensures a coherent public and governmental interface. More advantageously, a general-purpose national affiliate may serve as the new business development and consumer marketing affiliate for all the product divisions, thus enabling the office to be more customer-oriented and more flexible in shifting human and other resources as needed.

Thus the role of the country general manager as team leader may vary from that of a representative head to a weak or strong coordinative head, depending on the extent of diversification and self-sufficiency of the product and functional hierarchies. The role would be strengthened with control of the local management support services, the opportunity to review and reward performance and request the recall of team members for whose performance he or she would be responsible, and rank commensurate with his or her oversight responsibilities. Team members would work with their product and functional counterparts at continental or world headquarters as well as with the country general manager. The relative importance of these ties in the multidimensional global organization would vary according to conditions and circumstances – including the extent of corporate diversification, and the nature of the issue.

Develop cross-hierarchy, compatible systems and processes

Developing corporate-wide, compatible systems is necessary for the collecting and conveying of information vital for planning, programming and evaluating corporate projects. Cross-hierarchy coordination of efforts at the continental and country levels requires not only that these organizations be well led, but also that such leaders be well fed with the information regarding capital and operating budgets, management performance and potential, sales performance and projections, manufacturing input and output, and product development.

Coherency and strategic capability at continental and country levels requires inter-divisional as well as intra-divisional compatibility of information systems. Lack of compatibility not only frustrates interdivisional comparisons and collaboration but also retards and increases the cost of reorganization initiatives.

One of the major goals of the ICI reorganization has been the alignment of the information systems so that the territorial organization may more effectively support them. To the extent that the various international management teams and general managers are expected to provide cohesive leadership, they need the support of management systems which generate the information they need to access, plan and implement coordinated programmes.

Develop linchpin managers: beyond specialization

While well-shared values and well-built structures are indispensable to coherent and competitive organizations, they are ineffective without the managers who serve as the structural linchpins and culture carriers. The larger and more complex the organization, the more critical the management development process. Successful lateral as well as vertical collaboration, cross-border team efforts, and collegial styles at multiple levels rely upon a corps of managers who possess not only the requisite technical skills but also the interpersonal ones indispensable for teams sharing responsibility.

As multinationals have become more complex, management leaders have had to rely less on their authority to command and more on their general ability to work with and secure 'buy-in' from their colleagues. To thrive, mega-multinationals require management leaders capable of what Burns has described as 'the reciprocal process of mobilizing, by persons with certain motives and values, various economic, political, and other resources, in a context of competition and conflict, in order to realize goals independently or mutually held by both leaders and followers' (1978:425). To fulfil this mobilizing mission in the mosaic-like environment of diversified multinationals requires leaders capable of integrating the diverse product, function and national perspectives driving the corporate parts, reconciling the long-term and short-term goals, and accommodating global direction with local discretion. Effective leaders of complex organizations rely upon teams and networks that encompass the multiple dimensions of multinational systems. Team members and leaders share power not only vertically with those to and for whom they are responsible, but also laterally with those in positions to facilitate integrating product, area and functional efforts. Most critically, such leaders courageously and competently take responsibility in situations in which they do not have commensurate 'authority'.

Such effective multinational managers require a host of interdependent qualities. They need to be able to conceptualize ideas that exploit opportunities by integrating diverse strengths, and to coordinate and mobilize action by the complementary (yet competing) parts of the organization. And they need to cultivate and celebrate the corporate strengths – most notably its people – by appreciating them, developing them to their fullest potential, and focusing their use for maximum advantage. The very scope of qualities required suggests the value of teamwork and leadership.

To secure such leadership, multinationals have stepped up their efforts not only to develop managers capable of successfully participating in and teaching teams, but also to support such managers with systems which sustain such teams and their leadership. A number of multinationals have established practices which have generated a steady stream of candidates for their international manager posts. These initiatives have included not only recruiting career beginners and promoting from within, but also instilling in them from the outset a multidimensional appreciation of the corporate philosophy and practices. These initiatives have also emphasized interdivisional and international experience, enabled them by making relevant information accessible and stressing evaluations by team colleagues as well as 'bosses' – thus encouraging teamworking and networking, and placing a high priority on collegial efforts in the evaluation, compensation and promotion processes. Especially noteworthy initiatives are those that foster not only the development of home country nationals but also those from throughout the world.

Career-long management development

Career-long management development which embraces not only hiring career beginners and promoting managers from within, but also cross-border posting and recruitment-to-retirement, off-the-job learning opportunities, provides multinationals with the opportunity to develop an executive corps educated and experienced in the multifaceted complexity of a multinational's mosaic of parts. In filling their management posts, mega-multinationals generally select from among those whom they have earlier recruited directly from university (or from entry positions in other firms), and who have proven themselves in earlier postings. A few multinationals apply the hire-from-university and promote-from-within principles with rigour. Without exception the major Asian multinationals have long applied this principle to their own nationals, on whom they have long relied upon for filling not only the top corporate but also most overseas ones. A few companies, such as IBM and P&G, apply this principle with zeal in their recruitment and management promotion practices throughout the world. In fact, the zeal with which these principles are applied appears to be in direct proportion to the extent to which a multinational appreciates, articulates and advances value-sharing as a means of developing a more coherent and more competitive organization.

Tremendous investments of time, energy and foresight are required to recruit today for the management leadership that will be needed in one to four years, and in ten to forty years. The world will change, multinationals will change, those recruited will change and many will depart. Nevertheless, the practice of such a policy provides the most pragmatic means of developing management leaders – from the broad diversity of educational and national backgrounds required in a modern multinational – with an appreciation of the integrity of the corporate mission and vision, the interdependence of the corporate parts, and the importance of working in a collegial manner across hierarchical borders in order to maximize corporate advantages.

A career-long policy provides multinationals with the opportunity to give promising future general managers the broadening education and experiences that will test their ability to develop into the multidimensional managers needed in the coming decades. A career-long policy allows a manager to develop a variety of perspectives from which to build an encompassing vision, to establish an extensive network of alliances throughout the multinational, and to enhance his or her ability to work in power-sharing situations. Hiring young and promoting from within may appear to be a policy that only the larger multinationals can afford. The question that needs to be addressed, though, is whether multinationals can afford the risk of not having a sufficient pool of managers who already know 'who's who around here', 'the way we do things around here', and 'how to find their way around here'.

Educate managers for transborder leadership roles

To improve coherency at all levels, many multinationals have significantly increased their management programmes for developing the integrative and interpersonal skills necessary for the cross-border networking and team leading essential for mobilizing direction from diversity. Developing managers who can integrate processes, share responsibility and lead teams requires continuing education, focusing on broadening corporate perspectives and improving interpersonal leadership skills. The need for perspective-enhancing, power-sharing and process-meshing managers has an obvious corollary. With the need to reconcile so many perspectives, multinationals – more than most corporations – need to 'train and retrain':

> Work-force training and constant retraining – and the larger idea of the work force as an appreciating (or depreciating) package of appropriate (or inappropriate) skills – must climb to the top of the agenda of the individual firm [. . .] Value added will increasingly come through people [. . .]. Only highly skilled – that is trained and continuously retrained – people will be able to add value. (Peters, 1987:323)

As important as this point is for the workforce as a whole, it magnifies when applied to developing the managerial conceptual insights, interpersonal skills, and appreciation of corporate vision and values so vital to the art of transborder leadership. To cultivate such leadership many multinationals now invest far more in developing managers with the leadership skills required to serve not only as 'culture carriers' and 'role models' but also as consensus-formulators and 'change-facilitators' throughout the organization. No responsibility is more crucial to corporate-wide collaboration than that of managers from top down not only to espouse but also to practise the participation leadership styles that need to be cultivated. This requires not only corporate leadership initiatives to clarify corporate styles and values, but also increasing efforts to sponsor corporate-led education efforts to bring together managers from throughout the organization in order to cultivate shared values and bonding.

A number of European and American as well as Asian firms have stressed their education efforts by developing programmes that promote leadership skills and their companies' distinctive culture. They include GE's 'Work-out' and 'Best practices' programmes, IBM's cluster management, 3M's 'Leadership for growth' and Fiat's 'Capacità di Comunicazione'.

Efforts to break down the walls dividing multinationals require that management education efforts focus not only on updating their managers on changing environment and changing technology, but also on broadening their awareness of what the overall corporate objectives are, how the various parts complement one another, who the persons are with whom one can develop working relationships and networks of influences, and what they share. Education efforts focused on developing managers as part of a corporate-wide team are an indispensable means of developing their ability to look for the larger picture so vital to successful teamwork. They extend corporate contacts and develop border-transcending networks, especially if the programmes mix (selected) managers throughout the multinational. Such sessions help prevent 'in-basket-itis' (management's most prevalent disease). By helping managers take their eyes away from their 'in-basket' long enough to consider in a broader perspective what the most critical issues are which need to be addressed – by the company, their units or themselves – they also provide a means of preparing managers for new assignments, whose responsibilities may differ significantly from those in their current posts.

Ensure a variety of cross-border 'stretching' assignments

Providing promising managers with a variety of challenging cross-hierarchy postings helps them appreciate the variety of perspectives so essential for multinational management. Many multinationals already adhere to a policy of encouraging broadening interdivisional and international assignments for promising managers. P&G's country- and continental-category managers have all had multiple country experience. IBM managers have moved so often that they claim IBM means 'I've been moved.' Bayer managers must have had experience outside their home division and their home country in order to advance to senior grades. The most promising Mitsui managers develop a resumé that includes a posting as an assistant to a member of the corporate executive teams, an overseas assignment, and participation in an international executive education programme. Matsushita has just introduced a plan to send 100 of its most promising non-Japanese managers to Japan for one year. Royal Dutch/Shell and Nestlé have developed an international corps on which they depend not only for filling strategic international assignments, but also for nurturing the corporate ideology within the various national companies.

Many navies have a policy that no line officer may be considered for the rank of admiral until he has commanded a ship. Multinationals would gain from a similar policy: that no manager could aspire to a top management position without having had at least one assignment outside his or her home country and home division.

Particularly stretching would be an experience in developing a new venture; often heard is the comment that 'entrepreneurial opportunity was the most successful learning experience of my career' (interview, Art Davie, 19 June 1989). Such stretching assignments are especially vital for those managers whom multinationals have tentatively selected for developing and testing for senior posts. Such efforts confront the issue of length of assignments and extent of variety.

Managers may move so often that they do not appreciate the nuances of businesses they are managing, and do not 'develop the deep business knowledge they need to discuss technology options, competitors, strategies, and global opportunities substantively' (Hamel and Prahalad, 1989:74), thus avoiding making investments that do not promise a quick return. A number of steps may be necessary to counter this 'fast-move' syndrome. One would be to lengthen most assignments – as Mitsui has from 'about three' to 'about five' years. Another is to develop systems of performance evaluation that provide the opportunity to recognize and reward longer-term contribution.

Embrace diversity and corporate-wide management development efforts

Encouraging the development of managers from a broad diversity of national and professional backgrounds assures the interaction of perspectives essential for innovative and entrepreneurial management. Increasingly, multinationals recognize that for global synergy they require a heterogeneous mix of managers. This means they can no longer focus their concern for recruitment, management education and management postings on their home country nationals or on their core occupation professionals to the extent that many have. The efforts that P&G initiated post-World War II to recruit, post and promote non-Americans as well as Americans has helped it develop a corporate management of whom more than 30 per cent are foreign born and more than 60 per cent, including the CEO, have foreign experience. ICI has raised the percentage of non-British in executive positions to almost 50 per cent. To undertake such global management development efforts requires a cohesive, corporate-wide approach.

Select and monitor especially promising managers

Many multinationals, including Exxon, Royal Dutch/Shell, IBM and Mitsui, have centrally coordinated programmes for identifying and nurturing especially promising managers. Headquarters management resource offices not only provide coordinated direction to corporate executive evaluation and development efforts, but also arrange individual mentors who guide, counsel, criticize and defend assigned younger colleagues. The mentors' role has been enhanced when they are not in the direct chain of command.

With overseas posting such mentors are indispensable. These postings are often stressful, given the need to adjust to different country cultures (and perhaps different divisional cultures if the multinational has not been successful in establishing an overall one). International assignments are even more stressful when those assigned overseas believe they have been forgotten and passed by at home – and their repatriation experience proves that their fears were justified. Many executives have found repatriation to be even more stressful than expatriation. The provision of mentors helps. More important would be a more ubiquitous appreciation of the world-wide activities of the various parts of the multinationals.

Empower three-dimensional teams and leaders: beyond committees and matrices

To lead strategically coherent organizations, a multinational needs not only to secure power-sharing managers capable of orchestrating complexity, but also to provide them with the support they require to promote collegial interaction among the various staff support and operating hierarchies. The multiplicity of geographic, product and functional chains of command and communication form a three-dimensional maze of relationships that generates overlapping vertical hierarchies and innumerable horizontal and diagonal relationships among hierarchies.

For such complexity there are no simple solutions. Wishing for simplicity does not transform reality. Attempting to implement organizational strategies that ignore the importance of any one perspective or any one corporate part denies a multinational the opportunity to exploit its resources to their full potential. To coordinate cross-efforts, multinationals have used committees, matrices and teams. An increasing number of multinationals have embraced the concept of teams, which evokes the image of a group of players with specialized roles working together to win a common objective. To enable teams to win, though, requires sufficient coherence and sense of common direction to coordinate complex diversity. For teams to develop such coherence and direction, they need consistent multinational efforts to provide the resources, the rewards and the corporate backing, as well as the shared values, to support the team leadership required to enhance coherence and commitment to team efforts.

Supporting teamwork with sufficient resources

Effective teams need to be not only well led but also well fed with several types of resources. One type of support would be a minimal budget for continuing staff support and new initiatives that do not only clearly fall within one team member's responsibility. The efforts of a team and its captain would be assisted by a team 'adjutant' with a clearly transborder focus on a common agenda of decisions and follow-up actions. Such assistance would facilitate team meetings, improve teamwork, and increase the prospects of the various team players carrying out their part of the team mission. Such an assignment would provide an aspiring manager with a challenging 'stretching' experience.

Another type of critical support that would facilitate the efforts to achieve teamwork would be providing the team and their leaders with the information to plan, coordinate and evaluate their cross-border efforts. To do this, they require access to pertinent budget, personnel, product development, marketing and other information; and they need such information in a form that is comparable throughout the units involved in the team efforts. The development of such compatible systems was an integral part of the 1991 ICI reorganization – and a significant part of the projected $500 million reorganization cost.

A key element in strengthening the capacity of the teamwork would be providing the team leaders with a significant role in the performance review process and in the assignment of members into and out of the team. Providing a team leader with the right to request the reassignment of a member of the team strengthens the team leader's hand and the prospects of achieving 'buy-in' from the team members. As described earlier, such an arrangement strengthens the Sony Europe head, most of whose principal colleagues' operational reporting relationships are to their headquarters in Japan – not to him.

Support a shift to power-sharing with systems that reward teamwork

As multinationals move, and encourage their managers to move, towards more reliance on teams and responsibility-sharing as a means of integrating perspectives and increasing transborder collaboration, they face the problems long endured by committees and matrices. The delays can be long and costly. Many may not 'buy-in' to compromise and avoid the responsibility for implementing the decision. To many managers, whose traditional powers have been curtailed, to be told to continue to achieve results by exercising leadership and empowering people appears to be at best a placebo and at worst a top management 'cop-out' – and thus a cruel hoax. Power-sharing poses special difficulties for those who have long valued bold decisions and decisive actions.

Calls for more team participation and power-sharing would be more creditable and more viable if accompanied by continuing efforts to support and sustain team leaders. To support the shift to teamwork, multinationals need to develop mechanisms for measuring and rewarding group as well as individual performance. Such efforts require creatively developing the means of crediting team participants for their share in successful team efforts, with rewards such as pay increases, bonuses, promotions and choice assignments. Successful multinationals will continue to seek more effective ways of recognizing and rewarding collegial cooperation and cross-border commitment to corporate-wide efforts.

Provide team leaders with top-down and bottom-up support

To be effective, team leaders require not only team resources and rewards and leadership skills, but also the position, prestige and clear support of top management. Seniority in grade and experience, as well as a proven track record, provide a team leader with a clear advantage in conducting a team effort, especially one involving a diversity of participants. More important, a team leader's capacity to obtain consensus and commitment may depend on the awareness – on the part of team members as well as of the leader – that the team leader has corporate support that may be invoked when and where needed. The knowledge that such support is available is generally sufficient; such power seldom needs to be used.

To ensure such corporate support for cross-hierarchy teams, teamwork and team leaders requires well-established means of ensuring oversight and support of those whose perspectives are not protected and promoted by various corporate hierarchies. Thus, multinationals that are organized by product need to support functional and territorial lines of communication and oversight; those organized by function need to support product and territorial lines; and those that continue to be organized by area need functional and product oversight.

Such lines of communication would be especially effective if they extended up to and into the corporate executive team, with one or more members having area portfolios. With the rapid shift away from area-divided and area-driven organizations and the consequent threat to area-wide coherence, the presence of an area-focused line of communication extending from a country to a continent to the corporate executive team would enhance the prospects for supporting country-wide and continent-wide presence and coordination of corporate interests and initiatives.

But by far the most important support that leaders require is the bottom-up support not only of team members but also of all those whose participation is required to make cross-border action work. This depends on the continued cultivation of shared values, upon which the development of cross-border initiatives depends. Transcontinental enterprises will strengthen their competitive advantage only when and if employees throughout the organization develop a sense of extended family that fosters 'buy-in' and commitment. The most successful multinationals – the best of the best – will attract and keep the best global talent by creating an interactive, international and interdivisional sense of belonging within the transcontinental enterprise.

Thriving on multidimensional diversity and complexity, with well-led teams providing coherent direction

The present challenge of globalization and localization forces multinationals to find more effective ways to utilize the three dynamics of structure, staffing and shared values to orchestrate the three perspectives – geographic, product and functional –

more effectively (see Figure 9.3). The segregation of international operations from domestic ones has not supported globalized strategies; and the segregation of product lines – or of functional processes – has not allowed for the localized coordination of efforts.

The modular framework for a more strategically coherent organization that this agenda has outlined has been developed with one overall objective clearly in mind: to resolve the global–local dilemma so that the global organization may have the power to exert the coherent advantage of the interdependence of the diverse parts, and also that the local parts may be empowered to exercise the advantage of significant independence. Just as the ferment of reorganization in the early decades of the twentieth century led to the development of two-dimensional-type organizations, so the ferment of reorganization that multinationals are undertaking in the last decade of the century appears headed toward creating a new form of three-dimensional organization. In this process, the more pioneering, innovative efforts have frequently been those initiated by the multinationals that perceived their threats and opportunities most clearly; thus there is often a leapfrog syndrome, with those that appear 'best organized and most successful' one year trying to catch up a few years later (Peters, 1987:3–4).

The multinationals' profiles presented in this comparative book demonstrate the variety of steps being undertaken to meet the organizational challenge. Some of the

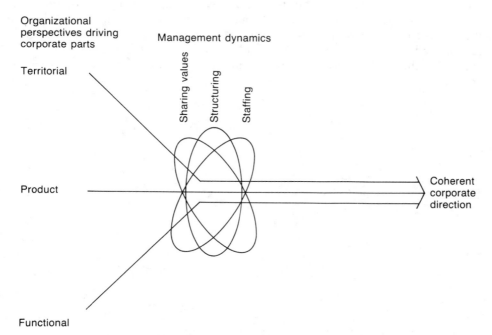

Figure 9.3 Reorganization for coherent corporate direction: three sets of management dynamics concerting three sets of organizational perspectives

organizational steps which multinationals have taken have appeared more cautious and more piecemeal than others, but the cumulative impact of these transitional efforts, as they have been adapted to existing corporate traditions, has already begun to point to some characteristics that future mega-multinationals may share. The more farsighted multinationals have begun developing their organizational strategy for the twenty-first century. Their leaders are focusing on who and what they want their organizations to be, how to foster transitions that build on their traditional strength in order to transform their present organization, and how to mobilize the bias for action required to transform an organization. The global moves tend to be ones which look to more consistency in the way the multinationals manage their domestic and international operations. The purpose of the agenda presented in this chapter has been to assist multinational executives in the process of envisioning their future organizational system. While multinationals differ dramatically, a number of the converging practices noted in the book have sufficiently proved their value to be especially worthy of consideration.

The vital ingredient of managing multinational globalization is leadership: not only transformation leadership to introduce and implement change, but also transnational leadership to make the complex organization work. Leadership provides the catalytic magic mobilizing the organizational dynamics essential for developing and implementing global strategy.

As multinationals prepare for the twenty-first century, the major ones have already embarked on radical transformations. Mounting global pressures will force others to follow them. Energetic multinationals will depend upon management leaders who can clearly outline what needs to be done and who can mobilize others to help lead the way. The more successful multinationals will be led by those who appreciate the merit of diversity and the inevitability of complexity and thrive on change.

Sources and methodology

This comparative endeavour has relied on a number of mutually supportive sources of information. A number of earlier studies, especially those by Chandler, have contributed to the insights from which have evolved the themes developed in this study. So have numerous books, articles, items of corporate literature (including annual reports and interviews); they have provided the basic sources of information which have supported the themes developed in this book.

The development of the multinational case studies, which provide the basic factual background supporting the major points advanced in the book, began with the design of a questionnaire and continued with the preparation of approximately 100 corporate profiles. Preliminary work was followed by intensive interviews with international managers.

Several factors have affected the choice of the multinationals whose corporate case studies form the major part of this book. The book focuses on 25 of the 50 largest (by sales) corporations in the world, not only because their size has magnified the issues the book is intended to consider but also to reduce the opportunity that random selection might prejudice my sample. Within this group I have focused on those multinationals whose primary business(es) were in one of the five major industries of the Global 50 – motor vehicles, electronics (and computers), petroleum, chemicals, and food (including soaps and cosmetics). I have included multinationals from each country represented in the Global 50 (except for Venezuela whose entry is government owned), fourteen of the top fifteen Global 50 (except IRI which is government owned), and a cross-section of distinctive organizational types. I have added the trading company Mitsui and Co., because it represented unusual features that add to the overall understanding of multinational globalization and localization. The profiles, as presented, thus include a cross-section of the world's largest industrial corporations by country and industry.

Those who have been interviewed included W.E. Berghmans, Steve Brown, William Bumpas, Steven Burke, Jan F.M. Candries, John Carrier, Young M. Chang, I.C.B. Clark, Dirk Craen, Arthur J. Davie, James C. Dess, Charles De Meyer, Pierre De Potter, Johan E. De Schrijver, John Egbers, Harald Einsmann, Eugene Foley, Stephen Fox, Toru Fukui, Dr Hanns R. Glatz, Mitsuya Goto, Eurfyl

375

ap Gwilym, Peter Ham, Dan Hamer, Andrew C. Harper, Dr John N. Horner, Dennis Ibarra, Tetsuro Inaji, Adriana Izvanario, Charles A. Johnson, Katsuhiko Kamazawa, Shoji Kato, Hyun-Mo Kim, P.J. Kohnstamm, Kees Kronbeen, John D. Largent, Dr Bruno Link, Desmond MacAllister, Paul Maglione, William Mainguy, Patrick Merckx, Takeshi Mitari, Setsuo Mizoguchi, John Muilenberg, Ryuji Muroya, Sean Murray, Kuni Nakae, Takashi Ohde, Antje Ostkamp, Takashi Osawa, Sabine Roobroeck, Dr Salvatore Rossetti di Valdalbero, Jack J. Schmuckli, F. Schuitema, Teruo Shimizu, Soung-Hoon Shin, Warren Shull, Dudley Smith, Noriuki Tagaki, Charles Thurlow, Hiroyuki Toda, Yasuki Ueno, Maria Vannoten, André Van Roi, David E. Veitch, C.P. Vlahodimos, Roland Wagner, John Weber, Tim Williamson, Alvin Wolf, Hachiro Yoshida and Basil Zirinis.

Many students, who were multinational executives or interns at the time of their studies, prepared background papers. These included José Bellod, Dimitri Boon, Marcel Bos, Karl Brauckmann, Paul Defraeye, Didier De Smedt, Jozef Doppler, Vassilios Fourlis, Sabine L. Gilette, Joëlle Glore, Patrick Henkes, A. René den Hertog, Diana Ibarra, Pradeep Jacob, Robin Lockerman, Patrick Merckx, Izabella Nowotny, Jozef Pieters, Cheryl Sedlacek, Frank Schoonbaert, Robert Vanderdonk, and Gus Weiss. Without their contributions this book would not have been possible.

Bibliography

Aaker, David, A. (1991), *Managing Brand Equity*, Hickman, NY: Free Press.

Abegglen, J.C. and Stalk, G. (1985), *The Japanese Organization: Aspects of its social organization*, New York: Free Press.

Aguilar, F.J. (1967), *Scanning the Business Environment*, New York: Macmillan.

Aguilar, F.J. and Hamermesh, R. (1981a), *General Electric: Strategic position – 1981*, Boston, MA: Harvard Business School, 381–174.

Aguilar, F.J. and Hamermesh, R. (1981b), *General Electric: Business development*, Boston, MA: Harvard Business School, 387–092.

Aitken, T. (1973), *The Multinational Man*, New York: John Wiley.

Alcatel Way (1990), Spring, 11.

Aldrich, H.E. (1979), *Organizations and Environments*, Englewood Cliffs, NJ: Prentice-Hall.

Allen, G.C. (1990), 'The concentration of economic control', in E.B. Schumpeter (ed.), *The Industrialization of Japan and Manchuko*, New York: Macmillan.

Allen, R.F. (1985), 'Four phases for bringing about cultural change', in Ralph H. Kilmann, Mary J. Sexton, Roy Serpa and Associates, *Gaining Control of the Corporate Culture*, San Francisco: Jossey-Bass.

Allen, R. F. and Kraft, C. (1982), *The Organizational Unconscious*, Englewood Cliffs, NJ: Prentice-Hall.

Almond, G.A. and Verba, S. (1963), *The Civic Culture: Political attitudes and democracy in five nations*, Princeton, NJ: Princeton University Press.

Ancona, D. and David, N.A. (1989), 'Top hats and executive tales: describing the senior management team', *Sloan Management Review*, Fall, 19–28.

Andrews, C. (1980), *The Concept of Strategy*, Homewood, IL: R.D.Irwin.

Aoki, S. (1980), *The Crisis of the Nissan Group*, Tokyo: Chobunsha.

Aoki, S. (1981), *Secrets of the Nissan S-Organization*, Tokyo: Chobunsha.

Applegate, L.M., Cash, J.I., Jr., and Mills, D.Q. (1988), 'Information technology and tomorrow's manager', *Harvard Business Review*, November–December, 128–36.

Ardagh, J. (1987), *France Today*, London: Penguin.

Ardagh, J. (1988), *Germany and the Germans*, London: Penguin.

Artzt, E.L. (1990), *Strategies for Global Growth*, Cincinnati: Procter & Gamble.

Asea Brown Bovori (1989), *Annual Report 1989*, Zurich.

Bacharach, S.B. and Lawler, E.J. (1981), *Power and Politics in Organizations*, San Francisco: Jossey-Bass.

Badaracco, J.L. and Ellsworth, R.R. (1989), *Leadership and the Quest for Integrity*, Boston, MA: Harvard Business School Press.

Bairati, P. (1983), *Vittorio Valletta*, Turin: UTET.

Baliga, G.M. and Baker, J.C. (1985), 'Multinational corporate policies for expatriate managers: selection, training, evaluation', *Advanced Management Journal*, 50, 31–8.

Barnard, C.I. (1968), *The Functions of the Executive*, 30th anniversary edn., Cambridge, MA: Harvard University Press.

Barnes, I. and Preston, J. (1988), *The European Community: Key issues in economics and business*, London: Longman.

Barnett, R.J. and Muller, R.E. (1974), *Global Reach: The power of multinational corporations*, New York: Simon & Schuster.

Barsoux, J.L. and Lawrence, P. (1990), *Management in France*, London: Cassell.

Bartlett, C.A. (1981), 'Multinational structural change: evolution versus reorganization', in L. Otterbeck (ed.), *The Management of Headquarters: Subsidiary relationships in multinational corporations*, Aldershot: Gower.

Bartlett, C.A. (1982), 'How multinational organizations evolve', *Journal of Business Strategy*, 3, 20–32.

Bartlett, C.A. (1983), 'MNCs: get off the reorganization merry-go-round', *Harvard Business Review*, March–April, 138–46.

Bartlett, C.A. (1986), 'Building and managing the transnational: the new organizational challenge', in M.E. Porter (ed.), *Competition in Global Industries*, Boston, MA: Harvard Business School Press.

Bartlett, C.A., Doz, Y. and Hedlund, G. (eds.) (1990), *Managing the Global Firm*, London: Routledge.

Bartlett, C.A. and Ghoshal, S. (1989), *Managing Across Borders: The transnational solution*, Boston, MA: Harvard Business School.

Bartlett, C.A. and Yoshihara, H. (1988), 'New challenges for Japanese multinationals: is organization adaptation their Achilles' heel?', *Human Resource Management*, 27, 19–43.

Barzini, L. (1983), *The Europeans*, New York: Simon & Schuster.

Bass, B.M. and Burger, P.C. (1979), *Assessment of Managers: An international comparison*, New York: Free Press.

Bayer (1988), *Annual Report 1988*, Leverkusen.

Beckhard, R. and Harris, R.T. (1987), *Organizational Transitions: Managing complex change*, Reading, MA: Addison-Wesley.

Beer, M. (1980), *Organization Change and Development: A systems view*, Santa Monica, CA: Goodyear.

Behrman, J.N. and Fischer, W.A. (1980), *Overseas R&D Activities of Trans-national Companies*, Cambridge, MA: Oelgeschlager, Gunn & Hain.

Bennis, W. (1966), *Changing Organizations*, New York: McGraw-Hill.

Bennis, W. (1969), *Organization Development: Its nature, origins, and prospects*, Reading, MA: Addison-Wesley.

Bennis, W. and Nanus, B. (1985), *Leaders: The strategies for taking charge*, New York: Harper & Row.

Bettinger, C. (1989), 'Use corporate culture to trigger high performance', *Journal of Business Strategy*, March/April, 38–42.

Beyer, J.M. and Trice, H. (1978), *Implementing Change*, New York: Free Press.

Blau, J. and Schoenherr, R.A. (1971), *The Structure of Organizations*, New York: Basic Books.

Bledstein, B.S. (1976), *The Culture of Professionalism*, New York: W.W. Norton.

Bolman, L.G. and Deal, T.E. (1984), *Modern Approaches to Understanding and Managing Organizations*, San Francisco: Jossey-Bass.

Book of Vital World Statistics (1990), London: The Economist Publications/Hutchinson.

Boorstin, D.J. (1973), *The Americans: The democratic experience*, New York: Random House.

Boyacigiler, N. (1990), 'The role of expatriates in the management of interdependence, complexity, and risk in multinational corporations', *Journal of International Business Studies*, 21, 357–81.

Brislin, R.W., Bochner, S. and Lonner, W.J. (1975), *Cross Cultural Perspectives on Learning*, New York: John Wiley.

British Petroleum (1977), *Our Industry: Petroleum*, 5th edn., London: British Petroleum.

Brooke, M.Z. (1986), *International Management: A review of strategies*, London: Hutchinson.

Brooke, M.Z. and Remmers, H.L. (eds.) (1977), *The International Firm: A study of management and across frontiers*, London: Pitman.

Brooke, M.Z. and Remmers, H.L. (1978a), *International Management and Business Policy*, Boston, MA: Houghton-Mifflin.

Brooke, M.Z. and Remmers, H.L. (1978b), *The Strategy of Multinational Enterprise*, London: Pitman.

Buchholz, R.A., Evans, W.D. and Wagley, R.A. (1985), *Management Response to Public Issues: Concepts and cases in strategy formulation*, Englewood Cliffs, NJ: Prentice-Hall.

Buckley, P.J. (1985), *The Economic Theory of the Multinational Enterprise*, New York: St Martins Press.

Buckley, P.J. and Cason, M. (1976), *The Future of the Multinational Enterprise*, London: Macmillan.

Burke, W.W. (1982), *Organization Development: Principles and practices*, Boston, MA: Little, Brown.

Burmeister, I. (1980), *These Strange German Ways*, 14th edn., Hamburg: Atlantik-Brucke.

Burns, J.M. (1978), *Leadership*, New York: Harper & Row.

Burns, T.J. (1989), 'Tests to target dependability', *Nation's Business*, March, 26–29.

Burstein, D. (1988), *Yen*, New York: Fawcett Columbine.

Business International Corporation (1970), *Organizing the Worldwide Corporation*, New York: Business International Corporation.

Business International Corporation (1976), *Designing the International Corporate Organization*, New York: Business International Corporation.

Business International Corporation (1979), 'Strategic planning for multinational corporations', New York: Business International Corporation.

Business International Corporation (1981), *New Directions in Multinational Corporate Organization*, New York: Business International Corporation.

Business International Corporation (1982), *World-wide Executive Compensation and Human Resource Planning*, New York: Business International Corporation.

Business International Corporation (1987), 'Restructuring and turnaround: experiences in corporate renewal', Geneva: Business International Corporation.

Business International Corporation (1990a), 'Managing today's international company', New York: Business International Corporation.

Business International Corporation (1990b), 'Organizing for international competitiveness', New York: Business International Corporation.

Business Week International (1988), 'Nissan is going native in Newcastle', 16 May.

Business Week International (1989a), 'Is the boss getting paid too much?', 1 May, 42–8.

Business Week International (1989b), 'Masters of innovation: how 3M keeps its new products coming', 10 April, 34–9.

Business Week International (1990a), 'War, recession and gas hikes: GM's turn around will have to wait', 4 February, 42–4.

Business Week International (1990b), 'Mighty Mitsubishi', 24 September, 38–41.

Butler, S. (1990), 'Cutting down and reshaping the core', *Financial Times*, 20 March, 22.

Calingaert, M. (1988), *The 1992 Challenge from Europe: Development of the European Community's internal market*, Washington, DC: National Planning Association.

Campbell, A., Devine, M. and Young, D. (1990), *A Sense of Mission*, London: Hutchinson.

Canon (1989), *The Canon Story, 1988–89*, Tokyo: Canon.

Caryle, R.E. (1988), 'Managing IS at multinationals', *Datamation*, 1 March, 54–66.

Casse, P. (1982), *Training for the Multicultural Manager*, Washington, DC: The Society for Intercultural Education, Training, and Research.

Chakvavarty, S. (1990), 'Philip Morris is still hungry', *Forbes*, 2 April, 96–101.

Chandler, A.D. (1962), *Strategy and Structure: Chapters in the history of American industrial enterprise*, Cambridge, MA: MIT Press.

Chandler, A.D. (1975), 'The multi-unit enterprise: a historical and international comparative analysis and summary', in H.F. Williamson (ed.), *Evolution of International Management Structures*, Newark: University of Delaware Press.

Chandler, A.D. (1977), *The Visible Hand: The managerial revolution in American business*, Cambridge, MA: Harvard University Press.

Chandler, A.D. (1984a), 'The challenge ahead: economic growth, global interdependence, and the new competition, Harvard Business School, 385–009.

Chandler, A.D. (1984b), 'The multinational enterprise', Harvard Business School Case 373–369, rev. 6/84.

Chandler, A.D. (1984c), 'The conglomerates and the multinational management of the 1960s', Harvard Business School 373–350, rev. 6/84.

Chandler, A.D. (1986), 'The evolution of modern global competition, in M.E. Porter (ed.), *Competition in Global Industries*, Boston, MA: Harvard Business School Press.

Chandler, A.D. (1990), *Scale and Scope*, Cambridge, MA: Harvard University Press.

Chandler, A.D. and Daems, H. (1980), *Managerial Hierarchies*, Cambridge, MA: Harvard University Press.

Channon, D. (1973), *The Strategy and Structure of British Enterprise*, London: Macmillan.

Chorafas, D.N. (1969), *Developing the International Executive*, New York: American Management Association.

Christopher, R.C. (1984), *The Japanese Mind*, London: Pan.

Clark, R. (1979), *The Japanese Company*, New Haven, CT: Yale University Press.

Cleveland, H., Mangone, G. and Adams, J. (1960), *The Overseas Americans*, New York: McGraw-Hill.

Contractor, F.J. and Lorange, P. (eds.) (1987), *Cooperative Strategies in International Business*, Cambridge, MA: Ballinger.

Cook, M.F. (1988), 'What's ahead in human resources?', *Management Review*, April, 41–4.

Cooke, P.N. (1986), *Global Restructuring and Local Response*, London: ERSC Environment and Planning Committee.

Craig, G. (1982), *The Germans*, New York: G.P. Putnam's Sons.

Cray, D. (1984), 'Control and coordination in multinational corporations,' *Journal of International Business Studies*, Fall, 58–98.

Crozier, M. (1964), *The Bureaucratic Phenomenon*, Chicago: University of Chicago Press.

Cusumano, M. (1985), *The Japanese Automobile Industry*, Cambridge, MA: Harvard University Press.

Cuttman, A.W. and Knudson, H.R. (eds.) (1972), *Management Problems in International Environments*, Englewood Cliffs, NJ: Prentice-Hall.

Daems, H. (1978), *The Holding Company and Corporate Control*, Vol. 3, Leiden, The Netherlands: Martinus Nijhoff Social Sciences Division.

Dalton, M. (1959), *Men Who Manage*, New York: John Wiley.

Daniels, J.D., Pitts, R.A. and Tretter, M.J. (1985), 'Organizing for dual strategies of product diversity and international expansion', *Strategic Management Journal*, 6, 223–37.

Davenport, C. (1989), 'America's most admired corporations', *Fortune*, 30 January, 64–77.

Davis, S.M. (1971), *Comparative Management: Organizational and cultural perspectives*, Englewood Cliffs, NJ: Prentice-Hall.

Davis, S.M. (1979), *Managing and Organizing Multinational Corporations*, Elmsford, NY: Pergamon.

Davis, S.M. (1984), *Managing Corporate Culture*, Cambridge, MA: Ballinger.

Deal, T.E. (1983), 'Journal of Applied Behavioral Science', *Culture: A new look through old lenses*, XIX, 501–2.

Deal, T.E. and Kennedy, A.A. (1982), *Corporate Cultures: The rites and rituals of corporate life*, Reading, MA: Addison-Wesley.

Decker, H. (1988), 'Bringing technology to the United States', *High Technology Business*, March, 44–7.

DeLamarter, R.T. (1986), *IBM's Use and Abuse of Power*, New York: Dodd, Mead.

DeRossi, F. (1982), *The Technocratic Illusion: A study of managerial power in Italy*, Armonk, NY: ME Sharpe.

Deshpande, R. and Websten, F.E., Jr. (1989), 'Organizational culture and marketing: defining the research agenda', *Journal of Marketing*, 53, 3–15.

Diamond (1991), 'Profit comparison of six groups', 25 May, 764–5.

Dobyns, N.L. (1988), 'More or less American multinational companies', *Across the Board*, February, 5–7.

Doe, P. (1989), 'MITI explains why Japan is no copycat these days', *Electronic Business*, 12 June, 80–1.

Doyle, F.P. (1990), 'People power: the global human resource challenge for the 90s', *The Columbia Journal of World Business*, 25, 36–45.

Doz, Y. (1979), *Government Control and Multinational Strategic Management*, New York: Praeger.

Doz, Y. (1986a), 'Government policies and global industries', in M.E. Porter (ed.), *Competition in Global Industries*, Boston, MA: Harvard Business School Press.

Doz, Y. (1986b), *Strategic Management in Multinational Companies*, Oxford: Pergamon Press.

Doz, Y. and Prahalad, C.K. (1986), 'Controlled variety: a challenge for human resource management in the MNC', *Human Resource Management*, 25, 55–71.

Drucker, P.F. (1954), *The Practice of Management*, New York: Harper & Brothers.

Drucker, P.F. (1964), *Managing to Results*, New York: Harper & Row.

Drucker, P.F. (1972), *The Concept of Corporation*, New York: G.Y. Crowell.

Drucker, P.F. (1973), *Management: Tasks, responsibilities, practices*, London: Heinemann.

Drucker, P.F. (1978), *The Age of Discontinuity*, New York: Harper & Row.

Drucker, P.F. (1980), *Managing in Turbulent Times*, New York: Harper & Row.

Drucker, P.F. (1985), *Innovation and Entrepreneurship*, New York: Harper & Row.

Drucker, P.F. (1986), *The Frontiers of Management*, New York: E.P. Dutton.

Drucker, P.F. (1989), 'Peter Drucker's 1990s', *The Economist*, 21 October, 22.

Duerr, M.G. and Roach, J.M. (1979), 'Organization and control in European multinational corporations', in S.M. Davis (ed.), *Managing and Organizing Multinational Corporations*, Elmsford, NY: Pergamon Press.

Dumaine, B. (1989a), 'Those highflying Pepsico managers', *Fortune*, 10 April, 64–8.

Dumaine, B. (1989b), 'Buying a Euro-stake that will thrive on the happenings of 1992', *Fortune*, 30 January, 50–2.

Dumaine, B. (1990), 'Creating a new company culture', *Fortune*, 15 January, 55–8.

Dunning, J.H. (ed.) (1971), *The Multinational Enterprise*, London: George Allen & Unwin.

Dunning, J.H. (ed.) (1974), *Economic Analysis and Multinational Enterprise*, London: George Allen & Unwin.

Dunning, J.H. (1985), *Multinational Enterprises, Economic Structure, and International Competitiveness*, New York: John Wiley.

Dunning, J.H. (1988), *Multinationals, Technology, and Competitiveness*, London: Unwin Hyman.

Dunning, J.H. (1989), *Transnational Corporations and the Growth of Services*, New York: United Nations.

Dunning, J.H. and Robson, P. (1988), *Multinationals and the European Community*, Oxford: Blackwell.

Dutton, W.S. (1949), *Du Pont: One hundred and forty years*, New York: Scribner.

Dyas, G.P. and Tranheiser, H.T. (1976), *The Emerging European Enterprise: Strategy and structure in French and German industry*, London: Macmillan.

Dyer, W.G. (1985), *Strategies for Managing Change*, Reading, MA: Addison-Wesley.

Economist (The) (1988), 'America, Asia, & Europe: Why it's Still a Triangle', 26 December, 51.

Economist (The) (1989a), 'The multinationals: eastern style', 24 June, 75–6.

Economist (The) (1989b), 'A new balance in Asia', in 'A survey of the Yen Block', 15 July, 5–8.

Economist (The) (1990), 'A survey of South Korea', 18 August, 5–20.

Economist (The) (1991a), 'Echoes of the 1930s', 5 January, 17–20.

Economist (The) (1991b), 'Inside the charmed circle', 5 January, 58.

Economist (The) (1991c), 'Jack Welch reinvents General Electric – again', 30 March, 59–62.

Economist (The) (1991d), 'Communities of interest: survey of international finance', 27 April, 40–2.

Economist (The) (1991e), 'New dreams at Deutsche Bank', 22 June, 85–90.

Economist (The) (1991f), 'Foreign investment and the triad', 24 August, 53.

Economist (The) (1991g), 'Hooked by Hollywood', 21 September, 77–8.

Economist (The) (1991h), 'Nice view from here', 24 November, 68–90.

Economist (The) (1991i), 'One Europe, one economy', 30 November, 35–6.

Edström, A. and Lorange, P. (1984), 'Matching strategy and human resources in multinational corporations', *Journal of International Business Studies*, **15**, 125–37.

Egelhoff, W.G. (1988), 'Strategy and structure in multinational corporations: a revision of the Stopford and Wells model', *Strategic Management Journal*, **9**, 1–14.

England, G.W., Negandhi, A.R., and Wilpert, B. (eds.) (1981), *The Functioning of Complex Organizations*, Cambridge, MA: Oelgeschlager, Gunn & Hain.

Estren, M.J. (1988a), 'Escaping the paradigm', *High Technology Business*, July, 18.

Estren, M.J. (1988b), 'The quest for clarity: seeking tools to improve communication', *High Technology Business*, December, 12.

Estren, M.J. (1989), 'Different drummers: adapting occidental steps to fit oriental tunes', *High Technology Business*, May, 9.

Evans, P., Doz, Y.L. and Laurent, D. (eds.) (1990), *International Human Resources Management in International Firms: Change, globalization, and innovation*, London: Macmillan.

Exley, C.E. (1988), 'On managing change', *High Technology Business*, May, 46–9.

Fallows, J. (1989), '*More Like US*', Boston MA: Houghton-Mifflin.

Fatemi, N.S. and Williams, G.W. (1975), *Multinational Corporations*, New York: A.S. Barnes.

Fayerweather, J. (1978), *International Business Strategy and Administration*, Cambridge, MA: Ballinger.

Feiger, G.M. (1988), 'Managing the new global enterprise', *McKinsey Quarterly*, Summer, 25–38.

Ferrier, R.W. (1982), *The History of British Petroleum, Vol. I: The Developing Years (1902–1932)*, Cambridge: Cambridge University Press.

Fiat (1988), *Consolidated Financial Statements of the Fiat Group*, Turin.

Fieldhouse, D.K. (1978), *Unilever Overseas: The anatomy of a multinational*, London: Croom Helm.

Fortune (1960a), 'Fortune Directory: 500 largest US industrial corporations', July, 131–50.

Fortune (1960b), 'Fortune Directory: 100 largest foreign industrial corporations', August 135–44.

Fortune (1965a), 'Fortune Directory: 500 largest US industrial corporations', July, 149–68.

Fortune (1965b), 'Fortune Directory: 200 largest industrial corporations outside the US', August, 169–80.

Fortune (1970a), 'Fortune Directory: 500 largest US industrial corporations', May, 182–218.

Fortune (1970b), 'Fortune Directory: 200 largest industrial corporations outside the US', August, 192–7.

Fortune (1975), 'Fifty largest industrial companies in the world', August, 163.

Fortune (1980), 'Fifty largest industrial companies in the world', August, 102–204.

Fortune (1985a), 'The 500: The Fortune Directory of the largest US industrial corporations', 29 April, 266–86.

Fortune (1985b) 'The International 500', 19 August, 182–222.

Fortune International, (1987) 'The world's 50 biggest industrial corporations', 1 August, D1–D33.

Fortune International (1989a), 'Largest US industrial corporations', 29 April, 161–209.

Fortune International (1989b), 'The biggest industrial corporations outside the US', 31 July, 33–80.

Fortune International (1990a), 'The 500 in the 1980s', 23 April, 88.

Fortune International (1990b), 'The world's biggest industrial corporations', 30 July, 42–112.

Fortune International (1991a), 'The world's biggest industrial corporations', 29 July, 63–106.

Fortune International (1991b), 'The world's biggest service companies', 26 August, 134–44.

Fortune International (1992), 'The world's largest industrial corporations', 27 July, 51–108.

Fouraker, L.E. and Stopford, J.M. (1968), 'Organizational structure and multinational strategy', *Administrative Science Quarterly*, June, 47–64.

Franko, L.G. (1976), *The European Multinationals*, Greenwich, CT: Greylock.

Franko, L.G. (1989), 'Use of minority and 50–50 joint ventures by US multinationals during the 1970s: the interaction of host country policies and corporate strategies', *Journal of International Business Studies*, **20**, 19–40.

Frederick, W.C., Davis, K. and Post, J.E. (1988), *Business and Society*, London: McGraw-Hill.

French, W.L., Bell, C.H., Jr. and Zawacki, R.H. (1983), *Organizational Development*, Plano, TX: Business Publications.

Friberg, E.B. (1989), '1992: moves Europeans are making', *Harvard Business Review*, May–June, 85–9.

Friedman, A. (1989), *Agnelli and the Network of Italian Power*, London: Mandarin.

Fruin, W.M. (1983), *Kikkoman: Company, clan, community*, Cambridge, MA: Harvard University Press.

General Electric (1989), *Annual Report 1989*, Fairfield CT, GE.

General Motors (1990), *Annual Report 1990*, Detroit.

Georgantzas, N.C. (1989), 'Share in: the missing link of MNC global strategy and structure', *Management International Review*, **29**, 19–34.

George, K.D. (1971), *Industrial Organizations: Competition, growth and structural change in Britain*, London: Allen & Unwin.

Geringer, J.M., Beamish, P.W. and deCosta, R.C. (1989), 'Diversification strategy and internationalization: implications for MNE performance', *Strategic Management Journal*, **10**, 109–19.

Gerloff, E.A. (1985), *Organizational Theory and Design*, New York: McGraw-Hill.

Ghoshal, S. and Bartlett, C.A. (1988), 'Matsushita Electric Industries Ltd', Harvard Business School Case, 9-388-144.

Gilbert, N. (1988), 'Foreign companies use democracy to prosper in the US', *Management Review*, July, 25–9.

Gill, S. and Law, D. (1988), *The Global Political Economy*, New York: Harvester Wheatsheaf.

Gladwin, T.N. (1977), *Environment, Planning and the Multinational Corporation*, Greenwich, CT: JAI Press.

Gladwin, T.N. and Walter, I. (1980), *Multinationals under Fire*, New York: John Wiley.

Glynn, L. (1984), 'Multinationals in the world of nations', in P.O. Grub, F. Ghadar and D. Khambata (eds.), *The Multinational Enterprise in Transition*, Princeton, NJ: Darwin Press.

Goddard, R.W. (1984), 'Manage', in *Everything Swings Off*, **XXIV**, 8–10.

Goold, M. and Campbell, A. (1987), *Strategies and Styles: The role of the centre in managing diversified corporations*, Oxford: Blackwell.

Granick, D. (1962), *The European Executive*, New York: Doubleday.

Greenwood, R.G. (1982), *Managerial Decentralization*, LaCrosse, WI: Hive Publishing.

Grosse, R. and Kujawa, D. (1988), *International Business: Theory and managerial applications*, Homewood, IL: R.D. Irwin.

Grub, P.O., Ghadar, F. and Khambata, D. (1984), *The Multinational Enterprise in Transition*, Princeton, NJ: Darwin Press.

Gubman, E.L. (1989), 'Getting the most out of performance appraisals', *Management Review*, November, 44–8.

Guzzardi, W. (1989), 'U.S. Business Hall of Fame', *Fortune*, 13 March, 68–74.

Hadley, E.M. (1970), *Anti-trust in Japan*, Princeton, NJ: Princeton University Press.

Halberstam, D. (1986), *The Reckoning*, New York: William Morrow.

Halberstam, D. (1989), 'Reflections on Japan, Inc.', *Business Month*, February, 45–9.

Hall, E.T. and Reed, M. (1990), *Understanding Cultural Differences*, Yarmouth, ME: Intercultural Press.

Hall, R.H. (1972), *Organizations: Structure and process*, Englewood Cliffs, NJ: Prentice-Hall.

Hamel, G. and Prahalad, C.K. (1989), 'Strategic intent', *Harvard Business Review*, May–June, 63–76.

Hamel, G., Doz, Y.L. and Prahalad, C.K. (1989), 'Collaborate with your competitors – and win', *Harvard Business Review*, January–February, 133–9.

Hampton-Turner, C. (1990), *Corporate Culture*, London: Hutchinson.

Handy, C., Gow, I., Gordon, C., Randlsome, C. and Maloney, M. (1987), *Making A Manager: A report*, London: National Economic Development Office.

Hannon, K. (1988), 'Girdling the gribe', *Forbes*, 26 December, 56.

Harris, P.R. (1985), *Management in Transition*, San Francisco: Jossey-Bass.

Harris, P.R. and Moran, R.T. (1987), *Managing Cultural Differences: High-performance strategies for today's global manager*, Houston, TX: Gulf Publishing.

Hasegawa, K. (1986), *Japanese Style Management*, Tokyo: Kodansha International.

Hattori, I. (1987), *Corporate Structure and Decision Making in Japan*, Tokyo: Sophia University Press.

Hayes, W. (1990), *Henry: A life of Henry Ford II*, London: Weidenfeld and Nicolson.

Haynes, W. (1983), *American Chemical Industries, 1886–1960*, New York: Garland.

Hearn, F. (1988), *The Transformation of Industrial Organization*, Belmont, CA: Wadsworth.

Heenan, D.A. and Keegan, W.J. (1984), 'The rise of third world multinationalism', in P.O. Grub, F. Ghadar and D. Khambata (eds.), *The Multinational Enterprise in Transition*, Princeton, NJ: Darwin Press.

Heenan, D.A. and Perlmutter, H.V. (1979), *Multinational Organizational Development*, Reading MA: Addison-Wesley.

Heer, J. (1991), *Nestlé 125 Years, 1866–1991*, Vevey, Switzerland: Nestlé S.A.

Heerding, A. (1986), *The History of N.V. Philips' Gloeilampenfabrieken*, Vol. 1, London: Cambridge University Press.

Heller, F.A. and Wilpert, M.A. (1981), *Competence and Power in Managerial Decision Making*, New York: John Wiley.

Herbert, T.T. (1984), 'Strategy and multinational organization structure: an inter-organizational relationships perspective', *The Academy of Management Review*, 9, 259–70.

Hickman, C.R. and Silva, M.A. (1987), *The Future 500: Creating tomorrow's organizations today*, New York: New American Library.

Hirschmeier, J. and Yui, T. (1981), *The Development of Japanese Business*, London: George Allen & Unwin.

Hofer, C.W., Murray, E.A., Jr., Charan, R. and Pitts, R.A. (1989), *Strategic Management: A casebook in policy and planning*, St Paul, MN: West Publishing.

Hofstader, R. (1989), *The American Political Tradition*, New York: Vintage Books.

Hofstede, G. (1980), *Culture's Consequences: International differences in work related values*, Beverly Hills, CA: Sage.

Hofstede, G. (1983), 'The cultural relativity of organizational practices and theories', *Journal of International Business Studies*, 14, 75–90.

Hood, N. and Young, S. (1988), 'Inward investment and the EC: UK evidence on corporate integration strategies' in J.H. Dunning and P. Robson (eds.), *Multinationals and the European Community*, Oxford: Blackwell.

Horovitz, J. (1980), *Top Management Control in Europe*, London: Macmillan.

Horsley, N. and Buckley, R. (1990), *Nippon: New superpower Japan since 1945*, London: BBC Press.

Howorth, J. and Cerny, P.G. (eds.) (1981), *Elites in France: Origins, reproductions and power*, London: Frances Pinter.

Hrebeniak, L.G., Joyce, W.F. and Snow, C.C. (1989), 'Strategy, structure, and performance: past and future research', in C.C. Snow (ed.), *Strategy, Organization Design, and Human Resource Management*, Greenwich, CT: JAI Press.

Hulbert, J.M. and Brandt, W.K. (1980), *Managing the Multinational Subsidiary*, New York: Holt, Rinehart & Winston.

Iacocca, L. with Novak, W. (1984), *Iacocca: An autobiography*, New York: Bantam.

Illman, P.E. (1980), *Developing Overseas Managers – and Managers Overseas*, New York: Amacom.

Imperial Chemical Industries (1990), *ICI World Data*, London.

International Business Machines (IBM) (1989), *Annual Report 1989*, Armonk NY.

International Management (1990), 'Invasion alert', December, 66–9.

IRC Co. (1990), *Current Business Conditions of the Toyota Group – Status of Toyota and its Keiretsu Practices – 1991*, Nagoya: IRC.

Isuor-Fiat (1990), *Isuor per L'Internazionalità*, Turin.

Jacoby, N.H. (1984), 'The multinational corporation', in P.O. Grub, F. Ghadar and D. Khambata (eds.), *The Multinational Enterprise in Transition*, Princeton, NJ: Darwin Press.

Jaeger, A.M. (1983), 'The transfer of organizational culture overseas: an approach to control in the multinational corporation', *Journal of International Business Studies*, 14, 91–104.

Jamieson, I. (1980), *Capitalism and Culture: A comparative analysis of British and American manufacturing organizations*, Farnborough: Gower.

Jeff, D.T. and Scott, C.D. (1989), 'Bridging your workers' motivation gap', *Nation's Business*, March, 30–2.

Johnson, C. (1982), *MITI and the Japanese Miracle*, Stanford, CA: Stanford University Press.

Jonquières (de), G. (1991), 'Barriers come tumbling down', *Financial Times*, 11 April, 11.

Junne, G. and Ruignk, W. (1988), 'Een Wereld van Handels Blokken', *Economisch Statistische Berichten*, 12 December, 1236.

Kanter, R.M. (1983), *The Change Masters*, New York: Simon & Schuster.

Kehoe, L. (1991), 'Key to success in managers' hands', *Financial Times*, 28 November, 15.

Khandwalla, P.M. (1977), *The Design of Organizations*, New York: Harcourt Brace Jovanovich.

Kieffer, G.D. (1988), 'Meetings of the mindless', *Across the Board*, July/August, 6–8.

Kikuchi, M. (1983), *Japanese Electronics*, Tokyo: Simul Press.

Kilmann, R.H. (1984), *Beyond the Quick Fix*, San Francisco: Jossey-Bass.

Kilmann, R.H., Sexton, M.J., Serpa, R. and Associates (1985), *Gaining Control of the Corporate Culture*, San Francisco: Jossey-Bass.

Kindleberger, C.P. and Audretsch, D.B. (1983), *The Multinational Corporation in the 1980s*, Cambridge, MA: MIT Press.

Kinlam, D.C. (1989), *Coaching for Commitment*, San Diego, CA: University Associates.

Kirkland, R.I. (1989), 'English spoken here, there (multinationals' corporate tongue)', *Fortune*, 19 June, 8.

Kirkpatrick, D. (1992), 'Breaking up IBM', *Fortune*, 27 July, 112–21.

Kirp, D.L. and Rice, D.S. (1988), 'Fast forward – styles of California management', *Harvard Business Review*, January–February 74–83.

Klein, J.A. and Posey, P.A. (1986), 'Good supervisors are good supervisors – anywhere', *Harvard Business Review*, November–December, 125–7.

Knowlton, C. (1991), 'Shell gets rich by beating risk', *Fortune*, 26 August, 51–3.

Kobayashi, K. (1991), *The Rise of NEC: How the world's greatest C&C company is managed*, Cambridge, MA: Blackwell.

Koestenbaum, P. (1991), *Leadership: The inner side of greatness*, San Francisco: Jossey-Bass.

Kolde, E.J. (1985), *Environment of International Business*, Boston, MA: Kent Publishing.

Kono, T. (1984), *Strategy and Structure of Japanese Enterprises*, London: Macmillan.

Korn, L.B. (1989), 'How the next CEO will be different', *Fortune*, 22 May, 11–13.

Korn-Ferry International (1987), *Board of Directors Fifteenth Annual Study*, New York.

Korn-Ferry International (1990), *Board of Directors Seventeenth Annual Study*, New York.

Kotter, J.P., (1979), 'Managing Exeternal Dependence', *Academy of Management Review*, 4 (1), 87–92.

Kotter, J.P. (1982), *The General Managers*, New York: Free Press.

Kotter, J.P. (1985), *The Power and Influence: Beyond formal authority*, New York: Free Press.

Kotter, J.P. (1988), *The Leadership Factor*, New York: Free Press.

Kotter, J.P. (1990), *A Force of Change: How leadership differs from management*, New York: Free Press.

Kraar, L. (1989a), 'Japan's gung-ho U.S. car plants', *Fortune*, 30 January, 78–85.

Kraar, L. (1989b), 'North America's new trade punch', *Fortune*, 22 May, 123–7.

Kriger, M.P. (1988), 'The increasing role of subsidiary boards in MNCs: an empirical study', *Strategic Management Journal*, 9, 347–60.

Krol (v.d.), R. (1989), 'A protected giant seeks the bottom line', *International Herald Tribune*, 3 July, 9–11.

Kuhn, T.S. (1970), *The Structure of Scientific Revolutions*, Chicago: University of Chicago Press.

Labich, K. (1988), 'The seven keys to business leadership', *Fortune*, 24 October, 58–65.

Labich, K. (1989a), 'Hot company, warm culture', *Fortune*, 27 February 44–7.

Labich, K. (1989b), 'Making over middle managers', *Fortune*, 8 May, 50–4.

Lall, S. (1983), *The New Multinationals: The spread of third world enterprises*, New York: John Wiley.

La Palombara, J. and Blank, S. (1976), *Multinational Corporations and National Elites: A study of tensions*, New York: Conference Board, Report No. 702.

La Palombara, J. and Blank, S. (1977), *Multinational Corporations in Comparative Perspective*, New York: Conference Board, Report No. 725.

La Palombara, J. and Blank, S. (1979), *Multinational Corporations in Developing Countries*, New York: Conference Board.

Lawrence, P. (1980), *Managers and Management in West Germany*, London: Croom Helm.

Lenzner, R. (1989), 'Tackling America', *The Boston Globe*, 19 March, A1–A6.

Leonard, D. (1988), *Pocket Guide to the European Community*, New York: Blackwell.

Lessing, L.P. (1980), 'Du Pont', *Fortune*, 11 February, 110–21.

Lewis, F. (1987), *Europe: A tapestry of nations*, New York: Simon & Schuster.

Lewis, J.D. (1990), *Partnerships for Profit: Structuring and managing strategic alliances*, New York: Free Press.

Liedecker, J.K. (1988), 'A delicate balance: the two functions of the CEO', *Management Review*, August, 18–22.

Lincoln, E.J. (1984), *Japan's Industrial Policies*, Washington, DC: Japan Economic Institute of America.

Lincoln, E.J. (1988), *Japan: Facing economic maturity*, Washington DC: Brookings Institution.

Lokon, E. (1987), 'Probing Japanese buyers' minds', *Business Marketing*, November, 85–90.

Lom, C. (1989), *1989 International Business Strategy Resource Book*, Fairfax, VA: Strategic Direction.

Longenecker, C.O. and Gioia, D.A. (1988), 'Please appraise me', *Across the Board*, June, 57–9.

Loomis, C. (1991), 'Can Akers save IBM?', *Fortune*, 15 July, 26–7.

Lorenz, C. (1990a), 'A drama behind closed doors that paved the way for a corporate metamorphosis', *Financial Times*, 23 March, 20.

Lorenz, C. (1990b), 'Re-appraising the power base of the regional barons', *Financial Times*, 26 March, 12.

Lorenz, C. (1990c), 'A cultural revolution that sets out to supplant hierarchy with informality', *Financial Times*, 30 March, 20.

Management Review (1984), 'Unlearning: technique for changing corporate culture', November, 7.

Mandel, M. and Murphy, B. (1989), 'Wake-up strategies for tired R&D projects', *High Technology Business*, February, 22–5.

March, J.G. and Olsen, J.P. (1976), *Ambiguity and Choice in Organizations*, Bergen, Norway: Universitatsforlaget.

March, J.G. and Simon, H.A. (1958), *Organizations*, New York: John Wiley.

Marquis Who's Who (1991), *Who's Who in the World 1991–2*, Wilmette, IL: Macmillan.

Marshall, C. (1989), 'Turnaround king', *Business Month*, February, 40–3.

Martin, D. (1990), 'Tough road ahead', *Prospects*, September, 8–9.

Masler, D. (1986), 'Japan's working wounded: in limbo by the window', *Across the Board*, June, 22–6.

Matsushita, K. (1984), *Not for Bread Alone*, Kyoto: PHP Institute.

Matsushita, K. (1988), *Quest for Prosperity*, Kyoto: PHP Institute.

Maucher, H. (1985), *The Nestlé Group's Development Strategies over the Last Forty Years*, Vevey: Nestlé.

Maucher, H. (1988), 'Future Aspects of Nestlé's global business strategies', speech in Tokyo, 9 April, Vevey: Nestlé.

Maxey, G. (1981), *The Multinational Automobile Industry*, New York: St Martins Press.

McCall, M.W., Jr., Lombardo, M.M. and Morrison, A.M. (1989), 'Great leaps in career development', *Across the Board*, March, 54–61.

McClintock, R.H. (1989), 'High-tech future of business requires advanced schedule of working retraining', *AMA Forum*, November, 32–3.

McLuhan, M. and Powers, B. (1989), *The Global Village*, Oxford: Oxford University Press.

Means, G. (1988), 'Globalization of world markets: the CEO response', *The Washington Quarterly*, Winter, 151–7.

Miller, E.L., Beechler, S. and Bhatt, B. (1986), 'The relationship between the global strategic planning process and the human resource management function', *Human Resource Planning*, 9, 9–23.

Miller, L.M. (1984), *American Spirit: Visions of a new corporate culture*, New York: William Morrow.

Mills, G. (1985), *On the Board*, London: George Allen & Unwin.

Mintzberg, H. (1979), *The Structuring of Organizations: A synthesis of the research*, Englewood Cliffs, NJ: Prentice-Hall.

Mintzberg, H. (1983), *Power In and Around Organizations*, Englewood Cliffs, NJ: Prentice-Hall.

Mitsubishi Public Affairs Committee (1990), *A Brief History of Mitsubishi*, Tokyo: Mitsubushi.

Mitsui (1989), 'Mitsui USA – An insider in the American Market', *Mitsui Trade News*, March/April, 2–5.

Mitsui (1991), *Annual Report 1991*, Tokyo.

Moad, J. (1988), 'Japanese pledge allegiance to U.S.: information systems strategies', *Datamation*, 15 February, 43–9.

Morgan, G. (1986), *Images of Organization*, Newbury Park, CA: Sage.

Morgan, G. (1989), 'Endangered species: new ideas', *Business Month*, April, 75–7.

Morita, A. (1986), *Made in Japan*, New York: Dutton.

Mosher, F.C. (1975), *Democracy and the Public Service*, New York: Oxford University Press.

Moyer, R. (1984), *International Business: Issues and concepts*, New York: John Wiley.

Murphy, J.M. (1990), *Brand Strategy*, New York: Prentice-Hall.

Nakamura, T. (1981), *The Post-war Japanese Economy: Its development and structure*, Tokyo: The University of Tokyo Press.

Nakane, C. (1970), *Japanese Society*, Berkeley, CA: University of California Press.

Negandhi, A.R. (1975), 'Comparative management and organization theory: a marriage needed', *Academy of Management Journal*, 18, 334–44.

Negandhi, A.R. (1979), 'Convergence in developing countries', in C.J. Lammers and D.J. Dickson (eds.), *Organizations Alike and Unlike*, London: Routledge & Kegan.

Negandhi, A.R. (1980), *Functioning of the Multinational Corporation: A global comparative study*, Elmsford, NY: Pergamon Press.

Negandhi, A.R. (1987), *International Management*, Boston, MA: Allyn & Bacon.

Negandhi, A.R. and Baliga, B.R. (1979), *Quest for Survival and Growth: A comparative study of American, European, and Japanese multinationals*, New York: Praeger.

Negandhi, A.R. and Baliga, B.R. (1981), *Tables are Turning: German and Japanese multinational companies in the United States*, Cambridge, MA: Oelgeschlager, Gunn & Hain.

Negandhi, A.R. and Prasad, S.B. (1971), *Comparative Management*, New York: Appleton-Century-Crofts.

Negandhi, A.R., Eshgi, G.S. and Yuen, E.C. (1985), 'The management practices of Japanese subsidiaries overseas', *California Management Review*, 27, 93–105.

Nelson, M.M. and Browning, E.S. (1990), 'Two years have done little to reconcile CGR to new boss GE', *Wall Street Journal*, 27–8 July, 1, 22.

Nestlé (1988), *Annual Report 1988*, Vevey.

Nevins, A. (1957), *Ford: Expansion and challenge*, New York: Scribners.

Nevins, A. and Hill, F.E. (1954), *Ford: The times, the man, and the company*, New York: Scribners.

Nevins, A. and Hill, F.E. (1962), *Ford: Decline and rebirth*, New York: Scribners.

Newsweek (1989), 'Giants under siege', 20 November, 26–31.

Nissan Jidōsha Kabushiki Kaisha (Nissan Motor Company) (1964), *Nissan Jidōsha Sangū Nenshi (A Thirty Year History of Nissan Motor)*, Tokyo: Nissan.

Nissan Jidōsha Kabushiki Kaisha (Nissan Motor Company) (1975), *Nissan Jidōsha Shasi (History of the Nissan Motor Company)*, Tokyo: Nissan.

Nulty, P.L. (1989), 'America's toughest bosses', *Fortune*, 27 February, 24–30.

Nulty, P.L. (1990a), 'How the world will change', *Fortune*, 15 January, 22–3.

Nulty, P.L. (1990b), 'Batman shakes BP to bedrock', *Fortune*, 19 November, 87–90.

Nunez, G. (1990), 'Managing the foreign services employee (managers and technicians)', *Advanced Management Journal*, 55, 25–9.

Nystrom, P.C. and Starbuck, W.H. (1981), *Handbook of Organizational Design*, New York: Oxford University Press.

Odiorne, G.S. (1984), 'Match organizational requirements to corporate human potential', *Management Review*, November, 49–51,

Ohmae, K. (1982), *The Mind of the Strategist*, New York: Penguin.

Ohmae, K. (1985), *The Coming Shape of Global Competition*, New York: Free Press.

Ohmae, K. (1987), *Beyond National Borders*, Homewood IL: Dow Jones-Irwin.

Ohmae, K. (1989a), 'Companyism and do more better', *Harvard Business Review*, January–February, 125–32.

Ohmae, K. (1989b), 'The global logic of strategic alliances', *Harvard Business Review*, March–April, 143–54.

Ohmae, K. (1989c), 'Planting for a global harvest', *Harvard Business Review*, July–August, 136–41.

Ohmae, K. (1990), *The Borderless World*, London: Collins.

Olins, W. (1989), *Corporate Identity*, Boston, MA: Harvard Business School Press.

O'Toole, J.J. (1985), *Vanguard Management: Redesigning the corporate future*, New York: Doubleday.

Otterbeck, L. (ed.). (1981), *The Management of Headquarters–Subsidiary Relationships in Multinational Corporations*, Aldershot: Gower.

Ouchi, W.G. (1977), 'The relationship between organizational structure and organizational control', *Administrative Science Quarterly*, **22**, 95–113.

Ouchi, W.G. (1978), 'Types of organizational control and their relationships to emotional well being', *Administrative Science Quarterly*, **23**, 293–317.

Ouchi, W.G. (1981), *Theory Z: How American business can meet the Japanese challenge*, Reading, MA: Addison-Wesley.

Palmer, R.E. (1989), 'Forget managers: what we need are leaders', *Business Month*, January, 69–70.

Pascale, R. (1984), 'Fitting new employees into the company culture', *Fortune*, 18 May, 28–40.

Pascale, R. (1990), *Managing the Edge*, New York: Simon & Schuster.

Pascale, R. and Athos, A. (1981), *The Art of Japanese Management: Applications for American executives*, New York: Warner Books.

Passer, H. (1953), *The Electronic Manufacturers*, Cambridge, MA: Harvard University Press.

Peet, W.J. and Hladik, K.J. (1989), 'Organizing for global product development', *Electronic Business*, 6 March, 62–4.

Pelkmans, J. and Winters, A. (1988), *Europe's Domestic Market*, London: The Royal Institute of International Affairs.

Peters, T.J. (1987), *Thriving in Chaos*, London: Macmillan.

Peters, T.J. and Austin, N. (1985), *A Passion for Excellence: The leadership difference*, New York: Random House.

Peters, T.J. and Waterman, R.H., Jr. (1982), *In Search of Excellence*, New York: Harper & Row.

Pettigrew, A.M. (1973), *The Politics of Organizational Decision-Making*, London: Tavistock.

Pettigrew, A.M. (1979), 'On studying organizational cultures', *Administrative Science Quarterly*, **XXIV**, 570–81.

Pettigrew, A.M. (1985), *The Awakening Giant: Continuity and change in ICI*, Oxford: Blackwell.

Pfeffer, J. (1981), *Power in Organizations*, Boston, MA: Pitman.

Pfeffer, J. (1982), *Organizations and Organization Theory*, Boston, MA: Pitman.

Phatak, A.V. (1983), *International Dimensions of Management*, Belmont, CA: Wadsworth.

Philips, F. (1978), *45 Years with Philips*, Poole: Blandford Press.

Pinchot, G., III (1985), *Intrapreneuring*, New York: Harper & Row.

Pitts, R.A. and Daniels, J.D. (1984), 'Aftermath of the matrix mania', *The Columbia Journal of World Business*, **19**, 48–54.

Pitts, R.A. and Tretter, M.J. (1984), 'Strategy and structure of US multinationals: an exploratory study (international organization structure)', *Academy of Management Journal*, **27**, 292–307.

Piturro, M.C. (1988), 'Decentralization: rebuilding the corporation', *Management Review*, August, 31–4.

Pochna, M.A. (1989), *Agnelli*, Paris: Hachette/L'Expansion.

Porter, M.E. (1980), *Competitive Strategy: Techniques for analyzing industries and competitors*, New York: Free Press.

Porter, M.E. (1985), *Competitive Advantages*, New York: Free Press.

Porter, M.E. (1986), 'Competition in global industries: a conceptual framework', in M.E. Porter (ed.), *Competition in Global Industries*, Boston, MA: Harvard Business School Press.

Porter, M.E. (1990), *The Competitive Advantages of Nations*, London: Macmillan.

Poynter, T.A. (1985), *International Enterprises and Government Intervention*, London: Croom Helm.

Poynter, T.A. and White, R.E. (1990), 'Making the horizontal organization work', *Business Quarterly*, **54**, 73–7.

Prahalad, C.K. (1976), 'The strategic process in a multinational corporation', unpublished doctoral dissertation, Boston, MA: Harvard Business School.

Prahalad, C.K. (1984), 'Patterns of strategic control within multinational corporations (headquarters control over subsidiary activities)', *Journal of International Business Studies*, **15**, 55–72.

Prahalad, C.K. and Doz, Y. (1987), *The Multinational Mission: Balancing local demands and global vision*, New York: Free Press.

Prahalad, C.K. and Hamel, G. (1990), 'The core competence of a corporation', *Harvard Business Review*, May–June, 79–91.

Quinn, J.B. (1980), *Strategies for Change: Logical incrementalism*, Homewood, IL: R.D. Irwin.

Rae, J. (1982), *Nissan-Datsun: A history of the Nissan Motor Corporation in the USA (1960–1980)*, New York: McGraw-Hill.

Randolph, B. (1990), 'When going global isn't enough', *Training*, August, 47–51.

Rapaport, C. (1991), 'Why Japan keeps on winning', *Fortune*, 15 July, 48–53.

Reader, W.J. (1975), *Imperial Chemical Industries: A history*, Oxford: Oxford University Press.

Reader, W.J. (1980), *Fifty Years of Unilever*, London: Heinemann.

Reischauer, E.O. (1977), *The Japanese*, Cambridge, MA: Harvard University Press.

Reischauer, E.O. (1988), *The Japanese Today*, Cambridge, MA: Harvard University Press.

Rice, F. (1988), 'Should you work for a foreigner?', *Fortune*, 1 August, 123–34.

Ridding, J. (1991), 'Back to the drawing board for Take-off Two', *Financial Times*, 5 June, IV–V.

Roberts, J.G. (1989), *Mitsui: Three centuries of Japanese business*, New York: Weatherhill.

Robey, D. (1986), *Designing Organizations*, Homewood, IL: R.D. Irwin.

Robinson, P. (1983), *Integration, Development, and Equity*, London: Allen & Unwin.

Robinson, R.D. (1964), *International Business Policy*, New York: Holt, Rinehart & Winston.

Robinson, R.D. (1984), *Internationalization of Business: An introduction*, New York: Dryden.

Robock, S.H., Simmonds, K. and Zwick, J. (1977), *International Business and Multinational Enterprises*, Homewood, IL: R.D. Irwin.

Rodgers, B. (1986), *The IBM Way*, New York: Harper & Row.

Ronen, S. (1986), *Comparative and Multinational Management*, New York: John Wiley.

Rose, R.L. (1991), 'How 3M by tiptoeing into overseas markets became a big exporter', *Wall Street Journal – Europe*, 2 April, 1, 12.

Rosecrance, R. (1986), *The Rise of the Trading State*, New York: Basic Books.

Rosenbaum, A. (1989), 'Olivetti hedges its bets while gambling on high tech', *Electronic Business*, 15 May, 91–7.

Rosenblum, M. (1988), *Mission to Civilize*, New York: Doubleday.

Ross, R. (1988), 'Technology tackles: the training dilemma', *High Technology Business*, September, 18–23.

Roussel, P., Kamal, S. and Erickson, T. (1991), *Third Generation R&D*, Cambridge, MA: Harvard Business School Press.

Royal Dutch/Shell (1988), *The Shell Review*, London.

Rugmann, A.M. (1979), *International Diversification and the Multinational Enterprise*, Lexington, MA: Lexington Books.

Rugmann, A.M. and Verbeke, A. (1990), 'Multinational corporate strategy and the Canada–US Free Trade Agreement', *Management International Review*, 30, 253–66.

Rumelt, R.P. (1979), *Strategy, Structure, and Economic Performance*, Cambridge, MA: Harvard University Press.

Rutenberg, D.P. (1982), *Multinational Management*, Boston, MA: Little, Brown.

Sampson, A. (1973), *The Sovereign State of ITT*, New York: Stein and Day.

Sampson, A. (1982), *The Changing Anatomy of Britain*, London: Hodder & Stoughton.

Sampson, A. (1988), *The Seven Sisters*, London: Coronet.

Saporito, B. (1989), 'Companies that compete best', *Fortune*, 22 May, 38–41.

Sara, K. (1987), *Alcatel: A strategic analysis*, New York: Northern Business Information.

Sasseen, J. (1989), 'Meeting mothers halfway', *International Management*, June, 48–52.

Sathe, V. (1983), 'Implications of corporate culture: a manager's guide to action', *Organizational Dynamics*, **XII**, 5–23.

Sathe, V. (1985), *Managerial Action and Corporate Culture*, Homewood, IL: R.D. Irwin.

Schaffer, R.J. (1989), 'Breakthrough strategists like to start small', *Business Month*, April, 99–101.

Schein, E.H. (1985a), 'How culture forms, develops, and changes,' in R.H. Kilmann, M.J. Sexton, R. Serpa and Associates, *Gaining Control of the Corporate Culture*, San Francisco: Jossey-Bass.

Schein, E.H. (1985b), *Organizational Culture and Leadership*, San Francisco: Jossey-Bass.

Schein, E.H. (1986), 'What you need to know about organizational culture', *Training and Development Journal*, **40**, 30–3.

Schisgall, O. (1981), *Eyes on Tomorrow*, New York: Doubleday.

Schitzer, M.C. (1987), *Contemporary Government and Business Relations*, Boston, MA: Houghton-Mifflin.

Schneider, S.C. (1988), 'National vs. corporate culture: implications for human resources management (multinational companies)', *Human Resources Management*, **27**, 231–46.

Schodt, F.L. (1988), 'In the land of robots', *Business Month*, November, 67–75.

Schoenberg, R.J. (1985), *Geneen*, New York: Warner.

Schumaker, E.F. (1973), *Small is Beautiful*, New York: Harper & Row.

Schwartz, H. and Davis, S.M. (1981), 'Matching corporate culture and business strategy,' *Organizational Dynamics*, **X**, 30–46.

Scott, W.R. (1987), *Organizations: Rational, natural, and open systems*, Englewood Cliffs, NJ: Prentice-Hall.

Seifert, B. (1991), 'Verwirrspiel', *Capital*, May, 148–55.

Senge, P.M. (1990), *The Fifth Discipline*, New York: Doubleday.

Servan-Schreiber, J.J. (1968), *The American Challenge*, New York: Atheneum.

Sethi, S.P. (1975), *Japanese Business and Social Conflict*, Cambridge, MA: Ballinger.

Sherman, S.P. (1988), 'GE's costly lesson on Wall Street', *Fortune*, 9 May, 72–5.

Siemens, G. (1977), *History of the House of Stone*, New York: Arms Press.

Simison, R.L. and Browning, E.S. (1991), 'Competition may cut Europe's auto making from Big 6 to Big 5', *Wall Street Journal*, 20 November, 1.

Sloan, A.P. (1986), *My Years with General Motors*, Harmondsworth: Penguin.

Smith, P.B. and Peterson, M.F. (1988), *Leadership, Organizations and Culture*, London: Sage.

Sobel, R. (1972), *The Age of Giant Corporations*, West Point, CT: Greenwood Press.

Sobel, R. (1981), *IBM: Colossus in transition*, New York: Truman Talley.

Solomon, L.D. (1978), *Multinational Corporations and the Emerging World Order*, Port Washington, NY: Kennikat Press.

Springer, C. and Hofer, C.W. (1984), 'General Electrics' evolving management system', in C.W. Hofer *et al.*, *Strategic Management*, St Paul MN: West.

Stinchcombe, A. (1965), 'Social structure and organizations.' in J. March (ed.), *Handbook of Organizations*, Chicago: Rand McNally.

Stopford, J.M. and Turner, L. (1985), *Britain and the Multinationals*, London: John Wiley.

Stopford, J.M. and Wells, L.T. (1972), *Managing the Multinational Enterprise*, New York: Basic Books.

Taucher, G. (1989), '1992: a competitive revolution', *European Affairs*, April, 53–60.

Tayeb, M. (1988), *Organizations and National Culture: A comparative analysis*, London: Sage.

Taylor, A., III (1988), 'Tomorrow's chief executives', *Fortune*, 9 May, 30–41.

Taylor, A., III (1989), 'How a top boss manages his day', *Fortune*, 19 June, 95–100.

Thompson, J.D. (1967), *Organizations in Action*, New York: McGraw-Hill.

Tichy, N.M. (1983), *Managing Strategic Change: Technical, political and cultural dynamics*, New York: John Wiley.

Tobacco International (1990), 'Philip Morris: the world leading consumer packaged goods company', 1 May, 4–6.

Tokyo Business Today (1990), 'Sony raises capital spending sharply', August, 45–6.

Tomasko, R.M. (1990), *Downsizing: Reshaping the corporation for the future*, New York: Amacom.

Toyo Keizai, Inc. (1990), *Japan Company Handbook*, Tokyo: Tokyo Keizai.

Toyota Motor Corporation (1988), *Toyota: A history of the first 50 years*, Toyota City: Toyota Motor Corporation.

Toyota Motor Corporation (1991), *The Automobile Industry, Toyota and Japan*, Toyota City: Toyota Motor Corporation.

Tse, D.K., Lee, K., Vertinsky, I. and Wehring, D.A. (1988), 'Does culture matter?: a cross-cultural study of executives' choice, decisiveness, and risk adjustment in international marketing', *Journal of Marketing*, 52, 81–95.

Tsurumi, Y. (1976), *The Japanese Are Coming*, Cambridge, MA: Ballinger.

Tsurumi, Y. (1977), *Multinational Management*, Cambridge, MA: Ballinger.

Tsurumi, Y. (1984), *Multinational Management: Business strategy and government policy*, Cambridge, MA: Ballinger.

Tsurumi, Y. (1990), 'From *zaibatsu* to *keiretsu*: Japanese industrial groupings are not exclusive cartels', *Basic Quarterly*, Summer–Fall, 9–16.

Tung, R.L. (1982), 'Selection and training procedures of U.S., European, and Japanese multinationals', *California Management Review*, **25**, 60, 61.

Tung, R.L. (1984), 'Strategic management of human resources in the multinational enterprise', *Human Resources Management*, **23**, 129–43.

Turner, G. (1986), 'Inside Europe's giant companies: Nestlé finds a better formula', *Long Range Planning*, **19**, 12–19.

United Nations Center on Transnational Corporations (UNCTC) (1988), *Transnational Corporations in World Development*, New York: UNCTC.

United Nations Center on Transnational Corporations (UNCTC) (1989), *United Nations Center on Transnational Corporations World Investment Report – 1989*, New York: UNCTC.

United Nations Center on Transnational Corporations (UNCTC) (1991), *United Nations Center on Transnational Corporations World Investment Report – 1991*, New York: UNCTC.

Valentine, C.F. (1989), 'Blunders abroad', *Nation's Business*, March, 54–6.

van Wolferen, K. (1989), *The Enigma of Japanese Power: People and politics in a stateless nation*, New York: Alfred A. Knopf.

Ventura, S. and Harvey, E. (1988), 'Peer review: trusting employees', *Management Review*, January, 48–51.

Vernon, R. (1971), *Sovereignty at Bay*, New York: Basic Books.

Vernon, R. (1977), *Storm Over the Multinationals*, Cambridge, MA: Harvard University Press.

Vernon, R. and Wells, L.T. (1981), *Manager in the International Economy*, Englewood Cliffs, NJ: Prentice-Hall.

Vogl, F. (1974), *German Business after the Economic Miracle*, New York: John Wiley.

Vossberg, H. (1984), 'Reorganization at Bayer from January 1984: the response to growth', *Bayer Reports*, **51**, 50–63.

Watson, T., Jr. (1963), *Business and Beliefs: The ideas that helped build IBM*, New York: McGraw-Hill.

Watson, T., Jr. and Petre, P. (1990), *Father, Son & Co. My life at IBM and beyond*, New York: Bantam.

Weinshall, T.D. (1977), *Culture and Management*, Harmondsworth: Penguin.

Wells, L.T., Jr. (1972), *The Product Life Cycle and International Trade*, Boston, MA: Division of Research, Harvard Business School.

Westney, E.D. (1987), *Imitation and Innovation*, Cambridge, MA: Harvard University Press.

Wheare, K.C. (1946), *Federal Government*, London: Oxford University Press.

Whyte, L.J. (1991), *The Automobile Industry since 1945*, Cambridge, MA: Harvard University Press.

Wilkins, A.L. (1983), 'The culture audit: a tool for understanding organizations', reprint from *Organizational Dynamics*, **XII**, 24–38.

Wilkins, M. (1960), *The Emergence of Multinational Enterprise: American business abroad from the colonial era to 1914*, Cambridge, MA: Harvard University Press.

Wilkins, M. (1974), *The Maturing of Multinational Enterprise: American business abroad from 1914 to 1970*, Cambridge, MA: Harvard University Press.

Wilkins, M. (1986), 'Japanese multinational enterprises before 1914', *Business History Review*, **60**, 199–231.

Wilkins, M. (1988), 'European and North American multinationals, 1870–1914: comparisons and contrasts', *Business History*, **30**, 8–45.

Wilkins, M. (ed.) (1991), *The Growth of Multinationals*, Brookfield, VT: E. Elbar.

Wilkins, M. and Hill, F.E. (1964), *American Business Abroad: Ford on six continents*, Detroit: Wayne State University Press.

Williams, I. (1991), 'Marlboro man rides a new range', *Business*, January, 41–5.

Williamson, G.P. (1989), 'At NCR it is the sixth sense that is counted on', *Business Month*, April, 103–4.

Williamson, H.F. (1975), *Evolution of International Management Structures*, Newark: University of Delaware Press.

Williamson, O. (1981), 'Modern corporations: origins, evolution, attribution', *Journal of Economic Literature*, **19**, 1539–44.

Wilson, C.H. (1954), *The History of Unilever: A study of economic growth and social change*, London: Cassell.

Wine, A. (1988), 'US headquarters in Europe', *The International Management Development Review*, **4**, 176–7.

World Bank (1989), *World Development Report 1989*, London: Oxford University Press.

Yamashita, T. (1987), *The Panasonic Way*, Tokyo: Kodansha International.

Yasuba, Y. (1976), 'The evolution of dualistic wage structure', in P. Huge (ed.), *Japanese Industrialization and its Social Consequence*, Berkeley, CA: University of California Press.

Yoshibara, K. (1982), *Sogo Sosha*, Tokyo: Oxford University Press.

Yoshino, M.Y. (1968), *Japan's Managerial System*, Cambridge, MA: MIT Press.

Yoshino, M.Y. (1976), *Japan's Multinational Enterprises*, Cambridge, MA: Harvard University Press.

Yoshino, M.Y. (1979), 'Emerging Japanese multinational enterprises', in S.M. Davis (ed.), *Managing and Organizing Multinational Corporations*, Elmsford NY: Pergamon Press.

Young, A.K. (1979), *The Sogo Shosha: Japan's multinational trading companies*, Tokyo: Charles E. Tuttle.

Young, S.D. (1987), *The Rule of Experts*, Washington DC: Cato Institute.

Youseff, S.M. (1975), 'Contextual factors influencing the control strategy of multinational corporations', *Academy of Management Review*, March, 136–43.

Zaleznik, A. (1970), 'Power and politics in organizational life', *Harvard Business Review*, May–June, 47–60.

Zeldin, T. (1983), *The French*, New York: Pantheon.

Index